Billingshurst's

A Short History of a West Sussex Village

Compiled by
Geoffrey Lawes

Peacock Press

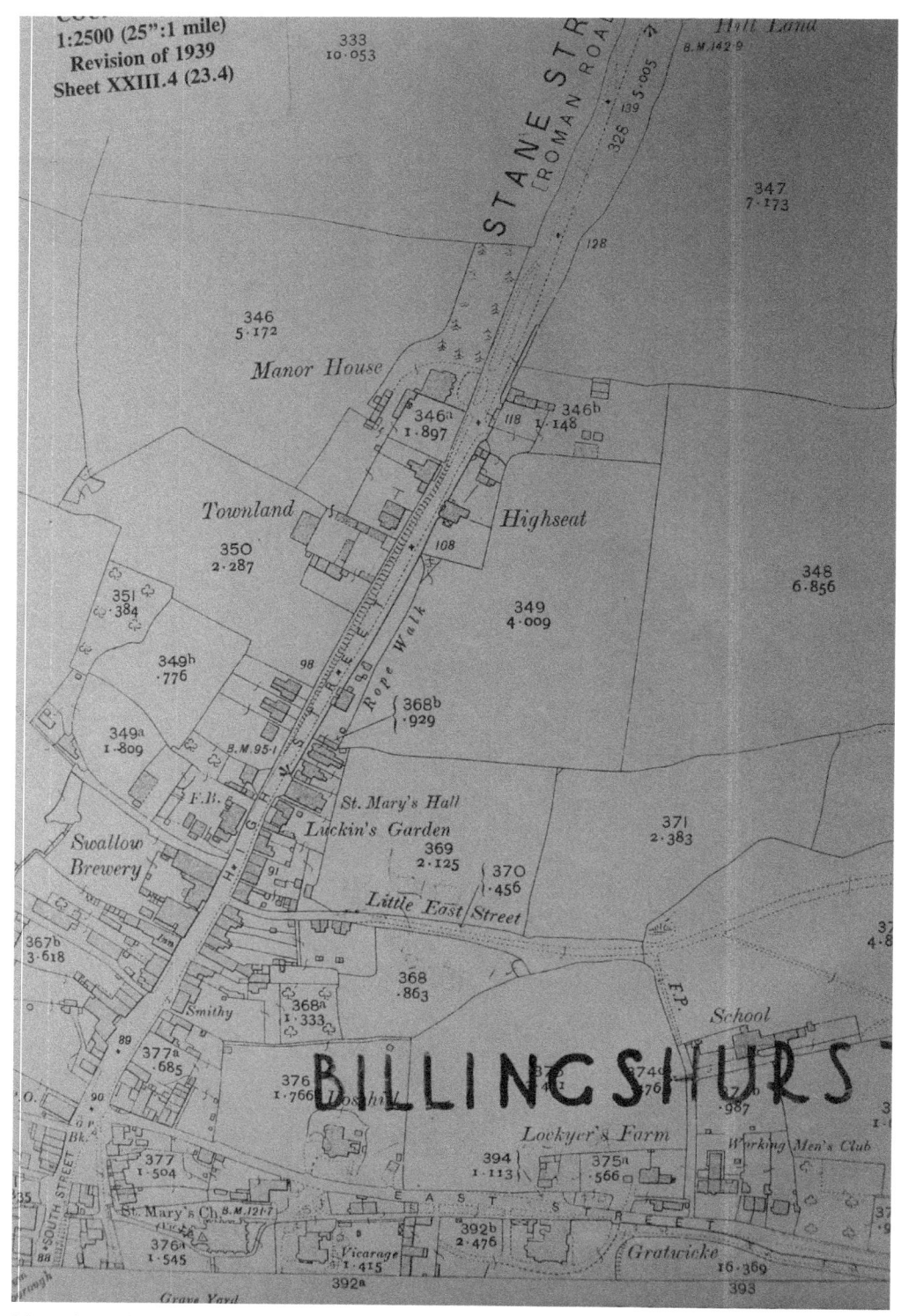

Map of North end of Billingshurst High Street 1939

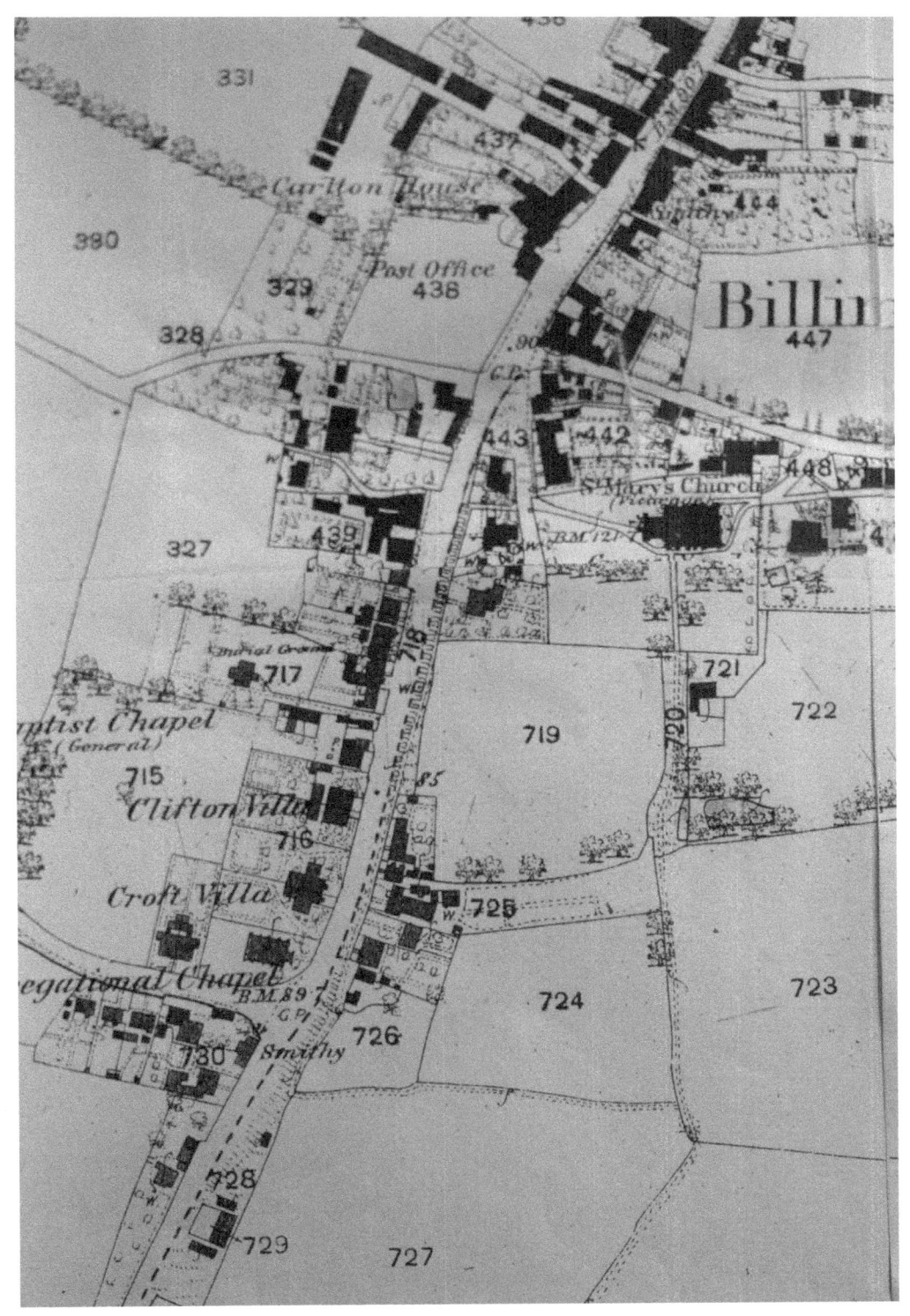

Map of South end of Billingshurst High Street 1877

High Street. Gingers House and Maltings, now the entrance to Jengers Mead

Billingshurst's Heritage

A Short History of a West Sussex Village

(Revised Edition)
Compiled by
Geoffrey Lawes

Village sign at the Community Centre

'There is nothing that more divides civilised from semi-savage man than to be conscious of our forefathers as they really were, and bit by bit, to reconstruct the mosaic of the long forgotten past'.

[G.M. Trevelyan]

Billingshurst's Heritage
© 2017 Geoffrey Lawes

All rights reserved. No part of this publication may be reproduced, stored in a retrieval system, transmitted in any form or by any means electronic, mechanical, including photocopying, recording or otherwise without prior consent of the copyright holders.

ISBN 978-1-912271-02-3

Published by Peacock Press, 2017
Scout Bottom Farm
Mytholmroyd
Hebden Bridge
HX7 5JS (UK)

Design and artwork
D&P Design and Print
Worcestershire

Printed by Lightning Source, UK

Contents

Village Civics 1
Local Democracy, Politics and Facilities .... 2 - 12
The Billingshurst Society 14
Evolutionary History 17
Before the 'First syllable of recorded time'. 21
Homo sapiens exploit the planet 24
The Ancient Britons and the valley where they lived 26
The coming of the Romans and their legacy 29
The Saxons colonise Britain 36
The conversion of the pagans 40
Fresh pagans threaten – the Norsemen 40
Saxon farming and later developments in agriculture 41
More new Christians – the Normans 47
Mastering the Wealden forest 48
The 'First syllables of recorded time' in Billingshurst.
The Church and its government 51
Early parish government 58
The Black Death 62
Feudal management of the County 64
The Manors of Billingshurst and district 65
Cocksbrook alias Hammonds north of East Street 67
Tudor times 68
James I and the Stuarts 72
Civil War. Charles I beheaded. The republican interlude 80
Restoration of the monarch. Charles II and the Church of England ... 81
18th Century – the Georgian era 83
The Unitarian Chapel 84
The 19th Century 93
Queen Victoria was crowned 100
The Officials of the Parish Vestry 106
1851 Census – the year of the Great Exhibition in the
Crystal Palace in Kensington 109
The Railway Age 111
Schools in Billingshurst 114
The Victorian regeneration 118
Hard times and good times 121
Death of Queen Victoria –the 20th Century 126

Hammonds House and Hammonds dairy farm	137
Kingsfold and Marringdean Road	140
Mr. Chitty's deeds – Mediaeval Farms	161
Ancient Buildings in Billingshurst	163
Pear Tree Farm and Frank Patterson	169
William Cobbett 1763-1835, Billingshurst Visitor	172
The Wey & Arun Canal	174
Rowner Watermill	181
The Tedfold Estate and Streele Farm	183
The Railway Network	188
Billingshurst Station	190
Gatwick Airport	191
Station Road Maltings and Whirlwind Limited	192
Printing in Billingshurst	193
Village Memories	194
Items of Interest	204
Murders in Billingshurst	214
Gardening and Horticulture	215
Billingshurst Horticultural Society	216
Beekeeping in Billingshurst	219
Billingshurst Institutions and Clubs	221
Leisure Centre	247
BBC Situation Comedy – Ever-Decreasing Circles	249
Retail Businesses in Billingshurst	250
Parbrook	251
Parish Yarns	256
The Weald School – A History	260
Oliver Reed and Josephine Burge	277
Billingshurst Primary School	278
The Hamlets – Five Oaks	279
Carnivals, Parades and Marches	290
The King comes to Five Oaks	294
The Hamlets – Adversane	297
Public Houses	301
Billingshurst Characters and Celebrities	309
Notable people with Billingshurst connections	310
Post-war Billingshurst	312

Building developments in the 70s 316
More recent developments.. 318
Possible future developments.. 323
The spirit of Billingshurst 328
Acknowledgements and Further Reading.. 334

Appendix 1 - Billingshurst Roads and Estates 2016 337
Appendix 2 - The end of the Georgian years 361
Appendix 3 - The early years of Queen Victoria 362
Appendix 4 - Mid-Victorian Billingshurst 364
Appendix 5 - Kelly's Post Office Directory 1867 367
Appendix 6 - Late Victorian Billingshurst 371
Appendix 7 - Early 20th century Billingshurst 374
Appendix 8 - Post-WWII Billingshurst... 380
Appendix 9 - Kelly's Directory of 1973 384
Appendix 10 - Occupants of Hammonds and Cocksbrook 388

Index 390

Foreword

Geoff Lawes came to Billingshurst in March 1974 to take up the headship of the Weald School - but it seems like he's always been here. Since then he has served the community at many levels. He is remembered by his colleagues and former students; he has served the Horticultural Society; he has contributed wider service as District & County Councillor. He has published on the history and development of the Weald School and on beekeeping.

We are told that when bees have found a good source of pollen they fly back to the hive and make a "waggle dance" to tell the other bees where to find it. This book may be Geoff's dance - it started as an account of the place in East Street where he lives but he soon discovered more nectar. It may encourage others to forage. This book reveals Geoff's love of knowledge "for its own sake" and displays his natural talent as a raconteur and teacher. Who better then to present a history of Billingshurst?

John Hurd, Billingshurst, October 2012

It is fair to say that Geoff Lawes has now truly earned his place among the small select group of village historians. His first book 'Billingshurst's Heritage' was critically acclaimed by his peers and is now into a reprint. I was able to see at first hand the work and dedication that went into that book as he travelled the highways and byways in search of knowledge of the many older buildings in the neighbourhood.

Subsequently, Geoff realised that he had accumulated a great deal of information beyond the self-imposed remit of this first book and, typically, he began to write another. This book is an extension of the earlier one and expands our village history to include the outer reaches of the parish. It also contains a wealth of entertaining anecdotal material for dipping into, consisting as it does of many humorous yarns and other accounts of bygone days as recalled by our village characters and other venerable citizens.

For those that regard Billingshurst as a town - which as it grows it will be hard not to so describe - these books are, and will remain, a wonderful contribution to the canon of the history of village life from which Billingshurst is derived. The book will dispense much knowledge and amusement for all who read it.

John Griffin, friend and neighbour.
December 2013

Shop and Wealden House, the Causeway, corner of East Street

Aerial view of Billingshurst 2008

Introduction

It is natural enough, as we tread the paths around our houses and turn the earth in our gardens, to ponder on what manner of men and women once trod those same paths and sowed seed in that same soil. How did those people earn a living; how did they lead their lives? What pressing business filled their waking hours? What have they left behind for us to enjoy; what were their names and who are their heirs who still carry their genes?

Prompted by such an impulse to find out more of the street where I live, East Street in Billingshurst, I gathered together information from authoritative local historians, jotting them into a notebook. Almost every house proved to have a story and posed a further question. I had originally focused on just one 17th century building, 'Hammonds', my immediate neighbour. But those further questions inevitably led to a wider delving into the research findings of other authorities until the notebook took the shape of an embryonic history. The vista widened from the story of one house to the whole street, which contained the 13th century church, the former workhouse, the old school buildings and other ancient houses with widely divergent histories, together with the echoes of other notable premises, now long gone. A study of the people of one street could not for long be divorced from their interactions with the rest of the village community, nor did it make sense out of context with the geography and history of the wider Sussex region. Consequently a concentric pattern grew from the Hammonds nucleus, and the result was a little book, *Billingshurst's Heritage*.

A fortunate factor that made the enterprise manageable was that the parish is an area remote from the coast, sheltered before Saxon times by ancient forest and not blessed with rich soils, so that it has been protected from intrusion, aggressive agricultural development and industrial exploitation until quite recent times.

The jottings began as a chronological 'line of time' to allow a reader a sense of the evolution and progress of Billingshurst through the passing of the centuries. This mode of presentation has remained as the basic structure of the village story as told in the first volume. It proved the simplest way of recording 'gobbets' of information, yarns and anecdotes which are not part of a general topic, and also the names and doings of particular people.

Interwoven among the chronological detail, were occasional essays on major themes which span long passages of time such as the development of farming, the evolution of parish government and the provision of schooling. Ever since man-like primates began to modify the face of the planet, human beings have dictated the superficial features of the landscape. Accordingly this account reached back briefly to those aspects of pre-history that scholarship and archaeological research have revealed to us. Conversely, at the conclusion it seemed appropriate to speculate on what may lie ahead for our successors who inherit the living space for which we are but briefly the custodians.

Coronation Parade 1911 – a field full of folk

"A faire field fill of folke fonde I there bytwene
Of alle manner of men, the mene and the riche,
Worchyng and wandryng as the worlde asketh"
[William Langland, 14th Century Poet]

In the Billingshurst Society's newsletter a member once lamented, 'Except for Wendy Lines' splendid photographic history, Billingshurst's history awaits an author. There is a bulging scrapbook for anyone brave enough to take on the task.' I have, almost by accident stumbled into this role. Volume 1 of *Billingshurst's Heritage* dealt mainly with the church and ancient buildings in East Street and the High Street. Other major areas were given cursory treatment or neglected. Volume 2 sought to remedy some of those major omissions. The first volume was arranged on a chronological structure while Volume 2 took the form of an historical miscellany of topics, with closer reference to affairs as they are today.

In 2014 and 15 Ms Hayley Nichols and her team of archaeologists from

University College, London conducted thorough searches in area once known as Cocksbrook and Crouchers in the NE quadrant of the village prior to the development of 475 new dwellings. Astonishingly they revealed extensive evidence of Iron Age settlement and Roman farmsteads. This runs counter to the received views of historical experts who believed that no Romans had ever made homes in the Billingshurst area or indeed elsewhere on the clay soils and oak forest of the Low Weald. Details of this matter and some other new information are included in the Revised Edition.

In compiling these combined history and reference books I owed an immense debt of gratitude to those many people who have contributed their expertise, memories and research to the body of knowledge about the village. It was my pleasure and privilege to assemble that knowledge, now, in this revised edition, conflated into a single volume. I have enjoyed recording the 'working and wandering' of Billingshurst's 'field full of folk' and offering this snapshot of the tycoons, the rogues, the affluent maltsters, the shopkeepers, the publicans, the community-minded leaders the craftsmen and the humble labourers who graced the fields and streets that we have inherited.

I have tried to present the story of the village in an objective manner, though doubtless my personal prejudices may have sometimes coloured my judgments. I apologise to anyone I may have offended. Necessarily many people, places and topics have been omitted. Detailed discussion of buildings such as South House, Hammonds and Kingsfold have to stand as representative of houses which have been passed over or given a mere mention. I hope that colloquial memoires, inventories, directories and other details of farm and village life, in peace and in war, will serve to illustrate the life of the people of Billingshurst in years gone by and as we experience it today.

Geoffrey Lawes, May, 2017

Village Civics

This historical miscellany of information about the village of Billingshurst begins with a description of the democratic structures that govern our lives. This may appear like a lesson in Civics most appropriate to young people, but it may also prove useful to those who find our multi-layered system of governance obscure and confusing. Basic information about the parish offices may be helpful and subsequent passages also open a window on the various clubs and societies that enhance the social and sporting life of the village.

Inflation and Money Values

Sums of money are sometimes quoted in the text about such matters as mediaeval fines and Victorian wages. In order to put the reader in mind of the effects of inflation and the varying purchasing power of Sterling, the following short table will offer a rough guide to the value of pounds and old pence at various times throughout our history.

Date	Value of a £ today	Value of a penny today (240 old pence = £1)	
1270	£1 = 835 pounds	1d =£3.48p	(d is an old penny. Two and a half old pence = one new p)
1313	£1 =712	1d =£3.00p	The cost of food varied greatly.
1413	£1 =686	1d =£2.86p	Today one hour's work buys at
1513	£1 =579	1d =£2.41p	least 12 lbs of good bread.
1613	£1 =161	1d =67p	In 1450 a farm labourer was paid
1713	£1 =129	1d =54p	2 shillings a week and could buy
1813	£1 =56	1d =23p	23 lbs of bread a day.
1890	£1 =96	1d =40p	In 1865, earning 14 shillings,
1910	£1 =89	1d =37p	he could afford only 4lbs a day.
1920	£1 =35	1d =15p	By 1912 it was 26 lbs. Now
1930	£1 =55	1d =23p	basic foods are much more
1945	£1 =38	1d =16p	affordable. Historically food
1965	£1 =17	1d = 7p	dominated most budgets. In
1995	£1 =2	200p	1800, they say, only 1 in 50
2013	£1 =1	100p	people wore socks!

Local Democracy, Politics and Facilities

In common with the rest of the country a Billingshurst citizen's democratic right to influence those who govern him, make law and to ensure they exercise it properly, has been for many years conducted through four layers of elected representatives. The lowest tier for well over a hundred years has been the Parish Council, formally instituted in 1894. For eight centuries before that the affairs of the parish were conducted by the Parish Churchwardens and subordinate officers and the magistrates.

The second tier of local government is the Horsham District Council, established in its present form in 1972/4. Prior to that there were three councils, Horsham Urban and Horsham and Chanctonbury Rural Districts. The third tier is the West Sussex County Council which has existed from the time when Sussex was formally halved in 1888. The top layer which makes national legislation is, of course, parliament, effectively the House of Commons. Billingshurst is part of the Horsham constituency, returning one MP. From 1997 this was Francis Maude. He was succeeded in 2016 by Jeremy Quin. Elections are held for all four bodies at four and five year intervals.

Each layer has particular areas of responsibility for which the duly elected representatives are accountable. Citizens often find this confusing as there is little evident publicity showing which body to contact and who is responsible for what. There have been unsuccessful attempts by Parliament to remove one layer, the County Council, in order to simplify local government. This was achieved in Brighton and Hove which became a Unitary Authority combining District and County functions in 1997. It is arguable that, ever since the end of the 19th century, power to raise taxes and conduct affairs has steadily shifted upwards to the centralised regime of Parliament and out of the hands of local electors.

The Parish Council is said to have only one statutory obligation, the provision of allotments. It has 15 elected members and employs a Parish Clerk and other clerks and assistants. It exercises influence over actions of higher tiers as it is, by law, a statutory consultee, for example on planning matters. Over and above that it has the option of providing amenities of its own choosing for the parishioners for which purposes it raises an annual local tax called the Parish Precept. To this end Billingshurst parish owns substantial land which it administers as sports grounds, recreational areas and gardens, allotments, public open space and as the site of the Community Centre. Its most important function is as a public forum and source of information where local people can seek advice, guidance and a medium through which to make known to authority their needs and grievances. Through its benign influence a complex web of voluntary organisations can flourish, adding to the quality of life of the village people. However it has no powers to make law itself beyond the rules and regulations of its own property.

Billingshurst Parish Council

Phone No: 01403 782555
www.billingshurst.gov.uk
email: council@billingshurst.gov.uk
Location: The Billingshurst Centre, Roman Way
15 elected parish councillors. Parish Meetings held monthly, supported by 7 main Committees and 10 Sub-Committees.
Parish Clerk:- Greg Burt

Chairmen of Council since 1895

Statistics

The village is among the top 15% of least deprived wards in England. 84% of households own a car which contrasts with a national average of 68%. Life expectancy for men in Horsham District is 79 and for women 83, the highest in Sussex. In 2001 the census found that 76% were Christian in religion, 94% were born in the UK and 98% were white. There were 122,088 people living in

Horsham District, 2.3 people per hectare. This was a 12.4% increase over 1991 figures. In 2015 29 crimes per 1000 people were recorded.

Other Village Bodies. The Community Partnership is a group of public-spirited volunteers who undertake research and attract funding and grants to organise facilities to meet identified needs. In 2011 the Partnership was awarded the prestigious Queen's Award for Voluntary Service. Amongst other things the Partnership was involved in the planning of the Leisure Centre, Jubilee Fields, Burnt Row regeneration, the fishing lake and the Childcare Centre as well as the initiation of hands-on services like the Lunch Club for the elderly, Billifest, a youth drop-in centre and the Eye Project.

The Chamber of Commerce supports the interests of some 80 businesses, shopkeepers and traders. It has staged an annual show called 'Billibiz' to publicise and help make prosperous the commercial life of the village and provides 'networking' opportunities through lunch clubs and other social events.

Horsham District Council, which includes three elected representatives from the Billingshurst ward, has its own specific areas of responsibility. The greatest of these is planning of housing development and the uses of buildings and business premises in accordance with the planning law of the land. This defines any development as "the carrying out of building, engineering, mining or other operations in, on, over or under land or the making of any material change in the use of any building or other land". To this end it has powers to grant or refuse planning permission according to established rules of its own making to those who apply for it and to prosecute anyone who fails to conform. This responsibility includes the particular form of use to which premises are put, alterations to properties and the protection of ancient buildings and communities through the designation of listed buildings and conservation areas. Billingshurst has such a carefully defined conservation area. It is also expected to keep up to date a locally determined twenty-year forward plan for future development, heavily conditioned by the dictates of the government of the day. On 27.11.2015 the Council adopted *The Horsham District Planning Framework*, available on its website.

Almost equal in importance is responsibility for the collection of waste, the one aspect familiar to most parishioners, and the policing of fly-tipping and other insults to the environment. The District also has responsibility for the actual housing of the public who do not own their own property which it exercises at the moment through an Association called Saxon Weald. Formerly the Council itself built and administered Council Housing. Much of this property has been sold to occupants and many consider that a new tranche of such development should be reintroduced to provide homes for those looking for affordable rental accommodation. At the time of this writing an extensive housing development authorised by the District Council in the 1990s is now maturing and many further piecemeal developments have sprung up. The District Council has recently granted outline planning permission, in the teeth of manifold local protests, for an estate of some 475 houses in the north east quadrant of the parish, with accompanying provision for improvements to the village infrastructure. The plans include an important road which will carry east-west A272 'through traffic' on to the Hilland Farm roundabout, so by-passing the village on three sides.

The District Council is a statutory consultee on many other matters such as hospitals and health, and like the Parish Council is empowered to provide leisure amenities, sports grounds, parks and gardens, and to support the arts through theatre, exhibitions and the Horsham Museum. The District Council is the Collector of Taxes for all forms of local government. It establishes an annual budget for itself to finance its own undertakings, but collects at the same time the Parish Precept, a sum to finance the Sussex Police Authority, and a much larger sum to provide funds to meet the County Council's requirements. This local tax, formerly known as the rates, is called the Community Charge and is levied on property, on a rising scale according to the value of the house. Business premises pay another separate rate.

West Sussex County Council is the top tier of local government which commands the lion's share of the Community Charge. This is largely the result of the County's responsibility for the provision of nursery, primary and secondary education up to the age of 18 for premises, and up to 16 for other educational needs. The general administration of education remains vested in the County, which decides, for example, school admissions, the designated catchment areas of schools and provides transport; but since 1989 control of curricula and school policies, powers of inspection and the use of taxpayers' money, has shifted locally to Governing Bodies and upwards to the Government Department of Education, and Ofsted, the national inspectorate of schools.

The County has other expensive responsibilities. Not the least of these is the disposal and recycling of waste which the District has collected. The County shares with the District the wider elements of strategic planning and has to look after coastal defences, provide for the County Fire Brigade and ensure the maintenance of proper trading standards, emergency services and transport. Even more relevant to most people is their responsibility for providing and maintaining roads and footpaths. The county also oversees the social services and provides public amenities such as the Library Service and the Public Record Office at

Chichester. Billingshurst elects one representative to the County Council every four years jointly with Rudgwick.

WSCC Public Library, Mill Way

There are other elected positions in local affairs. Parents elect some of the school governors and all citizens elect a leader of the all-Sussex Police Authority. Those in senior Cabinet positions were entitled to a supplementary allowance. The highest recent single person cost was £17,514. Similar, but more substantial, rates apply to the *County Councillors*. In 2014/15 their basic rate was £11,251. Cabinet Members could add £19,506 and the Leader's Allowance was £31,362. *All Councillors* are entitled to reclaim their necessary expenditure for travel and subsistence.

Party politics do not complicate discussion in the Parish Council. All the Members are 'Independent' so there are no manifestos or proposals for the future made known to voters at election time. Most electors are unlikely to know candidates personally so they are unaware of their ideas or any policies they may favour. In recent years there has been little or no competition for the 15 seats. At the time of writing there are unfilled vacancies awaiting volunteers. This is all in marked contrast to 1894 when 33 candidates were proposed. In those days elected Councillors enjoyed prestige among a smaller electorate, as they were already well-known for their active work in the village.

Though recent Councils have often canvassed public opinion on major issues as they arise and have researched proposals for village development, nevertheless the main role of the Council has remained that of a watchdog, passing judgment on the developments and initiatives of others. Proposals for change originate from many sources, the District Council, County Council, the Police, property developers, individual planning applicants, and creative development groups. The Community Partnership and the Chamber of Commerce, which now has seventy members, work in close collaboration to promote progress in village affairs.

However the Parish Councillors' judgments have most often been steered by the imperative to avoid risk and minimise expense. They have been reluctant to accept the cost and the burden of responsibility for initiating and overseeing onerous new undertakings. This has not proved to be a recipe for positive development and such negativity has often led to frustration among progressive elements in the community. Two examples of such dilatoriness are the failure to maintain the restored pumping site and picnic area created by the archaeological work at Burnt Row Cottages and a deliberate reluctance to approve a suitable central site for the provision of a purpose-built youth centre, a scheme known as 'The Eye Project', prepared by the go-ahead Partnership with well-researched proposals for feasibility and financing. This inertia has now lasted some six years.

The Parish Clerk is a salaried officer of the Council responsible for 'housekeeping', administering and implementing decisions, acting as the Financial Officer, providing a secretariat and offering legal advice and necessary information on all the Council's practices. It may well prove necessary, as the village population increases to that of a township and the financial precept increases proportionately, to upgrade this role to the status of a Chief Executive Officer. Such a provision of extra professional competence ought to inject yet more expertise into community enhancement. The volunteer Council members could then be actively supported in pursuing more proactive business. Attracting inward investment to offer employment in scientific and hi-tech light industry, promoting tourism, improving car parking, stimulating the arts and theatre, community social events and better amenities for youth and the elderly for example could ensue. In this way more adventurous leadership could be expected so as to improve the welfare and enrich the lives of all the people of Billingshurst who are expected to number some 12,000 by 2020 AD.

At District level politics ostensibly intrude, though at Horsham it has long been conducted on non-ideological lines, with most debate about levels of taxation and the quality of administration, rather than with matters of high political principle. A degree of common ground has existed between the Liberal Democrats and the dominant Conservative majority. Liberal Democrats have had control just once for only four years in the 1990s. Both parties have had the advantage of the wise advice from the Chief Executives and their staff of salaried public servants. The Labour Party has had only small representations on Horsham District Council which was Conservative for most of the early 20th century.

The County Council was for many years in the control of Conservatives and Independents, most of whom usually voted with the Conservatives against a small Labour opposition. During the 1980s the Liberal Democrats developed as the growing opposition group, and in the 1990s they took control for four years.

By 2013 the official opposition became the UK Independence Party which had won 10 of the 71 elected seats. However they lost them all again in May, 2017.

Jubilee Fields

Jubilee pitches and trail

The village playing fields are located immediately west of the western bypass. The main entrance is the first right-hand turn on the A272 road to Wisborough Green.

The Sports Pavilion, Jubilee Fields

The Sports Pavilion Bar – Jubilee Fields

The fields include association football pitches, a cricket field with pavilion, a fishing lake, a skate park and exercise path. The facility is managed by the Billingshurst Sports and Recreations Association.

An interesting archaeological site, Burnt Row, was thoroughly excavated in 2004 by the Weald School and Brinsbury College, revealing the foundations of a dwelling, renamed Weavers Cottage, a disused well and numerous historical artefacts. As Southern Cottage it had survived until at least 1935. It is now part of a country walk with picnic tables. The land, in 1603, belonged to one John Longhurst and is shown on maps as 'Burntrough'. The last known inhabitant was Edna Hayward who moved into West Street when the cottage was demolished. In the 1920s the cottage had a Coventry pump at the well to send water up to Tedfold Farm.

Other Facilities

The Community and Conference Hall off Roman Way is at the heart of the community and acts as host to a regular programme of clubs, educational and fitness activities, entertainments, meetings, elections and civic affairs. Examples are The Local History Society, The Community Transport Scheme (01403 787696), Film Nights, Short Mat Bowls, Yoga, and Rainbow Toddlers.

The Public Library is in the Mill Lane car park. (WSCC).

Public toilets are also found beside the Mill Lane car park.

Jubilee Fields Pavilion hosts Soccer and Cricket Clubs, The Angling Society, a weekly Youth Club and the Lions Club.

The Bowls Club is off Myrtle Lane, self-contained in the grounds of the Weald School.

The Recreation Ground off Lower Station Rd. has the Tennis Club and the Scouts, Guides, Cubs and Brownies.

Swimming Pool, gym, sports hall, studio and synthetic pitch are at the Leisure

Centre off Station Road beside the Family & Children's Nursery Centre.
Children's Play Areas are at Manor Fields, Cranham Avenue and Cherry Tree Close.
St. Mary's Room East St. hosts The Women's Institute, The Trefoil Guild and The Wednesday Group.
And St.Mary's Church is home for The Choral Society.
British Legion meets at various venues.
The Rotary Club meets, in 2016, at The Blacksmith's Arms, Adversane.
At the Women's Hall are The Dramatic Society and the Horticultural Society.
St. Gabriel's Hall, East St. hosts the Wine and Beer Circle and a playgroup.
Other playgroups are Dauxwood Pre-School off Natts Lane and the Community Centre.
62 allotment sites are at Manor Fields off Coombe Hill.
Waste recycling and a Community Tip for convenient disposal is at Newbridge Rd. by Jubilee Fields.
The Surgery – Roman Way 01403 782931
Mini-bus Association -01403 782695
Meals on Wheels (WRVS) 265280
WEA - 01403 784438
Adult Education – 0845 601 0161
Registrar of Births, Marriages and Deaths – 01243 642122

BEAT – Billingshurst Emergency Assistance Team. This is a volunteer group of trained 'responders' offering life-saving skills in critical circumstances. They operate in partnership with the County Ambulance Service. They offer oxygen and make available 16 defibrillators in the event of suspected cardiac arrest. 07930 416835

Community Gardens: Extensive works are ongoing to create attractive gardens and leisure amenities on the site of the old cricket ground and part of the former village football pitch.

The Women's Hall was built at the expense of the Beck Sisters, Ellen and Edith, keen supporters of Mrs Pankhurst and of female emancipation. They added the Mothers' Garden next door in 1926. Here the playground equipment was restored in 2003 at a cost of £25,000 raised by voluntary subscription, bolstered by the Lions Club and the King's Arms.

There are community facilities for public and private hire at The Community

Centre, The Women's Hall, St. Gabriel's Hall, St. Mary's Rooms, Trinity Reformed Church

Churches
St. Mary's C of E, East St., St. Gabriel's Catholic, East St., Trinity United Reformed Church, West St., Family Church –Community Centre, Unitarian Chapel off the High Street. Quakers meet at the Blue Idol, Coolham.

Schools
Billingshurst Primary School, 4-11 years, Upper Station Road
The Weald School, Comprehensive Community School, 11 – 18.

Community Recreational Gardens, Upper Station Road

Utilities
Piped water came to Billingshurst in 1911, coal gas from 1907 and mains electricity in 1934. The telephone was introduced, at first with a manual exchange with the few subscribers enjoying a two digit phone number. The automatic telephone exchange off Mill Way, now almost redundant, and a barrier to linkage between two car parks, was built in 1963 and extended in the 70s.

We often overlook the effect of the availability of ample clean piped water coupled with electrical light and power on the possibility of new industries and fresh job opportunities for village people. At last some light industries like The Whirlwind and its water heater successor could flourish and young men and women could find local work other than farm jobs, domestic service or the traditional crafts that had been practised in the village from time immemorial.

Western by-pass

Footbridge over the by-pass to Sports Fields

In 1993 the issue of providing a by-pass at the cost of extra housing which would finance it and other necessary infra-structure projects, mobilised public opinion more than anything before or since. Ten years earlier in 1983 The Billingshurst Society had canvassed opinion, printed numerous letters opposing the idea but finally decided to support it. The Weald School conducted a 10 point survey for a week and Mrs. Paton, Chairman of Governors, reported their findings. On two out of four days 15,600 vehicles travelled through the busiest part of the High Street in a 12 hour period 7 a.m. to 7 p.m. On each weekday more than 2.200 heavy vehicles were in the High Street during the same period. The school also conducted an opinion poll and found 74.4% were in favour of a by-pass despite anxiety about the cost, the likely loss of passing trade, 'concreting over the countryside' and unwanted extra development in the village.

The District Council had tabled a plan for a southern by-pass linking the A272 to the A29 through Daux Wood and crossing the railway line. An overcrowded Parish Council Meeting was followed by another in The Weald School Sports Hall attended by 800 people who unanimously condemned the scheme and favoured a western by-pass with a limited number of about 400 houses. The Council accepted this judgment and proposed three alternative western routes. One was chosen at a 'cost' of over 550 houses to be built in accordance with a design brief which complemented the traditional vernacular architecture of the village.

The road was opened in 1996 to relieve traffic congestion in the village centre along the A29 road from London to Bognor Regis. It is claimed to have reduced North-South through traffic by 40% to 10,000 per day. East-West traffic is estimated at 6200 per day.

Traffic through the High Street gave cause for concern even in the more leisurely days of horse-drawn coaches when vehicle movements were limited to a score of trips of stage coaches, freight wagons and private traps and carriages. The Burial Register notes that in March, 1839 Job Bridger, aged 13 was run over and killed by the Comet Coach and in 1842 Ruth Holden, aged 2, suffered exactly the same fate. Children could then play hop-scotch and cricket in the High Street. In the minutes of the Parish Council of 1909: 'carried unanimously that the attention of the County Council be called to the dangerous speeds at which motor cars pass through Billingshurst'. However by 1939 a writer lamented that he was obliged to drive through at five miles per hour because it was impossible to proceed faster in the continuous queue that stretched from Bognor to London. He called for the urgent building of a by-pass. By 1990, 50 years later, particularly in summer, matters were a great deal worse. The coming of the western by-pass may have reduced 'passing trade', especially for the motor business, but the relief from congestion and exhaust fumes has been warmly welcomed.

The housing development brought with it a number of improvements to the village infrastructure. As well as paying for the by-pass the developers were required to fund such things as Jubilee Sports Fields, the Community Centre, the all-weather pitch at the Weald, enhancements to the High Street and to make financial contributions for the schools and to give a £1M contribution for the new swimming pool.

The A29 follows the ancient Roman Stane Street for many miles. It was known at one time as 'The Devil's Road', supposedly because it was the only engineered road in the neighbourhood and seemed unnaturally straight compared with all other tracks.

The Billingshurst Society

Aileen Walker and Billingshurst Society Colleagues

In 1975, prompted by anxieties about planning and development issues, a group of like-minded village citizens founded The Billingshurst Society "to provide a forum for discussion on matters concerning the parish and to act as a channel through which members can make known their opinions to the appropriate authorities", meaning the Parish, District and County Councils, the MP, the Police Authority, etc. It campaigned for necessary improvements to lighting, drainage and crossings. It also sponsored such activities as the planting of three hundredweight of daffodil bulbs to help beautify the village and the designing of the village signs. It ran theatre trips, organised walks, held suppers, sponsored 'Made in Billingshurst' exhibitions and the Best Kept Village Competition. Its membership rose to over 800 people.

    Mrs. Aileen Walker, who was made MBE in 1998, was the leading light of the Society. She it was who did the pictures for the village signs that Mr. Gordon Simkin designed. She resigned from the Committee in 1988, when a warm appreciation was published in the bi-monthly news letter recognising her contribution to the village, her enthusiasm and knowledge of planning matters. The newsletter kept readers informed on all parish issues as they occurred in the agendas and minutes of the relevant Committees and, though non-political, took on a campaigning stance whenever it judged the majority of the numerous members so wished. In many instances its powerful influence proved persuasive, as about the Southern by-pass, and it welcomed the coming of Budgens Supermarket in 1986. But in the matter of many developments, it was less effectual and was criticised by some as striking an attitude of opposition to nearly every proposed change. When issues of development or conservation were in the balance its stance was generally opposed to expansion. John Richards, a notable local journalist, was a staunch pillar of the Society until he moved away to Boston. He wrote to say how his new community was uninformed by contrast with the useful service to the community that the Billingshurst Society provided. Nevertheless as the membership declined, older officers died or stood down and could not be replaced and meetings were sparsely attended the Society ceased to function in October 2005.

An influential member once wrote in the Society Newsletter: "I suspect that quite a lot of the people who came to 'the country' don't really like it – and won't be happy until Billingshurst looks like Purley…Do we need FEWER car parks, LESS street lighting, FEWER street signs?"

Robin Edgar, styled 'The Bard of Billingshurst' contributed a poem lamenting the passing of the old village character with the coming of the by-pass and housing estates:-

Progress – Well Change?
Sixty years ago 'twas mooted,
Ideas canvassed, schemes all touted,
Meetings called, the options shouted,
'Heated debates' – opponents clouted,
Scepticism, 'senses doubted'…
Finally protesters flouted –
Tarmac ordered, concrete grouted –
Billingshurst's surounderbouted.

Sad, but you are not the first
Small village to be by-pass cursed
Developmentally immersed
Until you think your seams will burst,
Until you can't recall the erst –
while shape of Billingshurst.
Progress now has done its worst,
So Goodbye little village-hurst

And Bonjour Greater Ville-de-hurst.

The Society was indignant about the development of 41 houses at Lakers Meadow, holding that the Butcher's Field should be preserved as open space or used as a car park and also opposed the building of Kingsfold Close. It considered that no playing fields should be built outside the Western by-pass. Its little publications were spiced up with anecdotes, memories and historical accounts to which this book is much indebted.

Evolutionary History

If we take the long view, the spot on the planet we call Billingshurst has enjoyed or endured a wide variety of climates and its surface has risen and fallen above and below sea level on untold occasions. Over the last 150 million years alone subterranean forces have heaved up the earth's crust into highlands. Those highlands have as often been weathered away to be redeposited under seas in the form of sands, gravels, chalk and clay layers. These layers too have been folded up by sideways pressure, only to be eroded once more by water and ice and deposited in new deltas to form sedimentary strata. To complicate matters further, the varying position of the earth in relation to the sun and alterations in its orbit have caused climatic changes over and above those occasioned by elevation. Also 'continental drift', the breaking up of a single land mass, has meant major shifts of a spot like Billingshurst to alter its position on the globe. Other cosmic forces led to five mass extinctions, each one almost destroying one world of evolution of plants and animals only to give an opportunity to surviving organisms to recreate a new and different one.

The mind-boggling time taken for all these changes, occurring world-wide, has enabled the comparatively recent emergence of flora and fauna as we experience them in Billingshurst. Now, as a result of evolution, millions of species of plants and animals live alongside us, Homo sapiens, whose own history dates back a mere 70,000 years. What follows is a brief resume of events and their consequences for wildlife and landscape in our area.

545 Million years ago

Cambrian period. First organisms – bacteria, multi-celled algae, plankton, sponges, Arthropods such as trilobites with an exoskeleton.

495 M

Ordovician period. Marine invertebrates, primitive vertebrate fish, snails, clams, corals and sponges. At the end of the period, there was *a mass extinction, wiping out approximately 75% of all species.*

443 M

Silurian period. Earliest land plants – lichens, liverworts, arachnids, millipedes, the earliest insects, jawless fish, big crab-like arthropods.

417 M

Devonian period. 'The age of fishes', Sharks and Rays with gills. Plants with roots and leaves –Forests of horsetails and ferns. 30 metre tall fern-like trees. Arthropods (with exoskeleton), vertebrates, fish. *Second mass extinction wiping out 70% of species. Many corals were lost.*

354 M

Carboniferous - Giant horsetails, mosses and ferns. Swamp-loving plants. Primitive conifers (Subsequently coal.) Amphibious reptiles, clams, crustaceans, giant dragonflies, cockroaches.

290 M

Permian period - conifer forests, seed-bearing plants, primitive ancestors of dinosaurs, birds and mammals, beetles.

248 M

The Triassic era began with the third and greatest mass extinction of 96% of marine and 70% of terrestrial life and ended with another fourth devastating extinction (75%). This is the Age of Reptiles. The first true mammals evolved, together with turtles, snakes, lizards and frogs.

205 M

Jurassic period – the triumph of the dinosaurs following the mass extinction. The 100 ton Brachiosaurus trampled cone-bearing conifer forests and the stegosaurus consumed horsetails and ferns. Circa 150 the Kimmeridge beds were laid down, now an oil source.
A major tectonic drift of land masses occurred, creating our present continents.

142 M

Cretaceous period – our main soils of Sussex were laid down, clays, sands and chalk, above the Jurassic deposits under shallow seas. Horsham stone and Sussex marble were deposited in the clay beds which contain fossils of early carp and freshwater sharks, crocodiles and turtles. The climate was sub-tropical. New groups of mammals and birds evolved living alongside dinosaurs, now often carnivorous such as Tyrannosaurus Rex. The famous sauropod named Titanosaurus, weighing 70 metric tonnes, which fed on tree tops, died in Patagonia 101.6 million years ago. Flowering plants evolved amid ferns and horsetails. Ants, gall wasps, early butterflies and moths, marine reptiles, ammonites and multitudes of marine life all flourished.

65 M

Tertiary era. *Following another fifth mass extinction* (75%) the dinosaurs vanished. The ammonites, many flowering plants and the pterosaurs [flying reptiles] all disappeared. This was the age when the mammals emerged. The ancestral horses, dogs, cats and pigs all evolved, for example, together with the first primates, ancestors of mankind (hominids). Rhinos, camels, rodents, hoofed herbivores. Grasses and other plants more similar to today.

The Wealden anticline, a great dome, was thrown up by folding upwards under lateral pressure. This loosened arch of rock subsequently was weathered away to leave the chalk escarpments, now known as the North and South Downs, and in Billingshurst clay soils at the surface characteristic of the Lower Weald.

500,000 years ago

The Paleolithic period. Boxgrove man, precursors of Neanderthal man and *Homo sapiens* had arrived in Sussex. Fauna included elephant, rhino, bear, wolf, hyena, mink and vole. Better not go down in the woods today! The climate was mild.

125,000 years ago

First of some 6 or 8 ice ages begin covering glaciated regions north of the Thames.

10,000 years ago

Ice retreating, Tundra conditions with arctic animals, reindeer, polar bears etc. [Many 'Creationist' thinkers believe that God created the earth at some point since this time!]

8,000 years ago

Mesolithic period. The land sinks, waters rise and the 'Continent was isolated'. The British Isles come into being. Our native trees evolved, elm, hazel, birch, pine, alder and lime. Warm wet conditions returned. Mankind has developed as hunter-gatherers, nomadic in life-style and using flint tools.

6,300 years ago

Neolithic first farmers were clearing trees for crops. Fauna now include wild boar, deer, beaver, wolf, and polecat. Ash trees grew. The lynx, reindeer and wild ox died out.

3,500 years ago

Bronze Age. More development on better soils and chalk with some clearance of wood (1500 BC) in valley bottom alluvium such as Billingshurst. Livestock farming begins on favoured sites.

2,700 years ago

Iron Age. Deeper ploughing. Weald forest still largely undisturbed. Native lime trees now (700 BC) extinct.

406 AD

Saxons arrive. Serious work begins around Billingshurst felling the native oaks and farming the fields.

Subsequently: The Normans brought in the rabbit. The black rat brought the plague in the 12th century. It died out in the 1950s like the red squirrel. The brown rat arrived in the 18th century and the grey squirrel in the 19th. The red deer died out then too. Wild polecats disappeared in the 1920s. Ferrets continued as domestic animals for catching rabbits.

Exotic plants from all round the world introduced by plant-hunters have been cultivated in gardens since the 18th century.

Although potatoes first came to Britain in Shakespeare's time they were treated with distrust for 200 years. Cobbett declared they were not fit for animal food. However about 1800, prompted by food scares of the Napoleonic wars, there was official promotion of potato growing in England. They became a welcome option for poorer people so that by Victoria's accession hot potatoes, buttered and salted were on sale in London streets for a penny each. (40p). By that time Billingshurst gardeners would have begun to grow them.

E.C.M Haes writes in his *Natural History of Sussex*, 'The Weald Clay is mainly of interest for oak woodland with its carpet of spring flowers, fine display of autumn fungi and great variety of butterflies and moths... It is gumboot country'.

In 1993, Ann Baczkowska, a District Councillor, wrote about Daux and Rosier Woods. "We walk the woods daily and often see Green Woodpeckers, Deer, Fox, Squirrel, Weasels as well as White Admirals and other woodland insects. We are told that the dormouse has been seen there and that the Nightingale is also heard. The woods are largely hazel coppice with oak standards, although other species such as Sweet Chestnut and Holly also grow there. The ground flora is varied and includes Butcher's Broom, Bluebells, Primroses and Wood Anemones, and there are two neglected ponds and a large wet area. We appreciate that Sussex is blessed with many high quality Woodlands, but we feel that Daux and Rosier Woods are of immense local importance as they are the only woods within walking distance of Billingshurst, and as such are enjoyed by many local people as well as wildlife, and are of great landscape value. We would like to see them protected from development." [When this was written the woods were under threat from a proposed southern by-pass.]

Woodland bluebells

Before the 'first syllable of recorded time'.

We have to assume that Billingshurst was no different from the rest of what are now the British Isles in offering living-room to *Homo sapiens* and probably to even more primitive hominids from the very earliest times.

500,000 BC

On the evidence of findings at Boxgrove, north-east of Chichester, on a land surface subsequently covered by a gravel beach, our earliest predecessors in the Middle Pleistocene period made flint axes in order to butcher wild animals like rhinos, lions, bears, wild horses and deer. This was *Homo heidelbergensis*, the common ancestor of the *Neanderthals* and *Homo sapiens*. The ones we know about lived on the former beach surface of a great lagoon at the foot of a former chalk cliff during a warm inter-glacial period when the old silt beach stood high relative to the sea. When the glaciers returned to the north the land sank. The waters returned, covering the leavings of the people who lived there with silt, together with gravel and outwash debris from the falling cliff. This preserved a rich archaeological record for us to find in the early 1990s.

These were probably some of the earliest hominids in Europe and it is most likely that they made group sorties in search of meat all over what is now Sussex. They had not yet made fire, had nothing recognisable as a language but were brilliant axe tool-makers and fashioners of spears. An iron-stained axe labled 'Rowner' exists from this time. Subsequently glacial episodes interrupted developments in this Palaeolithic, or Old Stone Age period. It is important to grasp how extensive was that aeon of time; half a million years! Equally we must remember the long sequence of radical changes of climate, sea levels, geology and landscape that occurred in that half a million passing years.

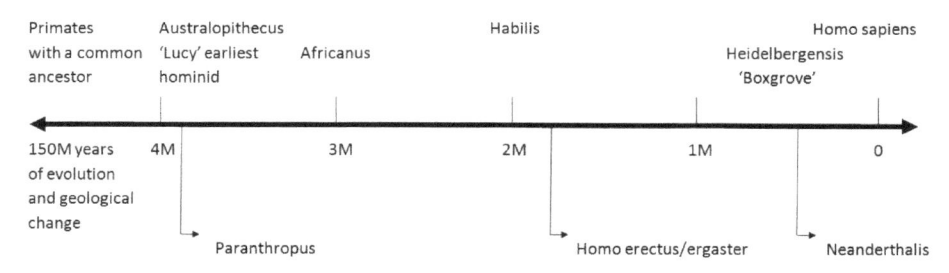

The descent of Boxgrove man and Homo sapiens

500,000 years was but a moment when compared with the 150 million years that preceded it when the underlying sedimentary rocks were laid down and then bent up into a great arch, only to be weathered away, leaving us the chalk North and South Downs and the Greensands and clays that outcrop between them.

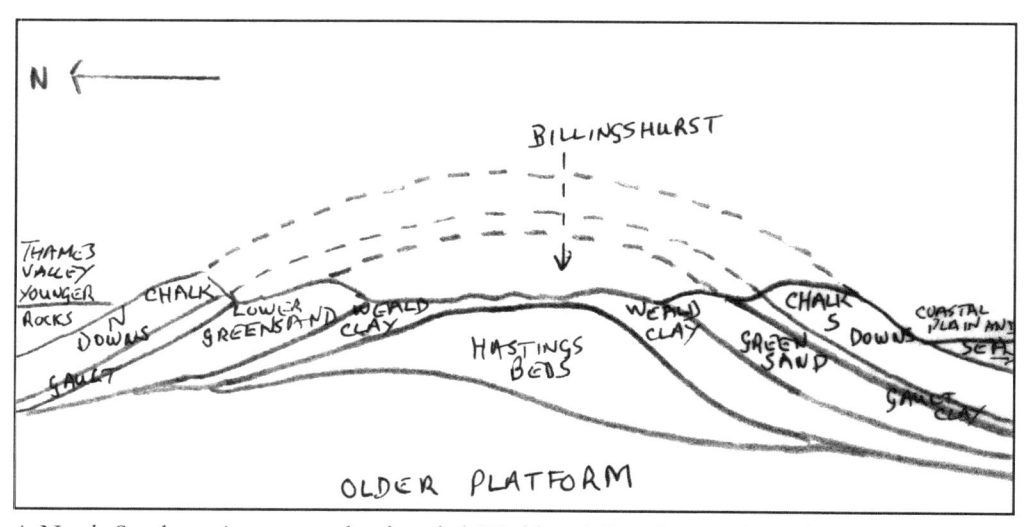

A North-South section across the denuded Weald anticline showing how the underlying rocks outcrop at the surface

40,000 BC

Neanderthal people were living in southern Britain some 40,000 years ago in what is now Pulborough. There is recently revealed evidence of occupation at Beedings Castle off Nutbourne Lane on the greensand ridge. They left behind several craftsman-like flint tools in Hampshire, Kent and elsewhere, notably beautifully made 'boute coupe' hand axes. They succumbed however and were superseded by Cro-Magnon man, the true *Homo sapiens*, also hunter gatherers and nomadic in lifestyle, but sophisticated enough to sew skins, catch fish and wear jewellery. They had discovered the benefits of fire.

It is likely that the Neanderthals would have explored and hunted along the Arun Valley and its tributaries even if they did not live there.

Homo sapiens exploits the Planet

6,000BC

From 12,000 BC, after the last ice-age, termed the Neolithic, or New Stone Age, climate change had altered the western European landscape into treeless tundra. *Homo sapiens*, by then, were hunting for the meat of deer and wild horses. In the period from about 8,000 to 3,000 BC, known as the Mesolithic, 'Doggerland', the land bridge to mainland Europe, was finally flooded by rising ice-melt and 'Europe was isolated'. Meantime in Iraq and Palestine quite sophisticated people were constructing the earliest buildings. There is much evidence that New Stone Age people were living in the Arun valley. A site at Okehurst, on sandy ground overlooking the Arun, shows occupation in a pit dwelling and the flaking of flints for at least 2000 years, longer than the present village has existed.

5,000BC

Socially developed people, recognisably 'modern' humans were known to have flourished as far north as the Orkneys in 5,000BC.

From then onwards the climate warmed, trees grew and boar and aurochs (cattle) entered the diet. Dogs and pigs were domesticated, horses trained to work. Sheep wool was made into cloth. There is much evidence of stone-age people living in the Billingshurst area. Local farmers are known to have gathered knapped flints turned up by the plough and a ground greenstone axe. They may well have been the tools brought in by hunters from the south in search of deer meat and skins. Flint flakes have been found in Daux Wood and Clevelands.

On the island of Papa Westray is a Neolithic farmstead, the oldest preserved standing building in northern Europe. A cluster of eight sophisticated dwellings, dating from 3,180BC and known as the 'Scottish Pompeii, is well-preserved at Skara Brae.

Axe heads found at Wisborough Green

4,000 to 2,000BC

The Neolithic time lasted from before 4,000 to 2,500 BC. This is the period of cave-dwellers and the rise of farming for sustenance – but not of dinosaurs. They were living a mere 150 million years earlier! Fred Flintstone deserves an Oscar for the most enjoyable anachronism of retro-science fiction. This is the era of henges, monuments and stone circles. Industrial flint mining was carried on at Cissbury, north of Worthing. There were flint mines at Blackpatch and Harrow Hill north of Angmering where excavations have revealed antler and ox shoulder-blade tools, flint axes, lamps and galleries. It was the dawn of religion, and massive public works like Stonehenge. There is much evidence that such people lived in Billingshurst, especially in the river valley.

Excavated flint pit at Harrow Hill showing galleries.

To 700BC

The Bronze Age lasted from 2,000 to 700 BC. That era is associated with beaker pottery, turned on a wheel, metal culture, using gold, silver, tin and copper and with long barrows and cremation urns and an economy based on mixed farming with livestock. Billingshurst had middle Bronze Age people dwelling locally on the evidence of five axes found 'near Hammers Farm' in the 19th Century, said to be in the British Museum. Bronze, a mixture of copper and tin, made stronger tools. In this era the greatest innovation of all time, the wheel, which was discovered in Sumer (modern Iraq), came to Britain.

A wooden wheel, probably from a horse-drawn cart of about 1000 BC, has been excavated at Flag Fen near Peterborough where a remarkably well-preserved causeway and many Bronze Age artefacts such as weapons and ornaments have been found.

The Ancient Britons and the valley where they lived

200AD

It is probable that our whole area was by now covered by the as yet unnamed Wealden Forest, so the earliest settlement would have been beside the local stream, feeding the River Arun which runs for some miles along the boundary of the present parish. Billingshurst lies in a broad valley, or better a three-sided basin, at the confluence of small streams rising from low clay hills to the South, East and North. Those streams met together, the main one running along what is now the High Street. Then it would have been a sparkling stream among the trees, but it now runs in a culvert, hidden from view since the beginning of the 19th century. It was once called the barrel drain, probably because barrels were used to create it. Water drained in from ponds in the Jengers area on the West, and off Billingshurst Hill to the North. The main feeder ran along the bottom of the steep sided Bowling Alley to the North East draining the area later called Cocksbrook. The water course then joins the Parbrook, again from the East, rising in the area round Great Daux running on the north side of Daux Avenue and now piped to the brook alongside Natts Lane. It then flows west forming a tributary of the Arun.

Hills to the North East form the watershed between the Adur and the Arun rivers at 120 feet above sea level, only a short distance beyond the East Street Hill. Places as close as Summers Place, Wooddale and Rowfold Grange drain northwards to the River Adur.

Any villagers then would have been 'Ancient Britons' speaking a Celtic language not dissimilar from Welsh, Gaelic and Breton. It is an open question whether they were really a Celtic race who had invaded from Gaul. The working of metals evolved into smelting and forging of iron tools and weapons – the Iron Age. Warring tribes developed. Those in our region were the Atrebates. These tribes had a King or Queen, nobility, middle and working classes and slaves. They built hill forts like The Trundle where many lived, worked and trained for warfare. They worshipped local gods and animals, the Druids, their priests, setting great store by human and blood sacrifices to appease their gods.

The geology of West Sussex dictated where earlier people chose to live. The loamy soils of the area round Chichester, extending eastwards to Brighton, gave the best farming opportunities to in-comers, and the chalk downs, together with the gault clay and greensand belts north of the scarp slope offered a welcome to successive invaders, much friendlier than the dense woodlands and intractable clay of the Low Weald. Iron Age Celts, Romans, Saxons and initially even the Normans chose to live and work on the 'Champion', as the favoured area is known.

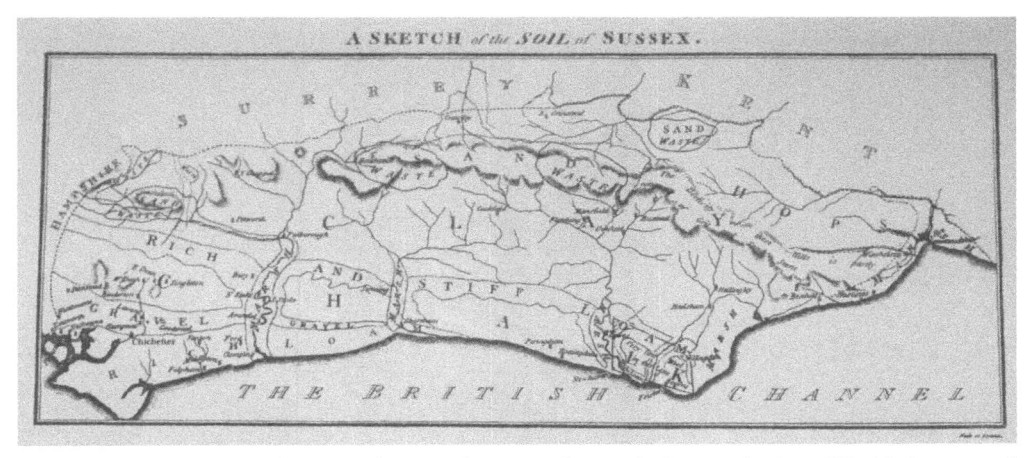

Sketch of 1813 showing the soils of Sussex, better in the south than in the Low Weald clay around Billingshurst.

To 43AD

The Belgae, a tribe from Belgium, arrived on the Manhood peninsula from 200 to 43 BC. Much of the rest of Britain was now a patchwork of forest and fields where tillable land had been exploited by clearing the trees. Our Billingshurst district would have remained largely dense woodland, since the trees and shrubs that flourished in the clay and the absence of firm roads in the winter mud created a formidable forest barrier. The English Oak, known as the 'Sussex Weed' (Quercus robor) dominated the flora. Just to the north iron ore seams might well have given rise to some deforestation though the earliest known iron workings were in the High Weald of eastern Sussex. Daux Wood remains as the closest descendant we still have of the original natural ancient Anderida Forest. To the south, Chanctonbury and Cissbury evolved into forts at this time.

Nevertheless during extensive archaeological investigations in 2014 on high ground north east of the Bowling Alley, named as the Nine Acre Field on the Tithe map, small quantities of residual Prehistoric finds were collected suggesting low level exploitation of the landscape. The earliest features of the site comprised drainage ditches and cooking pits of Middle Iron Age date (say 100 – 200BC), indicating early modification of the landscape and a more permanent human presence in the area. Very limited quantities of imported wine amphora fragments suggest there may well have been more permanent trade routes through the region during the Iron Age.

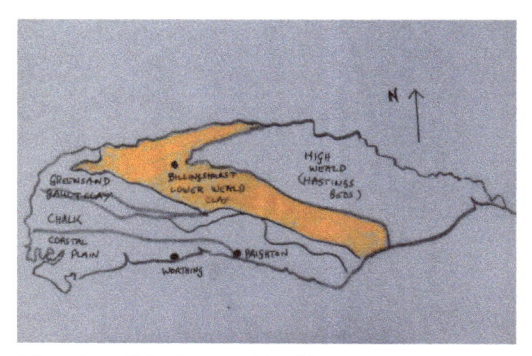

Excavated site of a round-house   The clay of the Lower Weald

The coming of the Romans and their legacy

43AD

The Roman Emperor, Claudius, profiting from knowledge of Julius Caesar's failed invasions of 54 and 55 BC, which had been ruined by bad weather, sent 40,000 invading troops to the south coast of Britain. They had the willing cooperation of the King of the Regnenses (the realm from Dover to Chichester) named Togidubnus who was one of the Belgae. He later became Tiberius Claudius Cogidumnus. Thus a tribal chief was enabled to build a spectacular palace at Fishbourne as a reward for his connivance in the subjugation of most of Britain as part of the Roman Empire. The Britons, speaking Celtic, would have been obliged to understand some Latin to stay on good terms with their Roman masters.

45 to 470 AD

The Romans established extensive settlements on the coastal plain at Noviomagus Reginorum, (meaning 'New Market') which became Chichester, at Fishbourne and Bignor. By 70 AD they had built the straight road we now call Stane Street (A29) as a post road link to Londinium. The nearest Posting Station for resting and changing horses is just south of Pulborough at Hardham. The next is north of Billingshurst at Alfoldean (Roman Gate). The Street alters its straight course by 7 degrees at North Heath to meet the Arun crossing at Pulborough and makes a slight bend beside where the stream flowed by the present High Street.

A conquering power must be able to move military forces quickly over the subject territory in order to suppress rebellion such as that by Boudicca and to challenge enemies at the borders like the Picts and Scots. The road itself, however, shows little evidence of military fortification. By creating Stane Street and subsequent extensions in all directions from Londinium the Romans achieved their security and access to the metal ores and other benefits their client state could provide.

It has long been thought that the Romans avoided any settlements or agriculture on the Low Weald clay, preferring to build their villas on the coastal plain, the chalk downs or on the greensand ridge. The received opinion was that the whole ancient Wealden Forest had remained in its original virginal state, or at any rate from the era of New Stone Age hunters and foragers.

It was recognised that there had been Iron Age iron working activity at the eastern end of the Weald and a Roman Villa westwards at Chiddingfold in Surrey but these were regarded as exceptions to the general rule. However about 2009 a series of round-houses and agricultural enclosures was revealed at Horley indicating that there had been some settlement in the Middle/Late Iron Age and in Roman times. As early as 1966 pottery from the 2nd century had been unearthed at Hills Place, Horsham. Further evidence of continual occupation came from excavations at Broadbridge Heath, again showing round-houses, enclosures and much pottery dating from C22 BC to 300 AD.

Next a significant revision of thought on the early first millennium history of the district came from work at Millfield, Southwater in 2012. A settlement dating from the 1st Century AD was found with some likelihood that its inception predated the Roman invasion of 43 AD. Here large enclosed space with drainage ditches encompassed an area of what was most likely pasture or arable land, originally subdivided, and with a probable round-house and many pits. There too was evidence of Roman activity in the 2nd and 3rd Century – coins, pottery and querns.

The recent Billingshurst findings east of Stane Street may be taken finally to disprove the accepted historical judgment. It is entirely reasonable to suppose that the building and maintenance of the Roman Road and sustenance for travellers along it, over a period of some 350 years, would have occasioned the development of small holdings and dwelling places on higher ground at a convenient distance from the highway wherever the forest was penetrable. Indeed the Iron Age finds suggest that areas in the Low Weald were utilised on a discontinuous basis by successive populations ready to meet the challenge of the trees and the mud. There are indications that in Billingshurst there was some small-scale exploitation in the Bronze Age though no actual evidence of settlement sites.

The archaeologists' report from 2015 researches reveals the initial actual settlement of the Billingshurst site occurred in the Late Iron Age/Early Roman period and comprised a rectangular enclosure containing a single round-house and a possible working area. Sherds of wine vessels dating from before the Roman invasion imply that there may well have been trading between the Celts and Mediterranean peoples and some more extensive use of the higher ridges east of the present village for husbanding animals and growing crops.

By the 1st to 2nd Century AD the small settlement underwent a major reorganisation with the excavation of a new settlement enclosure. An associated large stock enclosure was constructed to the north, along with an extensive field system extending to the east together with a drove/hollow way. Evidence of increasing exploitation of the area and its resources was given by small quantities of iron smithing slag in deposits of this date. Two cremations were identified both associated with the north-west entrance to the stock enclosure.

The settlement was abandoned by the middle of the 2nd Century (say 150 AD) and remained so until the 3rd Century when a final phase of activity occurred. Charcoal and pottery-rich deposits were dumped in the uppermost hollows of the enclosure ditches around the 3rd and 4th Centuries AD (200 – 400). However they were not associated with any contemporary newly cut features. Though there was no fresh settlement the deposits do indicate there were more dwellings in the wider vicinity. The final and clinching piece of evidence for late Roman activity in Billingshurst comprised a small hoard of 21 3rd and 4th Century Roman coins, identified in the uppermost fills of the 1-2 Century drainage ditch.

The new question posed by this discovery is what happened after the 4th Century when the Romans withdrew. One might speculate that, with the departure of the controlling masters, the Celtic slaves they doubtless employed would have decamped westwards rather than confront the Saxon newcomers or stayed to mingle with them. In all likelihood from about 390 to 800 AD the Saxons would have established themselves on the more tractable soils to the south and made only foraging or hunting expeditions along upper reaches of the Arun as has always been believed. The farms and dwellings would have been plundered for anything portable, then largely neglected. First the scrub, like that in the Bowling Alley today, and then the oaks would have returned. Thereafter as the Saxon incomers expanded their numbers and influence a fresh era of assarting would begin. With the coming of the Normans and the Manorial system of land management this process would have been completed and a permanent pattern of fields, woods and hedgerows established. It is conceivable that the Saxon clearances were often of a new generation of forest rather than of virgin woodlands of ancient prehistoric origin. However so extensive was the clay region that the concept of a great forest, self-rejuvenating from the continuous decay of fallen timber from time immemorial is still a valid supposition.

"I go, ---I come back!" was a much-loved catchphrase from Tommy Handley's wartime radio comedy 'ITMA'. It could well be employed as a pattern for mankind's relationship with the Low Weald of Sussex. There is evidence of some localised clearances by much earlier hominids, people of the Mesolithic (Middle Stone Age 9,000 to 4,000 BC) and yet more in the early Neolithic period (Middle Stone Age 4,000-2,500 BC) who left pits and flints to mark their presence. These fluctuating incursions may well have dated back some 500,000 years to the time of Boxgrove Man, *Homo Heidelbergensis*. Over a protracted epoch continual localised deforestation and human exploitation by glacial and post-glacial hunter-gatherers

Archaeological research October, 2014 on Nine Acre Field

followed by regeneration from the time of the last Ice Age (12,000 years ago) is by no means inconceivable. Such early activities were most likely of woodland clearings to encourage diversification in plant and animal species to improve foraging and hunting potential.

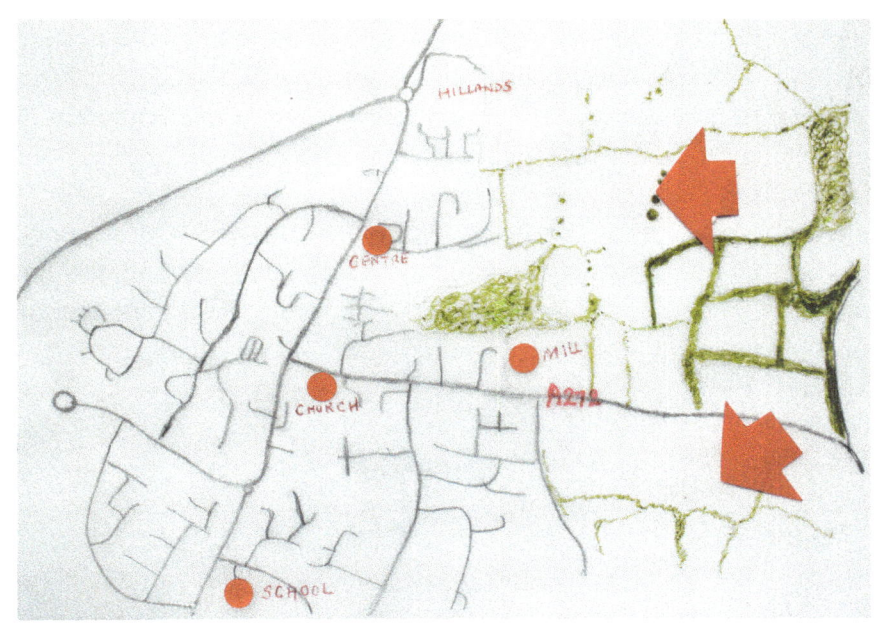

Pre-Saxon farmsteads east of Stane Street

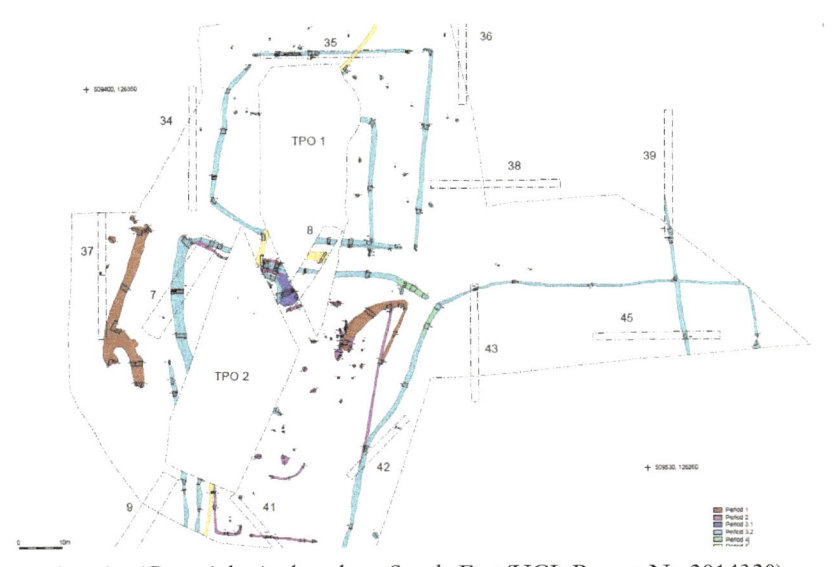

Excavation site (Copyright Archaeology South-East/UCL Report No.2014320)

Stane Street left a legacy on the economic and cultural landscape of Sussex. All subsequent roads were orientated in parallel, up to London and down to the coast, essential both for defence and for trade. The Romans did branch out eastwards from Stane Street, towards Lewes, at Hardham for example, in order to exploit iron ore in East Sussex. Generally, however, East-West routes were rudimentary and not developed. Even today only two major roads traverse the south of England, shadowing both the North and South Downs. The third route, the A272, linking East Sussex and Hampshire which crosses Stane Street at Billingshurst might well have given a nodal importance to the village were it not for the fact that it did not exist until recently. East Street merely petered out.

Most of the drove roads of Sussex mimic Stane Street in direction if not in straightness. Though there was one extending westward from Billingshurst towards Wisborough Green, a larger village than Billingshurst, one must assume that there was no significant trade on an East-West basis to call an important highway into being. Even the surviving railways echo the 'coast up to London' pattern initiated by Roman Stane Street. The lack of communication, east and west, no doubt as a result of the daunting forest barrier, has been proposed to explain the late arrival of Christianity to Sussex from Kent and Wessex where it flourished.

Until recently there was scant evidence of Romano-British settlement in Billingshurst; just a brick recycled into the church tower and some 2nd century coins including one of Marcus Auralius (161-180 AD). Alleged findings in a field at Five Oaks have not been investigated. However the recent discovery of farmstead sites suggests that they may have cultivated what were then exotic flowers, fruits and vegetables such as plums, mulberries and garlic as well as cereals. There were extensive gardens at the Palace at Fishbourne.

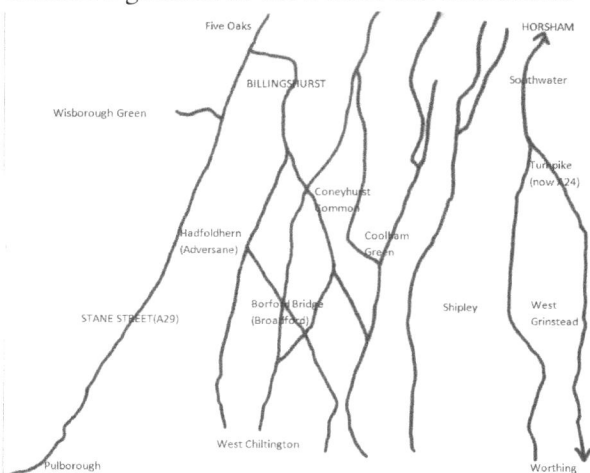

Sketch showing the old droving roads to the east of Stane Street from a map of 1795.
No road then ran eastwards beyond Coolham.

367 AD

As Roman power disintegrated at home, so marauding bands of Saxons were able to infiltrate the south coast of Romano-Britain, as they did elsewhere. But Romano-Britain still flourished. (Bignor Villa was built for example) until the incursions of 367. Christianity had reached Roman Britain around 300 AD under the Emperor Constantine.

The Saxons colonise Britain

To 477 AD

By 410 AD Rome had been sacked by the Goths, the last two Legions of Roman troops were withdrawn from Britain and the end of the Roman domination was inevitable. The incoming Saxons (or Germani) would occupy whatever settled sites they found and mingle with the Romano-Britons in situ, using them for labour in return for protection.

Aella came to Sussex. He was a pagan, worshipping Odin, King of the gods, Tiw, Woden, Thor and Freya (hence the names Wednesday to Friday). His son Cissa gave his name to Chichester. Roman buildings fell into ruins. The so-called 'dark age' of the Saxons began when they started on the work of opening up the wilderness of the Wealden Forest, beginning by 'turning the valley bottoms into water meadows, the forest margins into arable and pasture'.

Historians have always believed that Saxon settlement probably did not begin at Billingshurst until about 800 AD. However the archaeological findings of 2015, revealing two quite substantial Roman farmsteads about a kilometre east of the Roman Stane Street, suggest that some deforestation had occurred long before 400 AD. It is possible that the early Saxon invaders would have made some use of the access offered by Stane Street and of the areas on higher ground cleared of trees by the Romans and, even before the road was made, by their Celtic predecessors. However, any humble dwellings they raised would have left little footprint and any traces would have been disturbed or buried by later structures. More likely they would have left the settlements to deteriorate and revert to nature.

477 to 1066 AD

The Saxons, benefiting from the Roman road, cleared enough forest on fertile alluvial soil beside the streams to begin the village near what is now Lloyds Bank. Pulborough, which reached as far as Mole Country Stores and Newbridge with Rowner Mill, was then far more important, figuring in Domesday Book of 1086.

Billingshurst means 'a wooded hill of Billa's people' implying the knoll just up the A272 where the parish church stands. ('Bill' - head of a family, 'ing' - of the people, 'hurst' - wooded hill) The likelihood is that it was a small family settlement, not yet a parish or community, headed by one 'Billa' of indeterminate origin, rather than a populous Saxon tribe. The village was probably too poor and undeveloped to deserve to be named in the Domesday Book though Horsham does not appear either. Doomsday Book is a great, hand-written survey to assess the land and other resources available to William the Conqueror and the Normans in England as a database for the raising of taxes.   However it has been established that manors near the south coast utilised the acorns and other fruits of the woods growing in the heavy local clay for fattening their pigs. Parts of Billingshurst and Horsham therefore appear in the Domesday assessment, but only as outlying parts of their 'parent manors'.

The dwellings would most likely have been simple structures made by lashing three or more poles together at the top to form a conical circular or oval framework, then roofing it bottom to top with turf, bracken, straw, clay or other handy materials. Hovels of this nature, or of only slightly more permanence, were the dwelling places of the ordinary people of Billingshurst until quite recent times. For many centuries the common people would, at best, live in humble, impermanent timber-framed, single storey, chimneyless dwellings. The fine oak-framed buildings that have come down to us were all built for yeoman farmers or other gentry.

The residual Celtic speakers, many of whom had no doubt migrated westwards to Wales or Cornwall out of reach of the Saxons, would have been obliged to speak a new tongue, now named 'Old English', the language of the epic poem *Beowulf*. Few would have been capable of writing and certainly none in Billingshurst. *Beowulf* begins:

Hwæt! Wé Gárdena in géardagum	Listen! We --of the Spear-Danes in the days of yore,
þéodcyninga þrym gefrúnon·	of those clan-kings heard of their glory.
hú ðá æþelingas ellen fremedon.	how those nobles performed courageous deeds.

In 848 AD, The Anglo-Saxon Chronicle, the only comprehensive annuls we have, was written in the same Old English under the orders of Alfred the Great. Very few Celtic words had survived.

The Saxon people of Billingshurst would have only one name such as John or Alfred. Surnames came in quite slowly with the Normans. To distinguish people more exactly a second name might be attached from the place where they lived such as Greenfield, Coxbrook or Hurst. John and Tom might have sons named William Johnson and Walter Thompson. Another distinction could be based on their occupation such as Cooper, Smith, Wright and Carter or from a nickname, usually based on physical characteristics like Small, Sharp, Little and Long.

It is likely that boar, wolves and bears still roamed the forest as well as the deer, foxes and badgers and squirrels, then the red kind, which still survive. All wolves were cleared from England by Henry VIII's time. The Normans brought in the rabbits, kept in warrens for food and skins. The name Coneyhurst, meaning 'rabbit wood', implies that they were kept there.

Caedwalla, ruler of Wessex (685), and his successor Ine, became the local king of the area when he annexed Kent, Surrey and Sussex. It was then that the administration and system of law in divisions known as rapes and hundreds was devised. In return for protection the common people of Anglo-Saxon England were controlled, exploited for tax, rent, labour and military service by their tribal betters according to their holding of 'hides'. A Ceorl, or 'free' peasant farmer, typically had one hide of land. The Normans adopted and adapted the rapes to their own feudal purposes. Control was exercised through sub-divisions of land, the Manors, from the 'tun' or major administrative centre – in our case, Arundel.

Ultimately there were six Rapes in Sussex, Chichester Arundel and Bramber in the west and Lewes, Pevensey and Hastings in the east. The Rape of Arundel, granted to Roger de Montgomery in 1067, was the oldest and largest. He owned 83 manors. The Rape of Chichester was established from it in 1250, but the Rape of Bramber also dates from the 11th century, created from the Rapes of Arundel and Lewes. It was granted to William de Braose who controlled 38 manors.

Part of Speed's map of 1610 showing the Rape of Arundel

The responsible officers for each Manor were the Steward and the Reeve. The latter was a kind of foreman, estate agent and accountant to the Lord of the Manor and the ruling hierarchy. This basic administrative structure was systematised and defined by the Normans to facilitate their tax income and ensure their military defence. Geoffrey Chaucer depicts typical characters of Manorial England in *The*

Canterbury Tales as they had evolved in the 14th century – monk, nun, friar, parson, the man of law who was a magistrate, the Knight, who might have been Lord of many Manors, with his Squire and a yeoman forester servant, the self-serving reeve, the cheating miller and, at either end of the social scale, a rich Franklin, (a freeholding farmer), and a poor ploughman. By Chaucer's time the French and English languages had coalesced into the Middle English tongue and the Saxons and Norman people had merged into the English people without national distinction of social class. Chaucer exemplifies, in particular, that most cherished of English characteristics, a broad sense of humour.

By 1066, through constant warfare, England had slowly evolved into a single state, under the leadership of Wessex. Seven kingdoms had emerged on a regional and tribal basis, known as the 'heptarchy', comprising Wessex, Sussex, Kent, Essex, Mercia, East Anglia, and Northumbria. All but Essex had kings who, at some time, were accorded the role of Bretwalda, or 'overlord of the English Kingdoms'. There has not 'always been an England'. The country of the people who spoke 'Angl-ish', as opposed to Danish, was not spelt 'England' until the 13th Century.

The conversion of the Pagans

597AD - 681 AD

In 597 Pope Gregory sent Augustine to evangelise the pagans of Kent where Aethelbert, the King, was ripe for conversion. Subsequently Christianity spread throughout the land, and the first churches and abbeys were established. Most surviving early church buildings in Sussex date from the 12th century though earlier wooden structures may well have occupied the same sites. A significant change came in 681 when St Wilfrid made his second visit, beginning the conversion of the Sussex people to Christianity.

It is likely that progress into the forested Billingshurst Weald would have been slow. For that same reason local people would have shared little of the splendid Saxon culture now revealed by the Sutton Hoo treasure in Suffolk, or the educated court of Alfred, King of Wessex, or in the manuscripts of the monks at Lindesfarne. The earliest surviving West Sussex Saxon Churches are at Worth and Sompting [960] and the nearest at Bolney where the South doorway dates from about 900 AD.

Fresh Pagans threaten – The Norsemen

994 AD

Though most of Britain and northern France was constantly under the assault of the Vikings in Anglo-Saxon times, the present-day West Sussex area escaped serious intrusion and was never part of the Danelaw, established after the successful invasion of The Great Army from 866. The coming of the Norsemen had the effect of putting an end to two centuries of warfare between the Saxon kingdoms of the heptarchy. The Billingshurst area would still have been remote and inaccessible to raiders, and to a degree protected by the forts along the Saxon shore and the resistance of Alfred the Great. The Norsemen were defeated by Alfred in the 800s but they were still raping, pillaging and plundering the coastal settlements as late as 994 AD. King Ethelred paid 'Danegeld' to the Danes to get them to go away, but by 1013 England was ruled by Canute, a Dane who inherited from Svein Forkbeard, who had murdered King Edmund Ironside, Ethelred's son. The Norse Vikings had meantime colonised Normandy, so they did eventually rule Sussex and England.

Saxon Farming and later developments in agriculture

The three Rapes of West Sussex are parallel North-South slices of territory with an inherent economic geographical logic. Each had a coastal port, a river, a defensive fort and a share of the better coastal soils, the Downs, the greensand belt and a hinterland of the backwoods of the Wealden forest. This North–South orientation is echoed in the Drove Roads which, in our area can be traced along seven distinct lines, all running more or less parallel to Stane Street.

They are normally over thirty feet across, and, where metalled, have wide verges. When they wind through the greensand hills to the south, they narrow into deeply cut trenches where sand and sandstone have been excavated and passing herds have eroded the soil. There are about fifteen such roads detectable in West Sussex. They probably originated in Saxon times or even earlier and were fully exploited after 1066. Their purpose was the driving of stock back and forth to take advantage of woodland forage in season. Pigs were reared and fattened by rooting among the oaks for acorns and for beech mast and chestnuts, a practice known as pannage. The pigs' snouts helped clear the forest by disturbing the topsoil, breaking off saplings and the dense undergrowth. Many manors on the coastal plain had inland outposts of property reserved for this purpose. Ferring with Fure in Billingshurst is a prime example as is Climping with Clemsfold. Wherever the suffix 'fold' occurs in a place name, like Rowfold, Alfold, Slinfold, Kingsfold and Polingfold we can suspect some such north-south manorial linkage. (Old English 'falod' meant an enclosure for domestic animals).

Today livestock are carried in lorries, but up until Victorian times, pigs, cattle and sheep were moved on their own four legs, or even two in the case of Norfolk turkeys! Traffic along these roads ran from the Horsham area down to the lusher pastures and water meadows and more populous regions north of Worthing. There were the recognised links between coastal manors and their 'backwoods' properties. One drove road passes round Billingshurst and runs due South through West Chiltington. It is reasonable to speculate that, bearing in mind the simple dwellings of ordinary people, the early drovers would, temporally, move their dwelling places as well as their stock, whether they were the owners of the livestock or slaves or serfs employed by the tribal hierarchy. Dogs would have been trained to keep the animals under control. It was a kind of Wealden transhumance.

In 1256 the Bishop of Chichester, who was the Lord of many Manors, kept a moated stud farm at Drungewick, just north of Billingshurst, with 250 oxen, 10 bulls, 100 cows, 3000 sheep, goats and horses. Scrawny mediaeval oxen were but half the size of modern cattle and some would be slaughtered at Martinmas for winter meat as would the hogs. The meat would be salted to preserve it. Pike, tench, carp, perch and bream were kept in the stews, or fish ponds of Manors and doves in their cots. Carp were fed with pease and grew to 14 inches in four years. Bacon was the main meat meal of the moderately well-to-do and cheese the protein of the serfs, eked out by rabbits, thrushes, larks and larger game, caught or poached as opportunity offered. Impassable roads in winter would discourage the cultivation of arable crops to be marketed in distant towns. The sticky soils would have limited the growing of cereals to what was needed for subsistence. At the time of Edward III (c 1350) it was recorded: 'At Billynghurste in the Rape of Arundel...60 acres of land...worth 2d an acre and no more, and is of no value to sow, 'propter magnitutinem bosci', [close by great woods] but the pannage when it happens is worth 10s'.

Geoffrey Chaucer, in 'The Knight's Tale' written about 1382, has given us a list of native trees, being used in his story to build a funeral pyre, that might have been found in Billingshurst woods at that time:-

"...ook, firre, birch, aspe[n], alder, holm, popler,
Wyllugh[willow], elm, plane, assh, chasteyn[chestnut], lynde[lime], laurer[laurel]'
Mapul, [black- and haw-]thorn, bech, hasel, [y]ew, wipple-tree[dogwood]"

He omits elder and crab apple, but includes 'holm' which in Middle English meant 'holly'. Chaucer was retelling a story of ancient Greece when holm-oaks were revered, but that species did not come to England until Elizabethan times. Chestnut probably came in with the Romans. There are said to have been 110,000 sheep in Sussex in 1340. Red Sussex beef cattle, originally with white forward pointing horns were held in high esteem in the 18th century. They are believed to be refined descendents of original Wealden stock. South Down sheep are small but were celebrated for their wool as well as the texture of their meat. A man was expected to sheer fifty sheep a day in summer, hard work with hand-held clippers.

1. Sussex Cattle

2. South Down sheep

Much of England in the 15th century and through to Tudor times enjoyed an economic boom from the production and export of wool. This prosperity has left us a legacy of superb churches in East Anglia and elsewhere and the symbolic Woolsack upon which the Chancellor still sits. It is likely that the rich medieval farmers on the Champion would have shared in the bonanza and the Drove Roads would have been used to take advantage of pastures in the summer which had been won from the forest. The soils of the coastal plain, the chalk Downs and the greensand belt would have been preferable for wintering and spring lambing. The cold Wealden clay in winter would lead to foot-rot and other troubles though the shaws and woods offered the possibility of shelter.

It is probable that our earlier Billingshurst farmers would have kept their beef and dairy stock mainly for sustenance and as draught animals. Relatively few would have been for sale, driven to market on the hoof. The characteristic large hay-barns beside old farmhouses bear witness to systematic cropping of hay for winter fodder. Inventories made for wills list oats, barley, wheat, peas, beans, vetches and 'tares' for stock which were stored there. Cattle can better withstand the mud and poached earth than sheep. 'Grass upon wet land, corn upon dry'.

The Rev. Arthur Young in his celebrated book on Sussex agriculture of 1813 tells how Sussex oxen were normally bred for plough and haulage work from 3 to 7 years of age, and then fattened up for slaughter when 8 or more. Tractable willing working animals were kept going longer and the fractious beasts went earlier to the butcher. They were essentially dual-purpose animals, broken in to the yoke alongside older beasts at 2+ years. They ploughed in teams of 4 or 6 if the going was good and up to 10 or 12 in heavy soils. Their milk was a secondary consideration, though what the Sussex breed lacked in quantity it made up for in quality, rich enough to yield an average of 5 lbs of butter a week and 30 lbs of cheese a month from the skim milk. It was reckoned that a 100 acre holding of arable land required a minimum of a team of 8 oxen and 4 horses. Up to a third of the acreage would be used up to feed them summer and winter.

Young describes the standard rotation for the stiff clays of the Weald as 1. Fallow 2. Wheat 3. Oats 4. Clover and Grass for two or three years 5. Oats, Pease or Wheat. He deprecates 'fallowing', recommending turnips instead. He thinks much Sussex farming is old-fashioned and is in favour of the new threshing machines which yielded more grain than the flail and saved labour. He also regards shaws as a hindrance to the ripening of corn and poor sources of timber. Imported wood was just as good. The land should not be used for growing ships' timbers. Growing 100 year old oaks for the purpose was a waste of land. "Corn and cattle, mutton and wool, would mark the progressive improvement of the county and the Weald, in lieu of being covered in woods, would smile with plenty and prosperity". As far as the arable soils of Billingshurst were concerned he must have had reservations. Wheat, yielding only 16 bushels an acre, contrasted with 50 bushels on 6 foot straw at Felpham, using his own figures, was a loss-making enterprise, though necessary for bread. Profit came from the succeeding oats or barley and fodder crops.

At Hammonds Farm there is still a good deal of chalk in the old farm yard, clearly brought in more recent times to combat the winter mud where the cattle had to stand. Billingshurst is known at one time to have hosted two cattle fairs held on the Green on 8th November and Whit Monday mainly for the sale of pigs. On 12th September there was another bigger fair held at Hadfolds-herns, now elided into the name Adversane, where horses, cattle, pigs and corn were sold. There was a 'pork roast' in a booth on the Green where two tall posts and a cross beam stood. This feast marked the moment when pork was 'in season'. A fair was held at Shipley on October 21st. Arthur Young concludes that, 'The Weald of Sussex should be a grazing district. Large dairies with butter cheese and hogs; with beef and mutton for Smithfield'.

It would not prove expedient to plough up many pastures for wheat and barley until the coming of the Wey and Arun Canal in 1813, the railway in 1841 and metalled roads in Victorian times. Up till 1813 the Arun had been navigable for freight only as far as Newbridge. 'Timber, plank and all sorts of convertible underwood are sent from the Weald and the barges return with chalk, coal or lime'. During the brief life of the canal this trade was enhanced by the link via the Wey to London. The value of cereal crops had risen sharply in response to the Industrial Revolution, threats of the Napoleonic wars, and the rapid growth of population in the 19th century. Wheat trebled in price in twenty years so remedying Rev. Young's earlier criticism of loss-making wheat crops.

The London-Horsham turnpike began in 1758, giving better access to hungry markets. From then on we find millers and maltsters becoming the leaders of the community as arable farming became more profitable with good prices for corn needed to feed the rapidly expanding towns. The Corn Laws of 1815 protected farmers from foreign competition by tariffs. But until mid-century the high price of bread and low wages had brought great hardship to farm labourers. Things improved for them with the repeal of the Corn Laws. There were soon three malt houses in the village. This period also saw the growth of enthusiasm for gardening and allotments and the keeping of domestic animals, fowls, rabbits, bees and pheasants for sport.

After 1874 however the detrimental effect on arable farming of the repeal of the Corn Laws kicked in when growers could no longer compete with imported grain and meat. This devastated the profit from home-grown cereals so that much arable land reverted to pasture. Only milk, hay and straw could be sold at a profit and land values plummeted. As Wilde's Lady Bracknell put it, 'Land has ceased to be either a profit or a pleasure. It gives one position, and prevents one from keeping it up. That's all that can be said about land'. There was, however, still a market for dairy products.

See-sawing between arable and pasture continued. During the great depression following World War I much land was neglected as unprofitable. However from 1939, with the 'dig for victory' campaign, many meadows went under the plough under instruction from the War Agricultural Committees.

Small fields, characteristic of the Billingshurst district, do not suit well with modern harvesting machines. Post World War II prosperity has encouraged alternative recreational uses such as sports fields and equestrian paddocks and hayfields, at the expense of dairy farms, which have declined in profitability. More controversially many picturesque fields, not lucky enough to be deemed in planning law as 'of outstanding natural beauty', have been developed into housing estates to meet the needs and desires of incomers to the region. Dairy farming at Cocksbrook/Hammonds ceased when the Barnes Brothers retired in the 1980s. The dairy farms of Mr. Morris at Five Oaks and Mr. Voice at Adversane had also closed. Milk floats served the village from Five Oaks until the 1970s from a site now occupied by Civil Engineers.

1. Milk bottles of
Barnes of Hammonds

2. And Voice of Adversane.
The smaller 1/3 pint bottle was supplied to schools, sold at a halfpenny a bottle.

New crops such as linseed, peas and beans, maize for silage-making and oil-seed rape and Christmas trees have brought fresh interest to the summer landscape. 'Diversification' became the order of the day on farms, encouraging such stock as llamas, alpacas, goats, rare breeds of pigs, edible snails, trout lakes and maggots for anglers and local specialities such as cheeses and meats for Farmers' Markets. Utilisation for recreational use is increasing, mainly for horses but also for sports such as at Jubilee Fields in Billingshurst, or golf courses, as at West Chiltington and Slinfold. Setting land aside to promote wildlife along headlands or create environment-friendly parks and refuges is increasingly popular. In the mid 20th century several outlying farms concentrated on broiler chicken and battery-hen egg production in large sheds, but by the millennium more stringent humane legislation and the high cost of fodder and fuel had led to their closure.

We must conclude, however, that most of Cocksbrook would always have been meadowland, as indeed it has remained to this day. The patchwork of small fields was liberally interspersed with shaws and woodlands which not only offered food, but also shelter for stock, and oak timber for building, fuel and a refuge for foxes, deer and game. Coppicing was widely practised for faggots, sticks, hoops and palings. Cordwood was cut for charcoal and oak bark for tanning. Management of the timber assets was an important aspect of the lives of the people. Charcoal is still made locally and logs for winter fuel are readily available. Trading in fencing and timber building materials still prospers.

More new Christians – the Normans

1066

The greatest change came after the Norman Conquest of 1066, famously following the death of Harold Godwinson and his army at Battle in East Sussex. The Normans were bloodthirsty militant Christians who subjugated their Saxon predecessors and fraternised with them. They retained the Saxon land divisions and manorial customs, but superimposed their feudal rights, so that all lands ultimately belonged to King William the Conqueror, who parcelled out his properties to his Norman henchmen. The earliest Abbey was built at Battle by 1095, and Chichester Cathedral was resited from Selsey in 1075. Hardham Priory, 6 miles to the South of Billingshurst dates from 1248, otherwise surviving church buildings were from 1300 onwards, as indeed are the very oldest houses of the yeoman farmers. The monastic foundations in West Sussex were generally colonial outposts of mother monasteries in Normandy itself. The Normans built 500 forts throughout England much more quickly to consolidate their mastery. At this stage the integrated community, the 'Vill' or village slowly evolved.

The chief architectural contribution of the Saxons and Normans was their oak-framed hall-houses, many of which still grace our countryside. The 'wrights' sawed green oak into stout beams in saw pits or squared them with axe and adze. When they had cut them to make up a pre-tested, rectangular, jointed framework, the 'frame was raised' on a prepared site on firm footings, pegged with wooden pins and roofed with thatch or stone. Walls were often made of wattle and daub and the smoke from the central hearth escaped through a hole in the ridge, way above. Subsequently windows, chimneys and upper chambers and inner walls evolved, so that all of our old houses have been substantially modified as building technology and fashion dictated. These skills persisted for centuries, eventually being superseded by bricks and bricklaying in the 18th century.

Wealden House and The Green where livestock fairs were held

Mastering the Wealden Forest

When the Normans arrived the Saxon Andredesweald was by far the largest forest still remaining in England. The Venerable Bede described it in the 8th century as a region 'thick and inaccessible, the abode of deer, swine and wolves'. Its clearance and settlement for agriculture was a splendid achievement of our pioneer predecessors.

The question is who it was that cut down the trees in the area in and around Billingshurst so as to create the patchwork of small fields and pastures that have come down to us? When were the hedgerows laid to divide fields and mark off property boundaries? Were there, at some point, three fields subdivided into strips as in more fertile and workable soils of England? In the absence of written records we can only assume that most of this work was undertaken under the aegis and at the discretion of the Norman Barons by the Anglo-Norman peasantry by degrees throughout the 12th and 13th centuries. Some 'manorial strips' were cleared at Rowfold even earlier. The local controlling body for land north of East Street was most likely the Manor of Pinkhurst, with its head-quarters and Manor House in what is now Slinfold. Elsewhere in the village were the lands of the Manors of Wiggonholt, Storrington and Bassett's Fee.

By 1650 the farm strips on 'open fields' on the Champion had been enclosed. There is evidence of the 'common field system' on the Lower Greensand at West Chiltington, Ashington and Petworth. This agricultural system prevailed as the dominant pattern throughout England in a wide belt from Dorset north-eastwards to Norfolk, embracing the midlands and north-eastern counties. It led, typically, to the creation of three great fields in a village, divided into strips owned by different people, with further areas of uncultivated common land. Ultimately, and chiefly in the 18th Century, these big fields and commons were 'enclosed' to the benefit of profitable and large-scale productive agriculture and the richer landowners, but to the detriment of the peasantry.

However the heavy Wealden clay east of Billingshurst would not have encouraged development of the three-field system of arable farming. It is much more likely that there was progressive clearance by felling and grubbing up the stumps, known as 'assarting', in order to furnish small pastures of five acres or less. Enormous physical effort went into clearing the underwood bushes, felling trees and burning cut-over patches. The rooting of hogs helped the process but the clearance would have been an arduous pioneering challenge.

So Lower Weald farmsteads, like Cocksbrook would have been fixed when assarting was completed and would remain in that form. Great fields, farmed in strips on a three-year rotation, wheat, barley and fallow, never existed hereabouts and the land was 'enclosed' from the outset. While other enclosed regions of England were making huge strides in cultivation methods, stock breeding, drainage and fertilisation, modernisation and 'improvement' on the Lower Weald was at a standstill. Billingshurst yeomen would have run mixed farms, fundamentally sustaining their families and workers on a local and self-sufficient basis, rather than producing large surpluses to market for profit. The lack of good roads to a market and the intractability of the clay soils offered little alternative.

1. Oak framed 17th century Yeoman House, Southlands at Adversane

2. Stout Sussex Oak beams at Southlands carrying the chamber above

Draught animals employed would have been oxen. Because of the shape of their necks horses would have been strangled if yoked like oxen. The use of the horse-collar to enable horses to be used as draught animals was still a novelty in the 10th century. Oxen were still used in Sussex into the early 20th century. This very absence of 'improvement', of the clearing of hedges and copses to create profitable estates and accommodate machinery, has left us a legacy of the rich and various patchwork of fields and meadows, lanes, shaws and small farmsteads. It is a unique inherited landscape that is our duty to preserve and cherish.

Landscape historians are agreed that the forest had been colonised and the field pattern established by the time of the Black Death – 1348. Interestingly enough, this is the time when our scanty written record of our predecessors begins.

Characteristic of the area are the frequent 'shaws', some still evident. Many hedges of ancient origin have been narrowed to their present state in recent centuries. When fields were first won from the forest, wide hedgerows were left as divisions and boundaries, a good many of which survive as small woods also known in some parts of the country as 'rews'. Hedges can be dated by the number of different bushes they sustain reckoning on a gain of one new species every hundred years. Studies in Billingshurst have suggested that the most ancient are possibly those marking the boundaries of both parish and manor, such as that between Billingshurst and Rudgwick (12 species), next such manorial divisions as that between Marringdean and Hadfold (10 species) and most recent, in the majority, those managed hedges edging fields possibly planted between 500 and 700 years ago. The oldest hedges may indicate where fields may have been won from the forest by assarting. They were more than just boundaries since they were a valuable source of hazel nuts, blackberries, crab apples, bullaces, damsons and acorns. Blackthorn gave sloes and timber for tool handles and walking sticks. Wide hedges had underwood for faggots for baking ovens and farm use and were rich in birds and other wildlife. They offered shelter for rabbits and game and corridors for safe movement.

With the passage of time the feudal obligations of the peasantry, according to the custom of the Manor, to provide soldiering in time of war, labour in field service when called on and rent in money and kind to their noble Lord, were gradually diminished, but continued to be much resented and the occasion of periodic revolts.

The first 'syllables of recorded time' in Billingshurst.
The Church and local government

1215 AD

At the beginning of the 13th century we are at last able to make use of some written records of the ownership of land and 'messuages' or dwelling places in the village. Written documentation of the doings of the ruling classes are of course much more readily available. We know a good deal about King John who confiscated Knepp Castle, which was a fortified hunting lodge, and Bramber Castle and the signing of Magna Carta in 1215. Our sources of information about the relatively unlettered people, living and working in the backwoods, are necessarily more limited.

1274 AD

We do know that the earliest building in East Street is St.Mary's Parish Church. It was begun in the 12th century, possibly as early as 1100 A.D. At first it was under the aegis of the Priory at Arundel. In 1250 St. Richard, Bishop of Chichester, formed vicarages where he thought the monks were neglectful, so the earliest part of the church was built between 1160 and 1200. We do not know which Manorial Lord actually founded the present church. The most likely is de Braose of Bramber.

The first known Vicar was Thomas de Selhurst in 1274. With the dissolution of the monasteries by Henry VIII, the tithes passed to the owners of Okehurst where the Bartellot family were tenants of the Manor of Bassett's Fee. They had acquired it by marriage into the de Okehurst dynasty. They held it till 1579 when it passed to John Wiseman whose daughter married an Edward Goring of the family who became the eventual owners. Edward died in 1617. The Gorings held the Great Tithes until the 1860s when they auctioned it off. Many local Manors were originally church property gifted to the Abbott of Fecamp, a French monastery, so that they had Summers, Duckmore and Okehurst and Rosier. When the king thought it expedient to secure the profits to Englishmen rather than French, about 1450, he simply transferred the rights to a monastery at Syon in Middlesex.

A William Frye (1349) heads the next known list of Vicars. The oldest parts of the present building, apart from a Roman brick, are the 13th century tower and Lady Chapel with its crown post roof. The nave has a 15th century decorated oak-panelled ceiling with 117 carved bosses, fine tie beams and a 15th century early 'wagon' roof and timber framing. The tie beams are some of the oldest in Sussex, if not the most impressive in appearance, cut between 1200 and 1300 and closely resembling many in northern France. The 120 foot 8-sided spire was built on the old tower in the 18th century. It is covered with wooden shingles, originally of oak, but since 1972, of Canadian pine. Score marks on the south wall are said to have been made by medieval archers sharpening their arrows at practice after morning service. The Greenfield tombs in the churchyard have interesting epitaphs. That to Samuel' who died 1720 aged 48 reads:

'All you who pass this way along
Think you how sudden I was gone
God does not always warning give
Therefore be careful how you live'.

1. St. Mary's Church (rear view)

2. St. Mary's Church today

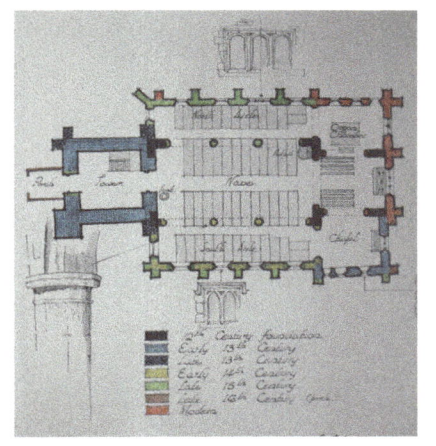

3. St. Mary's Church plan

Another famous Vicar, Nathanial Hilton, who died in 1655, was a stout Puritan so the Catholic images inside had to go! The children of John Downes, who was one of those who condemned Charles I to death were baptised here. John died in the Tower of London and escaped execution on the grounds that he had been bullied into signing the King's death warrant by Oliver Cromwell. He had been MP for Arundel and amassed a fortune from the confiscated royal estates. The Kings Arms is recorded in the Churchwardens' Accounts as having been 'struck out' in 1653, during the Republic, and money paid for 'setting and painting', after the restoration of Charles II in 1661.

In 1662 the Act of Uniformity re-established Episcopal worship and there were recriminations. On St. Bartholomew's Day two thousand ministers who refused to give their 'unfeigned assent and consent' to the Anglican service and re-established Book of Common Prayer were ejected from office. Rev. William Wilson, a non-conformist, and father of six sons was among them. He went into hiding and continued preaching at Arundel and Thakeham. He was arrested and had to appear at Petworth Quarter Sessions for continuing to preach, on the hostile initiative of a local magistrate and Thomas Oram, his successor at the Vicarage.

Quakers were particularly vulnerable. William Albury of Horsham wrote: 'Richard Shaw as he was riding jurny was sett upon by two drunken men in the town of Billingshurst and pulled of his horse and one of them drew a sword and swore he would kill him because he was a Quaker...one of these was a magistrates man and his master was in a drinking and would not come out to rebuke his man although word was sent him in that his servant was like to do a murder at the dore'. He also tells how John Pryor and his wife were fined at Petworth Sessions in 1676 for allowing a seditious meeting in their barn at Billingshurst in a manner not 'according to the liturgy and practice of the Church of England'. The informants were Penfold and Cowper and the Magistrates Weekes, Westbrook and Thomas Henshaw.

One Incumbent, in 1863, wrote lengthily to Mrs Botting who was taking over the business of Mrs. Trower's shop, protesting about intrusion on Glebe 'waste land'. Rev. G. Wells, 1792-1823, had made a careful map showing the Glebe Lands, some 13 acres in all, as a record of exchanges of strips of land with Sir Charles Goring to extend the churchyard. It was further extended in 1866 and 1926. However by 1974 the decision was made that there was no room left for more burials and an alternative cemetery has yet to be found.

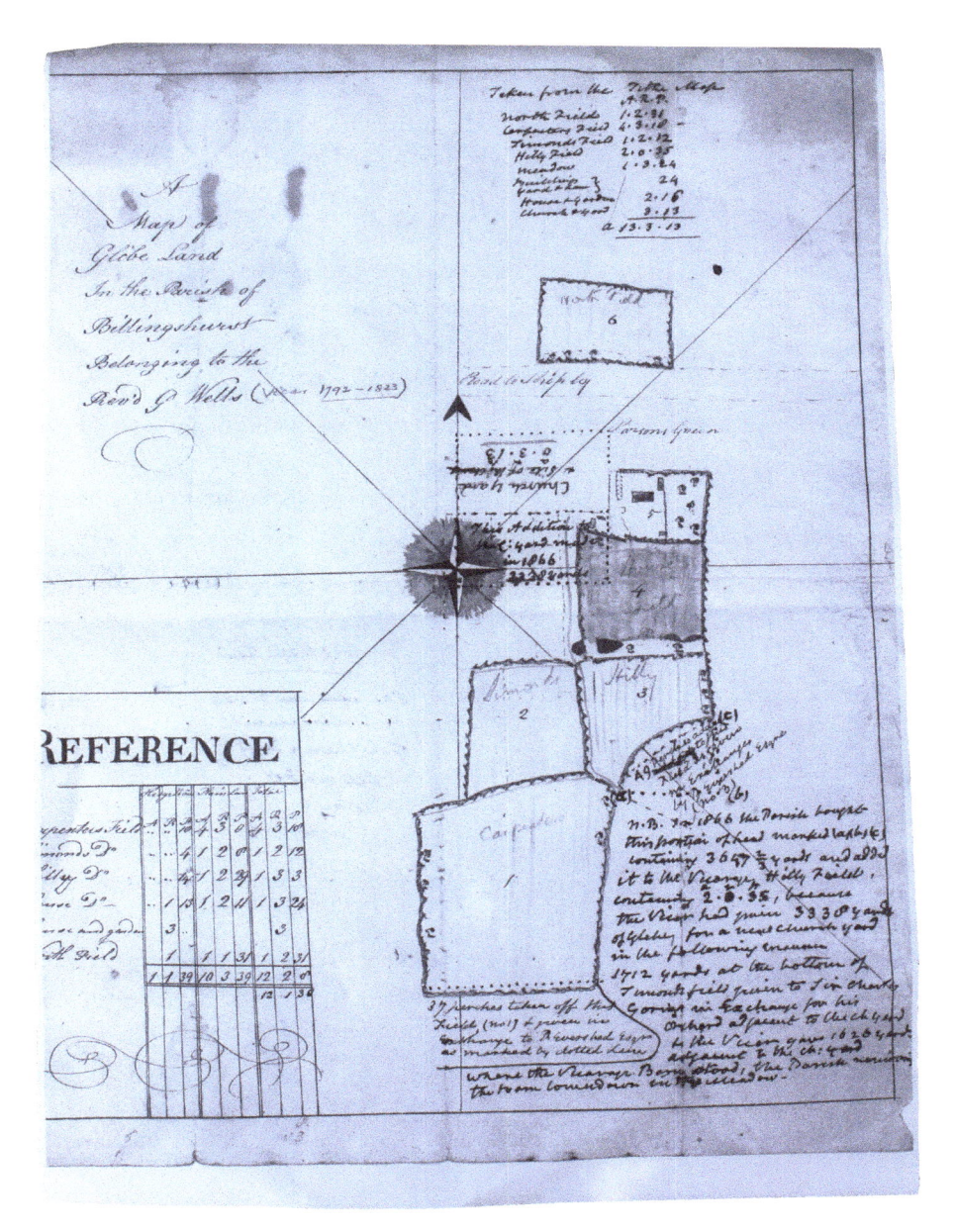

Vicar's map showing Church Glebe

The Vicar's Glebe land was originally extensive comprising most of the terrain East of South Street from Carpenters as far as the National Westminster Bank and also a field beyond East Street now called Rosehill. What is now the Carpenters Field estate occupied the majority of the territory. In 1635 it was recorded that modest rents were paid to the Vicar for the smithy land opposite the Chapel, Churchgate and Brick House on the corner of East Street where W.H. Hubert was the surgeon. Three parcels of land were known to have been sold off. Brick House is where the Nat-West Bank now stands, the so-called Village Green where the Causeway houses stand and space opposite the Chapel, where the smithy stood, now shops, was all leased at a modest 3 shilling annual rent, and it is most likely, a lump sum payment 'in a brown paper envelope'.

John Fuller was a one-time tenant of the Glebe lands. When he went bankrupt the Rev. Beath took the land in hand and farmed it for a time. He exchanged some land with Mr. Evershed, and then retired. He continued to live in Billingshurst as a farmer, until buried here aged 73. The land Mr. Evershed acquired became what is now Station Road.

Cecil Brereton (1886-1890) carried on a business, advertising in the *British Bee Journal*, selling swarms of bees, colonies and queen bees all over England.

There is a brass of Thomas and Elizabeth Bartlet (Bartellot) dated 1499. 'Pray for the sowels of Thomas Bartlet and Elizabeth which Thomas deceased the XXX day of Janever MCCCCLXXXXIX [1499]' of Okehurst, and 17th century alabaster murals showing the Goring family (1617) with five children, three of them infants. Sir Edward Goring received the Great Tithe and bestowed the Living. Richard Luxford is commemorated too. He died in 1654 and was married to a relative of Bishop Joseph Henshaw, Lord of the Manor of Bassetts Fee.

E.V. Lucas tells of a 'race which was held every Sunday for certain seats in the chancel and the tactical 'packing' of the same by the winning party.' He also relates that 'a noble carved chair used to be placed in one of the galleries for the schoolmaster [probably Henry Wright] and there he would sit during the service surrounded by his boys'.

Extensive Victorian restoration work was done in 1866 under the aegis of Rev. W.H. Bull and Henry Carnsew, with an architect Robert W. Edis. The result was described by Nikolaus Pevsner as 'rather disastrous'. Among other changes to the arches, two galleries were removed, a new font, pulpit and reading desk were provided, the present Vestry and organ chamber was built and three new east end windows filled with stained glass. Open seats replaced the owners' mixture of private pews. They demolished the school formerly attached to the Lady Chapel. Before 1866 the side chapel was used as a vestry, for Vestry Meetings. Then it moved to the tower. When Mr. Carnsew lost his young wife Henrietta Maria, he dedicated the East widow of the North Aisle to her memory. More recently the organ came in 1883; two new bells in 1897 and in the first decade of the 20th century a fresh pulpit, lectern and communion rails. Another stained glass window was added in memory of James Hall Renton J.P. by Major-General J.M.L. Renton of Rowfold Grange. The church plate includes a cup and flagon of 1631 and alms dishes of 1640. These have the initials of the contemporary Churchwardens on them.

In 1892 Mr. R. Morris of Five Oaks built a Mission Church there near the Inn, now demolished. A similar Mission Church came in 1928 at Adversane both premises being used for social events and meetings.

Modern students of church architecture can find Norman church building features at Wisborough Green, with characteristic round arched doorways built up to about 1180 and some 4' 6" wall, at Itchingfield where the North side of the nave is original Norman, with a round-headed west doorway, and at West Chiltington with wall-paintings and two round-headed windows. The church there dates from the early 12th century. The Church of St. Mary's, Horsham has two Norman doorways.

Early parish government

When we think of a Parochial Church Council today we expect it to concern itself with domestic and administrative matters about the church and churchyard, the congregation and the ministry of the clergy and their assistants. The modern Parson, in crude terms, is an employee of the Church Commissioners rather than the parishioners and has no explicit role in local government.

It is important to remember how much more significant were the Vestry Meeting, and the Incumbent who might have chaired it, in the administration of the parish from the 14th century until the late 19th. The Parish, as an institution, existed in Saxon times, but was fully realised after the Norman Conquest. Then the Lord of the Manor would contribute his tithe for the church building and its upkeep and expect his tenants to do the same, only keeping to himself the right to bestow the living.

By Tudor times the Hundredal and Manorial Courts were beginning to decay. Their administrative powers then passed to the natural successors, the Vestry Meeting. This was, effectively, a parochial parliament. So in the Billingshurst parish records, still preserved, we read not only of the maintenance of the church clock, bells, windows and the shingles on the steeple, but also of payments to maimed soldiers, paupers and children, of work on the almshouses and an emigration fund for people wanting to leave for America and Canada. As regards the church clock, a special 'Clock Field Charity' was set up to maintain it. One resident was alleged to have been guided home by its chimes in a fog and made a deed of 55 shillings a year to maintain it in perpetuity on the security of the Clock Field at Townland. This is probably a comfortable myth disguising the fact that the rents of small parcels of land due to their owners, the churchwardens, were taken in exchange for the pledge to pay an annual sum and to disarm the criticism of non-conformists who always wanted income to be spent on the poor rather than the fabric of the Anglican church. It was a shrewd deal in which valuable plots like the site of the Blacksmith's Arms and Manor House changed hands. In village politics the 'main chance' of private profit was often on the secret agenda. The Vicar Henry Wray Brown (1815-1830) was in dispute with parishioners unwilling to pay him their small tithes. A meeting was held, 'but no business was done owing to the disorder which prevailed'. He is safely buried under the church porch.

The power of the Parish Vestry Meeting to levy a church rate, from early times, led naturally to the administration of other levies, notably the Poor Tax. This was instituted to deal with the welfare of the indigent and the discipline of idlers and vagabonds. At first the Vestries worked in tandem with the Manorial Courts, but central governments, from Tudor times, had continually invested them with ever greater responsibilities. They were expected to look after the arms and welfare of the local militia and to appoint waywardens to attend to the upkeep of the dirt tracks that passed for highways. By nominating and paying constables they had responsibility for keeping law and order. The Vestry Meeting controlled tax budgets and as a result a select group of local notables became, as accountants will, the dictators of parish policy. They collected the rates and were in charge of how they were spent. W.E. Tate describes the parishes as 'miniature republics'. They enjoyed far greater community autonomy than we do today where authority is exercised to only a limited extent by Parish, District and County Councils but in most respects by central government legislation. In those days tax rates were agreed by the Vestry and ratified by the local Magistrates.

One drawback of that system was that worthy persons of a dissenting disposition, of whom there were considerable numbers in Billingshurst, tended to be side-lined. Baptists and Quakers and other non-conformists were not best-pleased to pay their taxes to the established church-goers and their tithes to the Anglican Vicar. By an Act of 1601 all Vestries were enjoined to meet at Easter to appoint Churchwardens and Overseers of the Poor. Non-conformist farmers duly took their turn as such officials.

Yet earlier in 1538, Thomas Cromwell had made Incumbents the Registrars of Births, Marriages and Deaths. They were to keep parish records in a 'sure coffer', secured by two locks known as the Parish Chest. St. Mary's had two of these, the older one of about 1700 containing scales to measure bread and flour. These were most likely churchwardens' tools to use as part of their civic duty to check weights and measures, a kind of 'office of fair trading'. The other chest in the tower dates from the 19th century.

Conscientious Vicars were well worthy of their hire, their financial reward coming from a share of the tithes and the profit of their glebe lands. At Billingshurst 'there is also belonging to the sayd Vicarage a yearely pension of five Nobles to be payd by the parson of the sayd Parish at the Feast of St. Bartholomew'. Tithes were meant to serve three purposes; to provide a living for the Incumbent, the maintenance of the church property and congregation, and the welfare of the poor. The Vicar had to be not only a farmer but also was often, in later times, expected to be the chairman of the Vestry administration as well as the spiritual and welfare guide to the parish flock. Every parishioner of some status was obliged to shoulder a share of civic responsibility, taking turns to be churchwardens. They were legally officers of the Bishop and normally appointed by the parish though under certain difficult circumstances the Vicar could nominate one of them. On one occasion in the 17th century it is pointedly noted that the appointments were 'of the whole parish'. The Vicar did not always get his way.

To supervise the work of the parishes, on behalf of the monarch, there was one constant force – the bench of Magistrates or JPs. They were normally landowning gentry or rich merchants, the 'squirarchy' of England, unpaid and hopefully imbued with the spirit of *noblesse oblige*, responsible for keeping the peace and enforcing justice. They had powers to fix wages and services, license liquor sales, discipline poachers and other felons and supervise the workings of the Poor Law.

These old democratic Parish Vestry arrangements were concluded by the introduction of elected Parish Councils in 1894, and for which there was initially great enthusiasm. Thirty-three people were nominated for election for 13 seats! Of recent years there have been barely enough nominations at the quadrennial elections to match the places available. However, the strict limits of parish income and responsibilities today are in marked contrast with the rights and responsibilities of our forebears. They alone were the 'welfare state', the police force and the administrators of matters now dealt with by central government and District and County Councils.

1894 was the turning point of the process. The caring responsibilities of parishes were superseded throughout the 20th century, notably when District Councils took on that role and even the duty of appointing Overseers was taken away in 1927, a process concluded by the Beveridge Report and the welfare legislation of the Attlee government in 1945.

We should bear in mind, however, that local government in former years, implied heavy local taxation on people with property. Today centralised regulation and social welfare depend on centralised collection, mainly through income tax and VAT. The parish precept is only a small fraction of the rates, collected by the District Council, and mostly spent by the County Council and Police Authority. Formerly income tax was minimal. Mr. Gladstone threatened to abolish it altogether. But the people of Billingshurst who were moderately well-off were faced with bills for Parish Rates, Poor Tax and tithes together with any feudal dues exacted by the Lord of the Manor. It is little wonder that several were rendered bankrupt.

Poor Tax was systematised by the Elizabethan Poor Law of 1601 which required the collection of a parish rate by the Overseers to provide food and clothing to those they deemed deserving. The idle poor continued to get a whipping. From 1662 only settled residents of a parish were entitled to relief. Outsiders were moved on to a place where they had a claim by birth or marriage. Tithes, in particular, were greatly resented, and not just by Dissenters. The Great Tithe on grain, wood and hay was payable to the Rector who was often a layman and an absentee. In the case of Billingshurst it was the Goring family. The Small Tithe, a tenth of everything else produced, such as milk, honey, eggs and vegetables grown on land tilled with a spade went to the Vicar. Payment in kind was abandoned in 1836 to general satisfaction. After that payments were commuted, paid in money as a rent, and by the landlords rather than the tenants. Tithes were not abolished until 1936.

It would, however, be a mistake to regard the autonomy of the parish as an idyllic, self-governing community, always exercising its 'little brief authority' with the best of motives, always addressing itself to the common weal. We may be sure the local worthies, traders and yeomanry, managed affairs to their own best advantage, trimming rates and investing in works to suit themselves. They would, for example, fine people for bringing paupers into the village who might prove a charge on the parish rates. But over and above that, then as now, real authority rested with the monarchs and their ministers, elected by a restricted franchise. These were the power-brokers of society who pulled the levers of control by Acts of Parliament, enforced by the Magistracy and backed by the militia. The Vestry worked within the law of the land, and when national policy changed the local leaders changed with them, after the fashion of the Vicar of Bray.

The Black Death

1348AD

At the Norman Conquest the population of England was about 2 ½ million, rising to about 5 Million by 1300.

However the major social event of this century was the Black Death which swept through England from the west country from 1348 to 1350. Some 1.5 million people died, about a third of the population. About 30 villages in the Downs were deserted. Though isolated, Billingshurst is unlikely to have escaped the death toll. Depopulation had the effect of improving the lot of peasant survivors whose labour, now in short supply, became more expensive to landowners. Our local forebears would have enjoyed progressively greater freedoms from feudal control and more opportunities to take on fields as lease or freeholders. The landowners could no longer rely on field service from serfs to work the land and were glad to commute the service for cash and willingly rented out their demesne to yeoman farmers. It is likely that some land won from the forest reverted to scrub, following the plague, not to be recovered until Tudor times.

The French word 'ferme', Anglicised to 'feorm', was used for a fixed sum paid to the Lord of the Manor as rent by a villein, a high status peasant working up to 100 acres. 'Feorm' gave us the English word 'farm' and the tenant the new and even more respectable title of 'farmer', the 'Yeoman of England'.

In 1381 an unpopular Poll Tax prompted John Ball and Wat Tyler to lead a popularist Peasants Revolt. The rich monasteries and lay rectors who took the tithes of the parish and parson were especially targeted, and there was much resentment of *heriot* where the best beast passed from the dead tenant to the Lord, of *merchet*; a fine on marriage; the enforcement of field work and the costly obligation to use the Lord's mill. The Statute of Labourers had attempted to fix wages when labour was scarce. The rebels captured London and, for a short while, looked to have secured the rights of free men, but brief concessions to placate the majority, followed by brutal suppression of the ringleaders, soon restored the status quo and the domination of the ruling classes. Nevertheless the uproar was such that serfdom withered away in England while persisting in continental Europe. Though Kent and East Anglia were the source of the main antagonists we may be sure there were repercussions in the minds of the people of Billingshurst as news of the rebellion spread.

[The customary administrative divisions as at Domesday (1086) are as follows:-

County or Shire.	Sussex was divided into East and West from the 12th century, but got separate County Councils only in 1888.
Rape	A group of Hundreds, with its own Sherriff. In Sussex it would embrace 40 parishes. Each rape had its own river, forest and castle.
Hundred	An administrative area, originally responsible for law and order, levying troops and raising taxes with its own court. Covered 100 homesteads or 'hides'.
Tithing	An area containing 10 households
Vill	A village
Manor	A major property or land division
Hide	8 Virgates (in Sussex, 4 elsewhere). Between 60-120 acres
Virgate	The land 2 oxen could plough in a season -20/30 acres
Ferlynge	A quarter of a Virgate

The residual powers of these divisions and their courts were seriously diminished in 1867 when County Courts were established, and in 1894 when Urban and Rural District Councils took on local administrative responsibilities.

Feudal management of the County

An important feature of Norman feudalism was their regularisation of the Manorial System. The King delegated control of a rape, at a price, to a Baron, a Tenant-in-Chief. He in turn subdivided his demesne to Lords of the Manors, often dubbed 'Knights', with similar rights and obligations. He often held land, his demesne, 'in hand', the Manor Farm or Grange, and parcelled out smaller holdings to serfs or villeins. They benefited from protection and the legal control of the Manorial Court of law. Some serfs' holdings were 'dependent', requiring military and labour services which were sometimes commuted for cash. Others were 'free' without such obligations, but held on copyhold for a rent. The term originates from the practice of giving the tenant a copy of the court roll as proof of his legal right. Tenure was usually hereditary, subject to a fee on changeover. Villeins' holdings could be sub-let. A village could embrace several Manors and a Manor could reach into more than one parish. Many Manors were gifted to Church Bishoprics and monasteries. Locally parcels of land 'paid suit and service' not only to Pinkhurst Manor but also to the Manors of Ferring and Fure, Bassetts Fee, Wiggonholt, Dedisham and Storrington. The parish of Billingshurst had several Lords of the Manor within its boundaries. The Bishop of Chichester owned Ferring with Fure. He was a major landowner of a strip two fields wide across the width of the parish including Woodhouse and Fewhurst. The Village Parish, which was the creation of the church, outlasted the Manors, which were legal property holdings deliberately created by the Normans.

The Manors of Billingshurst and District

The focal point of this history is an old building near the end of East Street called Hammonds. Hammonds Farm, alias Cocksbrook, is in the County of Sussex, the Rape of Arundel, originally held by the Norman Tenant-in-chief Roger de Montgomery, the 'Half-hundred' of West Easwrith and is part of the Manor of Pinkhurst. Roger, a senior commander at the time of the Battle of Hastings, was also gifted estates in Shrewsbury where he chose to live and die. While there he confronted the Welsh and won the land now known as Montgomeryshire. There is a hamlet in the cheese and apple region of Normandy, the Pays d'Auge, East of Caen named Sainte-Foy-de Montgommery where General Rommel was strafed in 1944 by one of Bernard Montgomery's airmen! A remarkable coincidence of names. It is quite near Falaise where William the Conqueror was born and the hamlet of Camembert, and the town of Liverot, a land of big cheeses.

Roger is said to have earned his magnanimous reward at the crucial Battle of Hastings. Here is one account of his part in the battle which depicts the mettle of the man and the violence of the struggle for England as depicted in the Bayeux tapestry. It is called 'The Story of the Saxon Knight':

'William sat on his war-horse and called out Rogier, whom they name de Montgomeri, "I greatly rely on you. Lead your men hitherward and attack them from that side!....The ground thus pointed out for the charge was the steepest and most difficult part of the hill....but Roger and his division did their work gallantly and were the first to break through the English stockade. Roger himself had a hand-to-hand encounter with a Saxon champion.... he wielded a Northern hatchet with the blade a full foot long and was well armed ....being tall, bold and of noble carriage. In the front of the battle where the Normans thronged most, he came bounding on swifter than the stag, many Normans falling before him and his company. He rushed straight upon a Norman who was armed and riding on a war horse and tried with his hatchet of steel to cleave his helmet, but the blow mis-carried, and the sharp blow, glancing down the saddle-bow, driving through the horse's neck down to the ground, so that the horse and rider fell together to the earth. The Normans were about to abandon the assault when Roger de Montgomerie came galloping up with his lance set, and heeding not the long-handled axe, which the Englishman wielded aloft, struck him down and left him stretched upon the ground. Then Roger cried out, "Frenchmen strike, the day is ours!"

Unfortunately other records show that Roger was still in Normandy at the time of the battle, looking after William's interests. He had contributed soldiers to the invasion force and was handsomely rewarded.

Much of Billingshurst was in the Manor of Bassetts Fee originally held by the Abbot of Fecamp. The Manor House in the High Street, an old timber-framed house erected in the early 18th century, now with a Georgian facade, was the main site. Henry V gave that Manor to the monastery at Syon in Middlesex. Wm. Garton was bailiff in 1535 and his son Francis bought it from Queen Elizabeth I. It subsequently passed to the Henshaws (1603-1690). Joseph Henshaw was a prominent divine, who became Dean of Chichester and Bishop of Peterborough. Philip Henshaw however is described as a lunatic. The ownership then passed by marriage to Bartholomew Tipping, then to one Collins, Thomas Clear and Maurice Ireland. Other Manors in the neighbourhood, creating a patchwork pattern of ownership, were Storrington, Wiggonholt and Ferring-cum-Furehurst.

In the Pinkhurst Court Roll of as late as 1872, we learn of the Lord of that Manor and his Manorial team:- 'The Court Baron of the most noble Bernard Edward, Duke of Norfolk, Hereditary Earl Marshal of England, Dewdney Stedman, Gentleman, Steward of the Manor, and Thomas Clear, Reeve'.

On the evidence of local history, of Messrs. Clear, Garton and Henshaw, the position of Manorial Reeve, Bailiff or Steward, was a sound rung on the ladder of wealth and social advancement.

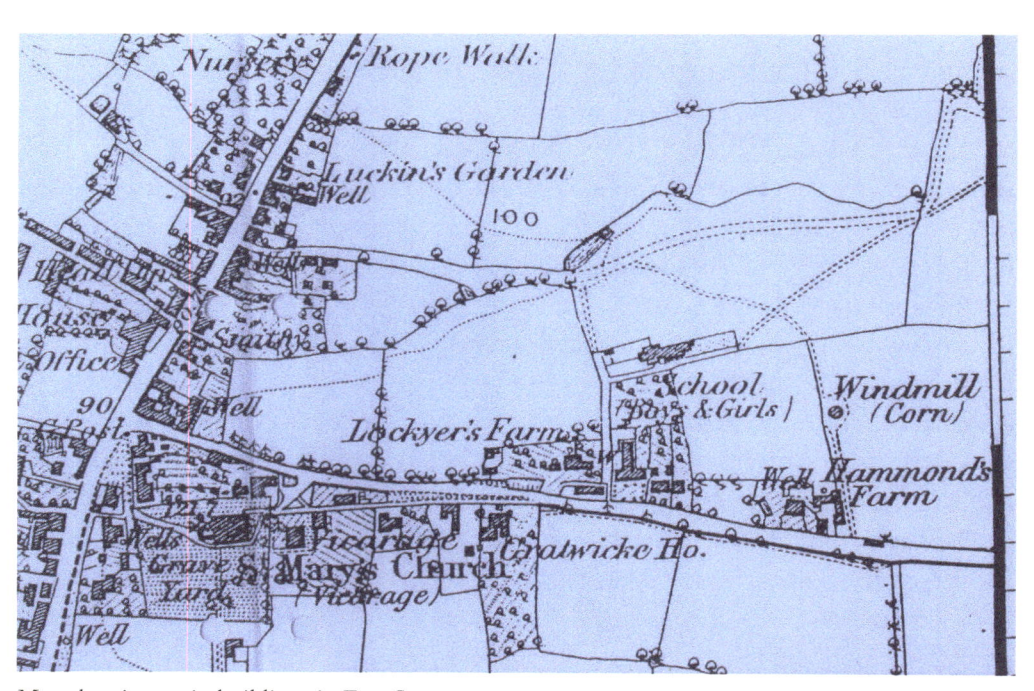

Map showing main buildings in East Street

Cocksbrook alias Hammonds north of East Street

1327/32

The earliest records of the area to the north east of Billingshurst, according to the documentation of John Hurd, suggest that one Johne de Kockesbroke or Cokkesbrouk gave his name to a piece of land subsequently known as Cockbrookes. [It is possible, of course, that Johne derived his name from his dwelling near a small stream called Cock's or Couk's brook!] The Lay Subsidy Roll of 1327 records the existence of Bellingesherst, with 41 inhabitants paying taxes.

Coxbrook, East and North of East Street, was a small part of the Hundred of West Easwrith, which comprised 12 parishes.

A lady called Alice Dawkes held 1 ½ virgates and a tenement called Crouchers. The parcel of land called Daux derives from her name and there was another area nearby called Broomfields. Coxbrook was larger that these other two combined.

There were 10 tithings in the Half-hundred of Easwrith. John Couk is one of those listed for the tithing of Billyngeshurste, amongst others like Somere, Gilmyn and Okhurst, names still extant in local place names.

1400AD

In the same year, when Geoffrey Chaucer died, William Dakons was paying 9s, 5d for Croucheslond and 5 shillings for Cookesbrouke.

Tudor Times

1485

With the accession of King Henry VII in 1485, Tudor monarchs brought peace and prosperity to England.

It is likely that Hammonds, as it was later called, was coterminous with Cockesbrook to the north of the present A272 described as one ferlyng. However it appears to cover about 60 acres. In the early16th century Crouchers and Cockesbrook, together making 90 acres, constituting a parcel of the Manor of Pynckhurst, was held by John Gryndfyld [Greenfield?] of Daks [Daux]. One Thomas Greenfield also of Daux died in 1578.

Hammonds House

Hammonds is not one of the oldest houses in the village. The aptly-named Old House at Adversane dates from 1470 and the farmhouse called Great Daux, with its black and white elevation and half-hipped roof of Horsham stone and a notable crown post, near the railway station, was also first built in the 15th century. [William Evershed, who founded the Unitarian Church, lived there as did his family for many generations. Dr. Arthur Evershed, born there in 1836 was a celebrated artist. His son Thomas, with Jane his wife and son John succeeded him].

Great Daux, 15th Century house

1557

Crouchers and Crockbrookes were assigned to Richard West, Yeoman

1564

Shakespeare was born

1559-1565

Church Porch

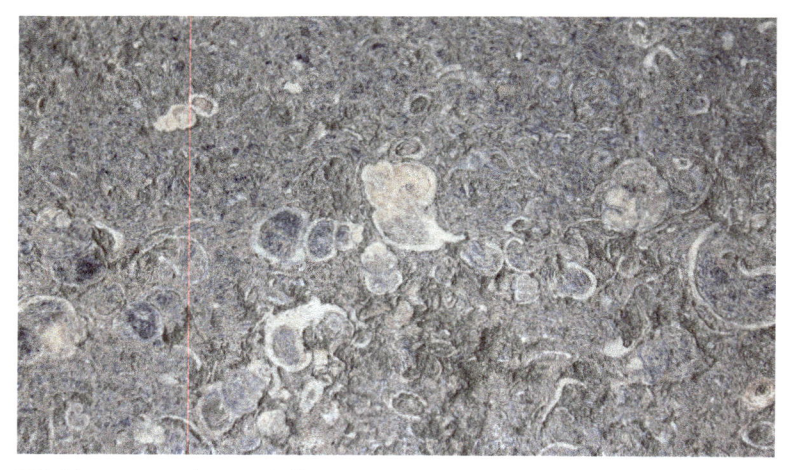

Winklestone on the porch floor

St. Mary's Church had its entry porch of brick and timber added in 1559, with slabs of winklestone or Sussex marble as flooring.

In 1565 Francis Garton, Gentleman, of Billingshurst took on a lease by copyhold for £140 for 10,000 years from Henry, Earl of Arundel of both Croochers, [tenement, yardland and one virgate] and Cockbrookes. To this he added a half virgate called Chesemans. William Garton had been the bailiff of the Manor of Bassett's Fee in 1553.

1581

In 1581 a lease passed to John Apsley and William Lee, yeoman for all three parcels

1591

Richard West, son Richard, wife Margery all die. The Inventory value of his property was £206. 3s

1600-1618

In these years one Isaac Bungar was active in both Wisborough Green and Billingshurst, buying up woodlands to make window glass, an industry that demanded copious amounts of coppiced timber for fuel. The industry had prospered in Elizabethan times at Chiddingfold and Kirdford largely because of skilled French Huguenot immigrants. By 1612 in Staffordshire coal became the preferred fuel and in 1615 the use of wood was outlawed by Royal Proclamation and Bungar was obliged to shut down his wood-fired furnace. Few traces of this industry remain in Billingshurst.

1605

In 1603 the Elizabethan Poor Law was enacted to deal with the perceived threat of rogues, vagabonds and the welfare of the destitute. About 1605 the Billingshurst churchwardens funded '4 little rooms for the poor of the parishe' fronting East St. in Gorefield, part of Cocksbrook, at a cost of £4-10s-2d. These almshouses cost the parish £1-1s-10d for mending and thatching in 1641 and were on record to 1661. They may have constituted the earlier workhouse accommodation, predating the 'Old Workhouse'.

James I and the Stuarts

1605

The Gunpowder Plot was thwarted. Bonfire Night was celebrated in Billingshurst for many years. The tradition has recently been revived.

1610

We learn that in 1610 William Lee still held three parcels of land. He alienated 20 acres to Edward Grinfeild. Both were ordered to do fealty' [take an oath of fidelity of the vassal to the lord].

1612

In 1612 John Fuste of Itchingfield left Lockyers Farm, south of East Street, to his grandson John Shelley. It later passed to John Charman, whose name 'Charmans' is also used for Lockyers.

1630

Anthony Haman [? Hammond] paid Church Tax for Coxbrok. He had married Susan Lee in 1603 and presumably acquired title to the property. The earliest parish register for the village dates from 1630.

1639

Baron Edward Apsley, Knight, had a tenement nearby called Hilland with Thomas Henshaw acting as steward. Anthony Hammond was noted as being at Cocksbrook, with Lee at the other two parcels.

It is reasonable to suppose that this prosperous period in the 17th century would have been the time when Anthony Haman and his Lee relatives had a tenement erected, probably with adjacent barns, cowsheds and similar buildings. However the grade II listing for Hammonds, as now established, describes it as an 18th century building – 'Two windows, Painted brick, Modillion eaves cornice, Half-hipped roof of Horsham slabs, Trellised wooden porch with door of 6 fielded panels'. It has a 'dentil course' under the eaves, a line of bricks arranged to look like teeth. The present restored adjacent barn with tarred weather-boarding probably dates from the 17th century.

Hammonds House shows three clear stages of construction. The frontage, under the Horsham stone roof, is the original part. It is quite possible that an earlier building stood on the same site. There may have been an outshot attachment on the rear north side. The central inglenook fireplace suggests an early date. The chimney stack echoes Elizabethan structures, but by serving hearths on two storeys with attic rooms above it hints at a middle 17th century date. The majority of our half-timbered houses were built between 1550 and 1650. One might speculate that the timber-framed house on three storeys with wattle and daub walls, both inside and out, was built some time after 1650. It then had major revisions at 100 year intervals in 1750 or so and again in 1852.

The first alterations to Anthony Haman's place would have entailed covering the original frontage with a brick skin and formalising the windows and porch after the fashion of the 18th century. Extra rooms were probably on the rear. At this point the west elevation may have been given its elaborate tile hanging as a defence against the rain of the prevailing wind and to enhance its appearance from the road. John Streeter would have had the necessary wealth at a time of prosperity in farming. By the same token when William Sprinks was prospering as a miller and farmer about 1850, landowner and tenant might well have undertaken the major conversion to a double roofed property when the mill and adjacent farm buildings were also erected.

1. Inglenook fireplace at Hammonds

2. Hidden date recording Victorian Extension

Inventories of goods and chattels left by Richard and Anthony Hammond, Anthony Haman's heirs, imply that the original house then had a central Hall with a table and seven 'joind stools' and four chairs. It had a Chamber or main bedroom above furnished with two feather beds and bolsters, 'bedstedles' a table and chests. Also on the ground floor was a Buttery or drink store and pantry with barrels, firkins and kilderkins (16 gallon storage casks). In the buttery loft chamber were kept a bed, a dozen pairs of sheets, two dozen odd napkins and half a dozen table cloths and 'pillow coats'. There was also a Milk Room with ten 'milk trees' [probably trays, pans used to settle milk ready for skimming off the cream], two cheese presses, a dozen 'truggs'. Again it had a lodging chamber above. This milk room was an indoor dairy where butter was made and cheese from skim milk.

There is no mention of third floor attic rooms, possibly because they had no possessions in them, and were used as servants' dormitories. On the ground floor was a Kitchen, with a table and forms, well endowed with twenty-four pieces of pewter, brass kettles and 'posnets' (3 legged pots) and iron vessels, a mortar, spoons, a shredding knife, candle sticks, salts, bellows, chamber pots, a warming pan, 'buckits', colander, basting ladle, a cleaver, spits and smoothing irons and a little 'foulling peece'. The Outlet Room or brew house was, perhaps, a utility space where there was a 'bucking tub' used for boiling clothes, a copper and mash tub where malt was mixed with hot water to form wort for brewing beer, and 'other lumber'.

1. Buttery vats

2. Butter churns

3. Cheese-making equipment

4. Cooking devices all as shown at Singleton Museum.

Elsewhere was the Malthouse, possibly in the High Street, where the malt was valued at £20 with the wire screen and 20 quarters of barley. In addition there was malting equipment –a vat, bushel and peck measures, 'linen and woollen wheels', an oast haire (haircloth used for drying hops) sacks etc. There was an outside barn with £7 of wheat grain and hay. They had one 'best horse' and a mill powered by a 'nagg' moving in a circle, 7 'smal pigs and 3 hoggs', 3 cows and one calf. The animals were valued at between £1 and £2 each. Anthony had bees and a 'beehouse' valued at £1.10s. There was a dung cart, a harrow and other 'husbandry tackling', tools, wood, 'faggats', a ladder and 'other lumber'.

A man's wealth, if he was not a landowner, rested in his possessions and the copper, silver and gold in his purse. It is easy to forget that there were then no branch banks or building societies in Billingshurst to care for the money of ordinary people in bank accounts, no chequebooks, no banknotes or safe facilities until the 20th century, and no Post Office offering 'postal orders' until the 19th. Goods and services changed hands for coins. Servants and wholesalers were paid in cash. [A private company had invented 'money orders' in 1792 and 'Postal Orders' descended from them. Very wealthy people might use City or provincial banks such as at Horsham who issued their own local notes, or make use of 'Bills of Exchange' to transfer money. The first coloured Bank of England banknotes were issued in 1927. £1 and 10s notes on white paper began during WW I to save gold and silver.] Farmers and traders, millers and maltsters would necessarily have been careful keepers of their business accounts, with a safe place to store their money, and reliant on lawyers to deal with their property rights and those of their heirs.

An Elizabeth I shilling

A 2d piece and two George III coins - 1806

When Richard died his apparel and purse were valued at £31 and Anthony's at £8. Business was done in cash and by barter. Richard had money for malt owing to him 'on book' for £9-15s-4d when he died. A man could will to his heirs the property he owned, the real estate he had legal title to and the cash he had stored in his keeping. He might be able to borrow from or owe money to others, with or without interest, against properly accountable legal documents, but the concept of a loan from a branch bank to buy or sustain property was quite foreign to country people. Our modern practice of getting a mortgage from a local bank or other lender in order to purchase property dates only from the 1930s.

Barclays Bank was first housed near its present site in an old building after WW I. While this was being demolished in the 1960s it moved to the Parish Room beside the 10 Steps then back to the present premises. Lloyds Bank enjoys an unusual 1960s design and the Westminster Bank came in 1929.

A good deal of financial business in the 19th and early 20th centuries would have been conducted through the Friendly Societies that acted as savings banks and provided mutual insurance against ill health and other calamities. Charitable semi-Masonic bodies met and offered a venue for local traders to make deals. The Rhodes family for example were members of the Royal Antediluvian Order of Buffaloes which met regularly at the King's Arms.

Malting was made easier in the High Street where there was a handy stream, stone slabs to cool the barley to allow it to germinate and cordwood for the kiln. The process was for grain to be tipped into a shallow pit to soak and swell. It was then drained and transferred to a 'couch', lying about a foot deep and frequently turned, creating heat and beginning to germinate. In a couple of days or so it was spread out on a growing floor until roots began to appear. The stem had swelled up and just before it burst out of the husk it was left to dry. It was gradually moved to the kiln for three or four days, separated from the fire by a wire screen. Next it was sieved to remove the shoots and stored for some months to develop flavour. Most work was done in winter when farm workers were free to help. Malt Tax was exacted from 1697, then 6d a bushel, rising to 4s-6d by 1804, with complex rules of production to safeguard the interests of the taxman.

At the rear of the original Hammonds building is a substantial addition extending along the length of the front with its own roof, built of stone as an extension, probably in 1852. It is quite possible that previous extensions on the back of the house were removed to make way for the Victorian addition.

East elevation of Hammonds showing the stone-built extension

West elevation showing decorative tile hanging

1640

By the will of Anthony Hammon, Yeoman, he makes 10 shilling bequests to the poor of Billingshurst, to his wife Susan, and his eldest son (also named Anthony). He also inherits Gilmans which his father had bought from John and William Penfold in 1632. Another son gets a featherbed, once his mother's at his house in Gaystreet, Chiltington. The third son, Richard, gets £5 when aged 21, and Coxbrook when Susan dies, plus a furnace from Anthony's house in Billingshurst. The fourth son Isacke also gets £5 at age 21 and the Gaystreet furnace. This son married Joan Nye in 1642. (He died in 1701). His daughter Anna got £50 at 21 or on marriage to Edmond Stringer, Susan similarly or on marriage to John Crutchlow, and his Godchildren a shilling each on request. A small bequest was often made in wills as proof that a person had not been unintentionally overlooked.

1642

Richard Hammond was duly noted as the holder of Cocksbrooke in the Manor of Pinkhurst in 1642.

Civil war. Charles I beheaded. The Republican Interlude

1649

William Greenfield, the elder, master butcher, willed Duckmore, Catshill and Lockiers, Hyle and Heathfeild to relatives. This is a considerable landholding East of Billingshurst. Lockyers is the farm south of East St and east of St Mary's Church, now Gratwicke Close. Duckmore lies north-east of Coxbrook. The Greenfields, who also occupied Summers, must have been very wealthy and influential citizens of Billingshurst.

Restoration of the Monarch, Charles II, and the Church of England

1660

Another prominent Sussex family, the Gratwicks, held Ifold Farm for 50 years which was part of the Billingshurst Manor of Bassetts Fee.

1665

In 1665 Richard Hammond and Matthew Weston were Churchwardens. They contributed to a fund for distressed Ancient Protestants, the Waldenses, who were being persecuted under the Duke of Savoy. There is clearly still a residual sympathy for Low Church values in the parish. The following year was that of the great fire of London. It is possible that Hammonds House was then built as his home.

1667

Richard was again elected Churchwarden along with Maurice Greenfield of Southhouse.

1675

Eight years later Richard was still at Cockesbrook. Thomas Stirt was at Dawks and Sigismund Stidolph of Headly at Broomfields.

1680

Richard Hammond, maulter [maltster], died in 1680. The inventory value of his property in his will was £98 -1s-11d. His eldest daughter Susan, born 1647, who was married to John Booker 1677, yeoman, of Rudgwick, gets 10s and a chest in the hall marked SH; his daughter Ann, married to R. Denn of W Chiltington, gets 10s; the youngest daughter, Rachel, gets £20. His son, Anthony is the executor and heir to the estate. Messrs. Pilfold and Ryde of Horsham are 'overseers'.

1682

In this year the last trial for witchcraft took place at Horsham. Only four out of eighteen witches tried in Sussex were found guilty and only Margaret Cooper of Kirdford was hanged, also at Horsham.

Isaac Hammond, Richard's brother, became Churchwarden in 1682. He paid £6.5s.6d to the Collectors.

Anthony Hammond, maulter and yeoman, died on the 9th January 1682 enjoying his property for only two years. His father, Richard, lived a long life compared to his son. The inventory of his goods and chattels valued them at £120.

By Anthony's will his grandchildren Jane and Reenald, (Ann and Denn's children), get £3 each, Susan's two children, John and Susan, £3 apiece, sister Rachel £80 from Billingshurst land and tenements and she shares the household goods with her sister Susan. Susan is the sole executrix. She inherits the freehold lands and tenements in Billingshurst, but if she does not pay Rachel her £80, then Rachel gets them! Susan's son-in-law, John Booker, and his heirs are to succeed on Susan's death.

1685

In 1685 The Manor of Pinkhurst reported the seizure of a cow from Anthony and Richard Hammond; both now deceased, in order to secure debts of 30s and 40s respectively. The malting business for the Hammonds seems to be faltering at the end of the 17th century.

1714

Queen Ann, last of Stuart's, dies.

18th Century – the Georgian Era

1725

The old Vicarage was built in East St.

At that time an expensive substantial stone-built dwelling called Tower's (or Towse?) House was erected east of the Almshouses. A will of Mary Champion of Frimley leaves her Billingshurst properties mainly to the Bartholomew family, with provision of £50 to buy Tower's, 'for the use of poor labouring men'. Dated ?? 1725. So began the 'Old Workhouse', originally a large T-shaped building.

1. The Old Workhouse original

2. Today

1731

In 1731 15 people are listed as taken in to the workhouse. Phillip Greenfield, possibly in charge, was paid for repairs to the workhouse and adjacent 'Clarks House'.

1738

In 1738 John Booker held the lease of Cocksbrook, '1d heriot, relief and services'. But in the same year, John Streater pays Poor Tax of £3. 15. 2d for Little Eaton and Coxbrook, indicating an imminent change of ownership. The fortunes of the heirs of the Hammonds were doubtless in decline and those of the Streeters in the ascendant. It was at this time that a host of special 'rates' for a wide variety of good causes were consolidated by Act of Parliament into a single Poor Tax.

1760-1840

Thomas Gratwick paid Poor Tax on a house in Lockyers south of East St. He died in 1766 aged 86. The house, buildings and yard together with six fields and meadows and a small shaw or wood were subsequently occupied by Henry Charman, William Smart, George Alwyn, Arthur Greenfield, Elizabeth Puttock and Mary Hughes, James Fuller, Phillip Puttock, a journeyman miller and nurseryman and Richard Hughes, a carpenter. This takes the story of Lockyers to 1840 or so. The Ordnance survey map of 1877 misleadingly places the name Lockyers on the north side of East Street.

The Unitarian Church

The Unitarian Chapel

1754

The Act of Uniformity of 1662 was intended to establish the supremacy of the Anglican Church and inhibit radical non-conformist preaching. Dissenters were prosecuted and imprisoned for heretical meetings called 'conventicles'. Two thousand Low Church clergymen refused to comply with the rules of the Act. Despite the penalties, ever since the Restoration of Charles II in 1660, non-conformists had met clandestinely in farmhouses in the Horsham district. Matthew Caffyn, a radical evangelist called 'The Battle Axe of Sussex', practised adult baptism and was imprisoned five times. He lived to 1714 but. by the time of his death, the 'Toleration Act' of 1689 had offered greater freedom of worship to all but Roman Catholics.

By 1721 a Baptist Meeting House had been founded at Horsham with two of the Trustees living in Billingshurst. In 1742 William Evershed, known as 'The Preacher' came to live at Great Daux Farm where he raised four children. From there he attended 64 Baptist Meetings at Horsham in 56 years! The Billingshurst members were keen to have their own chapel. So Evershed and William Turner, a farmer of Newbridge, bought land from Mrs. Elizabeth Sendell and her son Edward for three guineas (£3.30). They built the Chapel in what was then called South Street and transferred it to 10 Trustees for 1000 years in 1754. Extra land was acquired in 1759 and 1799 when William died. The Chapel still has a clock by Inkpen of Horsham dated 1756 and pews and coffin stands carved by James Knight (1787/8).

At first the Horsham and Billingshurst Meetings had joint Elders, but by 1818 a theological dispute about the 'laying on of hands' led to rupture and the installation of an independent Minister for Billingshurst.

The Registry and Baptistery, originally roofless, was added 1n 1825. Mr. Dendy Evershed published a comprehensive history of the Chapel in 1991, including a record of all burials since 1755. Baptism by immersion in an underground tank was practised till 1872, using water from a spring near the Women's Hall gate brought in buckets. When the water ran out sprinkling was substituted for general baptism. Marriages were solemnized from 1839. The Vestry was enlarged in 1886 which led to the making of a library with bookshelves, the only forerunner of the County Library in 1944. It was used as a Sunday School room, teaching the three Rs as well as piety. In 1887 the Jeffery family paid for a new roof and repairs.

An organ was installed in 1911 shortly after it was renamed The Free Christian Church [Unitarian]. Services steadily improved with rewiring and a new heating system in 1985. Some land was sold to CALA homes and subsequently an extension added in 1990. In 1999 the name was changed to Unitarian Chapel. Currently Community Arts are promoted at The Chapel' by 'Evershed Arts'.

Nicholas Pevsner praised the building, 'like a demure Georgian cottage on a knoll in a surprisingly big churchyard'. Besides Carters, Kensetts, Turners and Trowers there are 126 Eversheds lying buried in the graveyard. Many influential people in Billingshurst became Low Church adherents who did not attend St.Mary's Anglican congregation.

1766

In 1766 two men fell to their deaths while reshingling St. Mary's Church spire.

1767

Thomas Pacey, whose father was Thomas Pacy who died in 1715, a Yeoman, comes into the action, when it is reported in the records of the Manor of Pinkhurst that he had sold the freehold of the place called Hammonds and Cocksbrook to William Streater, miller of Billingshurst. Presumably he had bought it from John Booker about 1738.

Summers Place today

The area known as Summers on the road from Billingshurst to Five Oaks was owned in the mid 14th century by Richard Somer, on land presented to the Norman Earl Roger de Someri over a century earlier. Roger held two Knights Fees in Billingshurst and Kirdford, the gift of Edward I. In 1372 Richard made a purchase of land from William Newbrigge [Newbridge]. Summers was effectively owned and occupied by the Greenfields from about 1484 to 1690. It was part of the Manor of Bassett's Fee.

Thomas Bettesworth of London, a Merchant, who died in 1795 and is commemorated in the parish church, built a large and handsome Georgian mansion-house about 1790 which was demolished some eighty years later. It was rebuilt in 1880, designed by an amateur architect, John Norton, for Robert Goff who let the property to F.D. Leyland Esq. To improve his view Old Pratts, opposite the Drive, was demolished and two late Victorian cottages built nearer the village to replace it. They are now used as offices. The New Road, as we now call it, was a rerouting of the old road which ran much closer to the mansion. Summers Place was subsequently sold to Henry Carnsew and then to Major Pratt.

Col. Greenwell owned it from 1920 to 1945 when it became the Convent and School of The Sisters of the Immaculate Heart of St. Mary. In its heyday there were 40 boarders there and 120 day pupils. It closed in 1984 and until 2005 was Sotheby's provincial fine art auction house. This area is often spelt Somers in the records as in the tithing of Somere.

The boundaries of the Manor of Pinkhurst were defined [1766 to 1827] when the 'bounds were trodden': "W up Catshill to boundary (No.17) thence over the hedge into Cocksbrook and along the E side of Cocksbrook, leaving Duckmore on the right to (18) then up the N side of Cocksbrook to (19) by a stile, thence over the hedge and under the W hedges & then under the N hedge to (20) thence over into and under the N hedge of the Hammonds and Workhouse Garden to (21) in the Gore Fields hedge, thence round the Gore Fields and Old Platt, into a garden to (22) thence under the N side of said garden between Miss Pannells house in Billingshurst Street & Duckmore House in the Street held by the Manor of Bassetts Fee to boundary (1)".

1777

In the Report of a National Commission on Workhouses there are 45 places available in the Billingshurst institution.

1779

William Streater Senior was paying Poor Tax for Hammonds and Coxbrook in 1779.

1782

He paid Land Tax too. He also owned Taintlands and part of Gingers (Jengers) occupied by his son, also named William.

1795

William Streater Senior died in 1795.

By his will, he bestowed the Windmill and granary on Taintland and Gingers Farm to his Grandson William "with full and free liberty at any time with carts wagons and horses to and from the windmill". His son John got £700 from the estate, grandsons James and John [other children of his son, also named William] got £100 each at age 21 & 'and I hereby charge the windmill and the granary with the same.' His wife Elizabeth was to have £15 a year paid by his son William. [Messrs. Poltock and Holden were named as Trustees] – present messuage and tenement 'where I now live, garden, orchard farm barn lands etc. known as Hammonds and Coxbrook and wife Elizabeth the use of the messuage for life – to sell the same. His son William got Taintlands and Gingers (£15 payable to mother for life –'sans waste'). After his death the Trustees were to sell the property and invest the money towards the upbringing of his grandsons William, James and John.

Meantime in the wider world at a place called Speenhamland magistrates met and instituted a system whereby farm workers' wages were fixed, but when the price of bread rose above a critical figure they were to be paid a 'dole' from the Poor Rate. It was a disaster for all but the richer landowners. It kept wages so low that it pauperised honest workmen and weighed heavily on those who had to pay the Rate. The effect was clearly evident in Billingshurst

The Six Bells, formerly the farm house called Taintland

William Streater's will is the first real evidence of the house and property we now call Hammonds though it must have been built much earlier.

Taintland was a 16th century half-timbered farmhouse. It is now a pub in the High Street, the only house in Billingshurst with a continuous overhang or jetty along the whole first floor. It became a beer house in Victorian times. It was named Six Bells when St. Mary's Church belfry gained two more bells than the original six in 1897 to celebrate Queen Victoria's Diamond Jubilee. Bell Cottage is a 17th century building, originally thatched, which stands at the rear.

The old mill burnt down on Guy Fawkes Day, 1852. It is now only recorded by Mill Lane and Mill Way.

A hundred yards west of Hammonds House is Vine Cottage, built in the 18th century. About 1790 a brewer at the malting in the High Street lived there and in 1858 Thomas Baker, the 'Relieving Officer'. A Mr. Wm. Lorenzo Flight sold it in 1860 to the Voice family who lived there till 1919. Edward Voice who died in 1894 was a stone mason, plumber and painter. Between the world wars it was owned by seven different people, mainly maiden ladies. Miss Goddard and Miss Macintosh sold it, in 1953, to Miss Elder who sold it in turn to the late Alistair Morris, Chartered Surveyor. It has recently been extended eastwards.

Just west of the old workhouse is the 16th century or earlier Gore Farm house, one of the few Billingshurst buildings praised by Pevsner: 'half-timber frame, tile-hung front with a half-hipped gable at the w end: very pretty'. This judgement is despite the fact that the frontage is obscured by another building. Gore Farm is a late mediaeval hall house, though a floor and upper storey have been added, and it was extended in the 16th century, the addition now in separate ownership. The building was used as a tannery in the 17th century. It was recently offered for sale for £600,000.

1. Vine Cottage, west of Hammonds

2. Gore Farm house.

3. Bell Cottage

4. Horsham Stone roofing

1798

In 1798 Denyer and Carter, Churchwardens, and Turner and Greenfield, Overseers of the Poor, signed Articles of Agreement for Moses Chantler, a tenant farmer at Wooddale, to provide for the poor of the parish at a cost of £1000.

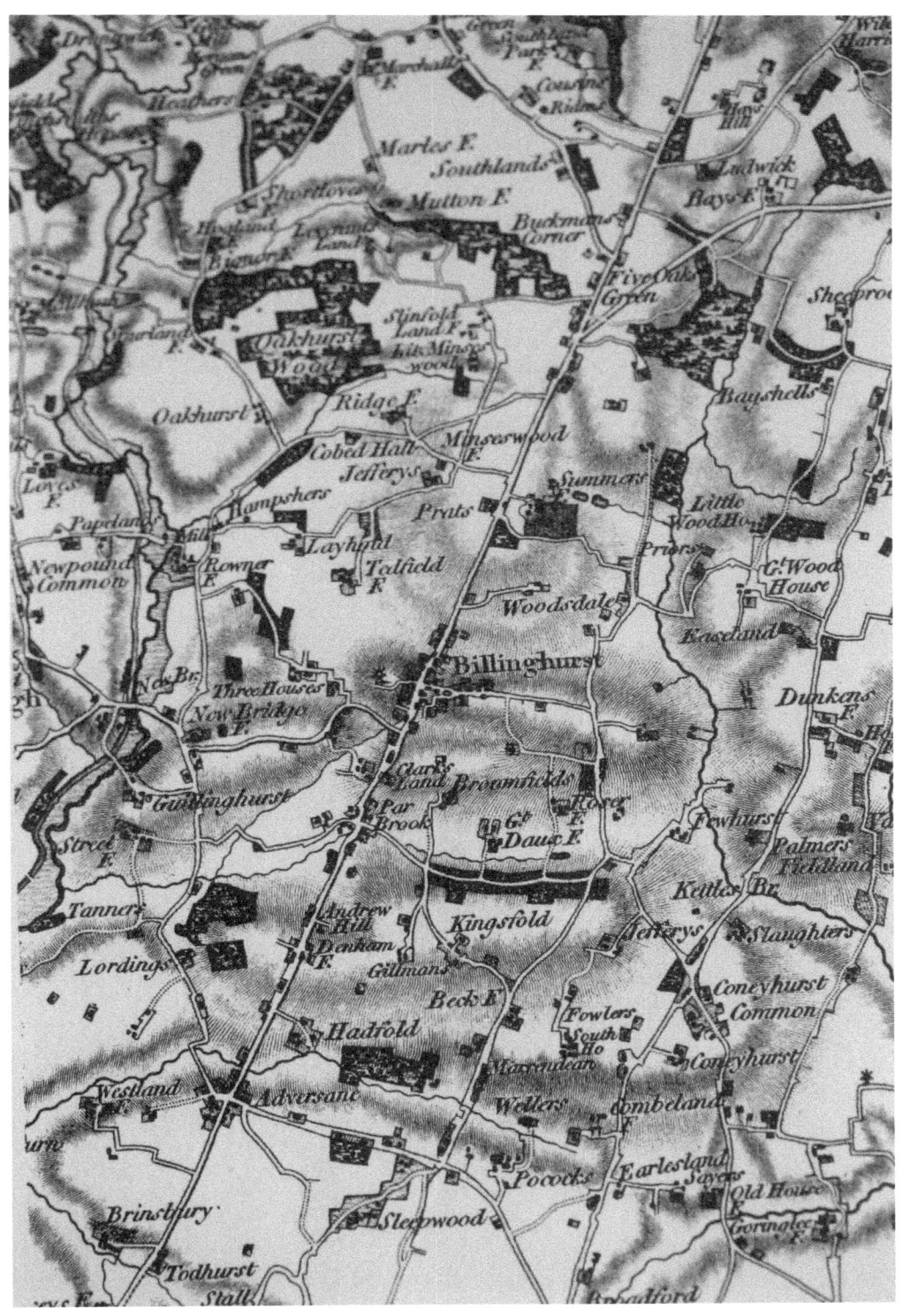

Billingshurst from Five Oaks to Adversane (1819)

A careful scrutiny of this authoritative map, dated four years after Waterloo, reveals significant features of Billingshurst as it was at the dawn of the industrial triumph of Victorian England. Many of the ancient place names and properties have our modern spelling, such as Adversane, but Guillinghurst, Oakhurst, Five Oaks Green and Woodsdale are exceptions.

The new 1810 Turnpike Road from Five Oaks to Horsham [A264] is depicted, as was the crossroads at Parbrook which then continued Natts Lane westwards to Newbridge. The present site of Station Road remains as open countryside. East Street is beginning to develop into what would eventually become the A272 through Coneyhurst to Coolham. A throughway to South House via Jeffreys Farm is shown, predating the present access off what is now called Marringdean Road. The old road made its way along a quite narrow strip of land, still well-defined by substantial hedges, which was an unusual feature of the Manor of Ferring and Fure.

The present New Road was a cul de sac and its predecessor from Wooddale ran close to Summers Place. Pratts is drawn almost opposite Summers. It was demolished to improve the view when the Place was rebuilt in 1880 and replacement cottages erected nearer the village. [Now business premises] A route off Newbridge close to the village, now lost, goes past Three Houses to Rowner.

The Wey & Arun Canal alongside the River Arun was only three years old when the map was made. It is precisely depicted.

The 19th Century

1801

The 1801 Poor Tax evaluation on William Streater shows him due to pay on Taintland and Gingers (41 ½ acres) with a house and Duckmore (54 ½ acres) with houses. This constitutes a considerable farmland holding. The widow of Wm. Streater Sr. and John Johnson were also taxed for part of Hammonds House. Sir Abraham Hume owned Brookfields, and Miss Leagatt Great Daux, both of which were occupied by Wm. Evershed. Lady Bartholomew owned Summers where Mr. Jeal lived.

1804

The Manor of Pinkhurst reported that Hammonds/Cocksbrook was held freely by William Streater, miller, a bankrupt. His business was clearly in trouble as was Europe, with the Napoleonic war well under way.

The Reverent P. Evershed successfully challenged the cruel 'sport' of cock throwing and cock fighting by pinning a critical poem on his church door. Weighted sticks called 'libbets' were hurled at tethered cocks. People used to come from miles around on Shrove Tuesday to see this gruesome spectacle.

1805

There was victory and tragedy. Nelson died at the Battle of Trafalgar in 1805.

1806

The Hammonds property, freehold land and tenement, was alienated by the assignees, that is to say, unpaid creditors, to John Streater, William's brother, a farmer. He may well have been bankrupt too.

William managed to father a bastard son, baptised Henry Roberson, by Charlotte Robinson at the Common Workhouse in East Street. The miller and Charlotte were to appear before the magistrates at the Half Moon, Petworth.

The family history of the Streaters suggests rich source material for an historical novel along the lines of Hardy's 'Mayor of Casterbridge' with its rags to riches theme and subsequent poverty and disgrace.

1809

John Streater was still paying rent and Land Tax in 1809.

1811

Charlotte, the mother of Wm Streeter's child, was baptised in 1789, married in 1811 and died 1842.

1812

Charles Dickens was born.

1814

John was paid 4d for carting stone from Stammerham, now the site of Christ's Hospital, for the belfry at the Parish Church just before the battle of Waterloo.

'Stammerham' actually means 'dwelling near a stone quarry'. Horsham stone is a thin, fine grained, calcareous sandstone laid down about 120 million years ago in the Cretaceous age of the dinosaurs, occurring quite close to the surface in an arc South and West of Horsham. Extensive old pit workings are evident at Cowfold. The Romans valued its tough properties in their building of Stane Street (= Stone from the Norse 'steinn') Street which runs through Billingshurst and subsequent builders appreciated the way it splits easily along the bedding planes for use as roofing slabs and walling blocks. We don't know what the Romano-Brits called it.

The Saxon term is first recorded in 1270 as 'Stanstret'.

Another valuable rock also occurs in the Lower Weald Clay. This is 'Sussex Marble', a compressed limestone composed of fossilised winkle-like gastropods (molluscs), which can be highly polished for fonts, tombs, mantelpieces, columns and fireplaces, and used for floor slabs as they were at St. Mary's Church. When the Billingshurst by-pass was built seams of the marble were exposed. It has been found at Stonepits in Marringdean Road. It is likely that it might be found under Hammonds as beds excavated at Coolham as recently as 1903 run West towards Billingshurst. The stone was laid down 125 million years ago. Though decorative it is not a rock suitable for building. Further south the building stone found in the Upper Greensand was deposited 110 million years back, and the chalk which contained flints for building and sharp tools is 100 million years of age. Eventually the Wealden clay of the Billingshurst area finally yielded a dividend with the development of local brick and tile making required for the vernacular architecture in the later Victorian expansion. At Wildens along from East Street is the site of a great brickyard with four kilns mapped in 1879. Here clay flower pots and tiles were made. There was also a brick field in Station Road, behind the first three houses in Silver Lane, another at the end of what is now Brookers Road and the Station Brickyard on the site of the current Gilmans Industrial Estate.

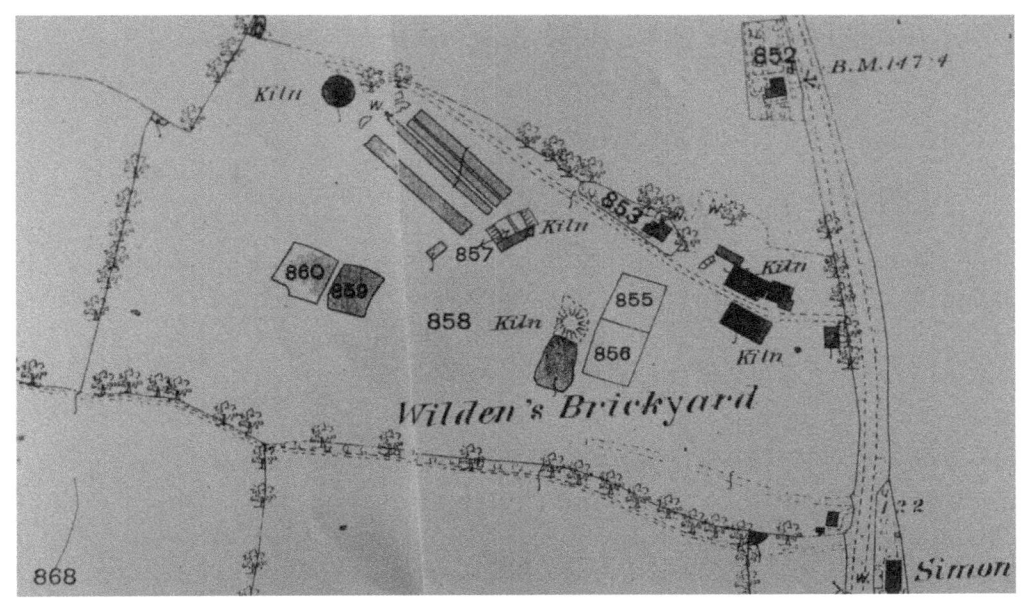

Map showing the Brickyard and kilns at Wildens

1816

The Wey and Arun Canal opened, linking London to Portsmouth. In 1817 27 tons of goods were moved from Arundel and a similar amount to London and a week later a similar cargo came back. For half a century it boosted local trade but with the competition of the railway it had become uneconomic and closed in 1863.

1817-1830

There was trouble at the Workhouse in 1817 when Renolds Totham, the Governor, was in debt and obliged to surrender his effects to his creditors. The Vestry advertised for a 'Man [without family] who understands the sack rope and woollen manufactory to superintend the poor house as Governor thereof' – no doubt to make simple work for the inmates- ; 'also for persons to visit twice a week with power to make or alter regulations etc.' In 1830 Simon Johnson, and wife, were appointed to care for the paupers, and later to superintend the road workers.

1822

John Streater and James Trower are now paying Land Tax in 1822.

1823

Streater was paying Poor Tax just for Hammonds House, while James Trower paid for Great and Little Rowfold, part of Priors, Hoile, Little Daux, and Hammonds. This is the first mention of the Trower family who figure significantly in later years.

1825

By the evidence from inscription over the door, "JS 1825" now lost, the East Windmill was built in 1825 by John Streeter with Richard Chennell as the miller. The walls of the mill would have been tarred to resist damp affecting the flour and to protect the walling stones from the weather. It was a smock mill raised on an octagonal stone base with an upper storey faced with horizontal wooden planks and a revolving cap designed to turn into the wind and carrying four large 'sweeps' or sails. The erection of a second mill in Billingshurst reflects the growing demand and profitability of cereals in early 19th century England. In 2016 the self-seeded ash tree within the ruin was felled. Archaeologists Nicholls and Green explored a 2 metre trial trench across the foundations from the SW doorway to the NE corner and a metre beyond. Their buildings report, commissioned with a view to subsequent preservation, established previously unknown features of the structure. The large central post hole revealed that the first 'meal floor' had been supported not only by transverse joists set in wall sockets but also by a stout central pillar. A post hole 0.7M outside the wall indicated that vertical struts had supported the 'reefing stage', a method unusual in Sussex but customary in Kent. This stage platform had encircled the top of the two-storey stone base, to enable the miller to adjust the 'sweeps'. The tall SW doorway served both storeys, constructed of locally sourced and crudely dressed stone, 4 M high and 0.54 M thick. A NE doorway, restricted to the first floor only, probably gave internal access to the reefing stage, for use when the sweeps were adjacent the SW doorway. Neatly chiselled graffiti included RIN(g?) which may well have been for the door-bell, WS for Wm. Sprinks, Mitchell Bath and JLV. They unearthed 101 items of domestic debris indicating resident families, such as pieces of a matching dinner service and a chamber pot. These ranged mainly from about 1900 to 1925. The occupiers were fond of thirst-quenching but non-alcoholic beverages, patent medicines and preserving jars. They had discarded numerous ink bottles, probably used for ledgers and accounts.

The East Mill

The young tree in the 70s'

Before the archaeological excavation

Pruning and stripping 2015

The dig in the Mill

After the dig, 2016

97

1827

Richard Chennell is now paying Poor Tax for his house, Hammons Land and the Windmill and Mrs. Evershed for Hammons House.

1830

The King's Arms, ancient coaching inn.

William Cobbett mentions The King's Arms in his 'Rural Rides'. He breakfasted well there. However farm workers were starving. They could not afford the high price of wheat caused by the demands and blockades of the Napoleonic Wars. (1803-1815). 1000 men assembled in Horsham, and compelled the magistrates to agree a wage of half a crown a day. The County Gaol at Horsham was swiftly filled with demonstrators! Fearing an attack on the gaol the Government moved in regiments of Life and Foot Guards. It became known as the 'Mobbing Winter'. Throughout England farm workers threatened magistrates, Poor Law guardians and rich tenant farmers by anonymous letters, signed 'Captain Swing' demanding better wages, relief from Poor Tax, an end to tithes and the destruction of new threshing machines, seen as a threat to employment. The name 'Swing Riots' was given to the insurrection allegedly from the name of the hinge on a threshing flail. Cobbett defended the rural labourers and was tried for sedition for his pains. He was acquitted.

One consequence of the riots was the Great Reform Act of 1832, and another the setting up of Workhouses in 1834 to give shelter to the indigent. This reform was deemed necessary because of the burden of poor rates. They had risen from £2m in 1785 to £10m in 1818. However the rioters were initially brutally suppressed, 19 being hanged, 644 imprisoned and 481 transported to Australia. The early Victorian recipe for dealing with the ever-threatening danger of insurrection by the underclass, the unprivileged majority of Disraeli's 'Two Nations', was a cunning mixture of the velvet glove, philanthropy with charity and social and political reform, and the mailed fist, punishment by imprisonment, transportation and execution. The workhouses were designed to deter any shiftlessness or welfare-scrounging by offering only miserable regimes, by separating families, and by providing only cheap food and hard labour.

1831/41

Billingshurst is recorded as having 1540 inhabitants. Corn was bought and sold once a fortnight at the Kings Arms on Tuesday evenings. The 'Comet' coach offered a daily service to London and Bognor.[Pigot's Directory].Fish was brought to the village from Worthing in carts drawn by four or five dogs.

1832

John Streater was still paying Land Tax but Richard Chennell and William Bridger were now the occupants of Hammonds.

Queen Victoria was crowned

1837

The 1841 Tithe Apportionment states that Phillip Puttock and wife Ann, their son Edwin and wife, a gardener and two young grandchildren lived at Lockyers house, and so did Richard and Mary Hughes and four children. However there is also listed Gratwick House and Garden, the responsibility of Richard Farhall, a Gentleman of Tillington, who seems to be the landlord of all Lockyers together with Woodhouse and Wilden's Land. He was affluent enough to have a vote in Horsham Polling District and perhaps facilitated the building of the great new house sometime in the 1830s. However the will of Arthur Greenfield suggests that Farhall was a trustee holding the property for the benefit of his sister Elizabeth Puttock, her good friend and housekeeper, Mary Hughes and Phillip, her illegitimate son. When they died the sale profits would revert to Arthur's nieces and nephews.

Gratwick House

Coach House and Stable of the house today

1834 to 1848

The year 1834 saw a new Poor Law enacted in response to low wages and the heavy rate demands of the Speenhamland system. 'Outdoor relief' was abolished and the 'workhouse test' imposed on applicants for public alms. Parishes were grouped together and enjoined to form Unions or central workhouses. Life in the workhouse was intended to be made deliberately unattractive to deter the shiftless. The likes of Charles Dickens in *Oliver Twist* exposed the inhumanity of this cruel process which separated husband, wife and children. Philanthropic sentiment slowly improved matters and the new Unions, run by elective Boards of Guardians were efficient, if unpopular.

It was decided in 1834 to pay the poorhouse master in East Street so much a pauper, depending on the price of good wholesome flour made from brown wheat. In 1836 Mr. Johnson was allowed to occupy the kitchen and pantry and two little rooms above, with a surveyor appointed to direct the necessary work. In 1838 the workhouse tenants 'had greatly abused the premises by destroying the windows and palings'. The Overseers had them boarded up. By 1839 the poor house was let out to James Fuller, a butcher, for £2 for one year. In 1840 the Overseers gave all the resident families notice to quit and to threaten those in the 'parish cottages' (almshouses) that unless they paid their arrears of rent by 1st Feb distress warrants would be taken out against their goods and chattels. Fuller's tenancy was then extended for 6 years at £10 per annum, with a cashback allowance of £4 for repairs, and agreement to give up the 'upper long rope shop' after due notice. It was duly taken down and sold in lots by auction in 1841. Fuller owed a year's rent of £10 so the Parish Officers were instructed to recover the money and recover possession. In 1848 there were just two caretakers in the old workhouse – 'no occupants allowed'.

By the Marriage Act of 1836 non-conformist and catholic people in Billingshurst no longer had to be wed by a Church of England parson, but could be married by their own ministers.

Kings Head Inn

Pigot's Directory of 1840 tells us of some of the personalities prominent in Billingshurst in the first years of Victoria's reign. The Reverends Henry Beath and Josiah Chapman were clergy and the 'Gentry' included John Ireland, John Napper, Magistrate, and George W. Wood at Summers. It states that The Duke of Norfolk is Lord of the Manor and holds a Court triennially. [A mistake! The Duke was not Lord of the Manor]. C.P. Goring. Bart. was Patron of the Living of St. Mary's Church. Professional persons included Wm. Boarer, day school, Matthew Caffin, land and timber surveyor, Peter Evershed, surgeon, and Henry Turner, Registrar of Births and Deaths and surveyor

Keepers of inns were Fred Peskett at The Blacksmiths, Adversane, a 17th century beer house, George Puttock at the Kings Arms and James Aylward at the Kings Head.

Shopkeepers and traders included David Baker, watchmaker, Cornelius Carter, blacksmith at Adversane, Stephen Evershed, Vetinary Surgeon, Edward Harwood, bootmaker, Adversane, Peter Kensett, grocer, draper and agent of the County Fire Office, Stephen Knight, maltster, three Lakers, tailors, leather sellers and hairdressers, George Puttock, basket, measure, sieve and hoop maker, William Sprinks, miller at Hammonds, John Voice, boot and shoemaker and Luke Wadey, wheelwright.

Many of these names have echoed down the years and are still familiar in the neighbourhood.

1840

Tithe acreage was assessed for payment by John Streeter and Wm Sprinks as follows: Garden Field 1.3.16 acres, Mill Field and East Windmill 5.2.17 acres, Hammonds House, Gardens and buildings 0.1.32 acres – about 8 acres in all. This must have included what is now Mill Barn and Hammonds, including the Garden Field now developed as 'Windmill Place'.

The workhouse plot, over an acre and occupied by Richard Farhall, the Lockyers landlord, had a separate tithe apportionment to be paid by Phillip Hughes and the 'parish cottage' was occupied by Abraham and Lydia Langley. (1841)

1841

The census of 1841 reveals that William Sprinks, aged 34 was now the miller of the East Mill (since 1839). He also ran the other older village mill. He had three wives; the first was Ruth who died in 1857 and was buried in the Baptist Chapel; in 1859, aged 50, he married a widow aged 47 – Sarah Seward; finally he married Ruth Older at St. Nicholas, Brighton in 1861. The second Ruth outlasted him by 6 years dying in 1891. William died 1885, and was buried at the Baptist Chapel. There were three children all by the first Ruth. William was named once again as the miller in Kelly's Directory in 1845.

1845

The children were William, b. 1830, Emily, b. 1834 who married Robert Bishopp in 1853, and Albert, b. 1838 who married Victoria Ann Worsfold, aged 20 and died 1880 aged 35. Albert Henry Sprinks died in 1887, aged 49. By 1874, according to the Sussex Directory, he was based at the Station Commercial Inn, licensed to let horses and a railway carrier. Mrs. Victoria Sprinks was still there in 1909. The Railway Hotel, as it was later named, sold beer brewed by Michell of Horsham. [Henry Michell (died 1874) was a wealthy local dignitary worth £40,000. He was a brewer, owner of pubs, brickmaker and investor in water and rail companies and friend of the Shelleys of Warnham. He left much of his wealth to his daughter Fanny who was married to Thomas Cowan who lived at Comptons Lea, Horsham for 20 years. Cowan became the most famous writer and 'Father of British Beekeeping'. Michell's son, also called Henry inherited the brewery business.] The present Railway Inn has a new facade.

1. The Old Railway Hotel

2. The present Railway Inn and former listed Signal Box

William Sprinks had two live-in servants, Edward Wells, 25, journeyman miller, and Charles Fuller, 19, manservant.

1848

In 1848 William Sprinks was named as a Constable, together with Joseph Dale of Five Oaks, Hez. Miles, farmer of Soil Farm, Adversane, John Nicholson, farmer, James Trower, draper of Billingshurst, James Towse, farmer of Kingshall, David Baker, Billingshurst a watchmaker and William Evershed, farmer at Tedfold.

Wm. Sprinks, miller, is on record as signing a Vestry minute. This set of local worthies, no doubt, were representative of the leading personalities of the Billingshurst community who conducted parish business through the Vestry Meeting.

1848 is remembered as the 'Year of Revolutions'. In England there was alarm among the ruling establishment when 150,000 Chartists assembled in London to present a petition for an extended franchise. As a result 100,000 special constables were recruited nationwide.

The Officials of the Parish Vestry

The position of Constable is the oldest parish official title. It was established by the 12th century as an appointment and executive authority of the Manor Court to enforce law and order. Thomas Grenfeld, Constable of West Easwrith in 1622, dealt with repairs to the Hundred Pound at Billingshurst where straying animals were constrained. Special Constables were instituted by Charles II to counter public disorder in 1673.

From 1842 the recommendation for appointments of constables was formally transferred to the parish Vestry, who also paid the wages, subject only to the approval of the Magistrate. The Constable had powers of arrest and the duty of constraining felons in stocks or cage prior to appearing before the Magistrate. They were expected to report crimes, deal with rogues and vagabonds, supervise alehouses, drunkards, lewd persons and other trouble-makers and conduct the whipping of stray dogs and vagrants as occasion demanded. One duty was to apprehend the putative fathers of bastard children! Their responsibilities were summed up as 'keeping watch and ward'. These duties were shared with the Churchwardens and Overseers and individuals often assumed two or more of the titles. They supervised the pillory and the ducking stool wherever that practice occurred. These were grave responsibilities and no doubt were often more honoured in the breach than the observance when entrusted to such as Shakespeare's character, Dogberry, who reckoned the best way to deal with a thief was to let him 'steal out of your company'.

The County Police Act of 1839 allowed Counties to establish a full-time professional Force which became mandatory from 1856. The Western Sussex Force dates from 1851. Billingshurst was fortunate enough to have its own Police Office and resident Sergeant and two Constables living in two houses in Coombe Hill throughout much of the 20th century but, of recent years, policing has been exercised by mobile units and Community Support Officers. The Station was sold off as residential property.

Churchwardens were officially established as officers of the church in 1127 as the proper 'Guardians of the Church'. They shared responsibility for vagrants and the poor with the other appointees, the Overseers, and for keeping the accounts of all parish business. The Billingshurst Overseers had numerous duties. They levied rates, registered and administered apprenticeships for poor young people in the parish, controlled censuses, alehouses and fire engines. Though unlikely in Billingshurst they dealt with brothels and pawnbrokers. They also registered electors until 1918. The office was not finally abolished until 1925. The parish officials often raised additional funds for the church by the equivalent of the church fete or jumble sale. This was a 'Church Ale' where home-brew was drunk at the 'Church House', a forerunner of the Village Hall. The Billingshurst Parish Room once stood beside the Ten Steps off the High Street. Overseers of the Poor administered the Poor Law from 1601 to 1834. After that they were just rate collectors and assessors.

1. Hairdressers and 10 steps today

2. Crisp's Barber shop built 1895, and the Parish Room

Waywardens were appointed to keep the highways in order. Up to 1835 roads were mended by 'statute labour' whereby certain wealthier parishioners had to supply the Surveyor with draught animals, carts and labour when he needed them. With the abolition of statute labour repair became a charge on the parish rates. Farmers did continue to help and regular 'roadmen' were appointed, familiar figures until after WWII when they were replaced by mobile gangs. From 1903 when the speed limit rose to 20 m.p.h. and cars became available the steady process of tarring of roads began. The Vestry records tell of how, in 1846, the making of a new road was let by contract and how the Workhouse Governor also supervised road workers. Haywards, guardians of fences and enclosures, saw to the upkeep of hedgerows.

One other official was the Parish Clerk. He was paid a salary and was often the Assistant Overseer. In 1833 there is a record of a vestry decision to discharge the Billingshurst parish clerk and appoint another.

1798 to 1854

There was, by 1835, a Union Workhouse at Petworth, originally built at Hampers Green in 1820 for 112 inmates. The 'Union' was of several parishes so that the refuge was provided centrally and more economically than separately at each village. The Vestry, advised by the Board of Guardians, decided to dispose of the Billingshurst Parish workhouse property. In 1850 the building and ¾ acre garden was put up for sale by auction at the King's Arms with a reserve of £225 together with cottages at Five Oaks, East Lane and a plot in Marringdean Road, together valued at £78.

Thirty-two burials are listed in the Burial Register from the poorhouse and later workhouse between 1798 and 1854 and two more from the Union, a large workhouse, which served five parishes. Billingshurst had three representatives on the Board of Guardians. From 1870 Billingshurst sent its indigent parishioners to Horsham Union rather than Petworth.

It is a matter of some regret that the earlier village records are scanty regarding the names and lives of the working classes except for those paupers at the bottom of the social pyramid. The honest toilers, who did the physical work of the village, lived in impermanent dwellings, owned no real estate, paid no rates and had no gravestones. The record that survives, like the timber-framed houses they lived in, is chiefly remembered in the lives and doings of the yeomanry, traders and tenant farmers.

1850

The Manor of Pinkhurst records in 1850 that John Streeter 'late of Lancing' has died and his lands at Hammonds or Cocks Brook were seized 'whereon a windmill is erected'. He and his wife Mary had lived as paupers in East Lane? But John's daughter, Mary Ann had married Thomas Trower of Rowfold so all was not lost.

1851 Census –
the year of the Great Exhibition in the Crystal Palace at Kensington

1851

William Sprinks was prospering as the miller and farmer of 52 acres at Shipley, employing 5 men. He had 4 servants – Wm Parker, a waggoner, aged 48, Thomas Voice, 16, general servant, Richard Tidy, 16, apprentice miller, and Charity Johnson, servant. She married Isaac Dean.

Foice Champion, a pauper shoemaker, and his son Edward, a ploughboy, lived at the Old Workhouse.

Edward Wells, journeyman miller and Jane his wife were now at Lockyers. They had five children. Henry Bridgewater, an unmarried farm labourer, lived there too with a housekeeper, Sarah Briggs.

The Vicarage

1852

Major alterations took place at Hammonds House. It became double roofed with a stone extension along the rear, provided with handsome tile hanging to the west elevation. The wattle and daub frontage had probably already been given a new brick facade. The date of the rear addition was established when an inner timber was stripped to reveal the workman's carved date. Regeneration work in

Billingshurst in mid-century coincides with a prosperous period for farming and the first influx of wealthy people from elsewhere.

1858

The present Vicarage in East St was built in 1858, designed by S.S. Teulon, a famous London architect of the Victorian Gothic revival, who supervised hundreds of church and vicarage restorations.

The Railway Age

1859

The opening of the railway station in 1859 altered the way of life of the people of Billingshurst for good. Hitherto the village economy was based, fundamentally, on locally produced food and shelter. People milked their own cows, butchered their own pigs, malted their own barley for their own ale, fashioned their own ropes and harness, quarried their own roof tiles, fired their own bricks, milled their own wheat, cut their own firewood, dug their own wells for water and made their own entertainment. The only imported items were sugar and spice and other ingredients that little girls are made of, and little luxuries they could afford to enjoy like tobacco, tea and coffee. Self-reliance and the necessity for neighbourly cooperation were essential. Tools to grow vegetables, wheels for the carts and horses to pull them, lime for the land and tithes and taxes to service the Vicar, the Workhouse School, the poor and the needy, all were locally forged, crafted or collected.

All movement was on foot or by horse. Certainly the old Roman Road had left Billingshurst the legacy of being a coach staging post. Carriers, using great wagons drawn by eight horses and guarded by a blunderbuss, operated regularly. The Comet coach, with twelve on top and four inside, left the Kings Head daily for London and the coast. But fares were so expensive that only people and light goods could be transported in or marketed at a distance. There were three turnpike gates between Billingshurst and Horsham alone. In 1820 a ride to London by coach cost £1-2s-0d, the equivalent of three week's wages for a farm worker! The Five Oaks Turnpike Trust netted £342 in the year 1845.

By the end of the 18th century those goods included tea, much of it smuggled, and sugar from the West Indies in sufficient quantities for them to become usual in the homes of cottagers. Formerly ale had been the main drink and honey the only sweetener.

Came the railway in 1858, came loads of coal and a gasworks and all the benefits of an industrialised society such as factory-made clothes and tools, imported bricks, groceries from all over the world, national newspapers and train tickets to London and the seaside. Local shopkeepers began to sell bread made from Canadian flour, Canterbury lamb and London beer and gin and cotton goods from home and abroad. Cotton often replaced the 'good old English' woollen cloth of earlier years, the stuff that in the late 18th century we were required by law to be buried in, on pain of a £5 fine for non-compliance. On the farms locally forged hand tools, sickles and scythes, flails and hoes, gave way to superior harrows and cultivators, and steam engines to power threshing machines and ploughs and stationary engines for workshops. Retail shops expanded and it became realisable to export local produce and indeed to multiply it by the founding of light industries like the making of flea powder and vacuum cleaners. For a time there was a cattle market just south of the station.

There was a downside of course. Although blacksmithing continued at Adversane and butchering and malting in the High Street, nevertheless a great many craftsmen on farms and in workshops were obliged to seek new work on building sites, in factories and in domestic service. A number emigrated to America, Canada and other Empire destinations. Workers in the coach and carrying trade at the Billingshurst Commercial Inns probably found employment from the railway and the Railway Inn was built. Harness and rope-makers, kiln workers, timber cutters, farm tool-makers, tailors, millers and ostlers gave place to the retail and motor trade, steam engineering, and the mending of bicycles.

Before bikes became popular in the 1890s ordinary Billingshurst folk had to walk everywhere. The bicycle transformed their lives in ways we scarcely appreciate. A horse would have cost a year's wages besides the provender and stabling costs. The commercial inns and transport businesses gained a temporary respite in the 20th century, with the advent of the internal combustion engine from cars and charabancs, only to lose trade again when the village was by-passed in 1994. Hill View garage, The Malaya, the Billingshurst Coach Station, Southern Counties and other outlets all flourished but finally disappeared to be replaced by dwelling houses and a Budgens supermarket. Many young people took off for work in London or the coastal towns.

1861

The 1861 census lists Hammonds, Mill House with William Sprinks still living as a widower with his son Albert and two different servants. These were Elizabeth Hutcheson, housekeeper, and Jane Aylward, dairymaid. Elizabeth Ewins, 13, was a visiting scholar. That same year William married Ruth at Brighton.

Moses and his wife Rhoda Wilson [nee Wadey], (a farm labourer) was in the Old Workhouse, with five children and a lodger, Edwin Puttock. Also listed are Mrs. Venn, whose husband had deserted, a seamstress aged 33 with four children, and Samuel and Barbara White, a brickmaker moulder with four children, one of whom, Ann, had a baby together with her brickmaker husband, William Richardson.

1862

By 1862 Mary Ann Trower, John Streeter's daughter, had died and her surviving husband, Thomas Trower, was reported by the Manor of Pinkhurst, to own the freehold, messuage and lands called Hammonds alias Cocksbrook.

Schools in Billingshurst

1. School timbers

2. Weald School

1865

In Shakespeare's time there was a keen regard for education. 'My brother Jacques he keeps at school and report speaks goldenly of his profit' [*As You Like It*]. In Billingshurst a religious Guild called The Brotherhood offered to pledge money to maintain a school. The road to Hell is paved with good intentions. Little tuition was available for poor scholars until the late 19th century.

The village school off School Lane in East St. was built in 1865, the gift of Henry Carnsew of Summers Place, and added to for infants in 1912. In 1972 it was used as a Church Centre and closed in 1973, though it was still utilised for some classes until 1991. It is now private residences.

Education that was available for a Billingshurst villager in the 18th century was in the type of child-minding institution known as a Dame School where a little reading and writing was taught by unqualified ladies. However lessons were provided even for pauper children in the Workhouse. The few moneyed local gentry would employ tutors and governesses and use the Grammar or Public Schools for their children. By reinvigorating Rugby School Dr Thomas Arnold had created an educational system for the landed gentry, the professional men and the new industrialists which served Britain and the Empire well. However it also served to weld together all the privileged classes into an exclusive old boy network which dominated the commanding heights in politics, the professions, the military and the judicature, to the detriment of the opportunities of a wider meritocracy. The legacy of that division of society remains with us.

During the 19th century elementary schooling for the less privileged slowly evolved, like most other social and welfare developments, under the leadership of the Vicar. There were a variety of private schoolrooms set up in the village for the lesser gentry such as The Crescent School in South Street. Wendy Lines tells of an Academy run by a Mr. Boorer, who may well have been aptly named, and of Miss Potter who ran a boarding school for girls. The Baptist Church had a school room and a library. More recently Mrs Murat ran St. Christopher's School on the corner of Daux Avenue and Audrey and Thomas Flynn had a boys' crammer prep school at Beke House in Marringdean Road. There was also the Convent School at Summers Place. Since 1961 at Ingfield Manor at Five Oaks, 'Scope', the charitable organisation which offers support for parents and conductive education for children with cerebral palsy, has enjoyed a national reputation for its service to disadvantaged youngsters.

The National Schools movement aimed to provide a school in every parish where orthodox Anglican doctrine could be assured and to establish Sunday Schools to reinforce the initiative. A Chartered School for Boys operated at the east end of the parish church. It was pulled down in 1866 when the church was 'restored'. Mr. Henry Wright was the Head. He and his son Ernest were Headmasters in the village for 68 years. 'Buzzy' Wright had a reputation for his enthusiastic use of the cane. He lived with his family at School House, and they helped run the classes. In those days all the teachers lived in the village. The village schoolmaster was modestly rewarded but, being literate, he could command esteem as Secretary of the Working Men's Club, counsellor and source of parental guidance.

'Lands he could measure, terms and tides presage,
And even, the story ran, that he could gauge.
While words of learned thought and thundering sound,
Amazed the gazing rustics ranged around.
And still they gazed and still the wonder grew,
That one small head could carry all he knew.
[Oliver Goldsmith 1770]

From 1833 government grants were available to charity schools subject to inspection by HMIs [Her Majesty's Inspectors]. The Revised Code of 1862 introduced the first 'National Curriculum', basically the three Rs for juniors and 'object lessons', an early version of 'show and tell', for Infants. Children were categorised into 'standards' or levels of achievement rather than by age, so that theoretically a slow learner, dismissed as a 'dunce', could stay in Standard I until he left school! Grants were only payable after the Inspector had certified acceptable results, punctuality and attendance. Thus the School Bell and the Attendance Register and keeping the Log Book were important tasks for the teachers who resented this system of 'Payment by results'. Billingshurst was at first a National

School under the aegis of the Diocese, but was taken over as a County School in 1910 when there were 240 children on roll.

In Victorian times demands for reform of the franchise and criticism of the poverty of ignorance by such as Charles Dickens and other evangelicals and philanthropists were prompting right-minded people everywhere to seek improvements to the literacy and numeracy of the work force. This was a special concern of Utilitarian thinkers who realised that expensive machinery and sophisticated engineering would be wasted without educated operatives. The culmination of this was the great Elementary Education Act of 1870 which set up School Boards to provide schooling everywhere, with qualified teachers, for children between 5 and 10. Attendance was not made compulsory though until 1880. The age of leaving was raised to 12 in 1880, to 14 in 1918, to 15 in 1944 and to 16 as recently as 1972.

Fees of a penny or two a week were still required from 1870 until 1891 when education became free. Payment by results was stopped in 1897. In 1902 School Boards were abolished and responsibility for education was vested in Local Education Authorities, which in West Sussex was the County Council. Characteristically the Parish Council took umbrage! A minute of 1905 reads: The Parish Council of Billingshurst view with great alarm and concern the enormous unnecessary and unreasonable increase in the cost of education since the local control has been vested in the County Council and ask the Council to give this matter their very serious consideration having due regard to the expenditure of the ratepayers' money.' Some of that expense will have been for the new mass-produced steel dip pens, with slit nibs required after 1870 to teach copperplate handwriting and for the cheaper powdered ink for the inkwells. Children at Adversane had the option of attending the school at North Heath.

At last there came some Secondary education when the school became 'all age'. Dr. Moreton was for many years the progressive and widely respected Headmaster (1937-51). Billingshurst School was the first in Sussex to provide hot dinners for the children in 1931 when Mr. Jeavons was the Headmaster. A dinner cost 3 old pence and 10% were free, served in a shed provided by the Beck sisters. A new Junior School and a separate Infants School were built at the entrance to Station Road in the early 1970s.

Cricket and football were played in the Bowling Alley and on the site of the present St. Gabriel's Catholic Church, with a Nissen hut as a changing room. Lent was the traditional marbles season for boys and skipping for girls. Good Friday was called 'Marble Day' or 'Long Rope Day'. Hoops made of iron, pop-guns made from elder wood, catapults and conker battles had their seasons.

A few clever children won 'scholarships', gaining places at Grammar Schools in

Horsham, Steyning or Midhurst. These 'all age' arrangements persisted until the Weald Secondary Modern School opened in 1957, taking in pupils at 11+ from many adjacent villages. Finally, in 1969 the Weald became Comprehensive and the Grammar Schools no longer recruited only selected pupils. Collyers School in Horsham became a Sixth Form College and the Girls' High School became a co-educational 11 to 16 comprehensive and was renamed Tanbridge House. The Weald School has been the subject of four major building extensions since its inception. It now constitutes an extensive campus with sophisticated modern facilities. It is the biggest employer in the district and is numbered among the best 10% of secondary schools in the country.

'Standards' persisted in primary schools until the 1940s. In 1879 a competent Standard VI pupil, ready to leave school, was expected to be able to: 'read with fluency and expression', write a short theme or letter with consideration for grammar, spelling and handwriting or write to dictation; to understand proportion, vulgar and decimal fractions; parse and analyse a short complex sentence; know the outlines of the geography of the world and of the history of England from Henry VIII to the death of George III.

A letter from Rev. Bull, the Vicar of 1870 states that the new school was built for 125 children but had an average attendance of 85. He also reveals that the old workhouse had been used as the parish school for several years past, when it was 'under government inspection'. In his letter he is proposing that the old workhouse dining room should become an extra classroom for 57 children, partitioned off to allow access to an upstairs room that 'used to be a girls school but is now a cottage'. He says that he, as Vicar, is the 'occupier' of the property given by the Patron of the Living and Lay Impropriator Sir Charles Goring, Bart. of Highden, Steyning, as long as Sir CG lives for the benefit of the schools. The income from cottage and garden rent are presently commuted to pay the school expenses. He seems reluctant to miss the opportunity of the extra school places, while recognising no immediate need, but fearful that if asked to build, presumably on the new school, he could not find the necessary £100, as indeed it was, in 1912.

The Victorian regeneration

1866

The Chancel at St. Mary's was rebuilt and a new font installed. The restoration work was paid for by Henry Carnsew of Summers together with two new stained glass windows. Luke Wadey and Owen Voice, local craftsmen, did the work.

1867

Two pieces of land were assigned involving Sarah Durham, widow, Peter Evershed, surgeon, and Henry Wells, Horsham, builder. In this year mantraps formerly used at Rowfold Orchard were abandoned.

United Reformed Church

1868

In 1868 Philip Puttock in his will bequeathed £343.16, invested in Consuls, the dividend to be paid to the Vicar and Churchwardens to distribute in bread to the poor of the parish. John Ireland left £91.14s, also in Consuls to relieve the Church Rate.

The Congregational Church was erected on the corner of West Street. A school was added in 1885. The site was formerly part of a four and a half acre market garden. In 1972 it became the United Reformed Church. Non-conformists had met under licence at Peter Draper's private house in Billingshurst after the Indulgence Act of 1672 but it was not until 1815 that a church with premises was founded by John Croucher of Hayes. He bought up the redundant octagonal officers' mess at Horsham used by the military gathered to resist a possible invasion by Napoleon. He had it rebuilt in Jengers Meadow, on a site now to the rear of the Jengers Mead shopping precinct as a meeting place for Presbyterians in Billingshurst. The Old Chapel and the cottage next door at Jengers were sold in 1889 and the adjoining Manse was then built on the new site. There is a memorial to the Rev. William Wilson M.A. who was ejected from the Parish Church at the Restoration under the 'oppressive Act of Uniformity'.

A 1680 sq yd plot in the south west corner of the Bowling Alley, then a five acre pasture field, was noted as ' in the possession of Henry Carnsew of Summers Farm and on it are erected a schoolroom, playground and master's garden'. On its south boundary is the Workhouse, owned by Sir Charles Goring and a piece owned by a Mr. Sadler of Chiddingfold and occupied by Sprinks, the miller. Sadler also has the land to the West of the plot. The remainder of the Bowling Alley is part of Duckmore farm, owned by Mr. Carnsew. The request was for a conveyance to the Vicar and Churchwardens for use as a Sunday School'

The Old School House today'

1871

The 1871 census reveals that William Sprinks was now aged 62 and married to Ruth, 52. He was now farming 140 acres and employing 5 labourers and a boy. He had three live-in servants, all about 18 years of age- John? Ervine, Henry Lellicot and Elizabeth Barnett.

Three families then lived at the Workhouse, four Lelliots and a lodger, two Reeds and a lodger, the Burchells with eight children and the Wilsons with two children and two lodgers. All were manual workers, woodcutters, farm labourers, gardeners, washerwomen, bricklayers' labourers.

At an auction at the Kings Arms James Wilson 'of Gratwick House', a civil engineer, bought Lockyers for £1090 from Trustees Farhall and Clear. A mortgage document (for £3500) suggests that 'a capital messuage' called Gratwick House with outbuildings a garden and orchard had formerly been occupied by Henry Carnsew, owner of Summers Place. It had been built on the site of a place named 'Hill House'. There was an adjoining messuage and stable.

In 1882 James Wilson bought Robin and Chime cottages.

Robin and Chine cottages

Hard times and good times

1874 +

This year marks the onset of the late Victorian agricultural depression. Cheap bread occasioned by imported wheat from Canada and America, and meat from the colonies and new world combined to undermine farming profits. Only dairy products, hay and horticultural fruit and vegetables could compete successfully with the overseas products of more favourable climates and soils. But in other respects the national economy was booming, with great fortunes falling to the well-to-do in banking, industry and trade with the Empire, while the yeoman farmers often faced bankruptcy. There were three such misfortunes in East Street alone. The numerous children of the poor often enough took off for the towns, the lads to find industrial and mechanical work and the girls a place in domestic service. Yet more bade farewell to their Billingshurst relatives and went off to Canada, Australia, Africa and New Zealand to seek a better fortune.

However rich town-dwellers, then as now, relished a 'place in the country' where they could relax or retire and enjoy the romance of the country-side and indulgence in rural sports, angling, hunting, the dog and the gun. Town money came to the rescue of the countryside. For example four substantial country mansions were established in Billingshurst bringing with them the wealth of their incoming owners and the opportunities for employment that their coming occasioned. There were hunting facilities for those with a taste for it and enough money and leisure to indulge it. There were Lord Leconfield's and Crawley and Horsham packs. The Warnham Staghounds worked Billingshurst and had point-to-points at Lordings Farm. Mr. Goff at Wooddales Farm had beagles. One of his followers was Dr. W.G.Grace, the famous cricketer.

Not the least of these benefits was the restoration work on St. Mary's Church and the building of the School in East Street. It is noticeable that though there is much sounder older building in the village and also much good Victorian property, nevertheless little remains to us from the Georgian period.

The coming of the railway had brought benefits for traders. Wooden hoops for barrels were exported by Henry Puttock from the Hoop Sheds by the station. Coppicing of hazel chestnut, ash and beech every seven years was a regular source of employment. The hoops were used for binding barrels, mainly for fishermen, but also for sugar, crockery barrels and tea chests. Carter Bros of Newpound built and sold their famous Unique straw elevator and industries such as the Gas

Works, Keating's Flea Powder manufactory and The Whirlwind Vacuum Cleaner factory, which made 400 machines a week, were able to flourish. The latter was built on the site of a malting in Station Road. It became Barralets Water Heaters in 1947 and is now Weald Court housing development. The American factory-owner, Mr. N.Ray Stiles, occupied Broomfield Lodge where Mr James King, the maltster once lived. He had the wall built that defines the former village cricket field in Station Road

These are emblematic changes. What had once been a farming village with a few shops for meat and groceries, bakers, shoes, clothes and basic everyday goods, with coaching inns and maltings, began to take on its present identity as a small marketing place and a dormitory, social and religious centre with light industry and service providers such as estate agencies, restaurants and secondary schooling for an extensive rural catchment. Mrs. Lines, local historian, has established that four shops paid rent to the church in the 15th century. The middle years of the 19th brought an explosion of shop-keeping enterprise and an expansion of retailing by independent traders once they had ready access to wholesale suppliers. This entrepreneurial spirit has continued. One chain store, International Stores, appeared between the wars, but it has been only recently that national supermarket chains such as Budgens (now Sainsbury's), Scats (now Mole) and Tesco have offered a challenge to independent businesses offering groceries, clothing, confectionary, ironmongery, computer services, and the like.

The Station Road Malting before conversion to a factory

1874

The Sussex Directory listed Wm. Sprinks as a farmer at Hoile Farm. He appears to no longer be the miller probably having retired. One H. Isted takes over, followed quite soon by W.F.Weller -1878.

1876

In this year the first great Ordnance Survey map was issued showing all the fields and woods. The accompanying book gave acreages and use as arable or pasture.

The signal box at Billingshurst Station was re-erected since it was built much earlier. It became a listed building as it was the only remaining example of the first standard box design. In 2014 it was dismantled and transported to the Chalk Pits Museum at Amberley.

1881

The census of 1881 shows that William Sprinks then farmed only 26 acres. He had two 17 year old servants, Mary Lindfield and Thomas Redman.

1884

The clock at St.Mary's, a half size replica of the clock at Westminster, was installed. A year before an organ had replaced a harmonium. Earlier there had been a musician's gallery prior to the 1866 renovations.

1885

The Manor of Pinkhurst reported in 1881 that Thomas Trower had died, who 'held freely the messuage and land upon which the Mill is erected'. 'He had no animal'. Edward Underwood of Billingshurst, miller, now held the premises. 'Fealty respited'.

William Sprinks, the old miller, of East Street died. He was buried at the Baptist Chapel

1890

Pinkhurst Manor reported: Edward Underwood, freehold, Hammonds or Cocks Brook.

1891

The following year Ruth Sprinks, nee Older died aged 73.

The next census in 1891 listed Edward 48 and wife Mary Underwood 42, farmer with servant Annie Blate 19 as in occupation of Hammonds. Edward died in 1923 aged 80.

Four Wilsons were still at the Workhouse cottages, but William and Ellen Lintott, (pale cleaver) with 3 sons and a stepson, Hale and Lucy Goodyer (carpenter) with 5 children and John Ewins (scripture reader) and Emma his seamstress daughter had replaced the previous tenants.

James Wilson, his wife Cecelia, Margery his stepdaughter and three servants were at Gratwick House but not for much longer.

In 1895 the sweeps of the mill were badly damaged when in charge of an apprentice.

1901

By the time of the 1901 census Emma Ewins, spinster, was in three rooms at the Old Workhouse as caretaker of the Working Men's Club. The club was founded about 1880. It had 150 members with Honary Secretaries, named Wright, Headmaster at the School, and Peacock in 1885, succeeded by Joseph Luxford, shopkeeper, until 1915. It was housed for two years at the old Village Hall in 1911. The members of the club no doubt had a hand in the 'firing of the anvil' ceremonial explosion in 1900 to celebrate the relief of Ladysmith during the Boer War. A long fuse of gunpowder led to a heavy charge packed under the smith's anvil where it was fixed to the block. When ignited it produced a satisfactory roar! It was traditional to celebrate 'Old Clem Night' in this way on 23rd November. St. Clement was the patron saint of blacksmiths.

Working Men's club building, Library Car Park, now a coffee shop

A purpose-built Working Men's Club was later erected in 1913 behind the Post Office off the High Street, the land being the gift to the village of Major General Renton J.P, DSO, OBE, DL, fruit farmer and horticulturist, of Rowfold Grange. In 1949 it had 200 members and plans for expansion. It later became a Social Club but afterwards declined and finally petered out at the Millennium. It is now a gift shop and tea room.

Death of Queen Victoria – the 20th Century

1901

Edward T Norris, 45, a rich brewer from Hertfordshire, bought Gratwick House in 1898. His wife was Jessie. They kept a butler and four servants in house with a stableman and gardener living in the stables. Sir Edward Lutyens designed a billiard room added on to the ostentatious building.

The body of Queen Victoria passed through Billingshurst Station on its way from the Isle of Wight to London in 1901

The village population was 1591 only 50 more than in 1840. Farming had been in depression since 1874 and few new employment opportunities were yet available.

Post Office

1902

The village Post Office was built with a plaque with an E for Edward VII. Now it is just a delivery office.

Looking East, with Hammonds Mill and St. Mary's on the skyline

Mr Malcolm Laker recorded notes of a conversation with Herbert Laker about the picture of Billingshurst taken from what is now Mill Lane. This abridged version adds colour to the Billingshurst scene in Edwardian days.

"Uncle Tom Laker bought the orchard from Mr. Ireland and this became the car park and library after it was sold to the Council. There was a barn at the corner of the lane now beside the Post Office. Uncle Tom bought the barn and first built his house on the site and then he built the shops and the bank, now a solicitor's office. The horse in the picture would have belonged to Willy Puttock who moved to Stonepits in Marringdean Road.

The barn in the picture is probably behind the Puttock's house in the High Street [Carlton House soon to become three shops]. The house on the left of the Church belonged first to Arnolds – the grocer, then to Billy Shepherd who took one of the shops that Uncle Tom built and then Billy sold to Walker's Stores. [Now an estate agents].

The Six Bells is on the right and the white house on the extreme right was at the top of the ten steps, a coal merchant lived there. Just left of the white chimneys is the dark side of the old barn which Tom bought. Where Rice Bros garage was (Budgens now) there was a red building which had been a grain store. Sid Streeter bought it and started a garage which Rice Bros took over. Sid did 18 months for fraud (some of this is libellous!). His mother lived in Bowling Alley Lane [Little East Street]. The poplar trees on the right are where the toilets are now.

The grocer's shop [on the corner of East Street, now a Chinese restaurant] was a blacksmith's shoeing shop belonging to Mr. Cook who emigrated to Australia. There was another baker's at the corner of Bowling Alley Lane, next door was a chemist's, then George Ware the draper, next 'Twinkle' Quick's the bicycle shop and then Henry Foice the butcher.

Other places in the village were Nellie Puttock's house who lived at Clevelands with her sister and Wildens bought by Teddy Norris, the brewer. Willy Puttock sold the big house that is Knights to an American [Ray Stiles] who bought the old malt house and built the factory for vacuum cleaners on the site.

There was a footpath from half way along the church walk [now under Carpenters] that came out on the main road by a saw pit used by Mr. Wadey who was the wheelwright on the corner of Newbridge Road [West Street] Opposite the Croft, another Laker's house, there was a private school where 'Grampy Laker' went to school, now a restaurant.

Rev. Stanley built a hut for the boy scouts in the grounds of the Vicarage before the First World War. Billy Renton of Rowfold made a donation for the Working Men's Club and Joe Luxford who had the sweet shop [on the East Street corner] went round collecting for the rest of the money. Joe had tennis courts in the allotments."

The village allotments, nearly five acres, began after the Great War. Another interesting business was basket-making from osiers grown at what is now Dell Lane. There stood three ponds and a dammed stream to nourish the willows.

Younger readers will not remember the retailing culture that still prevailed in Billingshurst up to the 1960s. Shopkeepers, often eminently recognisable personalities, displayed their goods safely on shelves behind stout counters where the scales and cutting and wrapping equipment stood. The shop assistants proffered sample goods on request, the customer made a decision, cash or a cheque changed hands, the deal was registered in a mechanical till and the goods were handed over, having been packaged from bulk on the spot by the seller. The system was economical of packaging and risk. It demanded a respectful personal relationship between vendor and customer, but was labour intensive and time consuming for both the management and customer. Goods had to be measured or weighed and priced, then wrapped. Customers had to wait patiently while others were served. The absence of refrigeration too made frequent shopping obligatory, since even outdoor meat safes and cool larders were unreliable safeguards against decay. Limited independent car ownership also favoured local village shopping. Groceries were often ordered in advance and delivered by rounds men on trade bikes or in a horse-drawn or motorised van. Bread vans, milk floats and door-to-door salesmen visited local streets and remote farms alike. The old system still continues in independent butchers, greengrocers, shoe shops, jewellers and other specialised outlets, but elsewhere, even for bulky and expensive items like boxed TV sets or containerised Christmas trees the 'supermarket principle' prevails.

Profits soared and the traditional shopkeepers could not match the supermarket prices. The system is fast, efficient, gives generous choice and must make economic sense, but it lacks the warmth and human interaction of the old way which afforded employment for many more people than today's less personal experience, where a trolley load of goods may be purchased without the exchange of a single word.

The first English supermarket was in 1948, but the new retail culture in Billingshurst came in the 1970s.

1906

Rev Stanley gave the Old Village Hall to the parish. The derelict East Windmill was badly damaged beyond repair by a gale. The hand-winded wooded cap was blown off. The following year the Gas Works was built.

1. Frank Patterson

2. Drawing by Frank

1909

Kelly's Directory of 1909 gives more interesting details of the village shortly before the Great War. The chief landowners were said to be the trustees of the late Henry Puttock of Carlton House, Mr. Goff of Wooddale who had Summers Place built, Mr. Shepley-Shepley, Mr. Schroeter and two Irelands of Manor House and Broomfield. Edward Ireland was Lord of the Manor of Bassetts Fee. The Duke of Norfolk held the Manors of Pinkhurst and Storrington. The Misses Beck are at Duncan's Farm, Norris at Gratwick, Maj. General Renton, subsequently Chairman of Governors at the Weald School, at Rowfold Grange, Ephraim Wadey, undertaker and brickmaker at Parbrook, James Wadey, builder was at Five Oaks, Frank Arnold the Grocer at Churchgate, Ellen Chart ran a girls' day school,

George Coombes farmed at Frenches, Mr. Crisp was the hairdresser, Mr. Foice was the butcher, the Huberts were at Rose Hill, one a physician and surgeon, the other the public vaccinator, and Frank Patterson (b 1871), the celebrated 'cycling artist', lived at Pear Tree Farmhouse, a 16th century building, on the road to Barns Green. William Carter was collector of rates and Alfred Head collector of the King's taxes.

1911 to 1960s

Rev Stanley started the local Boys Scouts in a room over Rice's Garage then at the Vicarage. After the Great War the troop ceased for a decade but was revived in 1928. It prospered at Clevelands stables and flourished thereafter. 'Salvage' – mainly waste paper- was collected during WWII and messages run for the Home Guard and Civil Defence. Scouts and Guides still prosper at the Scout Hut on the Recreation Ground.

The Billingshurst Band began in 1919, promoted by Mr. Luxford. The Miss Becks paid for the instruments and the uniforms. Sadly the band went into decline in the 1950s and the instruments were generously gifted to the Weald School, which had its own Wind Band.

Village events, such as the 1911 coronation party for George V following a floral parade, were held at Gratwick, the year Norris died. The family sold the estate in 1923. It was requisitioned during WW II. It then became a guest house. It fell into disrepair and was demolished in the early 60s to make way for Gratwicke Close, a row of well-designed terrace houses with garages, characteristic of the period. Specimen trees were planted on the green fronting East St.

Also in 1911 Dr. Hubert gave up his practice of over forty years at Brick House which stood on the corner of East Street. Dr. Hubert's son took over at Rosehill. The Vet, Mr. J Craft moved into Brick House.

Brick House on the left of East Street

    In the 15th century the Brick House site had been part of the Vicar's glebe. That oak framed house was built some time before 1635 when Henry Cooper, a maltster and inn owner used it and the adjacent croft as a maltings and brewery. One of his inns was The King's Arms on the site of Lloyds Bank and he had mortgages on The Star and The White Horse Inn, all three now long lost. His son Walter died about 1696 and was succeeded as maltster by Edward Laker who had married the Vicar Oram's daughter Ann. Edward and his widow were dead by 1719. The next maltster was Walter Longhurst, a Churchwarden. He was buried in 1768 by which time Richard Browne had taken over. He paid Land Tax for the Adversane malthouse too where first William Elmes then Charles Duke was in occupation. Maurice Ireland lived at Brick House from 1783. When Richard Browne died in 1787 his nephew, John Jefferies, had ownership.

    By 1820 a relative, Jacob Caffin was paying the Land Tax and Peter Evershed, surgeon, apothecary and General Practitioner, was the occupant of the house and Henry Mitchell had the malthouse. Peter was a healthy doctor, dying in 1884 aged 91. Jacob Caffyn, a very wealthy gentleman of Cuckfield, died in 1850. He had extensive property in Cuckfield, Charlwood and Ditchling. His buildings and nursery in Billingshurst which was occupied by John Allman went to his son Thomas. The 'field and close of meadow' and the houses and malthouse occupied by Peter Evershed, Henry Mitchell, Matthew Caffin, Joseph Kensett, Powell, Chantler, Coleman and Lander he willed to his son James Caffin. However by 1859 Henry Mitchell had written in his diary 'I had to give up three public houses...Kings Head at Billingshurst...gave up the old wretched Malthouse I had used for many years in the High Street'.

Peter Evershed had retired by 1870 when William H Hubert took over the practice in partnership with George Laurance, an Irishman. Ann Gravatt was his servant and William Vinall, his groom. Later servants were called Gosden, Taylor, Balchin and Ayling, names still current in the village. By 1907 his son, William A. Hubert, was also practising from Rosehill which became the surgery. In 1929 Brick House was demolished and the Westminster Bank moved in 'although not quite out of the builder's hands' just in time for the Wall Street Crash!

In 1920 the Parish Council applied, unsuccessfully, for a speed limit of 10 m.p.h. for the High Street and 100 yards up East and West Streets.

By this time the derelict East Mill had lost the remains of the smock tower, burnt as it was unsafe, and the stone base was in use as a store.

The Hubert family at Rosehill

1933

In 1933 significant boundary changes added a large area north of Brinsbury College and west to the Arun to the parish of Billingshurst. Previously this land had been part of Pulborough.

1934

Electric street lighting, the first in England, came to Godalming in 1881, but it was not until the National Grid was in place that a new light dawned. From 1934 mains electricity had arrived in Billingshurst and people could light their homes with the turn of a switch rather than a paraffin or gas lamp and, in due course, power their new radios from the mains, rather than with 'accumulators' and dry batteries. In 1895 the Parish Council bought fourteen 50 candle powered paraffin lamps and paid Mr. Bristow, the lamplighter, 10 shillings a week 'moonlight nights excepted'. Gas was substituted in 1911. It has been argued that electricity was more significant for the villagers than the coming of the railway. Steam engines pulled the trains until 1938 when electrification was completed along the line. Early telephones also improved the lives of traders and better-off people. The telephone poles and multiple wires that lined almost all the roads are now scarcely remembered.

The advent of the automobile in growing numbers from the 1920s gave welcome scope for enterprising businesses in the trade, and a steady decline in the use of broughams, landaus, Victorias and horse-drawn hearses. When Mr. W.T.Voice, grocer and proprietor of a cab and horse service since 1822, died after WWII all his expensive old carriages were sold to dealers from Edenbridge for £21 the lot, loaded onto a train and hauled away. Some are said to have ended up as props at Elstree film studios.

The coming of public utilities is often overlooked though they transformed the working and social lives of the people and are today taken for granted until things go wrong. Piped water had arrived by 1911. The North Sussex Gas and Water Company set up a reservoir at what is now Old Reservoir Farm, and a waterworks between Groomsland and Gilmans Industrial Estate. Also, by 1911, a sewage works serving much of the village had been established at Parbrook by Horsham Rural District Council. People no longer had to dig a deep cess pit in the back garden to empty the bucket in their outdoor privy. The original sewage tank was de-commissioned when the new works, created in the late 60s, was given a major re-development in the 1980s.

1914-18 and '39-45

During 1918-19 The Old Workhouse was used to house German prisoners of war. In June 1918 a single church bell was tolled 50 times to commemorate the 50th Billingshurst man to be killed in the Great War.

On Saturday, 4th Dec 1915, amid Rolls of Honour for fallen local soldiers, the

West Sussex County Times & Standard printed a report on a topic in marked conflict with many traditional favourite preoccupations of Billingshurst people; malting, brewing and enjoying hospitality in inns and beer houses.

"The first Temperance Meeting of a [monthly] series, arranged by M. F. Whitbourne, Pastor of the Congregational Church, took place in the schoolroom. An attractive programme drew a crowd of adults and young people of the village... He dwelt on the great need for this work...and urged that every young person should become an abstainer... Mr. J. Cramp showed by diagrams and pictorial posters the waste, folly and consequent loss accruing to the nation in spending the huge sum of £165,000,000 on alcohol, against the advice of the King and our greatest Generals and rulers when so much is deeded to prosecute the war to a speedy and successful issue....Alcohol, contained in all malt liquor, wines and spirits, he said, was a poison we had to avoid. At the end thirteen young people signed the pledge. The meeting concluded with prayers and recitations. ['Why doesn't father come home' by Mr.Gattings, 'The Temperance Story' by Mr. Nicholson, 'The Last Glass' Herman Bennet].

Strict 'Opening Hours' for the numerous village pubs were introduced by Act of Parliament in 1914 to help keep people sober for the war effort. They were not totally relaxed until 2005.

Italian and German prisoners were encamped in Marringdean Road during WWII, now the site of a small housing estate called Kingsfold Close. An air-raid shelter for the schoolchildren was built in the corner of the field behind the Mill bordering the Bowling Alley. Three bombs fell, one off the High Street and two in fields east of the Mill. Evacuees came to the village from London and were lodged in family homes. Forty men volunteered for the Local Defence Volunteers in 1940. The Battalion of the Home Guard, as it became, numbered 500 by 1944. They paraded at the old Village Hall with Battalion Headquarters at Gratwicke. The Royal Observer Corps kept watch for hostile aircraft at a post just beyond East Street. A painted board was in place there, said to have been a device which would change colour if there were a gas attack. Boys learned aircraft recognition and made model aeroplanes and older ones joined the village Air Cadets, many of whom later became RAF aircrew. They collected acorns for pig food and conkers used for making acetone for which they were paid 7s-6d a cwt. Admiral Holmes and Mr. Maille led a team of Air Raid Wardens. They distributed and fitted 3000 gas masks, billeted the evacuees, organised emergency feeding arrangements, and trained 500 people in fire guard duty. Land girls worked on the farms and were trained at Brinsbury. The Whirlwind Factory in Station Road was given over to making ammunition boxes.

The Home Guard March Past in the High Street

At Coolham an airstrip opened up to support the D-day landings of 1944. Large numbers of troops were assembled in Sussex ready for the assault on Normandy. In Billingshurst, Ingfield Manor was the Headquarters of the 1st Corps with a Royal Artillery Regiment, Infantry Workshops, a RAMC Casualty Clearing Station and two RASC Ordnance Ammunition Companies. At Wooddale was gathered another RA Regiment and a Royal Engineers Port Operating Company. Similar RE Companies were at Tedfold and Rosier Farm in a tented camp.

The Billingshurst Fire Brigade dates from 1938 and an Auxiliary Fire Service was formed. During WWII twelve firewomen were recruited and 50 fires due to enemy action were attended. In 1948 the Brigade was taken over from the Rural District Council by The County Council and re-equipped. In 1953 the present Fire Station, unlucky number 13, was built with Cecil Rhodes as the Station Commander and a total staff of 23.

Raymond Cecil Rhodes, centre, with the Fire Brigade staff

Evacuees arriving at the Station from Oliver Goldsmith School, Camberwell

Hammonds House and Hammonds and Little Daux dairy farm.

Hammonds is one of the old timber framed-houses in Billingshurst. The frontage to the A272 has a classic Horsham stone roof and a brick facade painted to keep the interior warm and dry. At the rear is an outdoor privy, still working, and a landscaped lawn and garden with a pond and two wells. The adjacent barn was partly demolished in the late 20th century but has been handsomely restored for ancillary use for the house. To the East are the restored remains of the old dairy farm buildings, converted in 1997 into a private house and renamed Mill Barn. The former milking parlour has been extended as a double garage and the calf sheds have become a secluded patio. The thick Horsham stone flooring of the derelict calf shed has been recycled as coping stones for a fish pond. The stackyard and farmyard is now an orchard and garden. In the years when it was a dairy farm a shed, still standing, fronted the road and was used to dispense milk to villagers either in cans or bottles printed with the Barnes Brothers trade mark. The dairy had its own well which still siphons water into a capacious Victorian brick-built L-shaped underground tank.

In 1931 Walter J Barnes and Sophie, his wife rented Hammonds Farm from the Trowers and Little Daux, from the Norris family of Gratwicke. The Barnes' had three sons, Jack, Leslie and Bob. Walter had kept a grocery shop at what became a restaurant at the corner of East Street. They lived there for five years before moving into Little Daux. Leslie worked for a time on the farm, then became landlord at the Limeburners' Inn and then worked for King & Barnes, the Horsham brewers. Jack and Bob had a milk round, and their own eggs. They kept rabbits, pigs and horses and 15 milking cows at Hammonds, cows and calves at Little Daux and bullocks on land at Duckmore. They worked hard for a modest living, making hay and struggling with the clay, typifying a small mixed farm in Billingshurst. Bob died in 1988 by which time they had retired. Mrs. Barnes, Bob's wife, wrote a memoire of her life at Little Daux which illustrates what life was like on a Billingshurst dairy farm in the mid-20th century. Here is an abridged version of her account;

"I was courted by Bob when I worked at the Toat cafe on the way to Pulborough in 1952. He took me to the pictures at Horsham the day George VI died to see 'Lady Godiva'. We married the next year, a simple wedding with a three-tier wedding cake that they photographed. We spent the evening watching 'Jane Eyre' at the Royal Court theatre in Horsham. At Little Daux there was a long kitchen with a stone floor and a big wire-meshed safe for perishable food – no refrigeration then and a cellar which often flooded. The kitchen had a 4-burner oil stove and a copper over a fireplace to boil the laundry. The family's favourite food was mince and dumplings. No one ever opened the big front door and the 'big room' was reserved for visitors. Granddad would watch the weather over the station. 'It looked bad over Will's mothers'; he would say when rain threatened. One end of our house went back to the 15th century. You could see the Downs from the attic on a clear day.

We kept three dogs and 15 cats. Henry, my favourite kitten got run over by the oil lorry. Water was pumped across the football field, really Jubilee Field. When it froze up it came by churn from Hammonds. We had to boil up water on the stove to have a bath. The toilet was an Elsan in the garden – often full when visitors were coming, so we had to dig a hole quickly. 'Burying the dead' I called it. I was content with the lack of amenities. I never knew anything else.

We had daisies, irises, honeysuckle, climbing roses and Virginia creeper, Victoria plums, two greengages and a good vegetable garden. We had a milking machine in the garden driven by an engine. Muddles of Ashington brought the animal feed. Butcher, baker and grocers all delivered to the door. Jack got his day-old chicks from the station and reared them in brooders warmed by oil heaters. About three fields of the 40 acres of Little Daux would be shut up for making hay, usually the old-fashioned way by cart to ricks. Later we had a baler. We did not grow wheat or barley.

When baby Nick came I had no washing machine – just the Raeburn and a black pot. Ironing was done with small flatirons heated up on the stove, or even on the fire with a poker. Then I had a paraffin iron with meths in the front and a pump to get it going. Then we got electricity! Just enough from our generator for lights at first. When it broke down we were back to Tilly Lamps outdoors and Aladdins inside. When we got 'mains' we could have a cooker, an iron and a fridge. All the hedging was done with a chopper and swap hooks with bonfires along the hedgerows. At first Nan did the milk bottling and when Bob went to school his Dad would pass him in the van with the parrot in a cage at the back. They retired to School Lane in 1963 and Jack and Bob took over, Bob replaced the copper with the Raeburn which proved hard to master – many burnt offerings!

Bob loved hunting and following the hounds. One day Nick was lucky to survive when Bob backed the tractor out of the shed at Hammonds, knocking him over, luckily into a pile of manure! It saved his life. Dr. Hope-Gill fixed his broken collar-bone. The cows were a mixed herd – Friesians, Red Polls, Guernsey, Shorthorns and Sooty, the Jersey. Heifers were reared on to join the milking herd. The bullocks were kept for 18 months then went to market. Roger Green took them in his lorry. They were hard to load up. The air was blue sometimes.

Frank Kitchener worked as cowman. The women, Nan, Joyce, (Leslie's wife) and I washed the eggs that Jack's hens laid ready for the packing station; Leslie made cream for the milk round".

At the time of this writing a small estate is now occupied on the former orchard at Trees, fourteen houses have been constructed on Hammonds Garden Field to the rear of Hammonds House and to the south of the Bowling Alley. This steep area of woods and scrub is proposed to be refurbished as a public amenity and wildlife sanctuary.

Kingsfold and Marringdean Road

It is tempting to suppose that the factor that determined the settlement of Billingshurst was the junction of Stane Street and the East – West route we now label the A272. However since the eastern arm, East Street, did not extend beyond Coolham for many centuries the High Street was really built west of a T-junction where the road to Petworth joined Stane Street, now called West Street. Much more important than the road east was the second road south, presently the fifth feeder route into Parbrook and Billingshurst. At Parbrook was a crossroads at the end of Natts Lane with a substantial farm track leading westwards on to Newbridge. The ancient road had not yet been named as Marringdean Road. It is said to have been called Billingshurst High Road. By tracing the outline of the history of its farms and people one can capture some sense of the characteristics and doings of the people of Billingshurst. One important estate on that road is Kingsfold.

Early records of Kingsfold

Twice in 1457 the Manor of Pinkhurst proclaimed that a tenement and land called Carpenters, late of William Kyngesfold was open to any heir with a rightful claim. "On the third proclamation came Benedict Browne who received the land –fine 20s." This was confirmed in 1460 in the Pinkhurst Manor Roll. However Carpenters is almost certainly not the land now called Kingsfold.

Which came first? Kingsfold, the place name or Kingsfold, William's surname? Posterity cannot readily resolve the 'chicken and egg' dilemma. Certainly there was a new bridge over the Arun, for example, so William Newbrygge probably earned his name from it. On the contrary Jengers or Gingers probably derives from one Oliver Gynguire who built it in 1370. But we can be less sure that a family called Kingsfold took their names from an estate in Marringdean Road. More likely that place was named after the men, and the original Kingsfold was elsewhere, perhaps at Warnham.

Certainly we know that about 1290 a Simon de Kingesfelde was witnessing title deeds to property in Shipley and in 1305 Matilde, widow of Robert de Kyngesfold, was conveying a virgate of land in West Grenestede and other land in Thakeham and Sepele (Shipley) to Simon de Kyngesfold and his wife Lucie. A John de Kyngesfold in the same year sold land in Rusper to another John, son of Symon de Kyngesfold. Symon's son, Rico de Kynggesfold granted land in 1316 to Mattheo de Apslye and Ffelice his wife to pay 2 shillings at two feasts in the year. The Kingsfolds were clearly people of means with ancient title to estates and their surname arose from the place where they first lived.

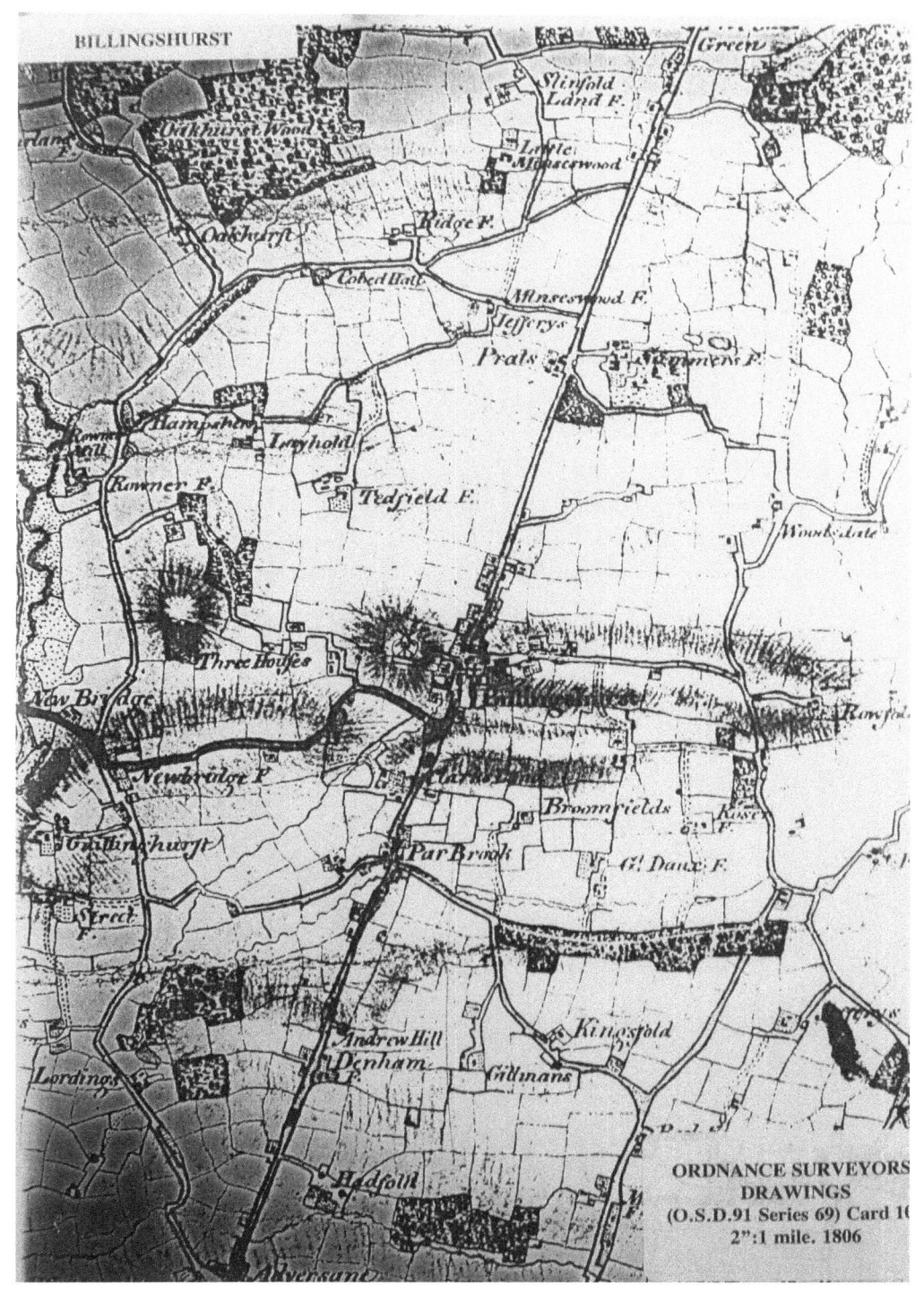

1806 OS map before the Station and its roads were built

In Tudor times in 1527 Richard Bakkes was licensed to let his tenement and land called Kingsfold for 3 years. Fine 4s. Redhoyse Land and Carpenters Land are held by baxe and cowp.(Cooper).

In 1530 Penfold 'The butcher in the dyke' has ownership of Kingsfold land.

John Cop or Cooper is in church records as Churchwarden that same year. There were many Sussex Coopers. The name derives from the trade of barrel and pail-making, a prosperous occupation when water was drawn from wells in wooden buckets and beer and wine stored in vats. There was one Cooper family of Strood, gentry at Slinfold, extant until 1715, which was influential locally and might well have had property in Billingshurst. The poet Cowper belonged to it.

In 1548 John Cooper had Kingsfold. He died in 1558.

By 1577 Master Stydolf held one tenement and half a virgate 4s8d p.a. He held land at Rowner.

In 1592 William Penfold paid church tax on Kingsfold.

With the accession of James I and the Stuarts in an Indenture of lease between Sir Thomas Palmer & Wm Penfold was granted in 1605 to Wm Penfold for 10,000 years 'for all that mesne farm in Billingshurst called Kyngesfold' – 110 acres. This was the year of the Gunpowder Plot.

1630 Cop paid Church Tax for Kingsfold.

1639 John Penfould of Kingsfold was a sidesman.

On 11th March, 1644 John Penfold was deceased.

The Commonwealth and Restoration Period

In 1648 the farmhouse was rebuilt by John Greenfield. We may speculate that the Greenfields were supporters of Oliver Cromwell and gained the land confiscated from the Penfolds, of a Royalist persuasion. Over the door are inscribed the letters IGM and the date, said to indicate John Greenfield and Mary his wife. Locally dug Horsham stone and winklestone was used in its construction. There is a chimney at each end of the structure. The narrow entrance bay with stairs was specifically designed as an entrance vestibule. English Heritage's description reads as follows: 'The Victorian frontage of the house conceals a single pile, two and a half storey, central entrance hallway house, dated 1648. Outshots had been added to the rear of the house by 1725. These were later converted to the second pile as part of the late Victorian alterations. The walls are of unequally coursed sandstone blocks with brick dressings to the windows. These were probably originally plastered to look like stone.'

1652 John Greenfeild of Kingsfold was a churchwarden, and in 1666 also a waywarden, and 1670 an overseer, all offices of the parish vestry. [1666 was the year of the Great Fire of London]. The Greenfield family had emerged as the most notable and wealthiest clan in the locality with extensive property in all parts of the parish for the best part of three centuries.

Aerial view of Kingsfold House

We first hear of them in 1504 when Edward Greenfield and his son Walter held "tenement and yardland called Le High Fure" by copyhold. The family were in possession of High Fure and South House for over 300 years until 1811. There is a record of a John Gryndfyld of Daks [Daux] in the early Tudor period and a Thomas Greenfield died there in 1578. In that same year William Greenfield of Daux married Mary Greenfield of South House. In 1610 Edward Grinfeild bought 20 acres of land at Coxbrook from William Lee. Researchers for Sotheby's believed that the land known as Summers was rented by the Greenfields from at least 1530 to 1690. A Richard Greenfield, carpenter, was buying properties in 1593 and one of that name bought Clarksland in 1645. In 1649 master butcher William Greenfield willed Duckmore, Lockyers off East Street and other extensive properties to relatives. He was known to have been at Palmers in 1645. Maurice Greenfield was at Southhouse in 1667 and acting as Churchwarden. A Phillip Greenfield was Churchwarden in 1688 and Overseer of the Poor in 1698. Samuel Greenfield of Greenwich, a waterman, bought premises in Billingshurst in 1702 and was buried at St. Mary's in 1720 aged 48; Maurice Greenfield, late of South House, died in 1752 aged 66.

"While in this life I did remain.
My latter days were grief and pain
Till God was pleased to give relief
None else could ease me in my grief"

There are continuous burials of Greenfields recorded from 1560 to 1675, and yet more later.

Arthur Greenfield lived at Gratwick in Dickens' time in the early 19th century. From about that time their fortunes seem to have faded and they do not feature in the Directories of the period as persons of note. A James Greenfield was a farmer and mealman at Adversane in 1858 and the surname has remained well represented in the district throughout the years. It is now more often found further south around Storrington.

In 1671 Goodman Greenfield was in occupation at Kingsfold.

The following year a new regal coinage was issued. This had farthing and halfpenny coins. Previously those denominations were made by actually halving and quartering small silver coins which were scarce, inconvenient and easily lost. Such was the shortage of small change between 1652 and 1672 that traders took to issuing their own tokens which were offered as change at shops to be afterwards exchanged for goods, serving as an advertisement and giving them credit for those outstanding and any that were lost. Nearly 200 different tokens were issued in Sussex, including a halfpenny one by Mathew Weston of Billingshurst in 1666 and nine in Horsham.

1685 Thomas Greenfield leased land from Katherine Garton (widow of John Garton of Pulborough) – Rowner Farm House and 120 acres.

In 1688 Philip Greenfield was in occupation.

1689 The Pannell Roll shows 'Phil Greenfeild of Kensfold' used the lands.

1712 Philip Greenfield died. Another Phillip succeeded, probably the one paid to repair the workhouse in East St in 1731.

The Penfolds and Coopers were still active in the village, conscientiously hounding the dissenting Quakers, though probably no longer from Kingsfold. We learn from William Albury, a Horsham historian, that at the Petworth Sessions in 1676 information was given by Richard Penfold and Thomas Cooper that: "John Pryor and his wife of Billingshurst and above five persons of sixteen years of age and upwards on Thursday 1st June last were present at an assemblye conventicule or meeting house under cover or pretense of the use of religion in other manner than according to the liturgy and practice of the Church of England Holden and kept in the Barne of the said John Pryor of Billingshurst by a certain person unknown to the said informers who did take upon himself to preach or teach and that the said John Pryor did wittingly and willingly permit and suffer the said building or conventicule in the said Barne contrary to the Act of 22 Charles II to prevent and suppress seditious conventicules.

We doe adjudge the said John Pryor and his wife guilty. In witness thereof: Thomas Henshawe, O. Weekes, William Westbrook."

Pryor was fined £20 and his wife 5 shillings. [Such constraints on freedom of worship were ended by the Toleration Act of 1689, apart from Catholics.]

Kingsfold passed in 1782 to Mr. Jno. Geering as the owner with Wm Towse as the occupier.

Victorian Times

Marringdean Road was not directly linked into Billingshurst as it is now by Upper and Lower Station Roads. These were built to service the Station which did not function until 1859. Originally Natts Lane from Parbrook was the junction to Stane Street, and, of course, there was no railway bridge to limit the access.

In 1858 Mr. J.Meetens is recorded as farming at Kingsfold, and in 1867, Mr. Shilcock.

1878 saw a menage indenture for £4000 from Geo. Carew-Gibson to H &W Farguhar (bankers and lenders of St Jas.) 147 acres Kingsfold Farm House and Garden.

1893 Indenture Oct 20th between W.R.Farguhar and A. Farguhar and Edwin Hunt.

The Early 20th Century

1902 Indenture Jan 29th Edwin Hunt and G.O. Bridgeman. Apl. 18th Indenture G.O.Bridgeman and W.B.Kingsbury. Deed Poll under hand and seal of W.B.Kingsbury.

1903 Power of Attorney to A. Julius, July 8th.

1903 Indenture Sept 9th Emily Kingsbury and T.N.C. Villiers, A. Julius, C.St. J. K.Roche & Cavendish Land Company. It was offered for sale by auction by the trustees, supported by the incentive of excellent development potential along Marringdean Road. "recently enlarged and judiciously restored...with well designed STONE GOTHIC ELEVATIONS, 166 acres with Frontages to both sides of a good Main road of about Three-quarters of a Mile, and affording some capital Sites for the erection of other Residences. There is capital Hunting. The Crawley and Horsham Foxhounds, Warnham Staghounds and Fishing. Water is supplied from...a reservoir pumped up to the house...with...three large storage cisterns and a modern windmill". The gardens and grounds boasted excellent shooting, lawns, a vinery and orchard house and two fish ponds with Jack (pike), Tench, gold and silver fish. Mr. Myram had one of the two cottages and also rented the pasture land for £80 p.a. –"Possession on 3 months' notice".

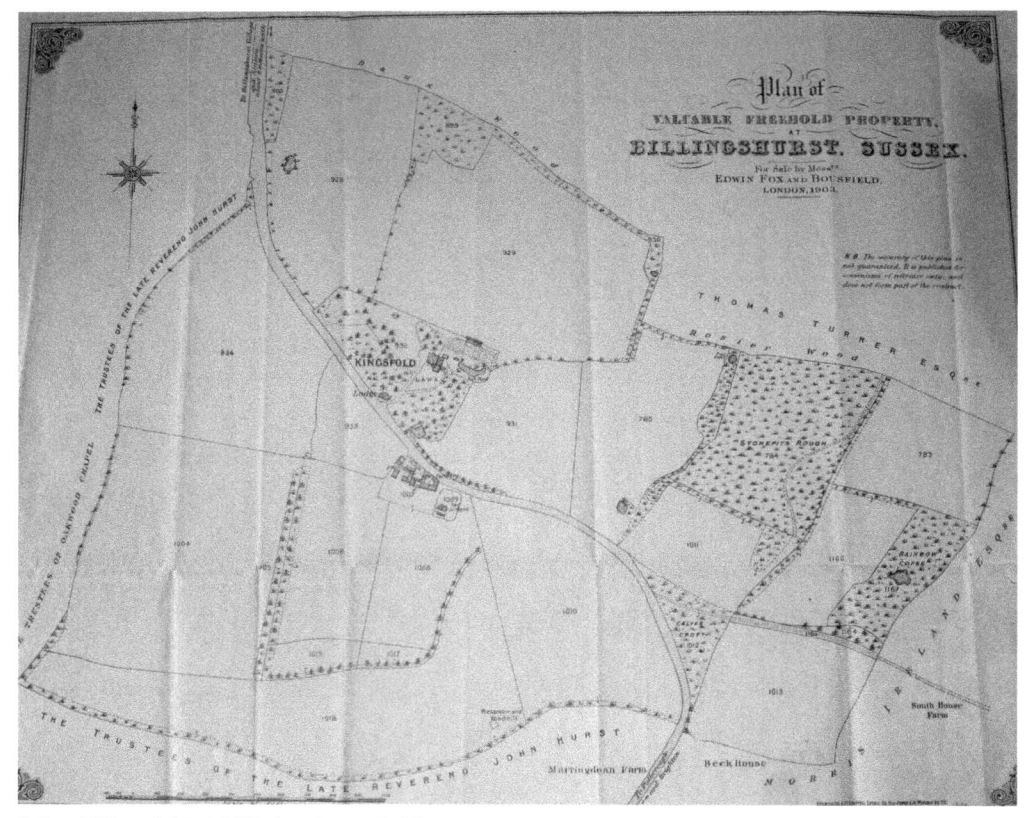

Sale of Kingsfold (1903) Auctioneer's Map

Ribbon Development

There are now in 2013 some 88 properties stretched along the ribbon development, mostly on the western side. Uncontrolled building along roadsides as practised between the world wars was legislated against in 1935 and more rigorously in 1947 when the Town and Country Planning Act circumscribed an Englishman's rights to his own castle and required the Local Authority to make twenty year building development plans for the estimated needs of the future.

The Englishman could no longer build wherever he liked, nor alter his house, add to it nor use it for any purpose he pleased without 'planning permission'. This was to be exercised, after consultation with his neighbours, by his local authority, following national guidelines determined by Parliament. One object of the Act was to protect the countryside so that long, straggling rows of houses were not erected so as to block out views of the rural scenery, to create traffic hazards by innumerable access points onto dangerous roadways, and ever-lengthening service pipes, drains and wires and journeys to shops and amenities as each tentacle slowly accrued. Marringdean Road is the most remarkable instance around Billingshurst and to a lesser extent along both West and East Street and along Stane Street at Parbrook.

The opportunity of development offered by the auctioneers in 1903 was taken up with enthusiasm, mostly by the building of larger, high value properties of distinctive, individual design. In Edwardian times a substantial country cottage could be built for £150/200.

In Dec 1903 Cavendish Land Co. conveyed the property to Sarah A Tucker who passed it in May of the following year to Samuel C Halahan. He became Chairman of the Parish Council for a time.

1904 Mr. Duffield, an estate manager, was regularly importing sheep from Scotland for fattening at Steepwood Farm. He took note of two unused hunting lodges, presumably available at a fair price. They had been imported from Canada in kit form. These he had transported to Billingshurst by rail and resited off Marringdean Road. One called 'The Brier Patch', home of Mr. Ken Longhurst still stands but its neighbour, called The Chalet' on the site of the present 'Long Acre' of the Lines family was demolished some thirty years ago.

Farm workers' Income

The average weekly earnings for a farm labourer in 1909 was 17s 6d (87 pence). It was not much for a man with a wife and children. A typical weekly budget, (quoted by Maud Davis), would be: rent 1s 6d, tea 8d, sugar 6d, bacon 1s 4d, Quaker oats 6d, 2oz tobacco 6d, cheese 9d, lard 9d, suet 2d, baking powder 1d, papers 2d, 1lb soap 3d, oranges 2d, currants 1d, pint of beer 2d, coal 1s 3d, 2 loaves 5d, milk 6d, butter 4d, oil 3d, stockings 6d, rest of baker's bill 3s. Total approximately 13s 6d. An allotment would cost 5s a year, but many villagers had gardens and could keep bees, rabbits and chickens. Another 7d a week might go to the Friendly Society to safeguard against any emergencies. Most items were priced using half pence and farthings. Meat, clothing, fuel, fares, furnishings, any extra 'luxuries' and any savings would necessarily be bought with the unspent balance of 3s 6d. It is not too surprising that children were expected to look for work as soon as they were aged 12. That year people over 70 were able to collect from the Post

Office the very first state pension, means tested and averaging 4 shillings a week. In 1911 Lloyd George introduced his contributory insurance scheme to provide for sickness and unemployment.

In the middle of WW I on Nov 15th 1916 S.C. Halahan sold Kingsfold to Col L.T.C. Twyford and on July 29th 1921 Mrs. Twyford passed the property to Mrs Fanny Clark.

The Later 20th Century and WWII

During WW II a prisoner-of-war camp, with pre-fabricated buildings, was established at what is now a housing estate named Kingsfold Close. The 12 acre site was originally called Finlanger Pasture. There is a record of a lease between James Champion and a William Firminger, a bucketmaker with premises in Billingshurst in 1712 and another about a William Firmanger dealing with Daniel Towse, timber hewer, in 1766. William Furlanger's daughter married an Evershed in the mid 17th century. This is most likely the source of that name. It is rumoured that the site was chosen by mistake by a government official who was told to requisition land at Kingsfold for the purpose (meaning at Warnham). He found Kingsfold, Billingshurst on his map and proceeded with the Marringdean site before it was too late to rectify the error. When the prisoners left in 1945 the buildings were first used to house homeless London families who had been 'bombed out' and later for stabling horses.

During WW II on 28th January 1944 a Hawker Hurricane fighter plane crashed at Steepwood Farm. Flt. Sgt. Wright survived. Another Spitfire came down in Daux Wood the following August. In 1943 a bomb-carrying Focke-Wulf 190 was shot down by a Mosquito night-fighter at Broadbridge Heath. The pilot, Fw. Jorga baled out and was captured at Cobb's Wood, Billingshurst. He was taken to his aircraft wreck the following day, much to the astonishment of schoolboys looking for souvenirs, which boys did in those days, often cycling for miles to 'incidents'. An Advanced Landing Ground was created at Coolham to support the D-Day Normandy Landings. Squadron Leader Horbaczewski, the Polish CO of 315 Squadron RAF landed his Mustang aircraft in France to pick up a fellow pilot and bring him home in his lap in the single-seater aircraft.

In 1943/4 20 Allied aircraft were lost in Horsham Urban and Rural District and two German craft crashed. Throughout the war 715 allied aircraft fell over the whole of Sussex, with the loss of 533 aircrew and 152 enemy aircraft crashed. 11,486 High Explosive bombs fell, about 90,000 incendiary bombs, 907 V 1s (Doodle bugs, flying bombs) and 4 V 2 rockets. Over 1000 people died and nearly 4000 were injured.

Farming and Business

Anglo-Saxon riddle: Who am I?

'My nose is pointed downwards; I crawl along and dig in the ground. I go as I am guided by the grey enemy of the forest, and by my Lord who walks stooping, my guardian at my task, pushes his way in the plain, lifts me and presses on, and sows in my track'.

After the war Kingsfold was back in the market. In June,1947 Messrs Lynn sold it to R. W. Cornell who owned it until July 25th 1952 when Cornell was succeeded by to Mrs. G.I. Scolding. Mrs. Scolding was obsessively keen on animals and tried to farm all her land with Shire horses. John Wilding, the horologist, who farmed at Duncans where the Beck sisters had lived, used to help her out with his tractor on the most intractable soils. She it was, who gave St. Mary's Church the original four wheels that are suspended with candles at Christmas-time, in memory of her equine friends.

Billingshurst clay is notoriously hard to cultivate, waterlogged in winter and baking hard and cracking in summer, so that many farmers had a second trade. Local historian, Hugh Kenyon, said that local clay was so hard to work that farms were seldom in the same family for more than two generations, whilst those on greensand lasted for ever. There is still one substantial working farm along Marringdean Road, Kingslea Farm, run by the Stocker family who are also Agricultural Contractors.

Farmers in Billingshurst usually had alternative strings to their bow, related to the opportunities and raw materials locally available. They could be millers, brewers and maltsters, timber dealers or run threshing tackle outfits for example, and deploy labour in winter when it was not needed on the land. A ready supply of skins would encourage various kinds of leather work –shoes, gloves and harness, which latter trade in tack and equipment for horse-drawn vehicles led to rope-making, blacksmithing and the craft of the cart and wheelwright. The demand for tiles and drainage pipes and building bricks encouraged the development of brick-making, using local clay. The exploitation of sandstone and winklestone offered another valuable alternative industry.

The answer to the riddle is: The plough!

The existence of Stane Street as a traditional route from London to the coast encouraged a continuing opportunity to offer ostling and staging facilities for horse-drawn transport and commercial hotel-keeping. There were numerous public houses for the benefit of both local people and the passing trade. This type of business was enhanced by the arrival of the motor-car and charabanc, especially when the practical range of vehicles was more limited than it is today, and road speeds slower and more hazardous. Cyclists and cycling clubs too contributed to hospitality businesses from late Victorian times.

More business was encouraged by the Wey and Arun rivers so that industrial development to feed distant markets could begin; and of course the coming of the railway triggered not only more shop-keeping but also a shift to light industry, the form of employment which still prevails.

One of the earliest of these factories was hoop and barrel making. The timber trade in all its forms, coppicing with 'standards', pollarding, collecting oak bark in spring for tanning, faggot making from the underwood for the baking oven, charcoal burning, fencing with oak, hurdle-making using hazel which was also used for thatching spars and wattle panels, basket-making with osiers, carpentry and general building had always flourished alongside arable and pastoral farming as normal local Wealden practices. Certain woods had special uses: ash for pegs, gates, bean rods, walking sticks, cart shafts, wheel felloes and tool handles; willow for cricket bats, elder for skewers, hornbeam for troughs, and way back, dogwood for arrows. From the time of the Napoleonic War it was customary to plant oaks widely spaced to secure short trunks and many curved branches providing *crooks* and *knees*, ideal for building ships' hulls. Oak bark was used for tanning and the timber made excellent charcoal. The Wealden topography had always dictated a complete integration of agriculture and woodcraft. Until wire became available, in the middle of the 19th century, cattle-proof hedgerows, usually with ditches and hand-made wooden hurdles, were vital to all farmers who kept stock. The woodcraft tradition is still honoured. Four Seasons at Coneyhurst, Potbury at Five Oaks, Burroughs at Fewhurst and many other suppliers, deal in charcoal, tree surgery, fencing and logging and there is an extensive wholesale fencing business, McVeigh Parker, established at Stane Street on the road to Adversane.

The older style of agriculture we would characterise as mixed farming, involving some arable fields for the growing of wheat, barley, oats and root crops. After 1874 when the price of wheat and barley fell because of cheap imported grain farmers ploughed less and turned to stock, especially dairying, 'From corn to horn' as the saying went. Most land remained as pasture, supporting horses, cattle for milk products and beef, sheep, pigs and goats, together with fowls for eggs and meat.

With the coming of WW II many pastures again went under the plough to grow wheat to save shipping in the hazardous conditions of war. Since then attention has shifted to more diverse crops such as oilseed rape, linseed, maize for silage, peas and beans. Most recently the number of dairy farms has shrunk to one as milk production and local distribution has proved uneconomic on smaller scale holdings and with the advent of refrigeration, supermarkets, and plastic containers.

Recent Ownership

On April 26th 1960 Mrs Scolding sold Kingsfold to Messrs. Tulloch and Maslin who held it for four years. The Maslin daughter, Jabeena, was a renowned horsewoman. She had all the old huts at the POW camp made into stables. She taught riding to all the schools in the area and was "Chef d'equipe' and trainer of the British Equestrian Pentathlon Team at the Seoul Olympics. Kingsfold was then sold to K.P.Hicks who was the owner for another six years until selling to Mr. And Mrs. Arthur Paton on 4th Jan 1971.

Mrs. Jane Paton was a magistrate on the Petworth Bench and an early Governor of the Weald School, acting with distinction as Chairman for many years until her retirement in 1991. Mr. Arthur Paton OBE, M.C. was born in 1916, the son of the Consul of Korea shortly after the Russian Revolution. The family later were in Moscow and Istanbul where father was Consul General. When Arthur came to school in the UK he had to forego the Cyrillic handwriting he had learnt from a White Russian Governess. He won a scholarship to Christ's Church, Oxford. He was summoned to Cardiff Arms Park to play rugby for Harlequins. He was commissioned into the 11th Hussars and won his Military Cross in desert battles in Libya and Egypt. On one occasion three armoured cars were shot up by a German aircraft. Luckily all the crews were having a brew-up some yards away. The sergeant, a former London bus driver cannibalised the three cars to make two, capable of returning them all to base. After the war he worked at the Foreign Office dealing with the problems of GI brides. Next he was into a fishing business in Kenya for four years and finally with the Bombay Trading Corporation from which hub he and his wife Jane travelled extensively in the Far East and the Mediterranean in the days before popular tourism.

In 2009 the Kingsfold property was sold for £1,100.000.

Other Older Buildings

There are other interesting properties along the road. One of the oldest which now gives the road its name is Marringdean Manor. Colin de la Mare, son of the poet Walter lived there for a time. Then the house was in poor repair. A visitor recalls seeing a bird's nest in one of the bedrooms. Other older timber-framed buildings, other than Kingsfold are Great Gilmans, South House and another small timber-framed dwelling.

South House is a hall house dating from the early 15th century. It was originally open to the roof before a chimney was inserted and the roof rebuilt. The chimney has a chamber halfway up probably used for smoking flitches of meat though some think of it as a 'Priest Hole'. Another curious possibility is that the house was first named 'Sow House' where pigs were used to clear woodland for cultivation.

South House, off Marringdean Rd. 2013

Great Gilmans is of 17th century date, or earlier, refaced with painted brick and weather-boarding.

Oakdean was one of the earliest erections after the 1903 sale. Mr. Jack Leaman lived there. He was a redoubtable village character, always smartly dressed like a pin-striped city stockbroker with a military air and authoritative voice. He had indeed been the Commanding Officer of comedian Spike Milligan during WW II and in his later years was the doyen of the Billingshurst British Legion and a stout supporter of the Dramatic Society.

Beke Place, a high status building, was where Mr Tom Flynn conducted a 'crammer' school to sharpen the prospects of candidates for the Common Entrance exam to public schools. The name is otherwise spelt – Beek and Beak.

Beke Hall, a Tudor house, originally built in 1495, was brought in pieces from Boxford in Suffolk by Captain Reginald Cosway in 1926 but burnt down in 1967 while being worked on by builders who were doing it up ready for Ms. Diana Dors.

Fure House in 1637 was known as Pocokes. High Fure is an Edwardian building on land which was part of the Manor of Ferring and Fure where the Bishop of Chichester was the Lord of the Manor. The many Manors with lands in Billingshurst were quite distinct from the ecclesiastical Parish. They originated as grants of land, under the feudal system, allotted to Lords who owed fealty, military services and paid taxes to the higher tier, the Tenant-in-chief of the Rape of Arundel. The Lords either farmed these economic units themselves, calling on labour from their tenants, or rented out the lands under 'copyhold' to yeoman farmers. They administered landholding rights and enforced the law through their own courts.

The actual Manor headquarters for Fure was way south at Ferring, but a strap of land, two fields wide from Fewhurst in the north east, through Jeffries Farm, South House and beyond High Fure to Greater and Lesser Woodhouse was an outlying unit of Ferring as a kind of colony. Students of hedge history, dating them by the number of species to be found, have postulated an early date to the distinctive strong hedgerow boundaries of Fure. Gervase de la Fure is first recorded as a tenant holding one yardland, paying rent of 7s 7d plus 4 hens and 25 eggs and required to perform services. Philip Hogheles (Howles) succeeded him in 1379 [Chaucer's time] at double the rent. The Pannel Roll of 1530 indicates that a Mr. Palmer had South lands and Gervase Goldings had South House though Jos. Grynfeild had the buildings and the land that was 'of old used by Maurice Grenefeild'. [There are farms named Palmers and Goldings in the north and east of Billingshurst. Sir Thomas Palmer had land at Five Oaks until 1609. He held Kingsfold until the last years of Queen Elizabeth I which he sold to William Penfold but the Greenfields had both that and Southlands by the end of the Civil War].

Edward Greenfield was in possession of High Fure from at least 1504 and his successive heirs held the High Fure land together with South House until 1811. Between 1563 and 1630 Robert and Morice Grenefeild are mentioned some 10 times in the Churchwardens' Accounts. In 1560 'Robert Greenfield bought for 3 shillings 2 black sheep, one ram, one ewe, which had been unclaimed for a year'. From 1609 to 1636 Maurice and Thomas were granted 20 trees for repairs and in 1617 the tenants of Fure were ordered to repair the parish pound there before the Feast of St. Michael the Archangel 'on pain of 20s'. [Michaelmas -29th Sept, a Quarter Day, traditionally the end of the farming year and harvest is over when roasted goose was eaten, lands changed hands and farm workers were engaged at Hiring Fairs].

Between 1636 and 1740 Greenfields and their relatives, the Slaughters (Slaters), acted as Churchwardens, Overseers of the Poor, Waywardens, Collector and Surveyor of Highways on 14 recorded occasions. Whenever a new heir took over a payment called '*heriot*' was payable, at early times the best ox and a fine to the manor court. The custom lasted until at least 1843 when Mary Allen had to pay £6 heriot and £100 13s fine on taking over from her late husband, William Allen.

Inventories

Four inventories of South House were taken just before and during the Civil War

(1633 – 1645). These records of the goods and chattels, stock and crops, offer us a valuable insight into the way of life of yeoman farmers in the 17th century. Some 16 rooms are listed on the site. In the following description the four inventories are conflated to identify significant items and the clerk's spelling as in the 1645 version is largely preserved:-

Imprimis: his wearing apparel and money in his purse - £10

In his lodging chamber [best ground floor room, also called 'The Parlour] – 1 bedsteddle, 1 feather bed, 1 straw bed, 3 blanketts, 1 rugge mat & cords & 2 bolsters -£5. I presse, 2 chests, 1 box, 1 side boord, table, 3 small chayres and 1 other little box- 15s.

In the hall – 2 long tables with frames, 8 ioyned stooles, 1 ioyned forme, 3 chaires, 1 glasse case, 1 glasse cuppboord, cushions and 1 old table - £2

In the buttery [an above-ground 'cellar'] – 6 barrells,1 long table, 2 stands, one old table, 3 flagons, baskets -£1

In the kitchin- 1 long table, 1 forme, 1 cradle, 4 chaires -£1: 1 dussen of pewter, 5 candlesticks, 1 lanthern & divers small peeces of pewter - £1.10s: 1 furnice, 2 brasse kettells, 2 skillets and 1 warming panne and an yron pot -£3 pott hangers, pott hooks, fire shovel & tounges and yrons and a dripping pan & s gridgeon ? spits -30s: a fowling peece and a sword, 1 stone mortar, 1 cleaver - £I: 5 payre of tyre sheets & 7 of towe sheets [?towel] - £4.: 2 fine table cloths, 4 of a courser sort, 2 dusson & a halfe of napkins, 4 pillowbers [cases] & other lynnen - £3: books, bottles, baskets & divers other small things forgotten - £1

In the Lower kitchen were a caldron, 4 posnets [3 legged pots], a trough and a coop [basket poultry pen].

In the chamber over the buttery [also called the loft} – 2 bedsteddles, one trundle bedsteddle,2 chaffe bedd, 1 straw bed, a rug, a bolster, matte & cords - £3. In the last two inventories it held 4 quarters of wheat, then flax and 3 bushells of buckwheat.

In the cheese loft, over the parlor: at first beds, tables chests and 10 cheeses. Later just beds etc. and a corslet and sword - £3

In his lodging chamber[the Little Chamber]- 1 bedsteddle,1 feather bed, 1 straw bed, 3 blanketts, 1 rugge, matt & cords & 2 bolsters - £5: 1 presse, 2 chests, 1 box, 1 side boord, table, 3 small chayres and 1 other little box -15s.

In the out or servant's chamber – 1 bedsteddle, 1 chaffe bed,1 blankett, 1 coverlidd and 2 old chests - £1

In the malting chamber over the Kitchen – flock, chaff or straw bed, rugge & cords etc. - £3

Wool was stored in the garret loft.

In the bake house – 1 powdring trough,1 tubb, 1 kneding trough, 1 stand, searchers and other lumber -£1.10s

In the smoke loft -12 flitches bacon, 4 flitches beefe, 3 quarters malt -£5. This room was later named oast house with an oast hair, a wimsheete, fatt, linen wheel, sacks etc. – 5s

In the milk House – powdering tub, 6 tragges [trugs], 4 butter crocks, 8 kivers [covers] etc. – 10s

In the wash house -1 renning tub [? for curdling milk with rennet], brasse kettells, a little kiver, a coop, 2 barells - £1 16s

In the brew house – 1 furnice, 1 mesh fatte, 1 keeler [shallow tub], 4 tubbs, 2 cheese presses etc. - £4

In the entry – great saw & other tools, poke [bag] of wool.

The farm dead stock comprised in 1645: shelve and other boards at Beeke wth other lumber – 13s 4d: weanes [wains or carts], plowes, 1 oxe harrow, 3 horse harrowes, 2 dungcarts, cheynes, yokes & other things - £6: boords, bees, planks & other things - £2: caseway stones, a grinstone, & 2 ladders £1 10s: 6 pronges, 1 sledg, 2 sickels, wedges, 1 yron ringer, mattocks, axes, bills, shovells, spitters [spades], augers, & other husbandry tools - £1

The live stock comprised: 7 hennes & a cocke 6s: 2 fowre yearling steeres £7 10s: 2 three yearling steeres £6 10s: 3 2 yearling steeres - £7: 9 twelvemonththings £11. [which suggests that the Greenfield wealth derived from beef and other meat!]: 6 kyne [dairy cows] £19: 31 sheepe & 12 lambes -£11: hogs & pigs £4 10.

Draught animals comprised 5 oxen - £20 and 1 horse, 1 mare & 1 colt with bridles & saddles -£6.

In store were: 20 bushells of oates - £1 10, wheate in the barne -£10, 3 loade of hay £3, wheate in the house -10s, wood, faggots, post and rayles £4.

In the fields were: 11 acers of wheate - £20, 26 acers of oates - £26, 5 acers of pease - £5

Early inventories show how all fabrics were relatively expensive before the industrial revolution. Wool was the main constituent and flax was grown to make linen. The value arose from the domestic labour involved in turning the raw materials into cloth, often the work of 'spinsters'. Bed linen was particularly valuable as were napkins and cloths. Clothing was often particularly identified and costed in wills. All households were working houses where the necessities of life were created from what nature and cultivation could provide. Money might be used for such goods as could be bought from pedlars, but much was won by barter and by do-it-yourself traditional craftsmanship.

The 'summa total' of Elizabeth Greenfield's estate she inherited from Maurice was £229 15s 4d.

This inventory of John Barkhall, late of Billingshurst, of 1692, illustrates the point about the high value of cloth and clothing to our ancestors:-

    Imprimis – his wearing apparel and money in his purse £5 -0 -0
        Item   - in his bedchamber one bed and all there unto belonging
£3 -0 -0   Two joyned chests, one box and the linnen in that chamber
£3 -1 -0   In the inner chamber one bed and all thereto belonging
£4 -0 -0   Two kine and a mare
£4-10-0   Six sheep
£1 -10-0 2 swine and six piggs
£2 -15-0   Item – on money
£45-0 -0

All the pewter, a silver bowl and three silver spoons only amounted to £7 -2 -0. Mr.Barkhall seems to have kept his cash under the bed or some other safe place! The value of a pound at that time was relatively quite low, about £45 in today's money, so John had the equivalent of over £2000 to hand.

Later History

Sussex marble at South House Stable (Coarse winklestone)

The records show that Sussex marble, the coarser of the two types of winklestone, was quarried. In 1634 Thomas Greenfield was granted a licence to dig and sell the stone for 7 years. Sarah Greenfield was allowed 'to dig marble stone at High Fure, burn it on her land [for liming the clay] and sell the same already burnt'. Maurice Greenfield was granted a similar licence for three years in 1641 'at Southouse' for 10 shillings. The superb barns and stable at South House have complete walls built of this Sussex marble. There was a 'horseway' linking Jeffries Farm via South House and Wellers to High Fure. The Manorial Court ordered Maurice, albeit he was a Collector and Waywarden, to repair it under threat of a twenty shilling fine in 1679. A later Maurice upset the Manor Court in 1727 when he ' required 6 timber trees for repairs to his customary holding in Fure, but licence was not granted to him as he had formerly greatly damaged and cut down trees growing on his holding without licence'. Copyhold had its limitations!

The Greenfields seem to have lost much of their wealth during the Napoleonic War. In 1806 High Fure and South House were surrendered by William Greenfield to Charles Farhall, yeoman, for £800, as a mortgage, then again in 1809 to George Henty of Ferring, and in 1811 to Peter Martin (Surgeon of Pulborough), comprising one messuage, 2 barns, 1 stable and 80 acres. These mortgages were duly paid off. In 1808 William had '5 sittings' reserved in St. Mary's Church pews. Finally in 1813 William 'surrendered [the property] for £3800 to William Allen, junior, of West Chiltington, in full and absolute purchase'. The Allen family held the property, raising and repaying three mortgages, until 1857 when Mary Allen, now a widow of Pulborough, was granted a licence to let the property for 21 years. The mortgage she raised from Edward Pettar of Petworth, Gentleman, was repaid in 1871. The acreage rose from 80 to 140. The Allen family probably included the wealthy maltsters who in 1857 cheated the revenue, as related here in the section about Adversane and graphically described in Deborah Evershed's book about the hamlet.

Other occupants, judging by the parish burial records, included May Johnson (1819), Esther and William Turner (1858) and Esther Luxford (1899). By 1879 Robert Evershed was hiring South House and Gardens and six fields. George Ireland farmed High Fure in 1890. In 1898 there is record of a mortgage between G.C. Carew-Gibson of Kingsfold and Lionel A. Vaillant when South House was included with other premises in Surrey and Sussex.

The property, together with Jefferies Farm was farmed by the Ireland family in the early 20th century. Listed as 'buried from South House' after the turn of the century were Solomon Wadey (1908) and James Hard (1919). Two months before the outbreak of WW II William Nash Wadey of Newbridge Farm, who already owned Steepwood and Jefferies Farm, bought South House farm for £1050. The estate was held in trust in 1960 and sold for £26,000 in 1965 to William and Pamela Harries. They held it or a year and then sold it on to a Dr. Louis Bohm of London, NW 11. Dr. Bohm broke up the estate, the moated farm 'Jeffries' going to Frederick Sopp, now a flourishing motor car business. The other land passed to Stanley Stocker, an eminent farmer. The house and 10 acres was conveyed to Nicholas and Maureen Rowe in 1965.

South House took on a more swinging look appropriate to the times. It was converted into a Country Club by the Rowes, equipped with a splendid bar, roulette wheel and all the paraphernalia of a well-concealed pleasure palace for a well-heeled clientele. They left for Pythingdean, Pulborough. Dignity and respectability were restored when Mr. C.E. and Mrs. Sheila Van den Bergh took it over in 1967. They re-established this fine house and stable building as two modern dwellings with total respect for what has remained from just short of a millennium of occupation and development. The main Barn was wrecked by the great storm of 1987 but it too has been restored by Robert Van den Bergh to its former splendour.

South House, barn, stables and pond

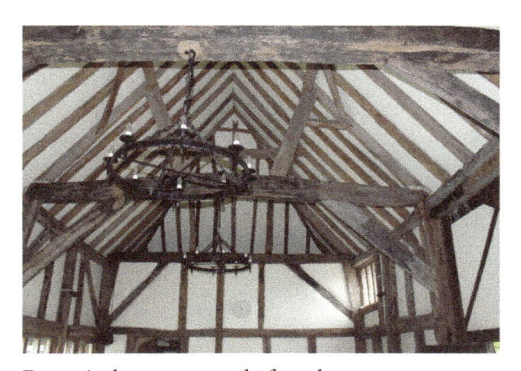

Barn timbers, restored after the great storm

Exterior of South House Barn

Mr. Taylor's account of his life as a garden boy, aged 14, at Kingsfold in 1932.

Written in 1977, slightly abridged.

We worked every day from 7 in the morning until 5 at night, 7 shillings a week. I don't remember any holidays in those days. There was Cherryman – he was the head gardener. He lived in the Lodge and Mrs Cherryman made butter in a churn at the back, proper little dairy there was there. One of my jobs was to bicycle two or three times a week to Oakdene and Clevelands with pounds of butter. Palmer, he was the under gardener and cowman, lived behind the wall. He was quite a character. He had an accordion, the kind with keys and one of the early radios set up with big loudspeakers – used to make a terrific noise. He'd lost his wife but he had several daughters. One of them worked as a kitchen-maid here. There was a big fat cook, wasn't very kind to her, used to make her scrub the kitchen floor and I'd find her in tears scrubbing this big floor. Palmer used to clean the windows and when he did the top ones I'd have to stand at the bottom of the ladder. The only trouble was he was a tobacco chewer and I'd be at the bottom dodging the bits he spat out.

There was a big Aga in the kitchen and the sink was the other side. I used to come in here to clean the knives, hundreds of them, valuable I think they were. The shoes too. I used to clean them in the garage, and there was an electric light engine next to it. I remember one man staying had the most enormous shoes – must have been a size 15.

Mrs Clark, she was a very old lady, all wizened and bent. She didn't go out very much. It was a big old car she had and Parminter was the chauffeur. He lived on the other side of the road. He didn't really do much work – used to spend his time polishing this car, but she'd only go out about once a month.

Outside there was the rose garden with roses in figure of eight beds. Mrs Clark would knock off the dead heads or spotty leaves and I'd have to pick up the bits. That's all they gave a boy to do in those days, just the dull jobs. Cherryman would cut the hedges and I'd pick up the cuttings. On wet days the two gardeners, they'd be in the shed sawing away and I'd be next door chopping wood, just the dull jobs. When they thought I was getting a bit fed up, they'd let me go over the field there and let me start the motor for the water pump in the mornings. That was an interesting job for a young boy.

We never used weed killer in the old days that I can remember, wouldn't spend the money on it. I'd be out with a knife pulling weeds out of the gravel. I lived over the road in Kingslea cottages. That was how I got the job in the first place because my father used to go to the Station Hotel for a pint on a Saturday with Mr. Cherryman. We boys used to hide in the bushes to see them staggering home, three forward and two sideways we always thought they took.

The plantation didn't have a nice path like this, but we used to spend a lot of time in the autumn sweeping up the leaves, pine needles and that. That was Mr. Gray's field over there. Gray was the farmer. They came from Somerset I think. He was a great character. He fell off a big hay cart and landed too heavy on his feet and he was stone deaf ever afterwards. It was his daughter married Mr. Stocker. In the field out there was an old donkey – if you touched him a cloud of dust came up. He was just a pet with a little shed for him.

We had good asparagus beds in the vegetable garden here. There were lots of polyanthus under the wall and over there where the swimming bath is was the compost. There was no grass on this side, just paths intersecting and there were raspberries, blackcurrants and fruit trees. I remember when a blackbird got to the raspberries under the net and Mrs. Clark came out. I caught the bird and she shouted at me, "Wring its neck" and again "Wring its neck" – I thought that was a bit hard. We used to weed round the pond by hand, but it wasn't as pretty as it is now.

Right up to where the wall is here there was great piles of coal, the big stuff, great huge lumps. That was another of my jobs, breaking it down with a hammer and I got grumbled at if I made too much dust. Down between these hedges there was a grass walk with herbaceous borders on either side'. The grass wasn't too wide and the borders went right up to the hedges. There were dogs' graves along the grass here (outside the cellar windows). Mrs. Clark had little hairy dogs, Cairns I think they were. You could hardly see their eyes for hair.

Mrs. Clark used the billiard room as a sitting room and there was a little conservatory with a door outside the kitchen window. That's where I gave my notice. Up the road I got 15 shillings [75 pence!] – that was double. Mrs. Clark couldn't believe it. "I can't afford to pay you that" she said.

We bicycled a lot in those days. I remember going all the way to London to see the Lying in State of George V. When we got there we had to wait about four hours in the queue. I wanted to have something to eat before we started home, but this other boy he said, "Wait until we get to Epson Downs". When we got there everything was shut. It must have been 4 a.m. when we got home. It quite put me off, doing it without any food!

Kingsfold Wedding

"Our England is a garden, and such gardens are not made'
By singing:- 'Oh, how beautiful!' and sitting in the shade,

While better men than we go out and start their working lives.
At grubbing weeds from garden paths with broken dinner knives."
[Rudyard Kipling]

From Mr. Chitty's deeds - Mediaeval Farms

In 1306 we learn from the deeds that one John le Pratt de Billingshurst granted land called Brokefield to Rogo Buchi de Shepele (Shipley), paying one red rose for it. He had the land from Elvicus the Bold. The Pratts owned several farms, and it is likely that Laura le Pratt married a Merlot, the family that owned Muntham House in Itchingfield from 1300 to 1877.

John Pratt's son, also John, granted land at Billingshurst in 1317 to Roge Buchi's son, also Roger. In 1318 Roger passed the lands to his brother, Lawrence Buchi. Witnesses to the transaction included Richard ate Putte (? Puttock) and Richard Gylemin (as in Great Gilmans?).

Lawrence's son Robert had land – meadows and a water mill – in Billingshurst and Shipley, which Robert Traylemere and his wife Maria 'held for their lives'.

Another Pratts Farm is marked on Budgen's map, opposite Summers, together with Pinkhurst, Muntham House, Itchingfield, and Hadfold. The Pratts Farm mentioned in the deeds is today a two-bay late 16th C end chimney-stacked house with extensions, refaced in brick in the 18th century.

In 1338 William de Hadfolde of Billingshurst granted 1 and ½ acres of land in Wassington to Robert Bouchi of Shipley. His name relates to Hadsfoldshern, Old English – Hadesfoldeshyrne – Hedefoldeshurne 1279 –Hadfoldsherne 1711 – Hadfordshern c 1800, corner of land relating to Hadfold (fold is an enclosure) – or Adversane.

Among the 40 or so names listed as paying a wealth tax in Billingshurst on the Subsidy Roll of 1332 are the following which have clear modern derivatives both as place names and surnames:

Johne de Pemefold – who paid most – Penfold

Robt le Tote – Toat

Petro Prat – Pratts Farm

Willmo Kockebrok – Coxbrook, East Street

Malill de Hadfold – Hadfold and Adversane. Hadfold was originally controlled by the Priory of Tortington.

John le Carpentir - Carpenters

Ancient Buildings in Billingshurst

There are 80 old houses in the Billingshurst area originally of timber-frame construction though they have all been altered and adapted through the years according to the fashion of the day. Twenty of these are in the heart of the village. All were first built for the more affluent yeoman farmers and traders. Subsequently they were often occupied by farm workers and humbler folk, but of recent years have enjoyed the status of antiquity and are eagerly sought after by well-to-do people of independent means. All 'listed' buildings are now strictly controlled by Horsham District Council to preserve their original features which are of special architectural or historic interest, as required by the Town and Country Planning Act of 1990. All buildings erected before 1700 should be listed and many up to 1840. Only St. Mary's Church is Grade I. There were 108 addresses in Billingshurst as entries listed at Grade II in 2013.

Fewhurst (late 14th century farmhouse) in Coneyhurst Road has a crown post and an end-aisle construction. The chimney extension uses local winklestone, which is also used at Jeffries Farm (part 17thC), nearby. An ancient L-shaped barn at Little Jefferies Farm was burnt down in 1969.

Pennybrooks, in Birch Drive set amidst modern housing, is a 4 bay house with two areas still open to the roof. Its original name was Broomfields, a name pre-empted by a Victorian building in Station Road while the old house lapsed into labourers' cottages until restored and renamed.

Okehurst

At Okehurst, beside the slab-roofed farm house, is the Clock Gallery in two bays and two storeys of about 1530. The ground floor was originally used for dairy purposes and the upper floor as accommodation for workers. In most of the older timber-framed houses the buttery, where barrels and bottles were kept, and the milk house were incorporated on the ground floor adjoining the hall. Here such rooms are provided in an out-house. Dallaway in his *History of the Three Western Rapes of Sussex'* (1811) says of this house:

"Okehurst is held in the honour of Arundel as parcel of the Manor of Bury and was a constituent part of it when Domesday [Book] was compiled. ....A family named 'de Okehurst' were the mesne tenants for many generations. In the reign of Edward IV Thomas Bartelott of Stopham, having married the heiress of de Okehurst, became possessed, and in their descendants it remained vested till 1579, when it passed to John Wiseman, one of whose daughters conveyed it in marriage to Edward Goring Esq., second son of Sir H. Goring of Bodecton, the immediate ancestor of Sir Henry Goring, Bart., the present proprietor." Edward Goring paid £340 for it in 1572. His monument is in St. Mary's s Church. Likewise Thomas Bartlet, MP for Midhurst, is represented in a monumental brass with Elizabeth his wife (1499). She was grand-daughter of William de Okehurst who fought at Agincourt. Okehurst was not a Manor House, in the strict sense, as the headquarters of a manorial court and demesne but part of the Manor of Bassett's Fee.

The Gorings sold it in the 1870s and the next owner we hear of is Shepley-Shepley followed by Peter Locke-King. The shield and baton of Sir Charles Goring, Sheriff of Sussex in 1827 adorns the Hall ceiling. Radiating from the shield are twelve pikes, each inscribed with name of a Botting. Smuggling was at that time going on along the Fosseways, and the story runs that the Sheriff's guard consisted of the two Botting brothers and the five sons of each of them, twelve in all. Pikes are said to have been better than firearms. William Botting was the miller at Rowner and Francis Botting farmed Okehurst in 1867. The Fielding family followed Hugh Locke-King.

Other listed buildings in Okehurst Road are Rowner, Spurland, The Clock House, Gatefield Cottage and Bignor Farm House, all 17th century in whole or in part. Frogshole and Pound Cottage are 16th Century.

South House, off Marringdean Road, is L shaped. It had a buttery with chamber above it, similar to Hammonds in East Street. The barn is 18th Century.

Great Daux is an early example, unusual for the area, of close-studding where the studs and spaces between are of similar width. It is 15th Century with a slab roof and diamond-shaped windows.

Buckmans (17th C) at Five Oaks is very unusual in that it is tile-hung all over. It has fishscale tiles.

Buckman's, Five Oaks with tile-hanging overall

High Seat (18th C) at the north end of Billingshurst has a wall with 'mathematical tiles' designed to look like bricks and a slate roof.

Old Cottage at Andrew's Hill is a 17th century 3-bay house with a central smoke bay.

Great Grooms, once also known as Parbrook, until recently the Jenny Wren restaurant, is largely of 16th Century date. It was named from a John Gretgrome and its early history dates from the early 14th century. Some floors are laid with Sussex marble and it has a bread oven inglenook fireplace.

At Marringdean Manor the south wing is 15th Century with a 16th Century crosswing.

Knob's Crook, Adversane is a 16th Century open hall house.

Fossbrooks, in Parbrook, a two-storey timber-framed building with plaster infilling with casement windows, is 16th century.

Fossbrooks in Parbrook

Duncans Farmhouse in W. Chiltington Lane, (17th C or earlier), has a Horsham slab roof.

In East Street are Gore Farm House and Hammonds.

Coombland House, Marringdean is 17th Century incorporating sandstone and red brick.

Great Gilman's, Marringdean Rd., is 17th Century or earlier.

Marringdean Cottage is 17th Century.

Grainingfold at Five Oaks exemplifies a mediaeval farmhouse.

Copped Hall, Okehurst Road, is an L-shaped house. The North Wing is 17th C or earlier.

Wynstrode, also in Okehurst Road, is 17th C, L-shaped.

Many of these houses have wide hearths built to accommodate standard four-foot cordwood logs. It was economical of labour to use long wood for fires until the invention of power-driven circular saws made 10 inch billets feasible for use in stoves and small fireplaces.

Wide hearth in South House inglenook

South of the Community Centre and Roman Way are modern apartments built on a former garage site where once stood a house named Whitehall beside the Rope Walk. These were owned by Henry Laker who dealt in harness and leather goods.

The northern High Street features more 16th and 17th century houses, their timbers now obscured by rough cast or peg-tiling. On the eastern side are No.39, 27 (Oak Cottage, 25 (Byron Cottage), 23 (Sleepy Hollow), 21 The Old Coach House), 19 (Stow Cottage), 17 and 13. Nos. 21 and 19 have Tudor chimneys. Five of these homes would originally have been two large houses.

Lloyds Bank (1968) presents a startling modern design, quite compatible with the disorderly miscellany of period buildings and architectural styles which characterise Billingshurst High Street. It occupies the site of a mediaeval Wealden house with a stone roof which became Argent's bakery and grocery in Edwardian times and Bernard Baker's Outfitters between the World Wars. A relic of the demolition, an ancient crown post, now rests at the Downland Museum at Singleton. Next door is another timber-framed house built at right angles to the road, now an estate agent's (No. 39).

On the opposite western side Nos.42 (Indian restaurant), 44-46 (estate agency),

54 (shop) and 56 (pharmacy) are all old timber-framed buildings, three of them with Horsham stone roof slabs.

Around the 'Village Green' are more timbered houses. No. 59 has been a shop for many years and more recently a restaurant. No. 61 has a half-hipped roof. 63 and 65 (Causeway and Tithe Cottage) were originally one splendid 'Wealden' house with a central hall, open to the roof, supported by a crown post and built at the time of Geoffrey Chaucer – 1400 AD. Opposite No.s 92 and 94 are timber-framed houses hidden under brick facades. Billingshurst's ancient inns are described in a later chapter.

Old cottages in the High Street

Pear Tree Farm and Frank Patterson

In 1898 Frank and Emily Patterson hired a derelict Elizabethan house at a rental of 9 old pence per annum (3 and a half pence). They had it repaired by a local builder and lived there for 54 years, renaming it Pear Tree Farm. Its old name was Hookers at Eastlands. It is a 16th century two storey, timber-framed building with a tile-hung south gable.

Frank was born in Portsmouth in 1871 of seafaring stock. His sailor father wrote for 'The Boys' Own Paper'. Frank attended Portsmouth Art School. There he set up a shooting gallery in the loft! He enlisted in the army in his teens but wisely bought himself out of it. To seek work he walked to London and began his career as an illustrator of books and magazines – mainly 'Cycling' magazine. He worked for the magazine for 63 years. He was an enthusiastic cyclist until 1909 when a leg injury restricted him to walking, sometimes up to fifty miles a day! His drawings were mainly not drawn from life however but based on pictures and postcards. He was a thoroughly reliable journalist, always on time, submitting up to ten drawings a week. It is estimated that he made 26,000 drawings, always displaying 'a joyful celebration of our beautiful countryside' [Gerry Moore]. He was an exemplar of the Golden Age of Cycling in the 1920s when touring to welcoming inns was a popular pastime. His riders would be dressed in plus fours, long socks, strap-over cycle shoes and an alpaca jacket, equipped with map, panniers and a saddle-bag. By contrast Frank himself dressed and behaved like a local Billingshurst yeoman farmer in tweeds, boots and gaiters who kept gun-dogs, though in fact he rented out his land, kept no stock and earned his living as an artist.

He did not drink tea, but had 4 and a half gallon barrel of IPA delivered from King and Barnes Brewery at Horsham every fortnight. He was a good shot, in demand at local shoots to boost the bag of pheasants, using his trusty hammer 12 bore shotgun with Damascus barrels, a perfectly weighted weapon in his grandson's opinion. Being a professional man he was often called on as a juryman. He saw this as a penalty and craftily arranged with the local policeman to be arrested and convicted for not buying a dog licence. In those days a criminal conviction was enough to debar you from jury service. In 1933 he found a piece of sandstone with footprints which were believed to be those of a stegosaurus dinosaur.

In 1934 he floated a correspondence course from Pear Tree Farm and produced a prospectus, 'The Patterson School of Sketching', but it did not flourish. One of his nephews was a pupil artist but they fell out when he tried to pass off some of Frank's work as his own. They never spoke again.

Billingshurst's Heritage

Pear Tree Farm by Frank Patterson

Frank and Emily had two daughters, Molly and Peggy. Emily had consumption and needed nursing for several years. Agnes came as a companion and when Emily died she and Frank married. They had two sons Jock Angus and Gordon Andrew, both of whom served in the RAF in WW 2. Jock's son Roger, now a retired master beekeeper of national standing, remembers only seeing Frank taken off to hospital by ambulance. In 1991 an exhibition of his work was staged at Sotheby's in Billingshurst. He died in 1952 and his ashes were scattered at the Farm.

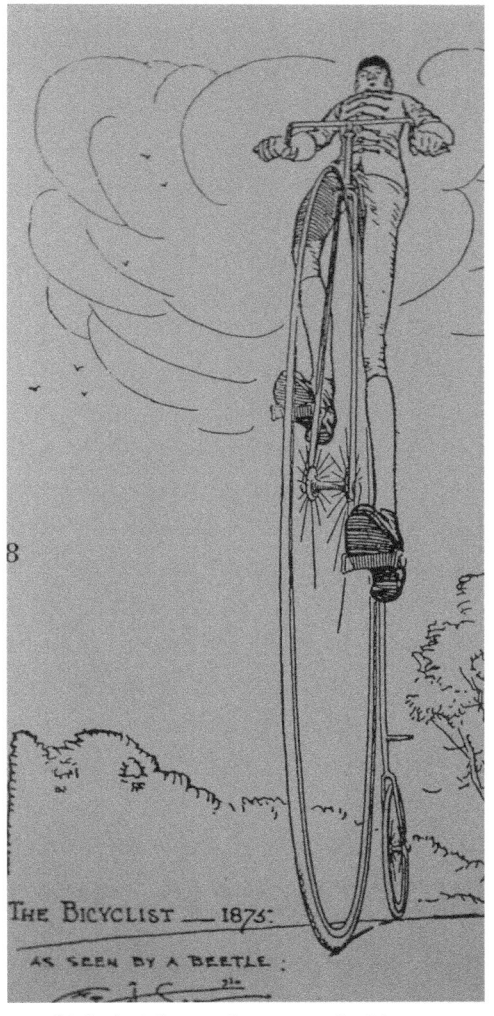

Frank's little joke on the penny-farthing

Frank greets a friend with his 12 bore

William Cobbett (1763-1835), Billingshurst visitor

Cobbett was a self-taught, anti-authoritarian agitator, and radical reformer chiefly remembered for his book 'Rural Rides'. He was a great champion of impoverished farm workers during the depression after the Napoleonic Wars, a whistle-blower against corruption on both sides of the Atlantic and an opponent of the Corn Laws. Yet he was a traditionalist who saw the Industrial Revolution as the ruination of rural society. Brighton Pavilion he likened to a turnip stuck on top of a box. However he holds Billingshurst and district in high esteem. "I saw, and with great delight, a pig at almost every labourer's house". "The people are very clean, the Sussex women very nice in their dress and in their houses". "This village [Billingshurst] is seven miles from Horsham, and I got here to breakfast about seven o'clock. A very pretty village and a very nice breakfast, in a very neat little parlour of a very decent public house [The King's Arms]. The landlady sent her son to get me some cream, and he was just such a chap as I was at his age, and dressed in just the same sort of way, his main garment being a blue smock-frock, faded from wear, and mended with pieces of new stuff, and, of course, not faded. The sight of this smock-frock brought to my recollection many things very dear to me. This boy will, I daresay, perform his part at Billingshurst, or at some place not far from it. If accident had not taken me from a similar scene, how many villains and fools, who have been well-teased and tormented, would have slept in peace at night, and have fearlessly swaggered about by day!

When I look at this little chap – at his smock-frock, his nailed shoes, and his clean, plain, coarse shirt, I ask myself, will anything, I wonder, ever send this little chap across the ocean to tackle the base, corrupt, perjured Republican Judges of Pennsylvania? Will this little lively, but at the same time, simple boy, ever become the terror of villains and hypocrites across the Atlantic."

Cobbett was angry about the enclosure of the 800 acre heath north east of Horsham by an enclosure act of 1813 secured by the Lord of the Manor, the Duke of Norfolk, the cost paid for by the sale of a small parcel of land. "A large common...cut up, disfigured, spoiled, and the labourers all driven from its skirts. I have seldom travelled over eight miles so well calculated to fill the mind with painful recollections". A verse of the time catches the spirit of Cobbett's criticism:

'The law locks up the man or woman,
Who steals the goose from off the common;
But lets the greater villain loose,
Who steals the common off the goose!'

He would have been yet more incensed had he lived to know how shrewd had been the Duke's investment in development land. 'By 1911 land thus acquired was fetching £850 an acre. No doubt as a small compensation to the burgesses of Horsham, he rebuilt the Town Hall, in a singularly ugly pseudo-Norman style' [J.R. Armstrong]. It has recently become a restaurant. Fortunately no enclosure acts affected the people of Billingshurst. There were no open fields or commons to be exploited because the farm landscape of small fields had originally been won by 'assarting' or grubbing up the trees from the time of the Saxons.

Horsham Town Hall

'Soon after quitting Billingshurst', Cobbett wrote, 'I crossed the River Arun which has a canal running alongside of it. At this there are large timber and coal yards, and kilns for lime. This appears to be a grand receiving and distributing place'.

The Wey & Arun Canal

The most remarkable archaeological feature in Billingshurst is the relic of an astonishing feat of engineering undertaken by our ancestors in the early 19th century. In truth it is an attribute shared both with Wisborough Green, since much of the enterprise was on the west bank of the Arun River, and also with Pulborough, since that village claimed the river frontage until boundary changes gifted it to Billingshurst in 1933. The Arun named after Arundel was originally called Tarrente or Trisanton meaning 'trespasser', and is recalled in the name of Tarrant Street in Arundel.

As early as 1641 a Bill was introduced to Parliament to link the upper reaches of the River Wey to those of the Arun by a canal between Cranleigh and Dunsfold. The Arun waterway, from the coast at Littlehampton, had been made navigable as far as Stopham Bridge at Pulborough in Queen Elizabeth's time. Cargo boats are even said to have been able to reach as far as Pallingham Quay by 1637. However the Bill was not proceeded with. A century and a half later, in 1785, The Arun Navigation Act was passed and the section between Pallingham and Newbridge opened two years later. The Wey & Arun Junction Canal Company was formed in 1811 and the Act of Parliament authorising the work between Shalford and Newbridge was passed in 1813 when construction began. An authoritative account is to be found in P.A.L. Vine's book *'London's Lost Route to the Sea'*.

In 1816 the Wey & Arun Junction Canal opened for business. At the opening ceremony in a spirit of euphoria at 'The Compasses' inn at Alfold an ox was roasted whole and the navigators who had done the spade work drank 200 gallons of ale. It had required the construction of over 18 miles of canal and 23 locks. It could accommodate 50 ton laden barges and cost £101,370. This is the equivalent of well over £100M today. It was a spectacular feat of civil engineering, of enterprise and of strenuous physical labour. Freight could now travel by water back and forth from the Thames at Weybridge via the Wey, the Junction Canal and the Arun to Arundel docks and the coastal harbour at Littlehampton. More importantly for strategic military purposes the government had secured a safe inland passage to Portsmouth when yet another canal linked Chichester and Portsmouth to Arundel. Ironically the security aspect of the project was never realised as the threat of French invasion was over after the Battle of Waterloo, only one year earlier.

Southwards from Loxwood Bridge beside the Onslow Arms are the following features:

Brewhurst Lock
Baldwins Knob Lock

Drungewick Aqueduct over the Lox River
Drungewick Lane Bridge
Drungewick Lock
Malham Lock
Rowner Lock
A272 Bridge (Newbridge)
[From here on we are on the Arun Navigation]
Orfold Aqueduct
Orfold Lock, now called Lordings
Lee Farm Lock
Pallingham Quay
Pallingham Lock – a double 'staircase' lock.

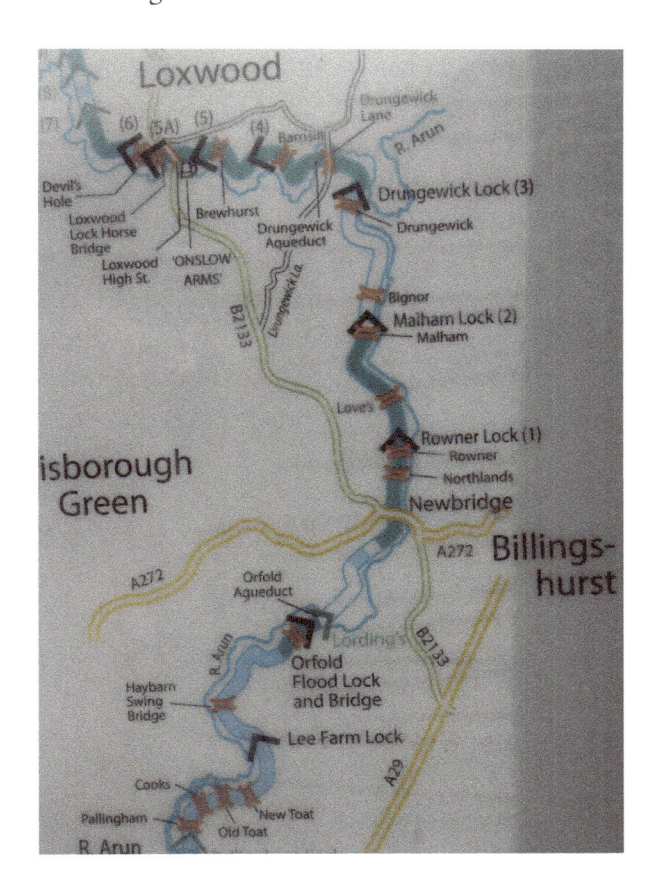

George Wyndham

The third Earl of Egremont, George Wyndham of Petworth was the main sponsor of canals in West Sussex. He is remembered as a patron of the arts who sponsored the emigration to Canada of thousands of poor Petworth folk. He saved the Arun Navigation Company from bankruptcy by buying shares. He also invested in the Portsmouth-Arundel link and his own canal on the River Rother. He bought 250 shares at £100 each, some 28% of the value of The Wey & Arun Junction Company. Dividends ceased altogether in 1865 and never exceeded 1%! By 1850 shares had fallen in value to £10. By a cruel twist of fate, the toll income had improved a little in the late 50s when the company undertook haulage of building materials for the new Horsham to Petworth rail line, the true instrument of the canal's own demise. The last dividend paid in 1865 was 6 shillings, about ¼ %. Closure was inevitable and the shareholders put the company into liquidation. The other two Navigation Companies, the Arun and River Wey (Godalming) Navigations, raised legal objection to abandonment, but after no buyer for the canal business could be found at auction in 1870, the necessary Act was passed and closure came in 1871 after which the land was sold off. The Earl's heirs were affluent enough to support the losses, though when George Wyndham died in 1837 he might well have still been nourishing hopes of better financial returns.

Wyndham was a power in the land, part of the influential Whig aristocracy. He, like Lord Byron, had an affair with Lady Caroline Lamb and is reliably reputed to have been the natural father of the young Queen Victoria's mentor and Prime Minister, William Lamb, Lord Melbourne, the statesman well commemorated in Australia.

He had some 15 mistresses and fathered over 40 illegitimate children. His nephew inherited the Earldom of Egremont and his eldest illegitimate son inherited his unentailed estates, the 1st Baron Leconfield.

Besides the goods mentioned by Cobbett, timber, coal and lime, the wharfingers dealt in imported groceries and shop goods, grain for the watermill, chalk, sand and gravel and seaweed for fertilizer on farms. Exported were timber, oak bark, hoops and other woodcraft products. The toll on a ton of coal from Arundel to Newbridge was 1s 8d plus 6d for using a tunnel at Hardham which by-passed a loop in the Arun.

The Working Years and Demise

Commercially the Wey & Arun Company enjoyed moderate success in the 1830s, paying that small 1% dividend but prospects steadily deteriorated. In the best year 23,000 tons of freight were moved. Most trade was from London, mainly coal and groceries, porter beer and pottery. Such things as bullion guarded by red-coated troops, furniture and soldiers' equipment went north. A wharfinger's house had opened at Newbridge in 1839 beside the entrance to the wharf. It continued in use until 1888 when the last barge to and from the south put an end to river traffic. At one time it housed a beer house called The Limeburners. It is now a private residence and The Limeburners Arms is on the opposite side of the river by Lordings Road, converted from a row of 17th century cottages. Rowner water mill on the Arun River was demolished in 1966.

Rowner Lock under reconstruction

Restoration

The Wey & Arun Canal Society was formed in 1970 and became the Wey & Arun Canal Trust in 1973. Enthusiasts have combined to rehabilitate the 'lost route to the sea' with the idealistic and laudable vision of restoring the entire derelict canal to the state of its heyday as a delightful leisure amenity. There are many obstacles. Many riparian landowners are reluctant to cooperate, some stretches have been built over, locks, bridges and aqueducts have collapsed. Nature has reasserted its dominion of the channel bottom requiring judicious reclamation from the wild before any dredging or restoration work can begin. The costs are formidable even with modern machinery and volunteer assistance.

Passenger barges at the Onslow Arms

Rowner Lock restored on the Wey & Arun Canal

The Wey & Arun Canal Trust has dredged half the old 18 mile canal bed, built a new lock and road bridge at Loxwood at a cost of £1.9M and restored 10 other locks, 24 bridges two aqueducts and many culverts. Rowner Lock, last used in 1871, was completely restored in 1982 having started in 1971. Pleasure cruises on three boats, the 'Wiggonholt', the 'Zachariah Keppel' and the 'Josias Jessop' (named after the consulting engineer) now operate from the Onslow Arms to Drungewick and northwards from the Inn as far as Devil's Hole Lock, (2012) and probably as far as Southland Lock in 2013/14. Once the stretch to Pallingham is repaired the waterway will be open for small boats to go all the way to Littlehampton.

Canal Tourist 1869 – a neo-Pickwickian idyll

J.B.Dashwood, with his wife and dog, stayed in the village on their sail-boat journey from 'The Thames to the Solent' at a time when the canal company was foundering and already up for auction. He wrote:

'Loxwood… boasts of a neat clean little inn close by the Canal side…although we did not pull up here but pushed forward to Billingshurst. There are five locks between Loxwood and Billingshurst. The country here is decidedly ugly with flat water meadows on either side. Just before reaching Newbridge…[the weeds] became so thick that it seemed almost impossible to cut our way through them.'

'We found Billingshurst a charming little place with a neat little Inn by the name of The Kings Arms…We had the gratification of sitting down to as good a dinner as I believe it is possible to get in a quiet country village! Fresh eggs, butter, bread, fruit, cream, all excellent with mutton chops done to a turn with excellent beer and a very fair sherry.'

'After dinner we took a stroll up the village…all seemed peaceful and happy; little family groups sitting at the entrance doors of their houses, others strolling up and down the hilly street, while the young ones besported themselves on all sides. Judging by the appearance of the old men we saw crawling about in every direction the place must be most healthy…for it stands on high ground and appears beautifully clean and thriving.'

'Next morning the Inn was a bustle by 5. Hot and cold water for shaving and baths to any amount and boots polished like mirrors. The breakfast is a capital one. Our little table was filled with cold meat, eggs, toast and coffee at our going hour of 5.45.'

'At a little before 7 o'clock we reached Newbridge where our boat lay quietly at her moorings, wet with the morning bath of dew…[at the first lock] we watched the lock-keeper's wife and two pretty daughters making butter in the early morning. Though flat the meadows on either side presented such a lovely English picture with cattle dotted about, …the larks sang aloft sending forth their melodious morning song and the banks of the Canal clothed with wild flowers of every hue and colour that we enjoyed this part of our journey almost as much as any.'

Barge Josias Jessop

Rowner Watermill

Probably the oldest recorded relic of the past in Billingshurst, though originally in Pulborough parish, is the watermill on the River Arun which may predate St. Mary's church. It is likely to have been included in Domesday Book of 1086 as one of the two mills listed in Pulborough. It was actually two mills of differing dates both raised on a small island to prevent flooding. A William Rowner, whose surname was taken from the place, had it in the late 15th century. He passed it to Thomas Stydolf in 1503, then it went to Richard West, a Billingshurst yeoman. In 1593, late Elizabethan times, 142 oaks were sold off to John Ede, woodbroker, of Wisborough Green. From 1678 Guildenhurst and Rowner were occupied by the Garton family of Billingshurst where John Garton is buried. From 1685 the Greenfields were in possession, having been granted an eight year lease, less one week, granted by Kathren Garton, widow, to 'Thomas Greenfeild of Kensfold'. This was for Rowner farm house with buildings and 120 acres. The mill is shown on Budgen's map of 1724.

In 1732 Richard and William Garton and 19 others petitioned Lady Elizabeth Goring, who had the rights to the Great Tythe, to continue to honour a verbal agreement on the rate to be paid over at Rowner House [2/6d in the £ of the rental value] and to keep up the enjoyable tradition "of being there treated with best ale and roast beef according to the said agreement with the late Sir, as hath usually been". The good widow gave them a dusty answer. In 1773 she turned them down in a letter from her Secretary.

The Carter family worked the mill from 1809 to 1842, succeeded by William Botting to 1870 and the Hammond family are believed to have been the last regular occupants. It is said that the mill was used briefly during WWII to grind animal feed. The West Sussex River Board inherited the mills in 1958 and, in the interest of the flow of the river, had them demolished in 1966. Only the wheelpit of the older mill remains.

Sketch of Rowner House

The only rival in antiquity to the Mill, other than the parish church, may be Newbridge itself, though not the present structure which crosses both the canal and the river. Records suggest that it was 'new' in 1279, implying that there had been a yet older bridge. Nearby was the site of the lost chapel of St. Elyn raised in the 14th century.

The Tedfold Estate and Streele Farm

The name Tedfold suggests that the place was an original Saxon settlement. John Hurd's researches reveal that in 1164, 100 years before St. Mary's began, it was held by a John Tregoz who was in dispute with the Abbot of Fecamp about a wood called Durehurst. The monks got the quarter next to Tuddesrode. Henry Tregoz was also in dispute in 1203 with a William Mordant, who provided him with a day's entertainment and a horse for his son and heir!

In 1321 the pasture of Toddesrode belonged to the Manor of Dedisham. In 1478 Thos Portbury, a tenant, stripped leaves from an oak belonging to the Lord of the land without licence. He suffered a 4 pence fine. John, the Elder, another Portbury is on record as paying 'to Our Lady of the Assumption 12d, the High Alter of the same church 12d, to the Chapel of Saint Elyn at Newbrigge 2d.' That Chapel is now quite lost.

By 1602, at the end of Queen Elizabeth's reign, the estate had passed to the Manor of Parham which leased it to John Wales for £4. A rent of 'reape sylver and horse sylver' was paid at 'midsomer' in 1605. By 1628 it was in the private hands of Anthony Wales and became a Manor in its own right. During the century and a half between 1628 and 1795 the ownership passed to Rich Haler, Wm Skinner and a farmer, Giles Brown. His son, also Giles, was a notable dissenting Anabaptist but when he married his first wife, Anne Naldrett, she put a stop to Baptists meeting at Tedfold. He was a Trustee of the Billingshurst Meeting House and an Overseer of the Poor. When he died in 1762 he was buried as he wished beside Anne 'who came to Church' in the Anglican churchyard.

It was written of the Baptists that 'They were more serious-minded than their neighbours but in Sussex they did not adopt extreme puritanical attitudes and behaviour. They enjoyed their smoking and drinking, went to fairs and to the races, watched cricket. Day by day they carried out their trades and occupations within the wider community and were often elected to serve as Overseers of the Poor and Waywardens'. After the deaths of Brown's sons, Tedfold passed to his three daughters. One of these daughters married John Evershed. He was Waywarden in Billingshurst in 1770 and another four years, and four times Overseer of the Poor up to 1805. In 1812 their eldest son, William, bought the estate from his mother and aunts. He and Thomas Evershed were often Overseers too. Three generations of Eversheds remained there until after the death of William in 1865.

The Greenfields were Billingshurst's most dominant agricultural family for several centuries but relatively little is on record of their doings and relationships. The Eversheds by contrast, who were also considerable farmers, were culturally and religiously important in the life of the village, albeit of a chapel-going rather than Anglican bent. The family has kept up and recorded its manifold membership world-wide. The family is thought to predate William the Conqueror. Thomas de Eversherd is on record in 1215. William Furlanger, a yeoman of Billingshurst had a daughter who married Thomas Evershed (1636 – 1695).

The Head of the family, Mr. John Dendy Evershed, whose father was born at Tedfold, has an article written by Sarah Evershed (1818-1907) in 1883 about her memories of Streele Farm where her grandfather lived amid the fields full of cider apple trees. She lived in Canada and her memoire offers an insight into domestic life in a Victorian yeoman farmhouse.

'On all the cottages flourished vines; some years the grapes ripened beautifully and they were always sufficiently good to make barrels of grape wine. The quince yielded ...enough fruit to make a barrel of wine....Grandpapa's gardens were well stocked with walnut, filbert, quince, medlar and rare apple trees....at the bottom of the garden the nightingale sang in the dewy evenings.' She describes the house with its inglenook fireplace in the hall where grandpa sat and smoked his long white pipe and read his Chronicle with the aid of his tortoiseshell spectacles, tied on with black ribbon. His clay pipes were put twice a week into an iron frame and burnt beautifully white and clean in the red embers of the big brick oven.

His counting house led off the Hall 'in which he transacted his business with his labourers'. On Saturday nights the cottagers came to pay their rents and the labourers trooped in wearing their heavy hob-nailed boots with their wooden tallies, notched for each day's work or a half notch if for only half a day and were paid accordingly. There were two staircases, one going to the principal bedrooms, one to the servants' quarters. The stone floored kitchen had a pump with a deep stone sink. 'Built in the chimney was a chamber large enough to hold many flitches of bacon and ham in process of smoking. On each side...in the chimney place were rough oaken settles for the use of the men and women servants. Beyond were seen two large coppers – one for boiling the clothes and the other for the lard, hogs puddings and sausages'. Faggots were used for heating the brick baking oven. The men drew their mid-day beer in the small beer room 'ad libitum' and in the milk house were the immense pewter dishes and plates used only at Harvest Home. To light the kitchen they used bundles of rushes drawn through the refuse lard. 'The youngest serving boy sat by the upright iron rush holder constantly moving up the rush as it burnt out while the women sat at their needlework, and the men wrote to their sweethearts, or sang the old English ballads'. October ale and 'small beer were brewed and cider in the brew houses'. Twice a week the big oven was heated, bread was made and when it was baked 'rice puddings and

Brobdignagian apple pies took their place'. 'The servants had plenty of bacon, cabbage and plain flour dumplings to eat or pork with cabbage steeped in vinegar. Grandpa had roast beef or veal or a slice of streaky bacon with his apple dumpling or tart. At bedtime the servants heated the beds with a large brass warming pan or a cradle made of hoops with an iron frame in the middle containing red-hot embers from the kitchen fire and by half-past nine everyone was in bed'.

Over 120 Eversheds are buried in the graveyard of the Baptist Chapel. 100 living Eversheds visited the Chapel in July 1999 at the fifth Family Reunion when Dendy was 87 years old.

The Tedfold estate was put up for auction but withdrawn because the reserve was too high and it was not sold until 1871. It comprised 420 acres, including the farms known as Tedfold, Leyhold, North Eaton, Jefferies, Coppid Hall (Coppid spelt with an 'i') and Old Hayes, or the Hole all in a picturesque and beautiful part of Sussex. There is no record of who bought it.

Auctioneer's map of Tedfold Estate

In August, 1920 Mr.C.E.G. Gordon offered for sale this large landholding in the northwest quadrant of Billingshurst parish. The sale particulars describe the estate as follows:

"A large family residence within a well timbered park, three farm homesteads with excellent pasture and arable lands, woods and plantations. The whole extending to 344 acres with vacant possession, for sale by private treaty." The description follows of 'An excellent family residence, in red brick …within a park of 90 acres, through which runs a long carriage drive with a picturesque Lodge Entrance.' There were 7 rooms on the ground floor with Adams mantels and French casements and 14 bedrooms all with 'modern grates' with access to balconies 'from which beautiful views are obtained'. There were 'ample offices' –Kitchen with large range, scullery, larder, servants' hall and butler's pantry, well-fitted cellarage and cool dairy in the basement, 2 coal sheds and W.C. and septic tank. Well water pumped by electricity and an electric power station 12 h.p. Pelapone and 54 accumulators installed 'this year'." [These Pelapone engines built in Derby are now collectors' items].

The gardens boasted ornamental trees in variety and a large spreading oak, kitchen and flower borders and shrubberies together with an orchard. There was stabling for four horses. The farm buildings included a large barn, a 14 horse cart-horse stable, cattle shed for 22, cow shed for 8 and loose boxes, a 3 bay cart shed with granary over, implement shed and stair over, chaff house and mixing house. The engine house was fitted with a Fairbank Morse engine mill, cake crusher, chaff cutter, root cutter and saw bench. There was a pump house in the yard and a range of piggeries – 'exceptionally good accommodation specially built for pedigree stock'. There were good quality grass-lands, 90 acres of arable and 21 acres of well-timbered woodland 'which affords good sporting'. 'Hunting may be had with Lord Leconfield's and the Crawley and Horsham Foxhounds'.

Ancillary holdings were Hampshires and Leyhold Farm, a small homestead with barn and sheds, and a pair of brick-built cottages – Leyland Cottages – formerly the farmhouse. In one field 'red sandstone is obtainable.' At Hole Farm, then in Pulborough village, was a 'picturesque old half-timbered cottage in black and white', a barn with threshing floor, a 6 horse stable and a 4 bay cattle shed. Additionally there were South Eaton Cottage, two other brick and timber dwellings (Weaver's and Burnt Row) and two five-roomed Ringwood Cottages.

These attractive sale particulars offer a picture of a well-to-do gentleman's estate just after the Great War, electrified but as yet largely unmechanised, but well equipped in traditional fashion for the enjoyment of mixed farming, high quality livestock and generously appointed as a prestigious rural seat for leisure and pleasure. The original building date of the house is unknown. It was modernised in 1831 when it was given a new brick front.

Subsequently it was up for sale again by auction in 1944 and 1966. Unsuccessful applications were made for various building developments at Tedfold Stud including one to build a by-pass and 300 houses in 1988.

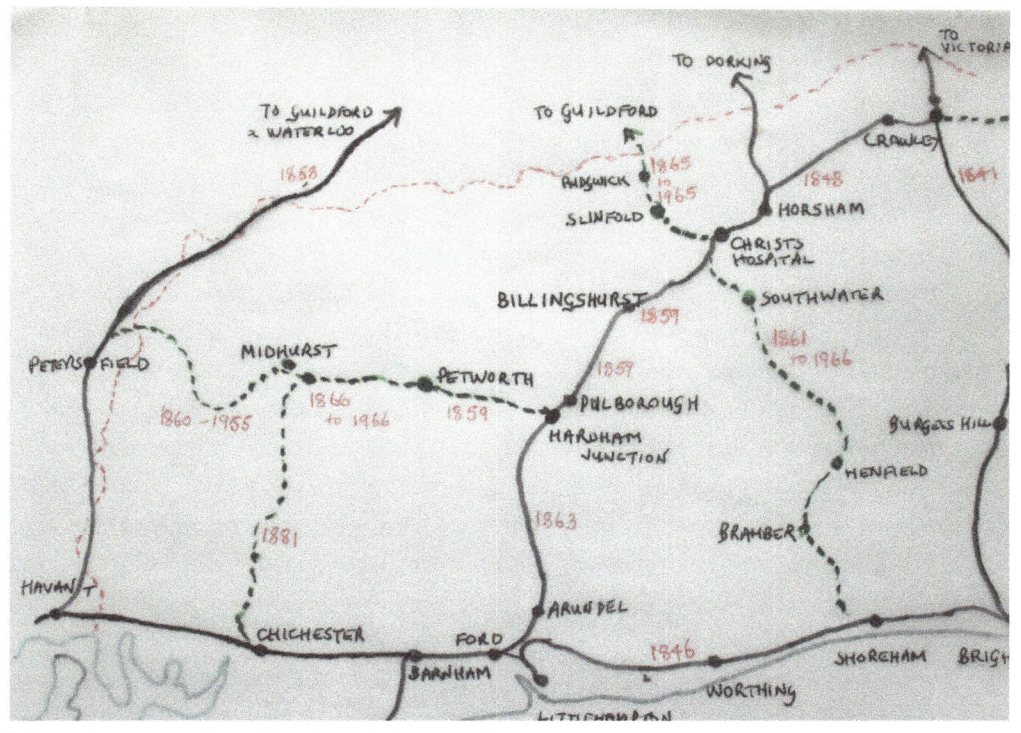

The railway network and lost branch lines

The Railway Network

The great British Railway Age was initiated in 1829 with Stephenson's Rocket and reached its frenetic climax nationwide about 1846 by then known as 'Railway Mania'. But in our geographical region the Railway Age flourished somewhat later, lasting for 100 years from the 1850s to the 1960s when Dr. Beeching's drastic recommendations were implemented and the network of branch lines that had grown up was mercilessly eradicated. The main factor which had made the railway uneconomic was the switch of freight from rail tracks to metalled roads. Lorries and buses ousted locomotives just as trains had replaced canal barges, even though passengers still made good use of the facility. At Billingshurst the railway service has continued, since the London-Portsmouth line has remained a strategic and economic necessity.

At first the only line from London to the south coast went from London to Brighton which was finished in 1841. In 1846 the London, Brighton and South Coast Railway Co. was formed as an amalgamation of five pre-existing enterprises. It had built a coastal branch line west from Brighton, first to Shoreham and then, circuitously, to Portsmouth. Shortly afterwards another rival company, the London and South Western Railway ran trains from London to Portsmouth through Surrey and Hampshire via Guildford and Godalming.

It was not until 1859 that serious progress was made on the third access, this time more directly to Portsmouth via Sussex, first to Horsham in 1848, next to Billingshurst and Hardham Junction in 1859. Four years later the line would push south, via Amberley and Arundel, to Ford Junction. (1863). This extension would link in to the coastal line already established westwards from Brighton via Chichester. Thus the first line south of Horsham through Billingshurst actually terminated on a spur to Petworth on what, subsequently, became a branch line to Midhurst.

Deborah Evershed catches the excitement of the very first steam engine to arrive at Adversane, which unloaded the household chattels for the new crossing-keepers' cottage (Thomas and Mary Smith) on October 10th 1859. A large crowd had assembled to wonder at this amazing occasion!

"Don't you go near it, George," Grandmother Deborah exclaimed …"It might blow up".

These three main lines survived Beeching's axe, but the branch lines which developed from the London-Horsham-Billingshurst-Ford line all succumbed.

The first of these ran from Hardham Junction by Fittleworth to Petworth in 1859 and on to Midhurst in 1866. North of Billingshurst another junction at Christ's Hospital allowed a new line linking West Grinstead, Henfield, Steyning and Shoreham (1861). The station itself was built between 1899 and 1902 when the school moved there from London. The Christ's Hospital junction caused yet another branch line to be built running north-west to Cranleigh via Slinfold, Rudgwick and Baynards. This line opened in 1856 and closed a100 years later, being adopted as part of the Link Way between The North and South Downs. Cyclists may still use part of the old railway from Christs Hospital through West Grinstead.

These local railway linkages were invaluable connections and in the days before sophisticated road transport and reliable roads they were welcomed by traders and farmers. They afforded ready routes to fresh markets, and also gave access to London and the seaside at acceptable prices and less expense of time to otherwise isolated people. A cheap day excursion from Billingshurst to the Crystal Palace, including admission, cost 4 shillings [20p], though cheap is a relative term. Most farm workers then would work for two whole days to earn that money. Before the trains came, coach fares were prohibitively expensive to ordinary folk. Mr. Thomas Ireland paid 10 shillings for a trip from Billingshurst to London in 1820, equivalent to some £40 today. When Mr. Pickwick was gadding about the country at that time Dickens' readers must have recognised in him a very wealthy gentleman.

The branch railways had become ridiculously uneconomic when Beeching made his report, and though today we might welcome having the routes back, it is questionable if we would try to reinstate the old service. Had the branch lines survived the 1960s the pattern of subsequent housing development in the region might have been quite different. It is the continued existence of the railway station that marks out Billingshurst as a 'sustainable location', so deemed by officialdom as vulnerable to further development.

In 1922 the two rival rail companies were amalgamated to form The Southern Railway, a company which was nationalised to become Southern Region of British Rail in 1948, only to be returned to private ownership by the Major government of 1993.

Billingshurst Station

The photographs from the footbridge, looking north, illustrate how the area has developed since 1922. Milk churns stand ready on the down line to go to the coast. Daux Road is a track to Great Daux Farm and beyond the platform are open fields.

View from railway bridge looking north

Recent view from same spot

In 2014 the antique Signal Box, erected in 1868 and a valued Grade II listed building, was moved away on a transporter to Amberley Chalkpits Museum. Part of the station building was demolished and the footbridge steps rerouted to allow for widening of the dangerous level-crossing.

At the crossing at Adversane a Gateman, George Piper, was still being employed until automatic barriers were installed in 1966.

Gatwick Airport

In 1957, the year the Weald School was opening, work was in progress turning an old RAF Station and former aerodrome and racecourse into Gatwick, London's second Airport. The world of the rabbit in Billingshurst was that year being rapidly depleted by myxamatosis but the human population was about to undergo rapid expansion, in no small measure as a result of the traffic of aircraft to and from world-wide destinations. Billingshurst is well-placed within the catchment area for staffing airport services so that much recent development of housing and light industry must be attributed directly or indirectly to the stimulus of air traffic. Pilots and cabin crew typically took up residence in restored labourers' cottages and new housing estates.

In many respects the airport has revolutionised and urbanised the lives of the people much as the steam train did in the 19th century, steam, smoke and cinders being only marginally more obtrusive than the roar of giant jets belching carbon dioxide and tracing vapour trails overhead. The coming of the railway transformed the distribution of consumer goods so that ordinary Victorian Billingshurst people could shop for such as Sheffield cutlery, burn coal, roof buildings with Welsh slate and enjoy products sourced round the Empire instead of depending almost entirely on things grown or made locally. They could afford a break and enjoy a plate of cockles at Bognor Regis too. Similarly the airport enabled a new and yet greater cosmopolitanism, bringing unfamiliar exotic foods, pasta, paella, pizza, tikka massala, won ton soup and 'genius' chicken wings. The chefs to prepare them came too in a more fluid society stimulated by international tourism and economic immigration. Billingshurst families ate paella and played golf on the Costa del Sol and drank wine and ate Camembert in Provence. Gardeners started to plant garlic and olive trees. Wine sales rocketed. In 1959 Gatwick handled some 368,000 passengers. Nowadays the annual figure averages about 33 million with up to 55 aircraft movements every hour from the single runway, nearly one a minute! Should a second runway be built there would be yet more development of housing in the village and the expansion of tourism, services and manufacturing.

Station Road Maltings and Whirlwind Limited

The old Malthouse in Station Road was owned by Mr. James King, (1824-84) maltster and corn dealer, who also had the maltings in the High Street. He lived in later life at Broomfield Lodge and had the wall built on his land which for many years formed the west boundary of the cricket field and is now embraced by the new recreational gardens. The Malthouse burnt down in 1883 but was soon rebuilt. The premises were taken over by Mr. N. Ray Stiles in the early 1920s and his company was eventually manufacturing over 400 Whirlwind Suction Sweepers a week. Further premises at the side were acquired for additional shops and offices. During WW II the factory made aluminium ammunition boxes. In 1947 Mr. Stiles sold the patent rights to what was only a moderately successful appliance, and the factory became Barralets (Pressform) Ltd. makers of water heaters, then Lorlins Electrical. Finally the whole lot was demolished and became Saville Gardens and residential accommodation.

The Old Wall

Printing in Billingshurst

From 1929 to 1941 Mr. Charles Tiller ran a printing business at Alick's Hill. He published a village news sheet up to the outbreak of war in 1939.

Oct. 3, 1936. — THE BILLINGSHURST NEWS. — 3

Streeter, K.O.M, (one of the founders of the Maple Leaf Lodge). Bro. Streeter said it was a great surprise to him to be asked to conduct the ceremony. He wished to thank their Worthy Chaplain for all the work he had done for the Lodge and the example he had shown to all brothers. Buffaloism had high ideals, and they would have to be supermen to carry them all out. One of the highest of their ideals was to elevate their brethren. The basis of the Order was charity. The Order numbered over seven million brethren in all parts of the world, and wherever a Buffalo went he would always find members to welcome him.

Bro. Gardiner thanked the brethren for their good wishes. He had enjoyed his visits to the Lodge and had met there men whom he might not have known otherwise. He well remembered on the occasion of the visit of another Lodge, one member coming up and asking him to shake hands as he had not shook hands before with a parson! The Maple Leaf Lodge had always been against anything that was lowering to the Order.

The Rev. Brother was given musical honours and cheers as he left the Lodge.

CHURCH SOCIAL.

All Parishioners (children under 16 excepted) are invited to meet the Rev. E. and Mrs. Streete at the Women's Hall on Monday evening next. Tea will be provided from 5 to 6.30 p.m.

FOOTBALL.

Billingshurst Wednesdays visited Arundel on September 23rd, and came home winners by four goals to nil. Phillips was the first to score with a long shot two-thirds to half way line up the field. Some minutes later a good pass from Hayes was taken by G. Voice, who scored a neat goal. "Mutt" also scored another goal soon after. Play was more even in the second half and D. Payne headed in the fourth goal from a good centre by R. Knight.

The K.O. Cup tie on the 30th was against Petworth (at Newbridge Road), who have been champions of the League for four years and are the Cup-holders. Billingshurst were up against a fine and fast combination, but held their own fairly well until after the interval. Petworth then scored a quick goal almost from the kick-off. Billingshurst attacked, and Pierce headed into the net from close up. The goal was dis-allowed for off-side, wrongly in our opinion. This rather made the homesters dispirited, and two more goals from Petworth put paid to the

---

Trinity Congregational Church,
BILLINGSHURST.

MONDAY, OCTOBER 5th, at 7.30.
RE-OPENING OF
TABLE TENNIS CLUB.
October—April.   Subscription 2/-.

THURSDAY, OCTOBER 8th, at 7.15.
OPENING OF
TRINITY GUILD.
October—March.   Subscription 1/-.

SATURDAY, OCTOBER 10th, at 3.
ANNUAL RUMMAGE SALE.
ADMISSION 1d.
All Gifts gratefully received.

TRACTOR FOR HIRE.
(WITH PRIZE PLOUGHMAN.)
ALL FARM WORK UNDERTAKEN,
including Sawbench Work.

Terms on application to
CULLEN, Grainingfold, Billingshurst.
Phone: BILLINGSHURST 50.

We can undertake Printing of any kind.
CHARLES W. W. TILLER,
The Printing Works, Billingshurst.

Billingshurst News – Ancient Order of Buffaloes

Village Memories

Things that have changed in Billingshurst since I can remember

Written by Mrs. G. Maria Ireland, who was born at Billingshurst Vicarage, May 5th 1837, the year of Queen Victoria's accession to the throne.

The Curfew Bell was rung at 5 am and 8 pm for a quarter of an hour from November 2nd to February 2nd. There was no policeman. An old man (watchman) walked about during the night.

A four-horse coach from Worthing to London came through the village and changed horses at the King's Arms every day. Vans went to and fro to London for grocery etc. Coal, Flints and all heavy goods came by barge on the canal to Newbridge, where lime-burning was carried on.

A small stream ran in the village between the pavement and the road from the Rising Sun [now long gone] to the Blacksmiths Shop. Mops were dipped in it.

There were two nursery gardens, one from Townland to the Rising Sun, used by Philip Puttock who left the money for bread to the poor. The other from the Baptist Chapel yard to the Wheelers Corner, was used by John Alman whose son John died in 1844. His favourite tree, a cedar, was planted to his memory in the Churchyard near the East Gate. [In 1978, a large tree at the east end of the church was felled by a gale].

There were two windmills, one on the hill by the lane near the Six Bells, burned down November 5th 1852, the other Hammonds Mill, the top blown off.

There was a pond and waste ground on Alex Hill where osiers were cut and stripped by the village women.

The Church was altered in 1866. Before that there were high pews all along the west entrance, with a three-decker pulpit by the middle pillar. There was no organ or harmonium but a Bass Viol, Flutes and other instruments, the metrical psalms being sung and a few hymns. The second service was held in the afternoon and no lamps were needed.

The Sunday School was held in a building attached to what is now the Lady Chapel, since pulled down when the Church was altered, used only as a Vestry and a Day School, when there was one. The Churchyard was enlarged about this time.

The Railway was begun in 1833 [sic. 1855 intended?]. At that time there was no house along the fields walk from the Vicarage to Kingsfold, except the farmhouses at Broomfields and Dawks and no road through from Alex Hill to Nats Lane.

The new Vicarage was built in 1858/9. The old one was on the same spot, facing north. The Hilly, Blacksmiths' Fields, the meadow and fields on the north side of the road by the shop was Vicarage ground.

Paraffin or Petroleum was not known. Candles were used, moulds and dips, some rushlights (pith of rushes dipped in fat). I once saw flint and steel used for striking a light. Tinder was used to catch the sparks and then small thin chips dipped each end in brimstone put to the sparks to make a flame.

Photography was unknown, and some people had their profiles cut in black paper. There were no bicycles or telegrams. There were three turnpike gates on the road to Horsham, one after Five Oaks, one at Lyons Corner and one this side of Broadbridge Heath which was then Common Ground. Dogs were used to draw carts. Fish was brought from Worthing drawn by four or five dogs.

[Rushlights were partially peeled rushes with the pith soaked in melted tallow. They burnt at the rate of an inch every two minutes. Tradition is maintained in 2016. A Hastings fishmonger still sells his fish van every week in the Library car park.]

Billingshurst Jottings by Ruth Kelleher

Ruth was born at the turn of the 19th Century

I don't think that many people know that our first library was in a hall at the back of the Baptist Chapel. When I went to borrow books I got to know the Librarian, a Miss Weeks, who lived in cottage at the entrance who showed me the little chapel. In the next cottage we met for meetings of the YWCA.

Across the road in Price's meadow we always had the bonfire and fireworks until the Misses Beck bought it and had the Women's Hall built

We had penny readings, so called, for a weekly variety show, all the local talent. One man always brought the house down when he came on stage in a Sussex 'cowgown' and sang Sussex songs. The Village Hall was always packed. One show I remember was Hiawatha. My eldest sister took the part of an Indian girl, never knowing that she would marry and go and live in Canada.

Courtney Laker had an orchestra; my brother played the violin in it, and there were always dances. We went to what was once a market hall in Myrtle Lane at the back of the Station Hotel. The music was provided by Len Voice on a cornet and by his future wife on the piano, which we all enjoyed.

Coronation Parade, High St. 1911

We went to all the fairs and shows. The first one was in the Jubilee Meadow at Little Daux, to celebrate King Edward's Coronation. We had sports and a nice tea and we all wore a medal.

Mr. Towner farmed at Rosier. I remember we picked cowslips in one of his meadows. Daux Wood was our delight when we gathered bluebells and other flowers and went blackberrying. Where the bungalows are now in Daux Avenue was our way to the woods. We danced in a fairy ring and gathered heaps of mushrooms there.

When we came to Billingshurst there was just one little post office in the High Street, one grocer, one draper, one baker and two butchers. We must have been good customers since at Christmas the grocer gave my mother a bottle of port; the baker gave a cake and the butcher 2lbs of his nice pork sausages. The butchers used to kill their own animals and all the boys used to go to watch.

Mr. Voice had a grocer's shop at the station and we went there to buy his nice lardy rolls. Across the road was a shop where we bought eggs at a shilling a dozen from free range hens in the field where Keatings is now.

Memories of Mrs. M.E. Marten, 1 Daux Avenue, born 1864 (abridged)

The village street had paving stones of all shapes and sizes. [In the High street lived] the Vetinary surgeon who was always called the farrier. Further up the road was the harness-maker; he had a long garden where there was a rope walk, and a man with a bundle of hemp in front of him could be seen walking up and down from post to post making a rope. Opposite lived a Currier in a shed close to the footpath putting the finishing touches to big pieces of leather. After the present Congregational Chapel was built the old one in the Jengers Meadow, an octagonal building which reminded one of a huge summer house, was used for Sunday School and entertainments called 'penny readings'. The Post Office was at a little shop at the beginning of the Church Causeway. At the top of Osier Hill was a pond, quite close to the road. This, at certain times of the year, was filled with osiers which were used for making baskets.

The old Congregational Chapel and Meadow House, Jengers Meadow

I also remember the brickfields in the Wildens. They were called 'The Potteries' and I well remember seeing flower pots made there as well as bricks in my very early days. Where the Post Office and the other new buildings now stand there was a meadow with a low brick wall upon which men used to sit and chat together about the affairs of the village.

Memories of Billingshurst- Tom Topper

Extracted from a talk with Mr. Mike Coxon, slightly abridged. Tom Topper was born in 1912. He had six brothers and two sisters. He came to Billingshurst in 1918, the end of the Great War and the year of the great flu epidemic

We lived near the Station, opposite the cricket field. The houses at the bottom of Station Road where the grocer and garden shops are now, used to be one big house. [Hereford House]. Then came the original houses and next a block of houses where the Malt House had been sited. Then there were two cottages and Brookers Road, beyond which were three or four more houses and Saville House (now Saville Gardens). An old man who lived at the Station used to come out on Armistice Day and blow the 'Last Post'. We kept two minutes silence. It was not organised – he just liked to do it.

Where there are now flats and a bungalow, which lies back a little, there used to be a big house, Saville House, occupied by Admiral Holmes. They had a big apple tree – I know because I scrumped the apples many times.

Beyond there was only hedge and field until you reached the Lodge (to Cleveland House), which is still there. They had conker trees all the way up the drive to the big house, which no longer exists. Then there was an empty field, and on that as you came down Alick's Hill, on the right, there was a wagon shed. (Carpenters is named after it [sic. This is a mistaken belief]). I remember the shed had a lovely beam across the middle, so you could hang from your feet.

On the hot summer days the steam trains used to catch the fields alight. We kids would say, 'The field's alight!' and rush out and stamp it out.

There was a shop at the Station, the post office and village shop. They had a taxi service with a Model T Ford. The driver would stand in the station saying 'taxi, taxi' and then he would run across to his brother in the sheds at the back and say, 'Jack her up, Percy, and get the handle going', because you always jacked up a Model T to start it. During the war the Canadian soldiers came and had the taxi, just for the sheer fun. They couldn't believe their eyes. This old thing must have been 20 years old before the war started!

People would take a taxi to Wisborough Green or Kirdford, for example, but if it was local they would only have the horses and trap. When it came by we kids would slip up behind without them seeing us and sit on the back axle. People coming along and seeing us sitting there would shout, 'Whip behind, Guvnor!'

We used to call the coaches 'charabancs' that came through the village. As they came over the hill we would call, 'Throw out your rusty coppers'. They were going to Goodwood races. Goodwood was a big week with lots of traffic and we could collect several pennies. The police stopped it. Kids were running all over the road amongst the traffic though it was only doing about 25 mph.

When there were police speed traps the AA man would stand in the road further down, so that members not receiving the usual salute from him, would know and slow down. This sort of warning was quite legal. Often a trap would be set just outside the village. The best local bobby we had was Sgt. Dutton who was here just after the war. [The AA men also worked at Five Oaks corner in Goodwood Weeks].

Not far from where we lived were the gas Works at the bottom of Groomsland

Drive. My brother, Bert, used to work there after the war in the mid-fifties, but when North Sea Gas came they were closed down, although the site is still there and they still use the pipes and controls.

As you go through Parbrook from Station Road, you pass the school playing fields and then, just before you reach the first of the new houses, there used to be a very old one with oak beams. My aunt lived in it, but when I was about 14 they knocked it down. Great Grooms was where the Jenny Wren Restaurant is now [currently a private house]. There is a footpath across the fields by the school, coming out by those new houses and when we were children we'd walk across to get skimmed milk from the farm. We always knew the direction from the whining noise of the separator, which sounded right across the field. [Cream separators were well established before WW 1 but milking machines, though invented in 1904, were adopted only very slowly].

Hillview garage was just one side of the road, the east, and was owned by Mr. Merrikin. Ted, his son, runs it now [recently redeveloped as private housing].

The original Hillview Garage

Where the Junior School is there used to be one big field running right down to the railway – as far as where the bowling green is – and then one awkward shaped field to square it off before the line. It was a lovely sight to see it being ploughed; two teams of horses, one going down, one up and the men walking behind them. At harvest time it would be stacked up with stooks and sheaves for the horses and wagons to come and pick up.

Then as you come further down Alick's Hill there was another orchard – I knew where all the orchards were! At the bottom two or three houses which are still there, and then, next to Badgers, on the other side of the bus drive was a baker's shop. It stood a little back from the road, and I used to work there as a boy.

The bake house itself was just at the back where Billingshurst Coaches are now [presently retirement homes]. Behind was an open field with a footpath to the Church and a pond.

As you go up the High Street there was a corn merchant's...not far from the Unitarian Church. Barclays Bank was an ironmonger's, but the slaughterhouse is still behind the butchers [now redeveloped]. As a lad I used to watch them kill the bullocks. After the war it was used for only pigs and sheep. Then come the King's Arms and Six Bells, and next to that, where a Building Society is now, was Miss. Laker's house. One of the rooms was used as a dental surgery. The dentist came out from Horsham on Tuesdays and Thursdays. West's has been a confectioners for years, but the Post Office used to be a barn. A farthings worth of sweets bought as much as 15p now [? 50p].

They used to play football on the Jengers then. There was no shopping precinct, but fields stretching away from the old white house and the red brick one, on whose site the old Congregational Church once stood. There was no Coombe Hill, and a footpath ran across the fields to Tedfold and finally to Rowner. It does still, but starts later because of the housing estates.

Turning up East Street from the High Street everything on the left is new until you come to the red-tiled farmhouse, Gore Farm, where the steam engines are [Lugg's Yard]. Up School Lane there are some old cottages; the one on the right hand side has been knocked down and the other rebuilt. Those on the left are still the same. At Hammonds, where Dr. Kilsby lived, there used to be a Mr. Trower and his two sisters. This old house was a farm once. I remember passing it in the evenings and seeing it lit by oil lamps. Just past it are the remains of the old mill. You could see the basic shape.

East Street rises fairly sharply from the High Street. The coal wagon used to go up pulled by a horse. There was always an iron shoe dragging behind one wheel so that if the cart slid backwards it would run into the shoe and be braked. The hill used to curve right round to the Church. At the top, where the Vicarage car park is now, there was a cafe. The old cottages, Rose and Chime are still there. Mr. Rhodes started his shoe business in the front room of one of them. Then, of course, came Gratwick Manor, with only fields between it and the Catholic Church.

To get to School Lane from Station Road we used to walk up the Church Path. At the bottom of the hill below the school was common land – The Bowling Alley. This was a great place when it was snowing. We used to slide down on tin trays.

Beyond the Catholic Church, by a big house called 'Trees', on the right was Red Lane where they used to play football. [Jubilee Meadow] The lane goes down to the Railway, past Little Daux Farm. I spent a lot of time in Daux Wood. In those days there were lots of brown squirrels, who nested in the oak trees. We used to climb up, take one of the babies and bring it home for a pet. We'd put him in a wheel like a gerbil and he would play in it.

One day when I was going through the woods a bird flew in front of me, looking as if it had a broken wing – so I ran after it, but once it had taken me far enough away it few off normally. I wondered why it had led me astray, flying a limping flight, just few yards ahead of me, so I retraced my steps, and sure enough, there was its nest with young in it.

In those days people had to make their own fun. Cricket was one amusement, and men came from far away to spend weekends playing here. There was no organised team for young people, but you could always go down on practice nights, and if you'd helped clear the ground of plantain weed, you'd be allowed to play while the team was practising.

Bonfire night was the big event, and as villages go, ours was a huge one, bringing in thousands to see it, one of the biggest in Sussex apart from Lewes. They used to build it where the Junior School is now. We were living at Hillview Cottage then and had a fine view. One year (1937) someone set it alight about three evenings before the night; but Colonel Drew came and said we would have one all the same, by hook or by crook. The farmers rallied round with tractors loaded with stuff. They had another bonfire built in two days flat, put an all-night guard on it, and ran electricity to it over the fence from our house. There was a Bonfire Society when I was a kid and the torch-light procession was quite intense and frightening. We used to watch it from the top of Alick's Hill where there was a high bank. The procession would wind down through Parbrook and past the Station, calling at all the pubs. They had fireworks and torches which they had made weeks before, at the back of the King's Head, their Headquarters.

When I was married I was earning only £2 a week and paying 1s-6d rent, and money seemed as short then as now. A new house probably cost £300! A trip to Littlehampton was terrific and one went to London once in a lifetime. No cars for us. We used to cycle everywhere. Street lighting was gas, and homes had it as well or, if not, oil lamps. But it was a great life all the same.

[Note: The Bowling Alley was not, properly speaking, Common Land, but an important footpath link from a Duckmore in the High Street to another Duckmore house near the present house of that name at Wooddale.]

Madeleine Woods also tells more of Tom Topper. His friend Cecil Rhodes' father the cobbler in East Street, also served as village lamplighter. He was so skilled at judging the distance from chain and stick that he lit the whole High Street without getting off his bicycle. Tom came from a family of 7 boys and 2 girls, headed by a fiery naval stoker. The Toppers supplemented their diet with nettle tops for greens, dandelion leaves and wild mushrooms. They had their hair cut for 3d a trim at Parbook and collected acorns to get 3d a bushel at Blunden's corn store in the High Street. The Miss Puttocks at Cleveland House provided their school caps and Major Renton gave them new boots at Christmas. At 13 Tom's friend Cecil was working for his father collecting boots from the grand houses where the cooks often treated him to a 'below stairs' meal. Tom's first job was fetching water and faggots for Lusted's bakery where he learnt the baker's skills. When he married he lived at Hillview Cottage paying 12/6d a week out of a £2 wage packet. There he caught rats by luring them into a dustbin and dropping the lid from a string suspended above. In those days you went to the Doctor's, with your shilling up front, sitting in the corridor of the Rose Hill surgery. Tom ran 'threepenny socials' at the Women's' Hall and used the collection to bake for and lay on a slap-up reception at the King's Arms Function Room for an unfortunate lady who 'had to get married'. This was so popular that he turned it into a regular weekend business launching Billingshurst couples into married life. Tom served on ten village committees including the Parish Council, Horticultural Society and School managers. Cecil Rhodes was 30 years with the Fire Brigade, 25 years as chief, rescuing cats from trees and pumping out water from High Street premises which flooded regularly until remedial work was undertaken.

Peter Stockwood remembers

Peter was a Weald School boy and has been 40 years at the School as Caretaker and now Premises Manager.

"I remember being caned by Mr. Gee for scrumping apples – "two strokes on hand, keep your thumb back" and how the bad boys would be marched back to his classroom as a further warning to other evil-doers. There was a terrific hailstorm in 1963 that dented all the green copper sheeting on the school roof. 6 oz hailstones, well over 2 inches across, fell from a tornado. Houses damaged and trees uprooted. Up at High Seat Nurseries Mr. And Mrs Hobson lost every pane of glass!

I used to see Diana Dors when I was a little boy at the Six Bells, then slim and glamorous with her red American sports car. I used to see Jimmy Edwards, the comedian, in the village too.

My school friend David Roberts slipped and fell into the flooded river at Newbridge and tragically drowned in 1959. The day before he had been selling goose feathers at the East Street School for a penny each.

I knew every tree in the orchard with a footpath running through where the Library car park stands. Mrs. Laker had apples, pears, plums and quinces and hazelnuts and lived in the High Street where the tobacconist's shop is now. The oak tree is still there.

Mr Cripps' the butcher's daughter owned a famous show-jumper pony called Stroller. They used to have gymkhanas just outside the village and kept the horses where Lakers Meadow is now. Marion Mould got Silver at the 1968 Olympics on Stroller. I read they won 61 international events.

When I was a boy I had a two hour paper round every morning all down West Street and out to Newbridge, then Lordings Road and Adversane, with lots of side turnings. Hard work in all weathers, snow, floods and storms.

I've long been an officer of the Angling Society and I've been all over the world diving and watching fish sub-aqua. Young Harry Enfield used to toddle down to watch us fishing at Rowner. I've seen him on TV shoulder a back-pack the way he saw us with our fishing bags"

Items of interest

In 1891 land south of East Street was purchased by Mr. E.T. Norris who had additions to Gratwicke House by his friend, Sir Edward Lutyens. Gratwicke Park was the venue for large fairs and, during the 1914-18 war used for the resting of cavalry detachments on their journey to Flanders battlefields. During WW II Gratwicke was commandered by the military authorities for a Home Guard Headquarters from Colonel and Mrs. Dudley-White, who had bought the property from Mr. Norris's soldier son in 1923.

In the early 1930s Mr. Hugh Maille bought part of Gratwicke parkland on which the present Catholic Church stands – a memorial to his daughter.

April 1982: ' There was great interest, indeed great excitement, when it was learned last month that the Southern Counties Garage had put in a planning application to demolish the garage, showrooms and workshops and the post office, and erect a large building incorporating a supermarket in their place'. [In the event the Post Office building stayed and a new office counter opened in Jengers Mead and Budgen's Supermarket was built]. In 2015 it was redesigned as a Sainsbury's Local.

Post Office and Budgens Supermarket

The old Village Hall was given to the village by the Rev. J Stanley and opened in 1906. Trustees included Rev. Stanley, Dr. Hubert and Mr. Joseph Luxford. Later an annexe was built to house a boys club. In 1939 the Education Authority booked the Hall for school purposes. Out of school hours it was used as a forces canteen and a Drill Hall for the Home Guard.

The Old Village Hall, High Street

Original Trustees of the Old Village Hall

The New Village Hall, now called the Community Centre, was officially opened on 30th January 1991. In that same year two other events of importance occurred. The new Doctors' Surgery opened in Roman Way and the Billingshurst Junior

School moved from East Street to Station Road. To mark the latter occasion the children made a symbolic march in Victorian costume.

The New Village Hall and Community Centre

Inside the Community Centre

Billingshurst surgery, Roman Way

Here is a report of a get-together at the Women's Hall in 1937. "The Social Evening on Thursday last, run by the Dinky Boys was a huge success…Games and competitions were organised by the Minister and Mr. Helsdon and were indulged by young and old. The great feature of the evening was a humorous item by the Dinky Boys which caused hearty laughter. Songs were given by Mr. Gravett and Mr. M. Harwood. Ronnie Radbourne gave a cornet solo and Mr. H. Morris told us some humorous yarns. Mr. Percy Wadey accompanied on the piano".

1999 - Billingshurst Millennium Map. "Chairman, John Hurd is working and reworking the actual map and Wendy Lines has compiled a draft list of Buildings to be included. She (Madeleine Woods) is to co-ordinate a growing team of artists (14 to date) to sketch out their ideas and paint in specific colours on the oak leaf corniches". (Madeleine Woods)

In 1940 the Sisters of the Immaculate Heart of St. Mary came to Billingshurst. Their Convent School at Newhaven had been damaged by bombing. They were first at the Corner House, Adversane, moved on to High Fure and in 1945 acquired Summers Place. There some 60 boarders and 200 day pupils formed a flourishing school which lasted until 1984.

William Evershed, who founded the Baptist Chapel with William Turner was born in 1717 near Lewes, and had no education except for reading. He was hired out as a farmer's boy but his ambitious nature overcame all his handicaps. He preferred Theology, Ecclesiastical, civil and Natural History subjects. It is recorded in his autobiography that, when following the oxen drawing the plough, he would have his task pinned to his shirtsleeve so that he could improve his mind at the same time that he was faithfully performing his duty to his master. In 1742 he took Great Daux Farm.

Elizabeth Carter, nee Evershed noted about another William Evershed, (1754 -1824):- [He] wore two fleecy nightcaps and then wrapped his head in a pillowcase. He wore a wig, so did his father and grandfather, but none of his brothers. Thomas Evershed (1680 – 1765) used to come to Billingshurst Meeting House wearing a cotton wig with one or two rows of little curls all round. John wore a bushy wig not a curly one. William wore curly one, large curls that he used to roll round his finger – his real hair was light brown.

The name Daux was current in 1369 in the name of Wiliam Daukes and it was also the name of Alice Dawkes who held one and a half virgates and a tenement called Crouchers in 1327. In 1400 there is a record of a William Dakons of Coucheslond. In Tudor times the name is variously spelt Daks when John Grynfyld bought it, and in Churchwardens accounts it appears as Daulkes (1563), Dawlks (1592) and Daukes again in 1630. In the will of John Sturt (1650) it is spelt Dawks but from then on it appears as Daux throughout the 18th century. Nevertheless the census of 1851 and that of ten years later has it as Dauks once more. Another authority writing about Great and Little Daux (pronounced Dorks) explains the word as 'Duhchae's hook of land', from the Old English Duhchaen hoc, written as Douwehok in 1296, Dawks in 1795 and Dorks in 1823.

St, Mary's Church Tower and Nave date from the early 13th Century. Subsequent additions are:-
Lady Chapel – c 1230
South Aisle - c 1280
North Aisle - c 1430
Spire 15th century
Porch rebuilt in 16th century
New clock   -   1800
Weather vane – c 1812.

The arms of the Garton family – three silver staves tied with a gold ribbon on a black shield – are on two of the church roof bosses. The Gartons, possibly originally from Yorkshire, had lands in Sussex in the 15th century and were probably enriched from the iron industry. Thomas Garton was vicar in 1478 and William, who died in 1560, was Churchwarden. In 1535 he was Steward of the Manor of Bassett's Fee which he subsequently purchased from Thomas Wroth who was gifted it by Queen Elizabeth. William's son Francis, 'Gentleman', became Mayor of Arundel twice. In 1588 he gave £30 to the Sussex Gentry Fund to help defend England against the Spanish Armada. The Manor then passed to Thomas Henshaw, a Royalist in Charles I's time, then his son Philip. After him was Thomas Tipping from Berkshire. His heir, Mary Anne, his niece, married Philip Wroughton. They sold to Collins who sold to Mr. Clear.

The Bongards of Wisborough Green were celebrated glassmakers until 1618. Isaac Bungar bought timber for his furnaces in Billingshurst and probably retired to a cottage in West Chiltington Lane called Horelands. Richard Greenfield, possibly the one who bought Clarks Land in 1645 and John Penfold of the family that once owned Kingsfold, were witnesses to the purchase deed in 1651.

Village worthies:-
Nathanial Short, weaver and Parish Clerk, paid £1 – 10s a year, 4 times married
William Frye, Vicar in the reign of Edward III
Old Ephrain Cooper, died aged 80, worth £58 in 1669, farmed Pounds, near Okehurst

George Hoare 75

Charles Pannell 79

Three village characters, Will Richards 74

John Gravett, 1530 paid 'to the light of Our Lady and St. Peter a cow for 10s, to be delivered to the Churchwardens'. Witnesses to a document dated 5th

Jan 1365 were Thomas Gyleman [Gilmans], William at Hull [?], Richard Somer [Summers] and Adam Goore [? Gore Farm].

Two cottages in West Street on the north side were so low that that someone leaning out of the bedroom window could shake hands with a person on the ground below. They were occupied by the Truelove family and known as 'The Bank of England'. Ambrose Truelove was the village chimney sweep. They are sadly long gone. Two Trueloves are named on the village War Memorial

We understood at the time of purchase that the building was Tudor, but have since learned that it, with the next door cottage, constitutes a Sussex Wealden House and dates from the late 14th or early 15th century! They are now listed Grade II and to think they were allowed to become derelict! [beside the Causeway] (Hilda Barton).

How many of you remember the floods in Billingshurst in the 1970s? My garden was inundated, and at 5 a.m. I was out in Stane Street rescuing my Grobags which were floating off to Pulborough! (Michael Smith)

Floods, 2nd June, 1981. A little old lady, Miss Williams, lived in the cottage beside the Baptist Chapel path. 'Her living room carpet disintegrated and her piano fell apart. Her neighbours had a summerhouse. When it flooded the water floated it over the hedge onto her lawn where it rested like a Noah's Ark. her. "That's not mine. I don't know where that came from!" (Michael Smith)

Tues. 2.6.81 'Two heavy thunderstorms. The Six Bells had water up to the ceiling. School trips to the Downs were cancelled. The buses were needed to ferry passengers as the stations were closed. Mr. Edgar rowed up and down the new lake in his canoe. (Paul Smith)

Verena Bristow, aged 81 in 1982, was born in one of the three cottages known as 'Weavers', now demolished, down a lane opposite The Smithy, which is now Mole Country Stores, on the Newbridge road to Wisborough Green. She then lived in Bell cottage behind the Six Bells.

Geoffrey Rhodes is the fourth generation of 'snobs' or bootmenders in Billingshurst. There could be a day when Rhodes and Son are no more. Geoff laments, "It's a dying trade. We can't get the materials. Lasting tack, brass tacks – we have to ask the manufacturers to hunt around the dusty corners of their warehouses. Modern shoes are machine loaded. Tanned leather is very difficult to get hold of and very expensive and oak bark leather is discontinued. No-one is taught about bends and butts and how to buy and select any more". Fortunately that day is not yet. The shelves are packed with footwear of every shape and size.

Clare Luckin, the 'Billingshurst Egg Lady' styles herself "The Reluctant Farmwife". She writes of milking the cows on a three-legged stool, of the awful smell of the three goats that ruined her roses. "Whenever the wind was in the right direction I had to shut all the windows. In due course (the billy's) actions bore fruit and we had four baby goats scampering about the place on their thimble-size hooves". She wrote of the one that escaped and destroyed the Doctor's dahlias and the large and unpredictable horses, bought for the children, none of whom took to riding. "My husband heard a rumour that the Indian restaurants, which were just becoming established in the area, used rabbit, named as chicken in their menus and that the local market paid well for them. In due course the shed became wall-to-wall hutches…they needed cleaning out every few days…I put a stop to that project on the grounds that I had enough cleaning to do with my own family without having a similar task with the rabbits…We have had pigs too, and of course, chicken, bantams and ducks – one hundred and fifty of them at one time, but I endure them for their excellent product, and one does not have to have a relationship with them, only one's regular egg customers, which is the best product of animals that I can think of".

Hoops were used for barrels for the fishing trade. Whole trainloads would leave Billingshurst Station for the northern fishing ports. They were also used for barrels for sugar, glass, pottery etc. and the smaller size for tea chests. The industry declined during WWI and the years after and wood hoops had been superseded by metal ones. The hoop shed was demolished by a gale in 1949.

Billingshurst in the 1880s always had its Corn Market, held in the King's Arms in the Market Room, still in existence, and a great deal of local trade was done before the advent of railways. (Phyllis Adam)

Frederick Mursell, 1930s Fish Salesman, advertises his goods in Charles Tiller's Newspaper:-
There's Haddock, Herring, Bloater, aye, and Kipper,
Such as will suit a hearty English skipper,
And tempting sole, or eels to make a "pie"
With perhaps Rock Salmon in my basket lie,
And Cod and Whiting with some other fish,
Await inspection – please bring out your dish!
P.S. For your "Cats" I've always bits and scraps.

W.A Shepherd, Universal Supply Stores, Church Gate advertises his beers:-
Elephant Brand Ale, or Stout and Oatmeal Stout 2/6 per dozen, net
Pilsener Lager Beer 3/- a dozen net
Fremlin's Family Ales and Stouts
All our beers (lager excepted) are bittered entirely with English hops.

Died on 14th March, 1849. W. Wadey, a carpenter of Billingshurst, aged 90. For many years he attended a dissenting place of worship 9 miles from his residence and lately he often walked 14 miles to a place of worship. He married May Holden in 1788, now 83. She brought him 11 children, 9 of whom are still living. He had 69 grandchildren living and 14 died. Eight young men, husbands of his granddaughters, bore him to his grave.

At the entrance to Dell Lane there used to be a large pond known as the Holy Well where people came to pay and seek cures. It was filled in by the developers.

The Church Path has no owner. Apparently it is 'no man's land', or perhaps Common Land. It belongs to the people of the Parish. It was properly call Holy Well Lane. Brenda Twine recalled the 'small tree hung pond' at the end of the path, subsequently filled in, which was the Holy Well.

Church Path from Station Road

The Green with Wealden House circa 1400 AD'

The Local History Society, guided by John Hurd, excavated a trench across the Roman Road at Parbrook in 1984 in conjunction with the Horsham Museum Society. The present road had been rerouted to the east, probably to avoid flooding and the site used for agriculture or waste. They dug a 6 foot X 66 trench. Beneath the overlying topsoil was the last road surface of flint, ironstone and clay, second was a possible mediaeval road surface of ironstone and clay, next the possible Roman foundations of large ironstone blocks laid on natural clay. This constituted the 'agger' which made use of a by-product of the local iron industry. It must have been in continuous use in this alignment at least until the end of the 16th century before the iron industry died out. The archaeologists had access to only one of the customary side ditches dug by the Romans. It was filled with clay and covered as part of the road thereafter. The road was estimated as being 10.2 metres wide, flanked by a wide and flat unmetalled surface.

"I worked at The Maltings in 1922/3 in the kitchen in the morning and a waitress in the afternoon. A plate of assorted cakes and a pot of tea was 10d a head. I worked from 8 a.m. to 6 p.m. for 7/6d a week. I remember a party of racegoers going home from Goodwood left a tip for 7/6d – a whole week's wages!" (Dora Allum).

"But we come to the countryside to see nature", they say. You won't see much nature in West Sussex. Almost wherever you look the landscape has been cut, dug, shaped and managed by Man. In fact if a farmer were to allow his farm to revert to nature, those same country-lovers would soon be complaining about 'that disgusting weed-covered eyesore' (John Richards)

Murders in Billingshurst

Miss Susan Lee, a student in the Lower Sixth Form at the Weald was killed with a knife by an employee of a local restaurant in 1978.
During the 1950s there was a double murder and suicide in the Argent family at Goldings Farm, Five Oaks which was subsequently renamed Oak House.
On Christmas Day, 2014, Jan and Julia Tshabalala were found dead in Groomsland Drive. Verdicts of Unlawful Killing and Suicide were returned.

Gardening and Horticulture

In all likelihood the very first Saxon settlers in Billingshurst built their simple dwellings on the small patches of alluvial and loamier soils they found beside the stream that rose from the Bowling Alley on land around about the present site of Lloyds Bank. The basic clay soils elsewhere would have discouraged tillage. Though they were fertile they were heavy to work in winter, liable to rot seeds in spring and apt to turn solid and crack in summer. The best prospects were alongside the Roman Road beside the stream. New Stone Age Celts probably tilled those soils. However recent evidence of Iron Age and Roman cultivation east of the road suggests that early Saxons too might have made some use of that area for a while. The scant population of the Low Weald was assessed, from Domesday Book evidence by historian Michael Wood, as between 2 and 5 per square mile and many of those people would have been transients, drovers, foragers and hunters on seasonal trips from the coastal manors. There the population was 20 + per sq. mile.

The early Ordnance Survey maps show how nurseries had developed south of Townland once run by Phillip Puttock and at (Lewkener's) Luckin's Garden on the opposite side of the High Street. To the south between the present sites of the Congregational Church and the Baptist Chapel where Croft Villas stand there were yet more nurseries with good fertile soils kept by John Allman the seedsman. All these plots of fertile soil, cultivated for hundreds of years now lie buried beneath houses, roads and other buildings erected since Victorian times. Elsewhere cottagers have grown their vegetable and tended their flower gardens with pride in their self-sufficiency. Fruit trees, raspberries, blackcurrants, roses and honeysuckle all flourish on the clay. Private enterprise has offered well-maintained allotments east of Little East Street. As late as 1972, High Seat Nurseries were still advertising themselves as Geranium specialists and offering cut flowers, 'particularly Iceland Poppies'. The Billingshurst Allotments Society was formed in 2009 and as a consequence the Parish Council has provided for new public allotments at Manor Fields. The Joyes, and their successors, the Watts, sold seeds and garden sundries for many years from their emporium at Hereford House by the Station. They were major suppliers of agricultural seed corn. Austin's Hardware store still supports Billingshurst gardeners.

Billingshurst Horticultural Society

In the Flower Show marquee 1969. Suited judges with Joe Kingston and John Sutton

On 6th September 1882 the village schoolchildren were given an extra holiday as there was to be a 'Flower Show' at 'Somers Place', courtesy of Mr. R. Goff. The Royal Sussex Militia Band was in attendance 'at the seat of Mr. Gough' as *The Horsham Advertiser* had it. So began the oldest village club, the Billingshurst Horticultural Society. The emphasis, in Class I, despite the title, was heavily on vegetables, with a few classes for fruit and flowers and a single one for honey. Cheerfully accepting of class distinctions, Class II section read:- 'Prizes to be competed for by Inhabitants, their gardeners or servants, occupying premises of more than £6 per annum'.

Only a few joint shows with Wisborough Green, Loxwood and Kirdford were attempted until the new century. There was one at Barkfold, Kirdford in 1884 and another in Billingshurst in 1887 at Summers. Unfortunately it rained all afternoon, disheartening the organisers, and no more shows graced Billingshurst until 1903. Mr. James Hall Renton then lent Rowfold Grange as the venue and was made President of the Committee. Mr. Joe Luxford was Treasurer and Mr. R. Morris of Five Oaks, Secretary, the latter two both being luminaries of the new democratic Parish Council. They served the Committee for many years. The Show on Wed. Aug 15th had an 'Industrial' section and was deemed a great success according to the Parish Magazine, with children's sports and Bandmaster Wallace and the 2nd V.B. Royal Sussex Band.

The show became an annual event, returning to Summers in 1904 and at Mr. Songhurst's meadow in 1909. The 1910 show was bigger than usual, featuring a floral parade through the village. Mrs Garton describes it in her time: "The Annual Flower Show was a big village event, held in station field, with two or three big marquees. Villagers exhibited produce, craft items, cookery and home-made wine, chutneys, jam, marmalade, rugs and always a village fair to go with it." The Flower Show was always held on a Wednesday. This was 'early closing day' in Billingshurst designed to give shop staff an afternoon off in compensation for working on Saturday mornings. A few businesses still practise what was once a common custom. Mrs. Lines, whose research this account is based on, reports that most early shows were held in the grounds of affluent landowners outside the immediate village. She presumes the parishioners brought their exhibits in wheelbarrows or carts borrowed from employers, or perhaps on trade bikes? Initially a new President was elected each year, and Major General Renton inherited the role together with his uncle's Rowfold estate.

The show ceased in 1916 but a best kept garden competition was held despite the war. After the war allotments came to Billingshurst and at some point the show resumed. By 1924 Mr. Luxford was both Treasurer and Secretary with a 20-strong Committee, including three Wadeys and the famous exhibitor Wally Wicks. There was a separate Ladies Committee too and a separate tent for poultry eggs and ducks! In the 30s the Women's Institute began to play a significant role introducing needlework and other domestic classes.

The Society still named itself 'Horticultural and Industrial' in 1934 when the site was Dr. Puttock's meadow, Alick's Hill. That show featured Skill Competitions and Side Shows, Teas, Ices and Light Refreshments, Messrs. F HARRIS & SONS' Noah's Ark, Roundabouts and Old English Fair. Many of the local gentry were made Vice-Presidents – Comptesse de la Chapelle, Lady Fielding, Miss Beck, Capt. Hall Renton. Other notables on the Committee have familiar Billingshurst names -Ayre, Puttock, Morris, Norris, Cripps , Sherlock and Harold Wadey, a long-time Society eminence. Watts and Sons at the Station handled the entry forms until the business closed down in 1992. The 30s were the Society's golden years, with 1,022 entries in 1936.

Up to 1939 the show was held in one or more marquees at a cost of £17-6s-6d. But during the 'phoney war' of 1940 the East Street School was pressed into service. With the war, by 1941 a threatening reality, the show was arranged but did not take place. Harold Wadey was then Hon. Secretary. The show closed 'for the duration of war' and did not resume until 1948. By then the event cost

£250, double the pre-war bill. A dance was held, there was a visit to Wisley and the word 'Industrial' was lost. In 1950 the chosen day was Saturday for the first time. Races were held, a tug-of-war organised and the Billingshurst Band played. In 1952 came an Exemption Dog Show. The presentation of cups was held on an evening in the Women's or Village Hall. In 1953 there was a special award to celebrate Elizabeth II's Coronation and in 1955 2,250 people attended. The site of the present primary school was one venue in those years and in 1962 it moved to the Recreation Ground, the band did not play and the attendance dropped to 1000. The sports continued in 1965 but there was no longer a fun fair.

The marquee, with its characteristic smell and atmosphere, proved too costly in 1970 and shifted into the Hall of the Weald School where it remained for 27 years until 1997. In 1972 when Mr. Beck and Mr. Kingston were the Honary Officers, the schedules included flowers, fruit and vegetables, floral art, cookery, needlecraft, handwork and painting for children, photography and honey, plus more domestic classes for WI members. In 1997 there was a crisis when Mr. Allan Dugdale, Rural Studies teacher at the Weald and Society Show Secretary, died but Mrs, Dorothy Lake stepped into the breach. In 1998 the show shifted to the new Village Hall, a smaller venue, and the live band and children's entertainer had to cease. The show now loses money and attracts some 600 entries, but other Society activities, visits, lectures, plant sales etc. keep the finances buoyant enough for it to make an annual donation to charity. Some 15 cups and trophies are awarded each year and 4 WI cups together with the Royal Horticultural Society's Banksian Medal, the National body which Billingshurst joined in 1926.

Beekeeping in Billingshurst

Beekeeping has been practised in the village since Saxon times. Honey was the only affordable sweetener available to country people until sugar became cheap enough in the later 19th century to replace it. Villagers and yeomen kept bees in skeps, killing the weightiest colonies with sulphur fumes in September to get at the honey and beeswax, until moveable frame hives were introduced in the 1870s.

Anthony Hammond had a 'beehouse' in the inventory of 1640 valued at about £150 in today's money. Rev. Cecil Brereton, Vicar of Billingshurst, (1886 -1890 and later at Sutton) had a sideline to his Ministering business. This was the rearing of swarms of bees and the raising of queen bees which he advertised for sale in the British Bee Journal for sale all over Britain, to be delivered by post or train. Beecraft was heavily promoted by the clergy and other well-to-do philanthropists in Victorian times. They thought that the poor 'cottagers', as they called them, could eke out their low wages and nourish their children by keeping bees, which required no land, could be collected as unclaimed swarms for nothing and could be kept in skeps that they could make themselves. Victorian thinkers admired 'self-help' and abhorred idleness, and the more politically astute advocating beekeeping as an insurance against revolt, such as the Swing Riots, by the potentially rebellious working classes. William Cobbett wrote: "He must be a stupid countryman indeed who cannot make a beehive and a lazy one if he will not... Scarcely anything is a greater misfortune than shiftlessness".

Thomas W. Cowan, for 40 years President of the British Beekeeping Association, married the rich local brewer Michell's daughter and lived for some 29 years in Horsham, latterly at Comptons Lea. He wrote that 'the importance due to the minor industry of beekeeping in promoting its work among the humbler classes of the community was due to the social position of (the Association's) patrons'. The Gentry and the Clergy, 'people of means', kept bees as an example to their flocks and many people in our district followed their example. Locally today's Billingshurst beekeepers belong to the Wisborough Green Beekeeping branch of the Association. Allan Dugdale, a pillar of the Horticultural Society and Tony Herbert taught the subject at the Weald School and there were formerly beekeeping classes at the village Flower Show. George Wakeford BEM, for services to beekeeping, was the local Beemaster who earned a living by attending to people's hives. He had some 400 colonies under his supervision in his heyday. George wrote a delightful autobiography, *Beemaster*, recently reissued as *Beemaster Revisited*. He died in 1985.

Weald pupils extracting and bottling honey

George Wakeford, Beemaster, showing a novice a queen cell

Billingshurst Institutions and Clubs

The Angling Society

The Society was set up in 1919 when Pub angling teams used to compete for cash. It has grown to offer some of the finest coarse fishing in the Horsham District. In Billingshurst the main venues are on the Upper Arun and in the recently constructed fishing lake at Jubilee Fields. The Society also offers facilities at Shillinglee and Malthouse Lakes, Wisborough Green, and along the Lower Arun as far as Lee Place towards Pulborough. Chub, bream, roach, barbel, little bleak and pike up to 26lbs abound on the Upper Arun and carp weighing up to 30 lbs. Migratory 15lb sea trout coming upstream to spawn have been landed but they are always put back. Jubilee Fields Lake, where children may fish free, has been stocked with 4,800 fish recently and 750 barbel were introduced at Newbridge but they have migrated downstream to tidal waters. Roach, tench, rudd, gudgeon and crucian carp are now to be caught. Membership is currently 250, fishing matches are held and training is offered for children and novices. Some 25 trophies are awarded each year. Meetings are held at the Weald School and informally at the Limeburners Inn.

Peter Stockwood, Membership Secretary, with a carp

Billingshurst Dramatic Society (BDS)

The BDS company

During WWII men were allowed for the first time into the hitherto exclusively feminine 'Women's Hall' so enabling enthusiasts to form a Dramatic Society with facilities, however meagre, previously denied them. In 1941 the Workers Education Association ran drama classes and produced Sheridan's '*The Rivals*' the next year. Encouraged by Dr. Moreton, the village school headmaster, a Dramatic Society was formed. Their first two productions were *Tobias and the Angel* by James Bridie and *Arms and the Man* by George Bernard Shaw, Britain's second greatest playwright. Any proceeds from the later were to go to charity, so with some cheek the members wrote to the great man, still active at Ayot St Lawrence asking him if he would donate the royalties they paid to charity. They got an emphatic 'no', but with the reservation that so long as they did the plays for themselves they need pay no royalties, but if they were for other people he wanted his share! Remarkably he offered his help with setting up the Society and the constitution he helped with is still in use today.

Shaw died aged 94 in 1950 but the BDS prospered under the influence of Dr. Bill Bousfield, Jack Leaman, Ron Oulds, Francis Crisp and Molly Church. Stalwarts John Farmer and Nevin Davis made an entry in 1958 soon followed by John and Rene Humphries, a group whose influence shaped the present Society. Pamela Leaman, a former actress, brought professionalism to the troupe. Her first production was Rattigan's *Deep Blue Sea*. Jack Leaman thought up the idea of the Patrons, a subscribing supporters club, who would get special booking privileges, and soon an annual party with copious refreshments. The President, C.G. Davis, Nevin's father had to pay £2 to guarantee the party against a loss! Jack Easton, Bank Manager and Chairman of the Parish Council swelled the Patron's numbers to 120. Jack died in 1990.

Notable plays were produced in the 1960s. Francis Crisp did *The Amorous Prawn*, Ron *The French Mistress*, Nevin *The Reluctant Debutante* and John Farmer *Present Laughter*. Ron's *Alfie*, in 1968, with John Farmer as the libidinous scallywag met with puritanical criticism but was a theatrical triumph, winning the County Drama Competition, as did Ron's *Tom Jones* the next year at the festival. There followed a period of developmental liaison with George Rawlins, the WSCC Drama Advisor, when BDS actors dominated the casts of County productions. These experiences deepened the members' theatrical competence and many memorable shows ensued.

In the 70s Chairman, John Farmer procured the rights to stage the first amateur performance of *O Clarence* (based on P.G. Wodehouse) with John Humphries as Lord Emsworth. Pat Gierth joined the company producing remarkable posters and set designs in a hall and on a stage offering little encouragement. Don Campbell produced *The Lion in Winter* and in 1974 John Humphries directed his daughter, Sue Pollard, in *There's a Girl in my Soup*. In 1977 Ian Harvey, who became a professional actor, produced a wonderful *Sweeney Todd*, a show complemented by the talented pianist, Craig Pruess. For the Queen's Jubilee Ron Oulds produced a splendid tribute, *Send ER Victorious*.

The Company offer the local people intelligent popular theatre on their doorstep, and is bold in its choice of genres, tackling verse drama such as Edwin Pollard's *Murder in the Cathedral* by T.S. Eliot, performed at St. Mary's, social themes such as *A Day in the Life of Joe Egg* and *Abigail's Party*, farce such as *Noises Off*, musicals like *Guys and Dolls* and pantomime such as *Aladdin*.

For all its manifest shortcomings as a theatre the Women's Hall offers advantages to the Society. It is centrally sited in the village, readily available for rehearsals and set construction and enjoys its own peculiar old-world ambience. Of course the good companionship of the band of Billingshurst thespians has thrown up a host of anecdotes about drying on stage, missed cues and entrances, ad libs to fill awkward pauses and embarrassing gaffes by people in the audience. Jackie Charman, gifted actress and Secretary of the Society could offer an Evening of Entertainment of such yarns. John Humphries, as Wishy Washy in *Aladdin* once brought up on stage a little Chinese child from the audience and a lady when offered a programme replied "No thanks, I've got one from the last play".

When in 1979 Edwin produced *The Crucible* the West Sussex County Times wrote:

'The Women's Hall can hardly be regarded as an inspiration even to dedicated actors. The stage is cramped, backstage infinitely worse, almost depressing. Yet time and again the Billingshurst players produce works there that often emerge head and shoulders above anything seen elsewhere'.

The Company, up to 2013, has staged 191 plays since its inception. A remarkable achievement and a demonstration of how great an asset the Society is to Billingshurst.

Rene Humphries and Nevin

Bowling Club

The Billingshurst Bowling Club is sited within the playing fields of the Weald School on three sides and on the fourth by Station Road Gardens. It is accessed from Myrtle Lane. A new pedestrian access, with disabled parking, has recently been built near the tennis court end of the Swimming Pool.

Mrs Puttock of Clevelands House originally leased the bowlers the land, carefully fenced off from her cattle, in 1932 at a peppercorn rent of 5 shillings a year. The freehold was purchased in 1968. Local tradesmen were the founders – Higgins the Ironmonger, Lusted the grocer, Crisp the barber and tobacconist, Cripps the butcher, C.E Wadey the builder and Watt the seedsman. At first the green had only three rinks, cut by hand mower at a charge of 6d an hour. The pavilion was 'basic' with a bucket and rota. The Club has been in continuous use by a band of enthusiasts except for the wartime years when it was utilised by the Red Cross and the Air Training Corps. In the early days matches were arranged against Graffham, Midhurst and Handcross.

Since the 1950s the Green was extended to six rinks, greatly assisted by the arrival of mains water and electricity. The original clubhouse was extended to include changing rooms, a kitchenette, lounge area and toilets. More recently a second pavilion has been installed for tea and refreshments after matches. Members reclad a Portacabin, previously used as a Parish Room at Clymping, and provided a pitched roof to complement the old clubhouse together with more toilets, available to the disabled. It has been named 'The Stocker Room' in honour of Jack who masterminded the project. An automated watering system has been an enormous advance on the loan of a standpipe and a long hose from the cricket club!

The Club now plays friendly mixed matches against 25 other clubs in West Sussex and Surrey, weekdays and weekends, afternoons and evenings with a full range of club competitions and friendly sessions. Newcomers are made welcome, all abilities are catered for and novices lent equipment and given free trial sessions. Garden seating is available for spectators.

The Bowling Club in 1960

Cricket Club

An early sporting newspaper called 'Bell's Life' of 1831 carried a report of a return cricket match between Billingshurst and Horsham, Nuthurst and Shipley. The Ordnance Survey map of 1869 shows a circle off Station Road marked 'cricket' which suggests that the game was played in the parish throughout the reign of Queen Victoria, possibly on the same site, though there was no Station Road until the railway came in 1859. Play continued there into the 21st century until fine new facilities became available at Jubilee Fields when the old pitch beyond the handsome wall was abandoned and redeveloped as recreational gardens.

Among the early players were the Hubert family, William Henry being a surgeon and his son William Arthur the village doctor at a house at Rosehill. They were renowned for hitting sixes over the houses in Station Road. Rex Haygate of a rival team, Wisborough Green, managed to hit a ball into a passing railway truck. No doubt a six was recorded for a lost ball, though it was recovered at Pulborough, the next stop on the line. The West Sussex Constabulary played their games on the village field and dinner was taken in 1878, as usual at the Station Inn where mine host was Sprinks, the miller's son. 'Later in the evening some capital songs were given'. W. Dalbiac was the Billingshurst demon bowler. The Eversheds, major Billingshurst landowners, like the Norfolk Edriches, once in 1892 fielded a complete family eleven, beating the village side in a low scoring, two innings match by two runs. Playing for Billingshurst, Rev Newcomb, A. Puttock and A. Hubert all scored 'golden ducks' and Maurice Ireland accumulated 4 runs. In 1885 W. Evershed went in first and 'carried his bat' scoring 90 not out against Horsham. In that year there was a match with Mr. Goff's team at Summers Place which is thought to have been another cricket venue in early Victorian times.

Ralph Wadey, dispatch rider during WWI

WWI disrupted cricket development, but interest revived in the 1920s with such stalwarts as Ralph Wadey of Five Oaks, R.E. Norris, Harold Wadey the builder, Arthur Spinks, Alf Burchell and three Bottings. Arthur 'Bumper' Voice provided transport from his Station Road business for the whole team in a Motor-van known as 'The Brake'. By the 30s the club could boast a Second XI. 'Old Winkle' (Bill Philips) was the groundsman. Again from 1939 war interrupted play though when peace came at last some Sunday cricket was permitted. In 1949 there was a danger of housing development on the site. Mr. Eric Puttock organised a fund-raising celebrity match with Sussex County and England players involved. Rev. David Sheppard, once of Slinfold, who opened the first Weald Sixth Form Centre and later became Bishop of Liverpool captained the side which also contained James Langridge, Jack and Charlie Oakes, Jim Parks and other famous players. Doug Wright and Godfrey Evans, England's wicket-keeper, played for Puttock's XI which won the match. Sufficient money was raised with a public subscription to see off the threat.

The club prospered. In 1958 the players made their first tour into Essex arranged by Secretary Tony Smith. They were well beaten in their first match against Tillingham, but rallied in their next game to beat the odds-on favourites, Rayleigh Cricket Club. More tours were arranged to the New Forest, Bath and Norfolk in the closing decades of the 20th century. David Sainsbury, sports master and notable rugby referee of the Weald arranged the Hunstanton, Norfolk tour and the bowler, Barry Taylor, the others. David scored a remarkable 150 against Blackheath. Other notables of the time were John and Mark Upton, Roger Patterson, Justin Millais, Jim Burroughs, Tony Petras, Cheeseman, Steve McMurrugh and Roger Lusted. Some weekends three of four matches were played on both Saturdays and Sundays. Originally there was only a small changing-room at the Weald School end of the field. The Parish Council provided a most-welcome wooden pavilion in 1962 but that is now demolished after falling into disrepair. In its heyday the club provided sport for ladies, both cricket and stoolball.

The advent of generous space and comfortable pavilion facilities at Jubilee Fields in 2006 has enabled the club to flourish in the 21st century. Friendly and convenient as the old ground had been, it was often in trouble from neighbouring residents who had balls landing in their gardens. Two teams now compete in the Sussex County League. The club takes part in the League Cup and holds many friendly games and practices throughout the summer months. Juniors are encouraged and catered for by age groups, under 10, 12 and 14s. They play in the Colts' League.

After the 2015 season, as a splendid sign of development, the Club was promoted to play in the Premier Division of Sussex County Cricket.

The Club with Cups and Trophies 1984

Steve Nicholls, Beryl Lusted, Barry Taylor, Roger Lusted, Roger Patterson, Dave Patten, David Sainsbury, David Rood, Chris Michael

The Club with pots of ale – Bath Tour 1981

The Billingshurst XI 1957

In 2002 Mr. Joe Sillett of Billingshurst scored a century with an old bat which had been so holed by woodworm that he had had to shave off curves from the top edges. Inspired by his triumph he designed a new prototype on the same pattern and subsequently launched a bat manufactory, trading as 'The Woodworm Cricket Company' which sold 200 bats in its first year and rocketed to 15,000 by 2005. The company mistakenly branched out into golf clothing. Sadly the rocket ran out of fuel, despite big-name sponsors such as Freddie Flintoff and Kevin Pietersen, and went into administration. It was bought up by 'The Sports HQ' in 2008.

Association Football Club

The Club celebrates winning the League and two cups 1962/3

Three club programmes

The club old brigade, 1920 division 2 Trophy

Gordon New with a few cups

Association Football in Billingshurst has a lengthy history, a game deservedly popular with generations of men and boys. The West Sussex Gazette recorded its formation in November, 1890 on the first Saturday, after Mr. Skinner's side beat Mr. Newcomb's 8 -5 in a promising trial

Rugby Football has predominated over Soccer at the Weald School since the early 70s. Prior to that soccer was played and earlier was much enjoyed at the old East Street School on a field where the Catholic Church now stands. It was also played in the first 15 years of the Weald. Keen rugby players leaving the school must now continue playing the game at other clubs such as Pulborough or Horsham. Young soccer players, however, are now well catered for by Billingshurst Football Club, which offers continuity and sporting fellowship for life, if they remain in the village.

The old soccer club played in many different places. The first field was Hill Top north of Manor House. In the 20s they moved to different pitches at Little Gilmans, the old cricket field, Tedfold Park, Jengers Meadow and Jubilee Meadow near Little Daux. The team took the name 'Jubilee Rovers' for that period. After WWII they played at a site off the present Forge Way, land under what is now Carpenters and the present Recreation Ground. A regular pitch was at last assured when the Parish Council bought an orchard due west of the old cricket ground in Station Road. Changing facilities were shared with the cricketers in the old pavilion. That has gone too and the site is now car parks, the Leisure Centre and a Nursery School. This was the home ground of the club until 2006 when another Jubilee Fields became available as one of the side-benefits of a large new housing estate. The additional bonus was the use of excellent changing and recreational facilities.

The game was successful and popular long before the Great War. In 1909 the team played Horsham in the final of the local league, but lost 3-1. In 1932 Mr. Joe Pavey played in the team that won the Intermediate Cup in 1932. "We never used to speak on the football field: now they are like a lot of parrots," he said. Before WWII there were about 15 players, taking part in the West Sussex Wednesday League. Wednesdays were commonly Early Closing Days. Mr. Dick Jestico recalled, "We used to cycle to and from matches and pay 2s a week to have our shirts washed". Nowadays the club attracts some valuable supportive sponsorship. Mr. Glaysher travelled to games in a furniture lorry. Play was suspended during WWII but several friendly matches were played against the Italian prisoners of war from Kingsfold Camp. After the war the club revived still wearing heavy duty shirts and boots.

By the 60s the teams were winning numerous trophies and turning the club into the present efficient outfit with regular training and a warm social fellowship.

A note in the Oct 1965 programme reads, "Old Sonny Harrison, used to be a Billingshurst postman and now is an old age pensioner. He has given us 10/- (Ten shillings) for this week's tea, sugar, milk and oranges. What an example for our supporters! Our Centre Half, Derrick Elliott was taken off to Worthing Hospital with a broken thigh. We are starting a small fund to help his wife during his twelve weeks in hospital".

In the Centenary year, 1990, the Club had 60 registered players with three teams playing in the Sussex League, the first team in the Premier Division. Today the club's facilities and its excellent website would startle the pioneers and they would surely envy the facilities, the keenness, the social benefits, not to mention modern boots, kit, handsome match programmes and playing surfaces on three senior pitches and a number of junior ones.

In a recent Programme, cost £2, the club history is briefly recorded. It played in the Horsham League until joining the WS Football League on its inception. It had won the Premier League title the year before 'under the management of Mark Betts and Malcolm Saunders'. They then ran three senior sides, the first team competing in the Sussex County League for the first time. The Reserve and third teams continued membership of the WSFL competing in Division 2 and Division 4. As a 'Charter Standard Club it also ran ten junior sides, upwards from under 7 years up to 16, playing in the Horsham District Youth League.

Following promotion in 2015/16 the club will play in Division 1 of the Southern Combination Football League for the first time in its 125 year history. To this end there will be a perimeter path around the pitch and a 50 seater stand. Floodlights, enabling mid-week games, are also planned, subject to sponsorship.

The Tennis Club

Tournament players 2008

Five club members

Installing the Floodlighting

Lawn tennis has been played in Billingshurst at least as far back to the years before the Great War. The 'Flapper' generation of the 1920s, among the well-to-do, embraced the sport as a socially welcome diversion for both men and women, unlike football, cricket and stoolball. The convivial game was an ideal meeting and mating point. John Betjeman's poem about Miss Joan Hunter Dunn catches the spirit exactly. Mr. Joe Luxford, grand panjandrum of Billingshurst, had a tennis court at the turn of the century and promoted the game and there is record of other courts at Lordings Road and Newbridge. It is likely that the great houses of old Billingshurst would all have kept racquets, nets and balls and made a screened grass lawn for the family and friends.

We first hear of an organisation to control the use of a public facility which kept minutes of its meetings on 13th October, 1949. The Village Sports Association met at the King's Head and nominated a Tennis Courts Committee and decreed court fees of a shilling (5p) an hour. The Parish Council has provided two courts, expecting to collect fees from the public hiring it on a casual basis. In practice arranging use, selling tickets and supervising etiquette and upkeep of the balls, net and other equipment was a demanding task and the Council welcomed the volunteers who came together to form the "Billingshurst Tennis Courts Committee". On 2nd Sept 1949 it was formed with Mr. F. Crawford as the leader, under the aegis of the Sports Association, which then had oversight of games in the village. The Council were pleased to delegate control of bookings to the volunteers, requiring 10% of the takings. Mr. J.B. Sherlock was able to report the gift of £250 from the Ministry of Education to promote the game and the loan of £50 from the Sports Association to be repaid within 10 years.

American Tournaments were arranged, matches against other village clubs keenly contested for the 'Wynstrode Cup' and social events provided for members. [Wynstrode is a17th century house in Okehurst Road where the Sherlock family lived] Dances raised small sums of profit, music by the 'Blue Quartet'. Jumble sales and Social Evenings were held. They even investigated some coaching for young players. Mr. Allan Dugdale, teacher at the village school ran the Village Youth Club and was allocated an evening for play. The Committee provided a simple pavilion measuring 20x15 feet. Calor Gas lighting was arranged. Sight screens were provided by using hessian sacks joined together and suitably treated. Hardboard was used to line the hut. They constantly harried the Parish Council as Trustees for repairs to netting and the surfaces of the courts. Mr. T. Topper was the go-between with the Parish Council. There was also conflict with Mr. Lawrenson about his building a wall to prevent 'the effluence from his works running on the courts'. A drainpipe was needed and they had to borrow the cricket club hose to clear the courts. They used the Railway Hotel's toilets and hired water from the Bowling Club at 5 shillings a year. They sought out a dozen tubular chairs from the closing down of the Maltings Hotel. Dances were held at Gratwicke House, hired from Mrs Page. In 1953 the Committee presented a Coronation Tableaux and won third prize. Regular suggestions of forming a Club were constantly rejected. The Parish Council was determined to ensure that the courts were available to the general public and not monopolised by a club.

Many of the group's doings are fondly reminiscent of the 1950s. The modern reader is taken aback by the effusive thanks to Col. B.C. Kerr for the gift of asbestos panels to line the pavilion. Raffle prizes were normally bottles of whisky and sherry, a box of chocolates and a pack of 50 cigarettes at whist drives and the like. The dance at Gratwicke in 1954 economised on the band by borrowing a radiogram. Tickets were 7/6d in 1956, the band cost £5.5s.0 and the profit two shillings and tenpence. The dance was deemed a success. When Mrs. Forster came to Gratwicke and charged £8 for hire and refreshments they went elsewhere. Meetings were held at The Market Room of the Railway Hotel or at the High Street pubs.

In 1962 the Parish Council sold the old courts and built two new ones encroaching slightly onto the football field. All play ceased until the work was completed.

In May 1963, the year John Kennedy was shot, forty people met at the Village Hall, Mr. Jack Easton, manager of Barclay's Bank in the Chair. It was decided to form a Tennis Club Committee to succeed the former Courts Committee. After meetings with Miss Joyce, Parish Clerk, the new Club secured exclusive use of the courts for 2½ days, (Tues. Thurs. and after 2pm Sun.) later 3½, at a rent £1 a week, plus use of the Youth Hut for changing, shared with the youth Stoolball team. The crying need was for a new pavilion and for the Club to take charge of maintenance and control instead of doing everything through the Council who had taken the courts out of use for resurfacing without notice. There were only 13 senior players left. More members were imperative. A plan to buy a Portacabin was rejected. Instead an elderly caravan was bought in 1966 renovated and furnished. A new agreement was made with the Council giving security of tenure and land for a pavilion. The club funds were invested in the new Premium Bonds! The idea of floodlighting was shelved. The club joined the Sussex County L.T.A.

Social events took in typical 60s style with barbecues, coffee mornings, wine and cheese parties, produce stalls, tombolas, a 'Cavalcade of Tennis' on Flower Show Day, sweepstakes, a bottle party at Gleniffer House, Slinfold and a Dinner-Dance at the Gatwick Manor Hotel. As the caravan steadily deteriorated the struggle for a pavilion began about 1967. The Council agreed to lease the site but funding, planning permission and bureaucracy were enormous hindrances. An offer from the then extant Stoolball Club to help with the fund-raising in return for a share of the building was politely declined. Mr. Easton, who was the second 'President', reckoned £2,400 would be needed. By 1968 they had assembled enough credit to place an order and secured planning permission from Horsham Rural. £540 Ministry of Education grant, £250 Parish Council, LTA loan £500, £109 donations, £90 interest-free loans, and £500 worth of guarantees! The new pavilion opened with a sherry party on 25th May, 1969. They sold the caravan for £20.

The Weald School courts became available in the 1970s as membership climbed to 94 seniors. There was now a continuing search for development. In 1975 floodlighting was installed costing £960 aided by a £500 loan from the LTA. Barry Barnes gave advice and service supplies. Prices rose sharply through to the 80s frustrating the demand for a pavilion extension, another court and more floodlights. Fundraising continued with the usual events which now included a barn dance. Annual membership rose to £20. By 1984 there were 110 senior members, but the fourth court would cost £6000.

Through the 80s the club prospered and in the 90s the 'old guard' gave place to new. Mr. Easton, doyen of the Club died in 1990. By the Millennium the roll of senior members had fallen to 53 and annual subs had risen to £65. The big question then was whether or not to move the Club to the imminent Jubilee Fields where a 4-court site was envisaged. A business development plan was drawn up in pursuit of grant aid, but in the event, like the rugby group, the Club voted to remain in its old quarters, with a renewed resolution to improve the facility. Its annual rent to the Parish Council had now risen to £1750 and the Parish, as Landlords, paid for basic maintenance and still required opportunities for casual public use.

Refurbished courts were opened in 2006 and new lights provided in 2008. Further refurbishment of courts 1, 2 and 3 and the provision of the long sought 4th court came in April, 2012 at a cost of £40,000. At this time new arrangements were made with the Parish Council. The Club were to pay a peppercorn rent rather than the current £2500 per annum, but from then on were entirely responsible for the upkeep of the facility, surfaces, nets, fences etc. The President, Di Burroughs, received the prestigious Tennis Sussex Robert Cushing silver salver award in recognition of her unstinting 30 years of service to the Billingshurst Club. Men's Captain and development officer, Rob Falkner, and Coach, Dave Almond, were also nominated for awards. David initiated a programme in 2013 for children from Worthing with disabilities. Adult membership is now £110 p.a. with generous discounts for the young and elderly. Casual users pay £8 for an hour.

In 2014 the club received funding to demolish the old clubhouse, dating from the 1960s, and replace it with a splendid, larger building with modern facilities for members and visitors. Also the courts were repainted in purple/green instead of the traditional green and terracotta.

Di Burroughs with the Wynstrode Cup

1984   David Watt, Ted Farmer, Jeremy David and Maggie Keyte

Di Burroughs remembers

I came to play at the Club in 1984 after a ten year break from tennis to discover that my short dress, frilly knickers and wooden racquet were no longer the done thing. They were as out of date as the Elsan toilet arrangements which required a rota to undertake the digging of holes in the days of the old caravan.

An intriguing mystery hangs over the Wynstrode Tennis Cup. The silver plaques go back to 1925 on the base of a splendid silver trophy intended by its donor, Mrs. Verling Sherlock, to promote competition and encourage fellowship among local village tennis clubs. Midhurst were the first winners, followed by Southwater. Billingshurst won it five times between 1932 and 1938. The competition continued throughout the 1950s, with a gap during WWII. A good deal of Committee time was spent debating how best to insure and protect the collectively owned imposing and valuable item. Sad to relate, Billingshurst were the last winners in 1960. Then nothing more is heard of the cup or of competitions in its name. No note of the loss is to be found in the minutes, so it seems likely that an end to inter-village rivalry was accepted without regret.

Then, out of the blue, forty two years later, the Cup was found in an attic in London and returned to the Mothersdales here in Billingshurst! There proved to be no enthusiasm locally to resume the old competitions between villages, most of which no longer had teams, so Billingshurst Club made use of it for the trophy for tournaments for five years. It has not been used since. Time for a rethink?

As for the future, we must keep up the impetus for improvement which will be the more likely with a new clubhouse and investment in young people. We can safely say that lawn tennis in Billingshurst has shed any snobbery, class consciousness and exclusivity and is now soundly based as a healthy mixed-gender sport with opportunities for friendly recreation as well as the development of skills at all levels. Novices are made welcome!

Billingshurst Choral Society

The Society (BCS) is an active and friendly choral group which sings in Billingshurst and the surrounding area. It currently has over a hundred singing members.

A chance remark, made at the right time, sealed the formation of the Society. Choral singing in the village had largely been confined to the church choirs, begun in 1985 when a group of singers joined together to sing madrigals. They called themselves 'Sundrie Voyces'. Following a successful concert at St. Mary's Church, a bass and experienced conductor, George Jones, commented that Billingshurst needed a choral society; a contralto, Jackie Bench, offered to do the administration. Much groundwork followed; visits to village church choirs, posting posters on notice boards, press notices in the local paper. As a reward 50 singers attended the first rehearsal at St. Mary's.

The Choral Society

By January 1986 a Committee had been formed, in the capable hands of John Cartmell, celebrated locally as a steam engine owner and enthusiast. Good connections enabled the employment of some of the very best soloists in the Society's concerts. Several up-and-coming stars travelled to Billingshurst who later rose high in their profession. Sarah Connolly CBE, opera singer, is just one example. From 1986 to 2000 performances had started locally, St. Mary's Church and the Weald School halls. Occasionally they travelled to Chichester Cathedral which has remained a popular venue.

George Jones has been the Conductor and Musical Director from the start. The Society has been performing a mixture of old and new challenging works ever since its inception. In 2000 AD BCS gave the first performance of the *Billingshurst Mass*, specially written by Stanley Vann, in Chichester Cathedral. The following year they performed the *African Sanctus* by David Fanshawe, a haunting mixture of African music and more traditional European melodies. The repertoire has extended recently with performances, in 2009 and 2011, of Will Todd's *Mass in Blue*, a popular and challenging jazz setting of the Mass. The following year BCS did Alexander L'Estrange's *Zimbe!* a celebration of the vibrancy of African music. 2013 saw BCS perform the UK premiere of Stale Klieberg's *Requiem for the Victims of Nazi Persecution*, as part of the Brighton Fringe.

In 2003 BCS and Angmering Chorale gave the first performance in the South of England of Karl Jenkins' acclaimed *The Armed Man*. The two societies travelled to New York in 2007 to join a performance of that work in Carnegie Hall. In January 2009 they returned for a performance of *Stabet Mater* in the Lincoln Centre. BCS formed part of the choir at the Royal Festival Hall to celebrate the reopening, following restoration, in 2007. They returned on stage there in October as part of a select choral group for the Royal Gala Concert to commemorate the same event. The choir perform regularly, by invitation, at the annual Brandenburg Festival in London.

BCS performs three major concerts annually, with the autumn concerts often in Chichester Cathedral and occasionally in Arundel Cathedral. Many concerts have been given jointly with the Angmering Chorale, also directed by George. The spring and summer concerts are performed at Billingshurst Leisure Centre at the Weald School.

The Society's Christmas Concert is usually performed at St. Mary's Church, which is also the rehearsal venue. Rehearsals take place there every Tuesday evening from 8 to 9.45 pm. BCS has a thriving social calendar and organises concert tours every two years. So far the Society has visited Belgium, the Loire Valley, Caen, Paris, Prague and Tuscany.

Bellringing

St.Mary's Church has a dedicated team of ringers and a peal of 8 bells, one of the best in Sussex.

Wendy Lines tells the story in an article in a Billingshurst Society Newsletter (No. 37 1982).

In the early part of the 16th century the sound of the bells in the tower was an integral part of the village life and from the Churchwardens' accounts we know that the bells were in constant need of repair and attention. In 1526 18 old pence were paid for "trussing of owre ilij th bell lytyll bel and second bell". On 1530 much work was carried out on the 'great bell' – 10d was spent on meat and drink when the bell was taken down and perhaps a jolly time was had after the hard work. The bellfounder however was not happy, because we find the item, "Paid to the bellfounder which was not content at the fyrst payment for the bell xxvjs viij (26/8d)" At the feast of All Hallows he was given a further fee and also paid 16d separately for food and lodging – for him and his horse.

At this time only four bells are mentioned by name, but there might have been five.

In 1532, in the reign of Henry VIII, the parishioners of Billingshurst undertook a mammoth task on behalf of one of their bells. They journeyed to a Reading foundry to have a bell recast. Expenses for "owre first goying to Redyng" were 5/7d. The carriage of the bell cost 8/- and the bell casting cost £6.0. 2d. Afterwards the suffragan bishop hallowed the bell and was provided with his dinner.

When Queen Elizabeth was on the throne in 1563 the bells were once again big news in the parish. Some 56 named parishioners and an unspecified number of 'bachelors' contributed to the recasting of the fourth bell. In 1580 a bellfounder must have been resident in the parish, because he rented two shops in the churchyard. Minor repairs were carried out constantly; for example "Item for taking downe the third bell and setting her fast in the stocks". Further recastings took place in 1593, 1616 and 1625. 1 shilling was spent on beer when it was loaded and 6d when "the bell was brought home". Think of the devotion, organisation, work and drinking involved on these occasions!

From the end of the 17th century the Churchwardens' accounts are not always so detailed, but in 1785 five bell ropes are regularly purchased. In 1818 the ring was increased to six bells. T. Mears of London this time recast or made the bells. The oldest of our present bells dates from then, as some bear this date and Mears' marks. [No 3 bell is dated 1812] At this time the bells were also hung in a new frame. The responsible officials in these years were Charles Farhall, Wm. King ,Guardian, Richard Puttock, Overseer, Thos. Clear, Thos. Lathy, both Churchwardens and the Rev. G. Wells.

The ring was increased to a full peal of eight in 1897 [to celebrate Queen Victoria's Silver Jubilee]. After the death of George III there is an interesting entry, "to js. Champion for ringing the bell on the interment of the late King".

Originally the bell ropes would have hung to the floor of the tower. Today there is a charming ringing chamber that probably dates from the eighteenth (?) century.

Perhaps next time you hear the church bells, you can ponder a little on their long history and of the people of Billingshurst who have rung them through the centuries.

Mrs Lines acknowledged her indebtedness to Mr. J. Newman for his transcripts of the accounts and to G.P.Elphick for his book, *"Sussex Bells and Belfries"*

Loading up the bells

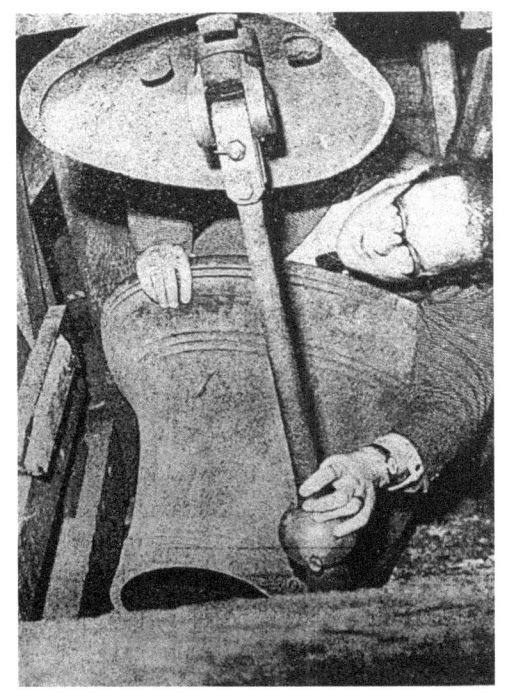

'Ring out, wild bells'

So far as we know then, three bells were installed prior to 1527, there were five in 1785 and a sixth treble bell was added in 1818. Two new bells were combined with the six in the belfry in 1897. In the 16th century accounts there is a record of constant expenditure on leather tongues for the clappers. The bells were no doubt silent during the Commonwealth period.

The Churchwardens Accounts in the Parish Records for 1823 reveal that they paid 7 shillings for beer for the ringers in 1821 and 5 shillings the following year, to James Fuller, landlord at the King's Arms, described as a public house. By 1823, however, James Trower of the King's Head was providing the beer. His hostelry was called an Inn and Wine House. By 1825 there was evidently no monopoly of the provision of beer for the bellringers at church expense as custom had shifted to George Puttock at the Blacksmith's Arms.

In 1965 the bells were again silent for a year having crashed to the church floor, mercifully harming no-one. Two were split so it was decided to recast them at Whitechapel at a cost of £1,500. Bell metal is commonly an alloy of copper and tin.

Lions charity bookshop

The Billingshurst and District Lions International Club maintain a comprehensive charity bookshop in Jengers Mead. Many people use this facility as an 'alternative library' paying a small price, subsequently returning books for re-sale. The club donates some £30,000 net on average per year from the bookshop and other sources of income to assist many worthy causes, both local and international.

The Lions charity bookshop, Jengers Mead

The Women's Institute

The WI movement started in Canada in February 1897. When Adelaide Hunter-Hoodless lost a child to gastro-enteritis she realised that women needed instruction in food hygiene and education as Homemakers and Citizen Builders. She worked hard to include Domestic Science in the school curriculum. The Farmer's Institute in Canada then formed a sister organisation – The Women's Institute. The movement thrived in the rural areas. In 1913 a member, Mrs. Madge Watts came to England to spread the word and establish the WI movement in the "Old Country".

Just after the end of WWI in January, 1919 a meeting was called in Billingshurst to encourage local women to form a WI. During wartime women had tackled many jobs formerly done by men, so they had greater expectations for themselves and a desire to share experiences, learn skills and better their education. A Billingshurst WI was formed. They still have a letter, dated 23rd Jan 1919, from the Board of Agriculture and Fisheries, Food Production Dept., welcoming the start. The rules were signed on 4th Feb. 1919 by the first Officers. A copy of the first six month's programme makes interesting reading. The lectures included Small Economies, Dressmaking, Pig Rearing, Keeping Fowls, Gardening and Keeping Rabbits. Also included were competitions, social time and, of course, tea.

A new nationally body was formed to govern the movement in England, with a Sussex woman as Chairman, Lady Gertrude Denman. She served for many years, building up the movement with the support of other strong-minded women. The organisation has three tiers. At the top is the National Federation followed by the County Federations and the local Institutes form the third tier. The Institute is a Registered Charity, and as such is non-party-political and non-sectarian but takes a wide-ranging interest in all matters, particularly those affecting women and their families. It does still preserve the crafts, cookery and needlework, most associated with the home, but takes pride in achieving recognition not only as 'jam makers' but also as women with much to offer in all walks of life.

Though not the first in Sussex, Billingshurst is among the first fourteen Institutes. Singleton takes the honours, founded in 1915. Nowadays the WI is thriving, meeting every month except August with an average of thirty members. Interesting speakers tell of events run by the County Federation, friendships are fostered and support offered to those who may be unwell or in need of help. The Institute meets with neighbouring WIs to share news and exchange programme ideas. The meetings are active and lively, eagerly anticipated by all the participants.

Leisure Centre

Billingshurst Leisure Centre

This community facility, built on the old association football ground at the approach to the Weald School off Station Road, was completed and opened for use in September, 2008 at a cost of £5.7 million. Karen Pickering MBE, an Olympic star and Britain's first world champion swimmer, performed the ceremony in the 25 metre, 4 lane indoor pool, equipped with a moveable floor. Alongside the pool is a 50 station Fitness Suite and reception and refreshment areas. Also available for hire on the Weald School campus are an all weather pitch, a gymnasium and a large four-court sports hall.

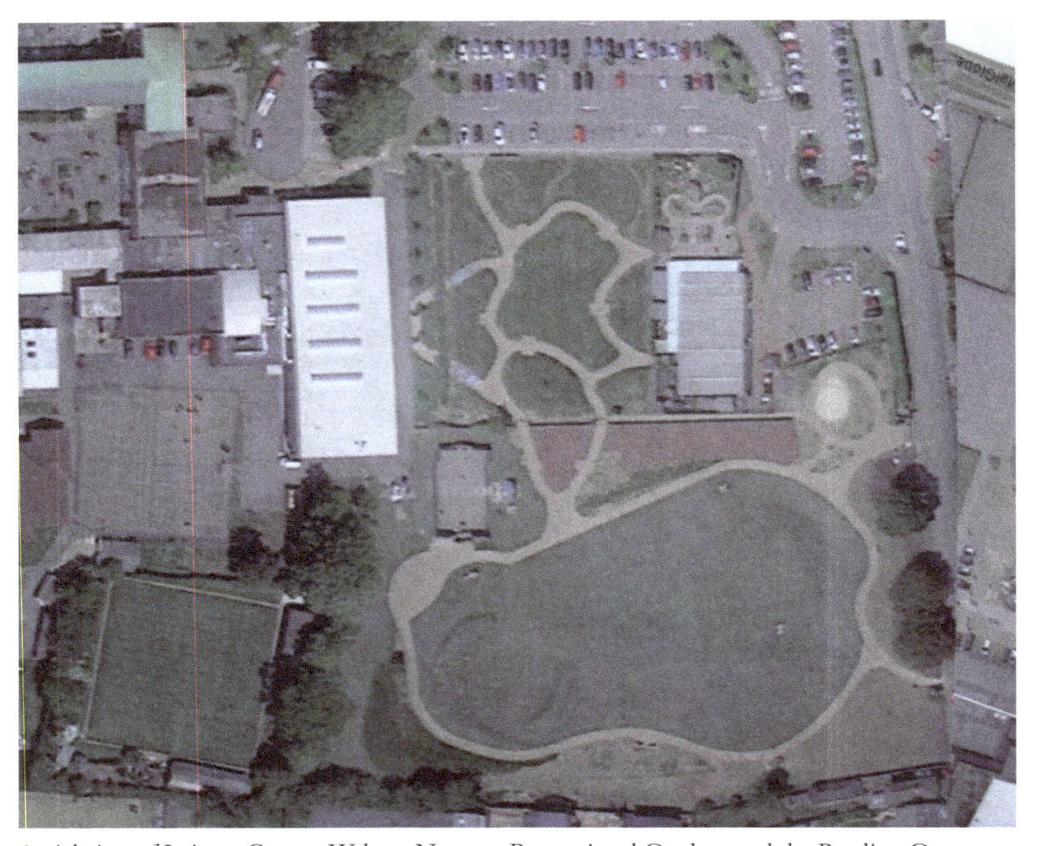

Aerial view of Leisure Centre, Wakoos Nursery, Recreational Gardens and the Bowling Green

BBC Situation Comedy – Ever- Decreasing Circles

This BBC TV programme was screened between 1984 and 1989. 27 episodes in four series were set in what was ostensibly a suburban close in Surrey. The filming was in fact mainly done in Dell Lane, Billingshurst and other Sussex locations. The series, considered by many critics to be one of the wittiest and intelligent productions of the Corporation, starred the late Richard Briers and Peter Egan. Richard played Martin, an obsessively orderly middle-aged committee man and Peter, his adventurous philandering neighbour, Paul, who had his 'salon' filmed in Lower Station Road.

Takeaway Restaurants, Lower Station Rd.

West of Station

Retail Businesses in Billingshurst

The earlier well-to-do businessmen in Billingshurst were the master butchers. The Penfolds (1530) and Greenfields (1649) are so described. Later men of affairs were the maltsters and brewers. They, together with the bakers, nurserymen, grocers, blacksmiths, leather workers, timber merchants and haberdashers supplied most of the needs of the people until well into the 19th century.

From Victorian times more shops opened and closed accordingly as fashion and perceived needs grew increasingly sophisticated. For example toys, bicycles, confectionary, fashionable clothing and hardware were in demand and services such as hairdressing, plumbing and photography afforded increasingly diverse opportunities for trading. Independent small shop-keeping provided a secure livelihood for many Billingshurst people until the challenge of the supermarkets and an increasingly mobile society began to rob them of their resident clientele. International Stores was the first national chain retailer. There is now one supermarket, one national convenience store and a large country store, not to mention massive competition from outlets in Pulborough, Storrington and Horsham, with other rivals readily accessible at Crawley, Guildford and on the coast. Enterprising entrepreneurs continue to accept the challenge offering local access to niche supplies and services such as computing, opticians, gifts, wine, travel and gambling with varying degrees of success. Regrettably however, as elsewhere, charity shops and empty premises continue to signal the steady decline of independent shopping. Many desirable outlets for books, art supplies, music, videos, antiques and other cultural desirables have faded away. Estate agents still prosper.

The Gastronomic Revolution

Kelly's Directory for 1962 listed only Jane's Tea Garden and the Shirley Cafe near the Station as places where one might buy a meal, together with the seven pubs which then dealt mainly in sandwiches and snacks. People did not eat out except on rare festive occasions. At Billingshurst since then there has been a truly remarkable gastronomic revolution. The businesses of the village can now be said to be predominately in the service of the inner man. Today there are no fewer than 28 outlets where hot food or ready meals may be purchased, eaten or taken away. In 13 of these it is possible to sit down and be waited on; 12 are 'ethnic' in character. They include 6 public houses, two fish and chip shops, a country store, supermarket, convenience store and two bakers.

Parbrook

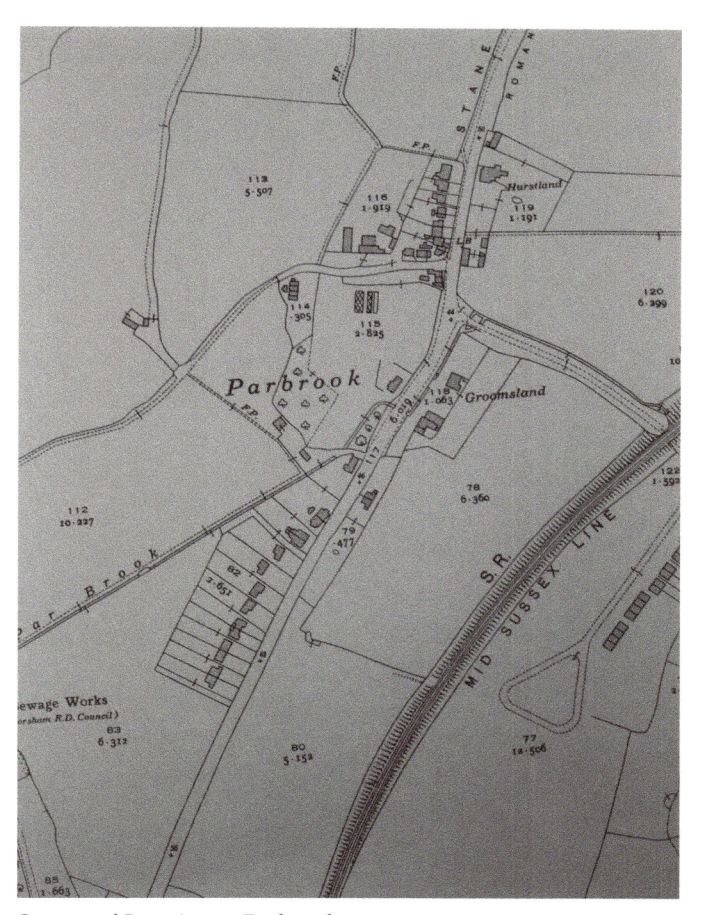

Staggered Junction at Parbrook

Street scene at Parbrook at the corner of Natt's Lane

South of Billingshurst along Stane Street lies the distinctive and separate set of dwellings beside the stream which is named Parbrook. The little hamlet stretches from Hurstlands, now a small estate in the corner of the Weald School playing fields, as far as Andrew Hill on the slope out of the valley on the road to North Heath, Adversane and Pulborough. Natts Lane is part of Parbrook leading off Stane Street beside the brook to join Marringdean Road and on towards West Chiltington. Before Station Road was built in mid 19th century all traffic from places south east of Billingshurst joined Stane Street at Hurstlands and could turn north to join the main Petworth Road or Billingshurst village centre and Horsham making it an important road junction. It was originally a crossroads with a more direct farm track going directly towards Newbridge at the Natts Lane junction.

The two oldest properties are Groomsland and Fossbrooks. Great Grooms about 1400 was recorded in the Fitzalan Survey as the property of John Gretegrome possessed of 'half a virgate [about 15 acres] 1s 8d & for ripeselver 1 cock, 2 hens 15 eggs and 9d'. The building has a chequered 20th century history. It became the Jenny Wren Restaurant for many years but has now reverted to private occupation, with another house recently built in the grounds. The barns and farm buildings were given planning permission for change of use to an office block and were transformed into an extensive antiques emporium for many years. It has recently become private apartments.

Sketch of Great Grooms

Fossbrooks was the home of Ephraim Wadey, the builder. He owned the brickyard at Gilmans, south of Natts Lane. This fine old timber-framed 16th century house with casement windows is now divided into two dwellings. The extensive builder's yard at the rear has been developed as a small estate named

Centurion Close. Groomsland Drive was built after WWII on the site of the old Brickyard together with the modern industrial estate called Gilmans.

Further north, opposite the Weald School, set back from the road is Cedars. Its original name in 1480 was Bondwick after its owner. Then when Laurence Clark married Mr. Bondwick's sister and took possession it was retitled Clarksland subsequently developing into a considerable farm estate. So it remained until 1912 when it was renamed Cedars.

Cottage life – by Mrs. Doris Garton, slightly abridged

"I was born in 1916 in a small primitive cottage in Parbrook, Billingshurst. My first memory is of my father coming home from the war in 1918 when I was two. I remember him opening his kit bag and producing a beautiful baby doll for me and a clarinet for my brother brought from France. Our cottage consisted of five rooms, sitting room, larder with shelves for keeping food and produce and a large scullery. All the downstairs rooms had flagstone floors and were very damp. The only floor covering was coco-matting, laid in strips and peg rugs made by my mother from old clothes. These could be replaced when the damp penetrated and caused them to rot.

The rickety wooden stairs led to two bedrooms, one door opening between the two. Under the stairs was our coal store. The coalman used to shoot coal straight from the sack into it. Imagine the dust! At the far end of the scullery was a large copper and built into the outside wall, a bread oven. The water was heated by faggot wood. My father had bought a piece of the wooded area nearby to provide faggot wood, pea boughs and bean sticks each year. He hired a horse and cart to bring them home

We had an outside loo which we flushed by taking pails of water with us on each visit. There was a well in the garden in which we used to keep butter, milk and meat. The provisions were placed in a bucket and lowered into the well by a chain. All vegetable fruit waste went into the hole for composting – true organic gardening.

My mother was a wonderful laundry woman and washed ironed and polished evening shirts and collars, worn in those days by the gentlemen for evening wear. She also goffered frilled caps and aprons worn by the maids for big houses.

I used to watch her heat the irons and polishing irons standing on bricks against the open fire. It was specialised work, goffering with tongs made hot in the red coals. My mother was a great wine maker so the larder with its stone floor was ideal for standing the crocks containing the fruit while it matured, feeding it from time to time with sugar candy. My mother bought spotted fruit from the greengrocer and put in a crock to soak to make wine. I used to go into the fields to pick dandelions, cowslips, winter pinks, parsnips, potatoes. The wines and ciders were made from all kinds of wild flowers, vegetables grown by my father.

My father worked in a small hoop yard, he was a hoop bender, these being used round barrels and casks. This was a small business at the end of Station Yard.

Making a bundle of hoops

Delivery of milk was by horse and trap, ladled from churns. Coal, bread, fish straight from the coast, all was delivered this way. We had steam trains. When I was about 9 a spark from a locomotive ignited a field of hay. Some livestock was lost with damage to sheds and some houses. People were evacuated from nearby cottages which I and my family were part. The fire brigade fought the fire with water from our garden wells and the brooks. Our well became permanently dry.

At the station was a taxi service run by horse and cab, some closed in carriages and landaus, used by ladies taking pleasure trips. The same family owned the station shop run by a small plump man [Mr. Voice] who always wore a bowler hat, selling everything from candles, sugar, tea, fruit and paraffin. No such thing as hygiene in those days.

I walked to school at the top of East Street. The Infant school had three classes and the big school was where we stayed until leaving at 14. I was taken to school by two older girls past the Vet's, where the Westminster Bank is now. It was a large house [Brick House] entered by a yard which housed an aviary and ravens. We walked up Rose Hill along a path on the top of a sloping bank where now stands the Rose Hill estate.

One big feature of the village was the Maltings Oast House. [It had, in its heyday, provided malt to the Swallow Brewery and run an in-house public house known as The Ship.] It was used as a 15th Century restaurant owned by a Scots family. All the waitresses wore long black flowing dresses, Dutch hats and aprons, 15th century style. I worked there, when aged 10, looking after a little boy of 2.

We used to walk across the Jengers meadow for picnics where now stand all the houses in Coombe Hill and Rowan Drive.

Opposite the current WI Hall there was an old corn merchant's, Blundells, sacks of corn and dog biscuits outside, and we kids used to help ourselves to the dog biscuits. Then there was the Unitarian Church and the butcher's where Cripps now is. Next was the King's Arms and Six Bells then the sweet shop owned by Lakers, World Stores, Post Office, Garage, International Stores, Drapers, Ironmongers, (Pilchers) Tribe the butcher, little cottages- old Mr. Jones had a clock business – a great character going round to all the big houses carrying his Gladstone bag and winding up the clocks once a week for the local gentry.

The only music we had at home was an HMV wind-up gramophone. We had a cabinet wireless powered by accumulators. Our lights were oil lamps and candles. Later we had a pump action Aladdin Lamp and then gas, a great step forward. The first street lighting was gas. A man used to cycle round the streets with a long-handled taper to light each lamp. [Mr. Rhodes].

I left school to start work after a disagreement with my father, who wanted to apprentice me in dressmaking with Hunt Brothers in Horsham. Being headstrong I wanted to serve in a shop but was not allowed, so I had to go into domestic service. There began a very hard but interesting 10 years, viewing and serving in many different households."

Farm work

"In the 1920s my father did contract to local farms at Parbrook. He would set off [from Hunston] at 6.30 am with his tools and hay knife strapped on his bicycle. According to the seasons he did hay cutting and tying, harvesting and threshing, thatching and land work, draining, ditching, ploughing with a horse, hedge-cutting and layering of hedges. He was also sometimes hired as a water diviner, using a hazel twig. Sometimes he would be away only returning home at weekends and at other times he was able to work locally. He also sharpened blades and shears using a home-made vice he erected in the garden".

Parish Yarns

Village Humour and other stories

In Sussex humour often involved jests at the expense of village rivals. This scrap of satirical verse is an example:

"Rudgwick for riches, Green for poors,
Billingshurst for pretty girls, Horsham for whores!"

Ridjik was the pronunciation for Rudgwick, (Wisborough) Green had the Union Workhouse, and Horsam was used for Horsham, hence the puns.

Bob Dames writes to the Billingshurst Society: We read last month that BILLA's people, having created BILLINGSHURST and moved up to BILLINGSGATE, finally settled in BILLINGHAM –what a long trek for a Saxon family all the way from London to near Middlesborough! Did they dilly-dally at BILLINGFORD in Norfolk, BILLINGBOROUGH near Grantham and BILLINGHAY towards Lincoln and later at BILLINGLEY near Doncaster? Who was it then, who settled in BILLINGTON near Bedford? Maybe they quarrelled with some of the family who traversed by BILLINGSLEY in Shropshire, thence to BILLINGE near St. Helens, Lancs. and finally to BILLINGTON north of Blackburn. Or, was the name BILLA a bit frequent like SMITH nowadays – and were they all different families? Think about it!

Billy Hoad goes courting in the rain at Billingshurst 1894

Billy Hoad grew up as a Horsham schoolboy. His fascinating 'Diaries and Reflections' are available online.

'Caught the 10.00 train to Billingshurst to pay first visit to Rose [who lived at Kirdford]. On arriving there found out the G. Baptist Chapel and went to service. While there the rain came on very hard so after chapel stayed in the schoolroom and had a snack I had brought with me with (the) Minister who seemed a very nice 'old Johnnie'. Stayed there till 3 then went to meet Rose. Found her then spent the afternoon under the railway bridge raining all the time. Went to chapel again in the evening. Only nine present including parson, choir, organist and ourselves but they still managed an anthem somehow. After service made for the station, caught the 7.37 train and got home soaking wet. Not a very good day for the first time!

The Railway Bridge, Natt's Lane

Scandalous behaviour and a lesson in tolerance

Reminiscent of Thomas Hardy's novel '*The Mayor of Casterbridge*' is the case mentioned by Harry Burstow in his book '*Reminiscences of Horsham*'.

"I have been told of a woman named Smart who, about 1820 was sold at Horsham for 3 shillings and sixpence. She was bought by a man named Steere, and lived with him at Billingshurst. She had two children by each of these husbands. Steere afterwards discovered that Smart had parted with her because she had qualities which he could endure no longer, and Steere, discovering the same qualities himself, sold her to a man named Greenfield, who endured, or never discovered, or differently valued the said qualities till he died."

The Haunting of the Kings Arms

Judy Middleton in 'The Haunted Places of Sussex' writes:

'As a coaching inn it is only fitting that a coachman should haunt it. On a cold February night, circa 1800, the coachman had imbibed rather too much beer and was unsteady on his feet. As he went to make his final check on the horses before turning in, he stumbled across the yard, missed his footing and fell down the well. It is said that it is exceptionally deep and his body was never recovered.'

Empire Day

"This was a special event, celebrated each year on 24th May. Parents attended our school at Billingshurst and Britannia and her attendants were always represented on stage whilst the rest of the schoolchildren represented the countries of the British Empire. All children wore white marguerites to school on this day. It was always celebrated in the morning and then we had half a day off."

Guy Fawkes Night

"The fancy dress competition was judged in the old village hall in the late afternoon. In the early evening everyone assembled outside the King's Arms to start a torchlight procession led by Billingshurst Band and bands from other villages.

The guy was carried on a cart of torches. Fireworks were let off – squibs, bangers and jumpers – as the procession wound its way around the village calling at one or two big houses and the Station Hotel and returning to the field at Alick's Hill which is now Hillview Garage and a housing estate. Here there was a very large bonfire. Someone would climb to the top of the bonfire to recite the bonfire prayer and position the guy, after which the fire was lit by torches. This was a major village occasion between the wars".

"One particular custom was for a man dressed as a devil to run to the top of the bonfire as the villagers recited their Bonfire Hymn – and then run down again as fast as possible before he got caught in the flames. The tradition came to an end one year when the 'devil' got badly burnt.

At Mr. Wadey's field beyond the Manor House there was the bonfire… Here poor 'Guy' was taken from the tumbrel and hoisted to the top of the bonfire. He must have made up his mind to make a quick job of it for he fell off the stake as soon as the bonfire was well alight and disappeared amidst the flames and the smoke. Mr. Radbourne read the 'prayer' from the top of the pile, and he too made a lightning disappearance as the flying torches went whirling through the air."

Bonfire Night
Remember, remember the fifth of November,
The Gunpowder, treason and plot.
I know no reason why gunpowder treason,
 Should ever be forgot.

Guy Fawkes, Guy Fawkes, 'twas his intent
To blow up King and Parliament.
Three score barrels of powder below,
Poor old England to overthrow

By God's providence he was catched,
With a dark lantern and a burning match.
Holler boys, holler boys, ring boys, ring.
Holler boys, holler boys, God save the King.

Additional lines were available for those of a particularly anti-papist disposition who recalled the burning of seventeen Protestant martyrs at Lewes in Mary Tudor's time:

A farthing loaf to feed old Pope,
A pennorth o' cheese to choke him,
A pint of beer to wash it down,
And a faggot o' wood to burn him!
Burn him in a tub o' tar,
Burn him like a blazing star,
Burn his body from his head,
And then we'll say old Pope is dead!
Hip, hip, hooray!

The bonfire was built on several different sites; one of the earliest was Price's Meadow where the Women's Hall now stands.

The Weald School, a history

In the Beginning

Weald School, Station Road entrance

The Butler Education Act of 1944 had decreed the creation of three sorts of Secondary School to be built to cope with the expected 'bulge' of babies to be born shortly after the armed forces had returned home from WW II.

The former 'all age' schools, such as Billingshurst off East Street, Pulborough and Wisborough Green, would be able to cope with extra children aged from 5 to 11 when the older pupils (12-15) were moved elsewhere. It was envisaged that the old dream of 'Secondary Education for All', previously enjoyed by only a small minority of children, might be realised. A Secondary School at that time was, normally, a selective Grammar School. All youngsters were now to be educated to the age of 15 in new premises designed to match the abilities and aptitudes of their pupils. The Grammar Schools, locally Collyers for boys and Horsham High School for girls, would continue to recruit the cleverest children from Billingshurst and district, selected by the '11 plus' or scholarship examination. They would be taught foreign languages, the classics and three sciences as well as the basic subjects. All the other children would attend new 'Secondary Modern schools' equipped and staffed to meet their assumed needs. These were broadly and mistakenly estimated to be largely non-academic and practical in nature, the 3 Rs, religious knowledge, woodwork, metalwork, technical drawing, domestic science, needlework, shorthand and typing, history, geography, physical education and in Billingshurst, rural studies. A third cohort was also envisaged comprising competent youngsters with a technical or commercial bent, who would be educated in Technical Schools. These latter were never actually built though one such existed for a while in Horsham.

So it transpired that on 12th September 1956, 80 pupils started secondary school off Station Road in the partially built Weald Secondary Modern School picking their way over planks laid in the mud. These children came by six coaches from local villages, but not at first from Billingshurst or Pulborough but as far afield as Cowfold and Petworth. 'First Year' boys wore short flannel trousers and school caps. In summer girls wore uniform frocks. Mr. Victor Gee, a headmaster from Bromsgrove, had been appointed at Easter to order equipment, recruit staff and prepare for the opening. Parents' Meetings were held at the Women's Hall. Only five classrooms were in use until after Christmas when 300 more children were enrolled. General Renton, horticulturist of Rowfold Grange, was made Chairman of Governors, and Mrs. Foster, nee Wilberforce, vice-chair. The children were tested on entry and allocated to 'streams', the cleverer A streamers having lessons broadly similar to grammar scholars, B streamers getting a good deal of practical tuition and those in the C stream offered simpler work and remedial lessons.

Early ideals of the Secondary Modern School

The parents of the children attending the school had high hopes for their youngsters but were understandingly disappointed that their offspring had been 'overlooked' by the 11+ examination. A 'Sec. Mod. School' was deemed 'second best' and an unproven asset. Adverse criticism of the green copper roof as being too costly for the education of people who were not high achievers did little to boost the morale of those who were enthusiastic for the new school system. An ideal education was envisaged as a ticket of entry to the 'officer class' as promulgated by the public schools and the Grammar Schools which were modelled on a similar ethos, curriculum and teaching practice. Most of the teachers there were university graduates who wore academic gowns. The pupils of these exclusive schools would be inculcated with a desirable body of knowledge and given the self-assurance and confidence that would authorise them to issue orders and expect to be obeyed; a ladder of success for those, with the high intelligence, tenacity, perseverance, and the necessary parental income, who wished to climb it.

Since 1951 Grammar Schools had prepared their more able 16 year olds for an Exam called Ordinary Level of the General Certificate of Education, which unlike its predecessor, the School Certificate, could be taken in just a single subject. [The older exam had to be passed in at least five approved subjects.] At the Weald the Governors supported the Staff in a determined effort to secure success in a public examination that would serve their aspirational pupils well and prove that all was not lost if a child failed at 11+ which, of course 9 out of 10 of them had. An early start was made using the UEI exam [Union of Educational Institutions] so that pupils who volunteered to stay on at school till 16 could achieve a valuable certificate to improve their career chances. This policy was highly successful. In 1960 the school had two girls who achieved Advanced level at GCE and in 1968 two boys gained places at University. By 1972 three-quarters of the students were taking extended courses taking a new exam, the CSE (1964) or the much desired O levels in a variety of subjects. Success in this demonstrable way brought enormous prestige to the Weald, soon recognised as one of the more desirable Secondary Modern Schools. Parental support was generous. By 1961 they had raised enough money to build a swimming pool. Anxiety about youthful rebelliousness as exemplified by the fashionable 'Mods and Rockers' led the County Council to provide the school with a Youth Tutor, and in due course, a purpose-built on-site Youth Wing for day and evening use.

Up until 1989 Heads, Staff and Governors of schools were responsible for both what was taught in the curriculum and how lessons were conducted. They were unconstrained by a National Curriculum, but strongly conditioned by their training and accepted good educational practice as recommended by the advisory service of the County Council. The Secondary Modern ethos of the time expected schools to broaden children's horizons by hosting visiting speakers, promoting sports, music, drama and the arts and by opening the pupils' eyes to the world of work and life in Britain and abroad. The Weald management responded well and it is fair to say that the initiatives of those years by the Secondary Modern Schools have left our present schools a legacy of breadth in education which we would be ill-advised to overlook in pursuit of narrow academic examination scores.

Mr. Gee was especially concerned to promote foreign travel. Under his influence many hundreds of Weald students visited Copenhagen, Amersfort in Holland, Germany and St. Augulin in France. He was a long-term trustee of the Central Bureau of Educational Visits. In 1968 he led 60 British Children to Lucerne where a plaque commemorating the centenary of a visit by Queen Victoria was unveiled by the Mayor. More local destinations were also exploited regularly like Cobnor for sailing, London for the National Association of Youth Clubs, Lodge Hill, the Lake District and local shows and theatres.

Mr. V.V. Gee. Headmaster, 1956 to 1974

Going Comprehensive

In 1965 Anthony Crosland, Wilson's Education Minister, issued Circular 10/65, a document which was to change the face of secondary education for the next half century. Local Authorities were asked to reorganise their schools 'along comprehensive lines'. The Conservative members of WSCC were against making changes, but the Independents, who normally backed the Conservatives, took a different view and supported the various proposed schemes. These involved creating three Sixth Form Colleges in West Sussex, served by 11 to 16 schools, several Middle Schools and, as in the case of The Weald, some few 11 to 18 all-through Comprehensives with their own Sixth Form. When 300 Weald parents attended a meeting to hear about the proposals for going comprehensive by 1969, all but one voted in favour. Billingshurst district parents were well aware that the 11+ exam was a game of snakes and ladders, played at too early an age, and there were 9 snakes sending you back towards 'go' for every single ladder leading to the glittering prizes. The new system would bring with it up-to-date buildings and equipment and a better-qualified staff.

From 1968 children of all abilities and aptitudes living in the catchment area and not in private schooling would come to The Weald, the 11+ exam having been abolished. The school would be fully comprehensive by 1973. By that date also the raising of the school leaving age to 16, called 'ROSLA', obliged all children to be prepared for a public examination, either the Certificate of Secondary Education or O Level. Some 25% of each school year group would have to stay on rather than leave to find jobs. Pessimists predicted disciplinary disaster but in practice the staff and students coped well. Though behaviour did deteriorate somewhat during the 80s 'punk' years, nevertheless good order prevailed and the dreaded 'ROSLA', was soon forgotten. The young are now expected to be in either training or education until they are 18!

A Change of Headteacher

This was Mr. Gee's chosen moment to retire to finish his days in 1992 in Norfolk.

Mr. Geoffrey Lawes, a Headteacher in Brockley, South London, was appointed in his place to begin in the summer term of 1974, bringing his experience of by now well established London Comprehensive schooling. Among early appointments was that of Miss Angie Clark, confirmed as Senior Mistress, a position she had held in the last year of Mr. Gee. She had come to the Weald as Head of Girls' physical education. No-one made a longer or more conscientious career at the school than Mrs. Burroughs, as she later became. She retired only in 2013.

Subsequently numerous changes of policy ensued. For example corporal punishment was discontinued. Mr. Lawes championed abolition in two national TV debates. The House System and division into Upper and Lower Schools disappeared. Forms were no longer streamed for registration and 'setting' was introduced for teaching purposes, so that children were taught in groups according to their ability in particular subjects rather than by a general assessment. At that time it was a fashionable judgment that good 'pastoral care' of pupils was just as important as any other aim in education and that large schools needed sub-division so that no child became an overlooked anonymous unit. Consequently each year group was allotted its own permanent staff under the management of 'Heads of Year' acting, for welfare and disciplinary purposes, like schools within a school. The excellent tradition continued of extra-curricular activities, music, drama, sport, visits and foreign exchanges. Association football gave place to rugby union. The familiar uniform school blazer and badge and logo gave way to a V-necked jersey, and the Sixth Form were allowed smart casual dress. The influence of ever-increasing numbers and the admixture of higher ability pupils together with a major building programme of laboratories, a new Sixth Form Centre, opened by Rev. David Shepherd, Bishop of Liverpool, and a teaching block boosted morale. By 1979 some 22 students were beginning degree courses, two of them at Oxbridge. A successful Modern school had morphed into an equally successful comprehensive. The teaching staff of 1981 had had at some time 40 of their own children on the school registers, a silent testimonial of their confidence.

Progress has continued unabated so that today over 90% of Weald pupils achieve 5 or more passes at the current equivalent of the old O level, the GCSE, grades A to C. [The CSE and O Level were merged in 1988.]

Community Schooling

A popular concept from 1976 onwards was that of the 'Community School' successfully pioneered by Cambridgeshire Village colleges. In a nutshell it envisaged the use, by the whole community, of expensive school halls, classrooms, gyms, swimming pools, libraries, playing fields, educational equipment and teaching expertise. They ought not, it was argued, to be used exclusively by secondary aged children. Anybody in the neighbourhood should be enabled to use or hire the facilities from the cradle to the grave. By uniting adult education, youth provision, and providing crèches and hosting clubs, societies, public meetings and celebrations, a Community School could make available both continuing education and public amenities and leisure facilities, comparable to a small local university. Older 'late developers' could enjoy refresher courses and learn new skills. The premises would be particularly welcoming in school holidays and at weekends. The beauty of it was that the taxpayer had already paid for it. Mature adult students could study for A level with the Sixth Form on payment of a small fee. Evening classes were arranged to meet in local primary schools. A crèche was opened in a school hut, the origin of the present Wakoos.

The concept was enthusiastically adopted at the Weald in 1978. A Community Tutor was appointed in liaison with Horsham District Council to run the thriving Evening Institute and Youth Wing and to organise lettings of the premises. The Parish Council held its meetings in the Library, there were regular discussion group and Society Meetings, the Annual Flower Show used the Hall, Sports Clubs hired the pitches, dances, music concerts, keep-fit rallies and carnivals were held. Together with a handful of other West Sussex Schools the Weald was officially designated a Community School by a supportive County Council. During 1988 25,000 customers paid to use the Weald Recreation Centre. The previous year 80 Adult Education Courses were run with 2,386 enrolments, plus 246 for children of junior school age. Where did it all go wrong? The answer was, of course, 'Events, dear boy, events'.

Economic strictures and troubled times

Progress was made during the late 70s and 80s in the face of difficult political and economic circumstances. Financial constraints meant that the maintenance of buildings was most often left to working parties of staff and parents, and fund-raising was a necessary means of securing minor building developments. Numbers on roll continued to swell resulting in dangerous overcrowding in narrow corridors. Temporary buildings proliferated. 1536 pupils were on roll in 1982, a figure similar to today. In 1983 some temporary relief was obtained as a result of a complex fund-raising collaboration of the County and District Councils, the Sports Council and the local parishes to build the Sports Hall and changing rooms and a new library, so designed as to create a quadrangle west of the old Assembly Hall. The designation as a Community School helped to secure these funds.

Then in the mid-80s there came industrial turmoil. Chancellor Lawson announced £500 M of public spending cuts. The teachers' unions were seeking a pay award to remedy ten years of steady deterioration of their salary. At the Weald between 1984 and 1987 a fairly normal service was maintained through a difficult period of 'work to contract' by staff. [withdrawal of goodwill to do anything other than teach their classes]. Only by dint of introducing a 'concentrated school day' was it possible to deal with supervision of pupils at break and lunchtime. When, after months of national discord peace was restored to the teaching profession, a short interlude of peaceful reconstruction followed.

The so-called 'Continental Day' was continued, the afternoon sessions becoming periods for voluntary clubs and extra-curricular activities, with two separate home runs on the buses. This lasted until the next set of major political interventions in the life of the school.

In 1988 all schools had to adopt the American style grade numbers for school Years, so that what had been the 'First Year' of secondary school became the 'Seventh Year' and the Upper Sixth was 'Year 13'. Curiously the 'fossil' term Sixth Form has persisted.

This was the first of a flood of more profound changes. Teachers were now subject to a tighter contract. More importantly, the school curriculum, hitherto determined by Staff and Governors, was to be prescribed in some detail by the Government. The National directives would shortly swamp the school with paper in pursuit of 'one size fits all' reforms which were over-ambitious, over-prescriptive and, after much wasted effort, proved unworkable. The documents required a so-called 'entitlement' range of subjects which it was felt necessary for every child to follow, regardless of its age, ability or aptitude. Silk purses could be created from sows' ears. Every student could learn a foreign language, for example.

The political consensus was that English education was in a parlous state, desperately in need of drastic 'reform' from the wisdom of governmental 'experts', and it was reckoned no longer wise to leave the curriculum, and to a great extent how it was taught, to teachers and governors. Not surprisingly the Weald management which had conscientiously tailored its own curriculum to the needs of local pupils resented this imposition of a national orthodoxy but were obliged to comply. Teachers began to make some limited use of Information Technology. From 1985 another sea-change in practice swept away the traditional crafts of woodwork, metalwork and technical drawing, needlework and domestic science, together with the lathes, forges, benches and circular saws in dedicated rooms. They, and their teachers, gave place to computer science, design and technology, correctly assessed as the working media of the future. In retrospect we may have washed away the baby with the bathwater. Traditional craft skills still remain in constant demand.

In 1989 Mrs. Burroughs returned to the Weald after a ten year break to raise a family in the role of Head of Special Needs. By this time children who found school a challenge, abused as 'Dunces' in Victorian times and offered poorly resourced 'Remedial' treatment more recently, now attracted extra funding and individual support. Wherever possible they were taught in 'mainstream' rather than 'special schools'. It was to Mrs. Burroughs credit that with the Weald quickly established such a service to successive groups of disadvantaged pupils.

A new Head, new initiatives

In 1991 Mr. Lawes retired after 17 years as pilot of the Weald and Mrs. Virginia Holly, a Deputy Head from a school in Greenwich was appointed.

Efficiency and progress needed, in the Thatcher government's view, to be brought about by vigorous competition between schools, so that parents could select the good schools and failing schools would either wither away or could be disciplined and reorganised. The key instrument would be the exercise of parental choice of secondary school at 11+. To further that choice, annual league tables of measurable achievement such as examination successes and attendance would be published. The accompanying tool was a new machinery of 'accountability'. Governors were required to publish written policies on all aspects of school life such as bullying, health and safety, illegal substances and sex education. Regular assessments would be carried out on all schools by an inspection regime called Ofsted. Its judgments would be published for the benefit of parents and for remedial action by local authorities when deemed necessary.

The effects of this were mixed. Sharper competition did develop between local schools in pursuit of 'top billing' and energy was invested in advertising and public relations. School uniform was elaborated. However enhanced parental choice for Billingshurst catchment parents had little effect. They had always been free to select other schools providing they could afford their own transport. Parental choice is an urban concept where there is practicable access to alternative schools. In practice Weald annual enrolment stayed steady and of recent years the school has been fully subscribed by satisfied parents of the neighbourhood. A series of excellent Ofsted reports from their first introduction has endorsed their encouraging judgment.

Mrs. Holly soon made some changes. The Continental Day was discontinued as it breached certain new legal requirements for hours of tuition and the focus of practice was, of necessity, subtly shifting to improving pass-rates in examinations. Standard Achievement Tests at 14 were introduced to support the regime. A substantial budget surplus was invested in a more attractive redesigned entrance to the school. A public Gold Awards Annual Prizegiving Ceremony in the Sports Hall was instituted to promote the growing prestige of the school and the successes of the pupils. Mrs. Paton resigned as Chairman of Governors and was succeeded first by Mr. Tony Bolden who declared that the Governors should 'market the school'. When, in 1993, four pupils won Oxbridge places public esteem indeed stood high.

Mr. Bolden was shortly succeeded by Mr. G. Puttock. For a short time there was some anxiety lest falling rolls would cut back available school resources. Since 1990 schools had been obliged to manage their own finances, being granted an annual budget according to the number and age of pupils on roll. The management was then free to spend this on teachers' salaries, ancillary staff and equipment as they thought fit. This was just one example of how power over policy and practice was shifting away from the County Council both to the Head and Governors locally and also to central government in respect of the curriculum, inspection, institutional discipline and financial provision. Responsibility for funding the Sixth Form was removed from the LEA and entrusted to a new agency called the Further Education Council. Special subsidies were then offered to schools which could earn themselves special status for particular excellencies. The Weald explored 'Technology Status' and was eventually duly rewarded, though it underwent some turmoil in the process.

The national purse-strings were now loosening. The 1996 school budget was for £3.25 million. A splendid new library, the school's fourth siting, was opened in March by the Duke of Kent and permission given for a new music block. There would soon be an all-weather pitch and 'Solutions', a fitness suite, as an enhancement of the Community School. Some playing fields had been lost to the major development of 550 houses and the building of the western by-pass, and £1M was promised for a new swimming pool. The reduction of traffic on the A29 at last allowed the possibility of a major lay-by and coach park. From the school's inception in 1956 the need to use Station Road as a bus park for 17 coaches twice a day had proved a daily hazardous headache for the staff and local residents.

Sadly in 1997 the pioneer Governor, Mrs. Pamela Foster died, a lady whose counsel and wise judgment had contributed to the growth and achievements of the Weald.

A Hiccup in Progress

Enormous energy by two staff members was now dedicated to achieving 'Technology Status' which required sponsorship with local businesses and a commitment to develop and propagate good practice. British Aerospace was highly cooperative. However negotiations and details of the bid for government funding were limited to the Head and her small circle. £147,000 worth of support was promised from local businesses. The rest of the staff, hitherto always accustomed to consultation, began to take umbrage. The bid for recognition was successful, ready for a start in 1998, one of only 18 such approvals nationwide. The Governors were delighted but many staff felt side-lined and unconsulted.

Meantime other negative issues emerged. Rolls had fallen and would not revive for two years until new pupils arrived from the new housing development. Resources would probably shrink and certain unwise expenditures and promotions were being called into question in the staffroom. There was disapproval of the Head's presidential style of management which frequently deliberately excluded the advice of the three popular Deputy Heads. Matters were exacerbated when she announced that one of them would be made redundant with other teachers to help meet the expected financial shortfall. The Governors backed the Head and Chairman, entrusting them with any necessary decisions. They also foolishly turned down the scheme for a bus park lay-by. The Senior Management Team in response devised a set of alternative proposals to balance the budget without recourse to any redundancies.

The staff rebelled. In February 103 of them signed a crucial document giving a vote of no confidence in the Head's ability to manage the school. The damage was done. The story spilled into the local newspaper. The Governors supported the Head, but the County Council sent in a team of officers for a week to explore the situation. No bulletin was issued but Mrs. Holly, who had been on sick leave, resigned to take up a temporary post with the Central Bureau of Educational Visits.

Adverse publicity was minimised by this resignation and the rapid restoration of good relationships by Mr. Bunker, the Director of Education, drafting in Mr. Ted Hickford from Midhurst Grammar to restore morale as temporary Head. In this Mr. Hickford was eminently well-qualified by experience and personality. He paved the way for the next Headteacher, Mr. Peter May, to put the school once more into the public good books. He joined in January 1999 from a headship in

Witney, Oxfordshire. Mr. Puttock had resigned in exasperation as Chairman of Governors, and Dr. Graham Parr took on the responsibility.

21st Century Schooling

After those few steps backwards the staff, pupils and parents and governors were enthusiastic for a new leap forward into the 21st century which with evident vigour the new Head was keen to promote. Technology status led to a marked investment in Information and Communications Technology. The computer now began its significant invasion of the classroom as a standard medium of research and instruction. Within a year 230 stations on the internet network came into operation, all with e-mail and internet access. Through all the difficulties exam results remained excellent. A 66% pass rate at GCSE (A-C) was recorded. An 'exceptionally good' Ofsted report in 2000 boosted morale. By 2002 the Weald had won two Achievement Awards and the Head attended a celebratory reception at Highgrove hosted by Prince Charles. The school adopted a web-site and the new parking area off the A29 came into use. When the whole school visited the Millennium Dome they saw former student Matthew Clark in his role as the leading acrobat.

Mr. May then pressed for a necessary new capital building programme. New teaching methods and technology demanded more generous and more specialised classroom spaces than the traditional 'chalk and talk' way of working. Science, Information Technology and Business Studies were particularly short of proper facilities. The Sixth Form had far outgrown the facility of 1974. Financially prospects were more promising. The school annual budget was just short of £4 M. Teachers salaries and conditions of service had improved. By 2002 two thirds of the Year 11 pupils entered the Sixth Form and many of those who left went into further education or training. Education had moved a long way from the anxieties about 'ROSLA to 16' back in 1972. Over 100 students each year were by now leaving the Sixth Form for university. The 'Trug', a battery-powered car built by Weald enthusiasts, was featuring in national newspapers for its success on the Goodwood circuit. These were winning days.

In 2003 a new burgundy school uniform was adopted and a fresh logo, the fourth symbolic oak tree in the school's history. A year of construction work lay ahead, valued at £3 M. This produced 7 new science labs and 5 lab makeovers, 8 classrooms, 3 business studies areas and a modern Sixth Form Centre to replace the 1974 structure, now totally inadequate for its purpose. The Weald main entrance had always been hidden from the highway and presented an unattractive architectural spectacle. The bold new buildings offered a striking modern aspect for passers-by on the A29. Internally the rooms showed high quality workmanship and a welcome spaciousness in contrast with the older school premises.

Burgundy uniforms

The Sixth Form Centre from Stane Street

Teachers were by this time relieved of much clerical and welfare work by a rapid expansion of non-teaching support staff. In 1956 they had been two in number. By 1990 they had risen to 32 and by 2007, including part-timers, the head count of ancillary staff had risen to 69. All classrooms were by now connected to the computer network and the Weald had become licensed to broadcast its own radio programme and showcased their work at two national conferences. A survey revealed that 94% of the pupils had access to a home computer! By 2005 400 computers were in use in the classrooms.

When in that year children invited their grandparents to a 'Generation Game' to show them how school work was being done it transpired that 50 of them had been pupils of the school themselves, underlining the fact that the school could no longer be regarded as a dubious experiment in social engineering but was a thoroughly respected local institution, widely admired for its excellent service to the community. It may not have produced as many cabinet ministers as Eton College, but for the vast majority of children, it had provided a sound liberal education and a springboard to fulfil their life chances. The ready sale of property in the neighbourhood and, regrettably, the enhanced price of it, bear eloquent witness to the satisfaction of incomers to the district.

The school continues to be thought of as a Community School but not with the same justifications that found favour in the late 20th century. The generous sporting provision of Jubilee Fields and the fine new Parish Hall, [lately designated The Community Centre], following major housing developments, removed the imperative need for the hiring of pitches, social gatherings, the Flower Show, conferences and civic meetings. Competition between schools discouraged the school management from offering generous access to Tom, Dick and Harry who might disturb the polish on the floors and interfere with the keeping up of appearances. National disquiet about deviants who might harm children led to anxiety about strangers and tight security measures to control access to the premises. Any dilution of resources on non-statutory causes was to be avoided in pursuit of more targeted objectives. The Youth Wing dwindled, its customers coming to regard a return to school in the evenings as unwelcome, a view which, strangely enough, had not troubled their older brothers and sisters. For a decade from 1978 the Governing body had entitled itself 'The Community Council' to reflect its wider responsibility, but the 1988 Education Act so prescribed the format of Governors' Meetings that it reverted to standard form. Finally responsibility for adult education was removed from the County Council and the funding for the Community Tutor discontinued. Adult education classes, once so valuable for socializing reasons and self-improvement, eventually disappeared altogether. Thankfully the Pool and Leisure Centre and the new Wakoos nursery have kept the Community School concept alive.

Wakoos – Billingshurst Family and Children's Centre

The school was now eligible to apply for another 'special status'. A bid was submitted to become a Sports College and this was awarded in 2006. The upshot was that the Weald became a district sports hub, the CSSSP [Central Sussex Schools Sports Partnership]. The catering work of the school was taken in-house rather than let to contractors, or as in the early days, run by the County Council. Planning was soon under way for the new 25 metre, 4 lane enclosed swimming pool and leisure centre at a cost of £5.7M to the County, District and Parish Councils. It was to be ready by 2008/9. Meantime Midhurst Grammar School was in difficulties as a result of unsatisfactory Ofsted reports and Mr. May was seconded to take charge there, jointly with the Weald.

Aerial view, 50th anniversary in 2006

There then began a remarkable new project. This was to build a school of 25 classrooms with a working party of 23 staff and students at Katale, north of Nairobi in Kenya, at a cost of £50,000 to be raised by the Weald. The Lions club contributed £6,000, the funds were raised and the project was successfully completed.

In 2007 the school celebrated its half century, entertaining many hundreds of visitors, including a small distinguished group of the original staff at the opening in September, 1956.

In December 2008 Mr. Peter May retired and Mr. Peter Woodman joined as Headmaster from Avon Vale High School. There were developments. The school is now organised once again on a House system, but with the difference that tutor groups are arranged so that each unit, with its permanent teacher-tutor, consists of pupils of all five ages from 11 to 16. The Tutor Group will belong to one of five Houses – Wilberforce, Elgar, Austen, Livingstone and Darwin, symbolising five branches of study and the initials spelling WEALD. Tutors and House Heads care for the children's welfare and discipline and monitor their progress in studies. They are assisted by two Directors of Learning who monitor development through Key Stages 3 and 4. House competition for the House Cup is exercised in all aspects of school life, for example attendance, library use, sports achievements, and house points for good work and behaviour, calculated by computer.

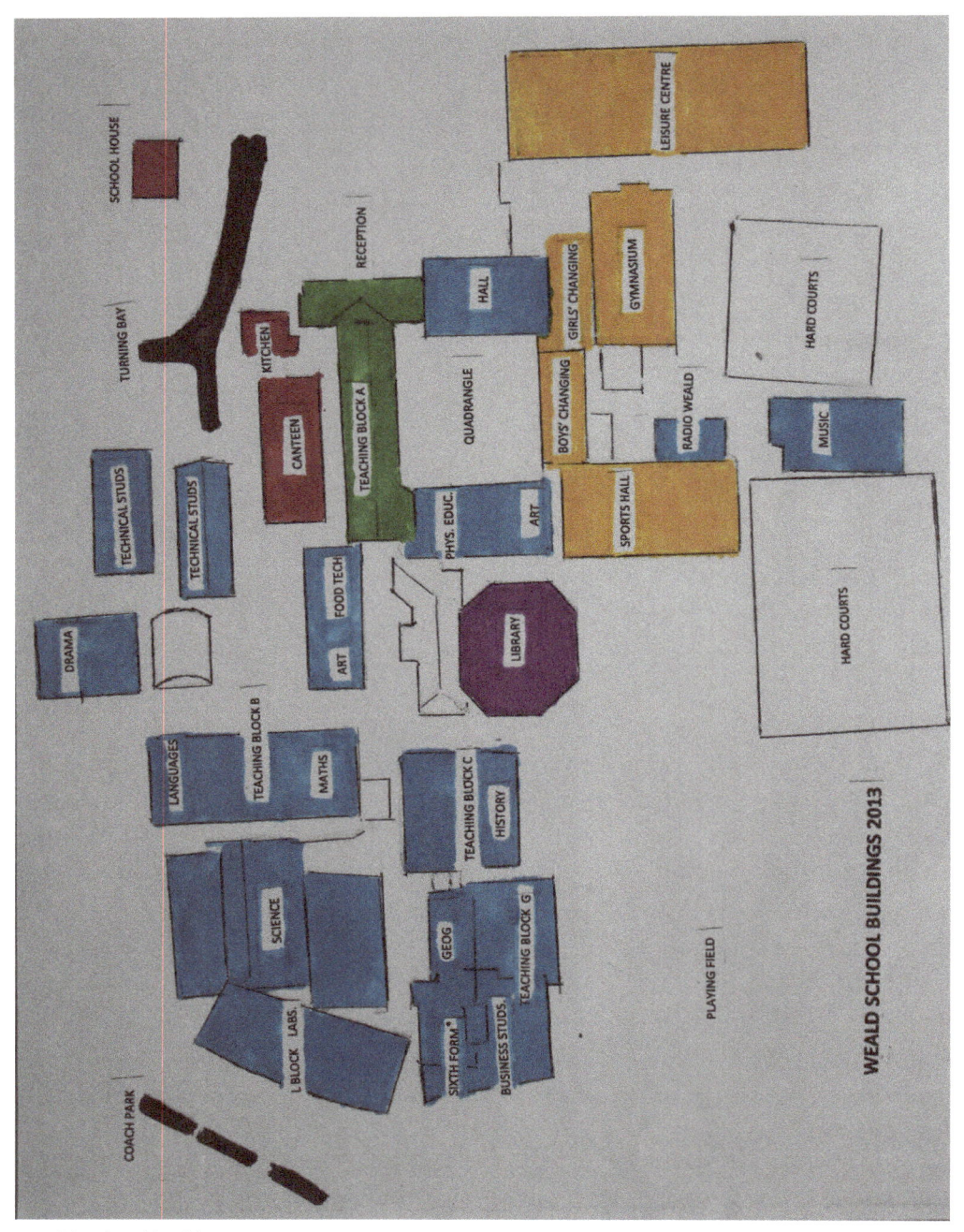

Weald School buildings

In 2011 and 12 the school had a £2M refurbishment and building programme.

The former Youth Wing was reborn as a Drama Studio.

Since 2006 the school has raised £200,000 for Kenya schools enabling 50 classrooms to be built. Radio Weald broadcasts on 87.7 FM for a week in July and regularly in school. Since 2008 it has broadcast on the internet. In 2006 the 'Slippery Trug' battery-powered car was UK Champion in the National Greenpower Car Competition. Its successor, the 'Black Bullet' came second in 2010 and 11.

Communication with parents is enhanced by an excellent fortnightly Newsletter, e-mailed to them and available on the school website. In the past 12 years over 40 members of staff have sent their own children to the school. Examination results are highly commendable. In 2013 91% of the students gained A* to C passes at GCSE. 70% of them had both English and Maths passes. 99% of A level entries were successful, 7% with A* grading and 60% at A* to B. In November 2013 Ofsted, the National Office for Standards in Education, having recently inspected the school, graded the Weald as 'Outstanding in all areas and outstanding overall'.

Local housing developments in Billingshurst parish, lifting the population to 12.000 by 2020 AD, together with those of other villages in the school catchment area, will require places for 2000 students. To that end a £3M expansion and modernisation programme is ongoing in 2016. Obsolete facilities are being upgraded and some 40 extra classrooms constructed on the campus. A new teaching block will rise on the former tennis courts beside the Sports Hall.

Weald School Alumni include:

> Billy Twelvetrees - England international rugby union footballer.
> Hinda Hicks – popular singer
> Tim Hincks - President of Endemol, TV company
> Matthew Morrison – barrister
> Lynsey nee Miller – JP
> Mandy nee Miller – Hd of Dept. Universite de Meaux
> Killa Kela - (Lee Potter) – beatbox musician
> Michael Coupe – CEO Messrs. J. Sainsbury
> Piers Hernu – writer and editor of men's lifestyle magazines
> Bryce Wolfe – Australian financier
> Mark Hubbard – YMCA sports director, basketball USA
> Dr. Paula Richards, Fellow of Royal College of Radiologists
> Alison Garland – actress
> Katie Blake (Beale) – actress
> Laura Poot – President Oxford Union

Messrs. Crabbe, Hogan, Jones and Verheul all Doctors of Medicine
Roger Patterson – National authority on beecraft.

Oliver Reed and Josephine Burge

Just after Christmas, 1980 the Weald School was the unwelcome focus of a storm of tabloid journalism. Oliver Reed, a popular film actor of tough-guy characters, with a well-cultivated reputation for roistering pranks, arm wrestling and drunken exuberance, lived in Ellens Green with a pink rhinoceros at his gate. He is well-remembered for a male nude-wrestling scene with Alan Bates in 'Women in Love'. Jo Burge, a keen young horsewoman, was in the Lower Sixth Form. The press got hold of the story that she was absent with flu, but had been recovering in Barbados in company with Oliver Reed, a man 27 years her senior.

The paparazzi took up positions at the front gate of the school, where police Sergeant Dick Parrott and a colleague also took up camp. David Elling, Head of Sixth Form and Pat Bush, Deputy Head, smuggled Jo in and out of school under a blanket in the boot of a car, until Jo's mother wisely decided that Jo should leave school, in view of her social commitments. These resulted in marriage in 1985 and a partnership which endured until Oliver died in 1999 in Malta. He is buried at Churchtown, County Cork. Oliver claimed to have drunk 106 pints of beer on a two-day stag party binge. Mr. Elling described Jo as 'a smashing young girl, an elfin type, never a raving beauty, but a quiet sweet person'.

Billingshurst Primary School

The history of primary education in Billingshurst up to 2010 is described elsewhere in this book In that year the separate Infant and Junior Schools on the Upper Station Road site were combined under the direction of one Headteacher and a single Board of Governors. Extensive building work accompanied the reorganisation, providing spacious classrooms and well-designed areas for outdoor learning. There are two Halls, well-stocked libraries, an up-to-date ICT suite, a music room, kitchen for hot meals, a food technology area for children, outdoor areas and playgrounds.

Helen Williamson MA is the Headteacher of the school which caters for up to 630 boys and girls from age 4 (Reception) to age 11 (Year 6). Pupils normally leave for Secondary education at the Weald School, or elsewhere if parents so choose. She is supported by some 34 Assistant Teachers, a Business Manager, a large team of Teaching Assistants, Ancillary Staff, Lunchtime Helpers and Cleaners. The school was rated 'Good' by the Ofsted Inspection Team in December, 2015. An informative account of the school curriculum and policies on partnership with parents, music, sports, after-school clubs, pastoral care and individual support of pupils, school uniform, enrolment and visiting opportunities is available on the school website: www.billingshurstprimary.org.uk Phone: 01403 782789

Billingshurst Primary School, Upper Station Road

The Hamlets – Five Oaks

Five Oaks sign

The Norman Manors

The Normans from 1066 controlled law and order, collected rents and arranged for services and military forces by the feudal Manorial system. The King parcelled out his kingdom to his henchmen in return for Knight Service, in our case to Roger de Montgomery whose fiefdom was the Rape of Arundel. They in turn allocated 'Honours' to favoured parties, who were in charge of one or more Manors where rents were collected from tenants and courts of law held.

The most important Manor of the 20 or so with land in Billingshurst parish was Bassett's Fee, originally possessed by the Abbott of Fecamp, which also held lands in Rudgwick, Pulborough, West Chiltington, Slinfold and Kirdford. In Henry V's reign the ownership passed to the Abbess of Syon Nunnery in Middlesex. In the village centre it held property west of the High Street, Townland, Gingers and Taintland. Rosier and Okehurst were also part of the Manor but probably were acquired later. In the 15th century Manor House in the High Street was the residence of the Steward of Bassett's Fee. When Henry VIII dissolved the monasteries the Manor passed into lay hands and by the 19th century, a timber merchant, Mr. Clear was Lord of the Manor. He got into dispute with the Puttock's who lived where Austin's is now, over heriot, a sort of death duty. He sent two men to collect two animals but the mighty Billingshurst Puttocks rebuffed his demand.

At Five Oaks, lands east of Stane Street were in the Manor of Pinkhurst, with a Manor House at Slinfold, under Roger de Someri whose name is recalled at Summers Place. [In 1372 Richard Somer bought a house and garden in Billingshurst from William Newbrigge (Newbridge) paying 6s a year and one rose, to the Lord of the Manor.]

Lands west of the road were gifted to the Bishop of Fecamp in Normandy as part of the Manor of Wiggonholt. The Lords of the Manors' agents, the reeves and stewards, collected the Manorial dues. Billingshurst parish was parcelled out to a score of Manors since, in the earliest times, the woods were allocated for swine to forage in as outlying territories which belonged to the more southerly parent manorial headquarters. Other Billingshurst manorial lands included Pounds, Arundel, Ferring and Fure, W. Chiltington, Storrington, Marringdean and Guildenhurst and, of course, Bassett's Fee.

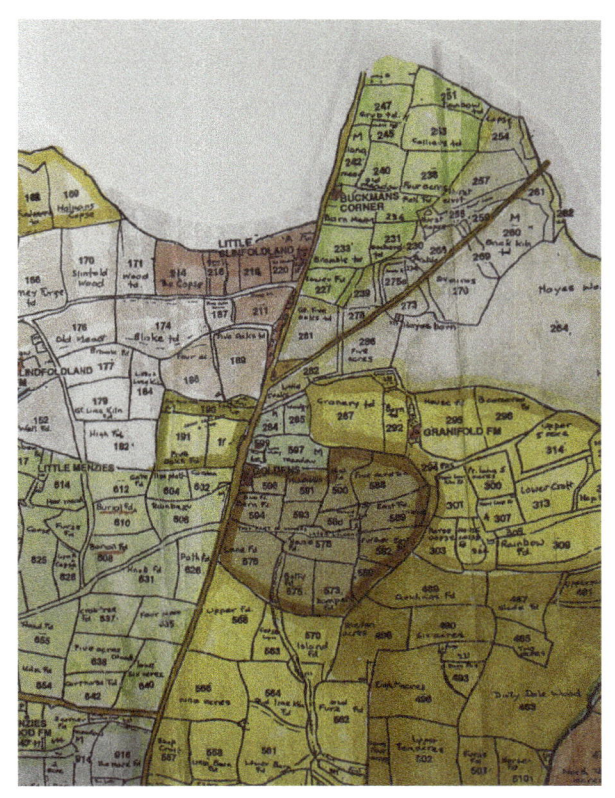

Tithe Map, 1841, of Five Oaks

Mediaeval Manors were grants of land to trusted Knights allocated in return for military service and rents to the feudal hierarchy, the Barons and Tenants-in-Chief, and ultimately the King. They had their own courts to control property rights and maintain law and order. Some lands were farmed 'in hand' but most were divided up among yeoman who paid rent, rendered labour services on demand and military service when called upon. They were effectively economic agricultural business units deliberately structured to entrench and defend the Norman body-politic. They were quite distinct from the ecclesiastical and civic institution which was the parish, expected to care for all the people, body and soul. This feudal format withered with time, particularly after the dissolution of the monasteries which had been major Lords of Manors, and when service and military obligations had been commuted to money payments.

Origins

The name of the cluster of houses and farmsteads where the A29 road to Guildford joins the road from Billingshurst to Horsham is first recorded on an estate plan in 1651 showing the whereabouts of trees. It is tempting to suppose that the road junction determined the growth of the settlement but as the Horsham road was not built until 1810, as a business venture in order to build a turnpike, this is an unlikely origin. Prior to that travellers to Horsham had to go further north and make their way via Hayes Lane through Slinfold. Unlike Parbrook and Adversane the area had no convenient streams either.

More probably the close conjunction of several thriving farmsteads straddling Stane Street led to an accumulation of dwellings which comprised the hamlet north of Billingshurst. The map of the Rape of Arundel (1819) names it Five Oaks Green. It also identifies 'E. Griningfold' on the way to Horsham and Buckman's Corner en route to Slinfold or Bucks Green and Rudgwick.

The name Buckman, incidentally, was substituted for the old name Buckmott in deference to a family of that name living nearby. Rev. Henry Beath, Vicar of Billingshurst lived at Buckmans Corner.

Grainingfold House was farmed by Joseph Dale in 1855 and ten years later by Thomas Chesman, followed by William Belcher and Haramand Scott by 1878. Later occupants were the Cullens who had aircraft landing there.

17th Century Five Oaks

In 1609 100 acres of land identified as Slinfoldland in the Manor of Wiggonholt was leased from Sir Thomas Palmer, the Elder, to Thomas Haylor.

The name Five Oaks occurs on a deed of 1622 where Jonathan Hayler sold 11 acres beside Stane Street 'where there stand five oaks'. We can conclude that the oaks stood near Slinfoldland west of Stane Street in Wiggonholt Manor. (The Manorial documents of 1832 contain a bill from John Allman, nurseryman of Billingshurst, for replacing a 30 foot oak which presumably some errant citizen had cut down against the custom of the Manor.)

Slinfoldland is now known as Fold Farm.

The 1622 deed reveals that Jonathan Haler, yeoman, leased the 11 acres known as Toms Field to William Clayton, husbandman, of Rudgwick. This stood west of Stane Street between Buckmotts Corner and Billingshurst on the north of Minstrells Wood, also known as Winstrills Wood or Menzies. He made up and sold another 17 acre landholding called Little Slinfoldland, now called Five Oaks Farm. On these grounds early cottages were built originating the hamlet. Present day 1 and 2 Fieldings Cottages are most likely on the site of the house that Clayton had built in the 17th century.

James Cooper and Thomas Penfold were witnesses to the 1622 deed. Gentlemen with those surnames were known to have had property at Kingsfold at that time before the Civil War.

Eight years later John Nye of 'Five Oaks House' (built on 'Five Oaks Land') is known to have paid Church Tax for bread and wine and the wages of the Parish Clerk. Possibly this was the house now known as Chequers. A subsequent farmer, Cornelius Voice, tenant of people called Sharp, renamed his holding The Chequer House and Land. A Checker House was a beer house so it may have been the predecessor of the Five Oaks Inn.

Mr. Voice went off to Canada in 1834 under the emigration scheme sponsored by Earl Egremont. Luke Wadey and wife Sarah, a carpenter and wheelwright, followed Mr. Voice in 1839 as a tenant and by 1861 had become a farmer with 60 acres, some of which may have been won in a wager! He had a big family, remarried a widow Sarah Jupp and employed eight men. His firm did the restoration work on St. Mary's Church. By 1871 he had 180 acres, a groom and a servant. Three of his sons were carpenters, James married to Jane, David married to Harriett and Isaac who was a wheelwright. Another son, Frank, was the blacksmith. All had big families. By 1890 we know that James' widow was in charge of 'Mrs. Jane Wadey & Sons, builders and contractors, plumbers and house decorators'. The farm bothy beside Chequers was renovated in 1979, now renamed Shire Cottage.

Later Buildings

Near Chequers was another farmhouse called Goldings or Goldens Farm in Pinkhurst Manor. It is now Oak House. Richard Bettesworth Denyer inherited it from his mother, together with Summers Farm in 1810. His great uncle, Thomas Bettesworth, a London merchant, had been the tenant at Summers in the 17th century and, in 1729, had permission from the Manor of Bassetts Fee, to which it belonged, to knock down a 12 roomed house and erect a stone building with a polished marble porch. (The Lord of the Manor House of Bassetts Fee was Maurice Ireland living at Billingshurst. ['Fee' is a short form of 'fiefdom', meaning a feudal grant of land]). Robert Goff of Poole bought the freehold of Summers in 1880 and commissioned John Norton to design the present edifice. It became a convent school in 1945 and Sotheby's sale rooms in 1984. It is now elaborately redeveloped as the main feature of an upmarket housing estate. As for Goldings, it was owned by Mrs' Louisa Maas at the end of the century, the land being farmed first by John Thorne and then Mrs. Mercy Penfold and her family. They delivered milk in Billingshurst.

The old Five Oaks Inn

The Five Oaks Inn as rebuilt before demolition

The actual Five Oaks hostelry is first recorded as a public house in 1838 with Peter Towse as the landlord. Previously a widow lady, Mary Seamar paid Land Tax in 1780 on her house on Mr. John Croucher's land. She left it and a shop to her daughter Mary. That Mary married Richard Hoad who held it till 1808. Then James Holden took it on, only to sell it on to Maurice Ireland, then the leading shopkeeper in Billingshurst. Mr. Towse took the tenancy in 1831 and by 1851 was described as a grocer and innkeeper.

19th Century – the new Horsham Road

John Croucher was a substantial land owner of Hayes House in Slinfold parish at the turn of the 19th century. He was a Dissenter and founder of the Congregational Chapel at Billingshurst. He organised a company to promote a new turnpike road in 1810 from Five Oaks to Horsham and profit from the tolls. The road also provided a prestigious new access to Hayes House. Tollgates were set up at Hayes with William Wilson as the gatekeeper and another at Lyons corner. One of Croucher's supporters was Richard Bettesworth Denyer who lived at Goldings in 1841. That gentleman's ancestor had had Summers Place built.

[The Bettesworths were linked by marriage to the Bartellots who had themselves gained possession of Okehurst by marriage. There is a memorial plate in Stopham Church commemorating 'Anne Bartellot, eldest daughter of Thomas Bettesworth, gentleman, cousin of Sir Peter Bettesworth, Knight, late the wife of Walter Bartellot, gentleman' (1690) Anne, nee Bettesworth, was herself descended from King Edward III.]

Well-to-do Incomers

In the late 19th century several rich men indulged themselves in country seats in and about Billingshurst. Land was relatively cheap from 1874 when the agricultural depression began, but several prosperous and nouveau-riche had enough money made in business elsewhere to set themselves up as country 'toffs' and enjoy the good life and sporting facilities available there. Improved rail and road access had made this practicable. The local farms were becoming unprofitable so the traditional farm owners were pleased to sell their lands at a mutually satisfactory price. Butlers, grooms and domestic help were readily available amongst the poorer villagers, eager for work. Perhaps the most egregious example nearby was the purchase, in 1908, of the enormous ancient Cowdray estate by Weetham Pearson, a Yorkshire-born Bradford contractor and Mexican oil tycoon. In Billingshurst Goff of Wooddale, Carnsew of Summers, Norris the brewer of Gratwicke and Hugh Fortescue Locke-King, doyen of Brooklands motor-racing circuit were just four of many such wealthy incomers. Their advent signalled the decline of the older yeoman social hierarchy of the district, the Greenfields, Streeters, Puttocks, Lakers, Irelands and Eversheds for example. The new circle of gentry enjoyed their mansions, their gardens, their servants, their country house weekend parties, their hunt meets, their pheasant rearing and shoots, all the pleasures of the fashionable glitterati who adorned the belle époque. Professor Asa Briggs describes it as 'the golden age of the country weekend...of the new business tycoon, of the Gaiety Girls, of the bustle and top hat, and above all of the golden sovereign'.

Their Legacy

The well-to-do brought in money for village improvements and stimulated the local economy through their building ventures and sophisticated needs for catering, transport and services. Eventually they were the later sponsors of local industry, as in the case of the American Ray Stiles and the Wyldes who ran the Thomas Keatings flea powder enterprise that came from London in 1927. The mode of living of the wealthy incomers made ordinary folk aware of the bountiful Victoriana newly available, the books, newspapers, magazines, the photographs, the finer clothing, the home furnishings, the exotic foods and drinks we read about in Mrs. Beeton, all the trappings of foreign trade and the industrial revolution that their parents and grandparents had known little of and had managed quite well without. The villagers now wanted bikes and bananas, greenhouses and a good time on holidays, pianos, photographs, china ornaments, proper football boots, fancy goods, table linen and finer foodstuffs. The 'toffs' introduced Cobbett's simple village folk to a new acquisitive society that placed value on the accumulation of 'things'. This material progress was to be brutally interrupted by the outbreak of the Great War in 1914.

Hugh Locke King c.1880s. Photograph taken in Vienna. (Brooklands

Hugh Locke-King inherited Slinfoldland and other major holdings which included Rowner, Okehurst where he lived and more land in Rudgwick. According to Dr. Peter Brandon, Locke-King's estate embraced fourteen farms and ran to 2,700 acres. He envisaged it as a 'shooting game estate', not only rearing some 3000 pheasants each year but also teal, mallard and other water fowl. His Brooklands adventure, demanding bricks made from Okehurst clay and the employment of 2000 building workers, had depleted his fortune by the time the race track opened in 1907. Locke-King's father Peter, scion of many aristocratic families, by profession Barons, Bishops and Bankers, including the philosopher John Locke, and an MP for 26 years, was an astute land and property developer who amassed a fortune valued at well over £30M in today's money. The Five Oaks estate was a part of it. His son Hugh inherited most of Peter's fortune and by injudicious whims managed to spend most of it too.

He lost a small fortune on a food preservation scheme. He then bought and developed, in sumptuous style, like an oriental palace, an Egyptian hotel with 80 rooms in 1886 to ensure his own luxury accommodation. The great dining hall was an exact replica of a Cairo mosque but every effort was made to satisfy the English taste, with a golf course and a swimming pool, both the first in Egypt, tennis courts and magnificent riding stables. Mena House named after the earliest of the Egyptian Kings (4400 BC) stands still in the shadow of the Great Pyramid, early visitors including Sarah Bernhardt, Arthur Conan-Doyle and the Prince of Wales. The project cost him £35,000 equal to two and a half million pounds today and ran at a loss. It has enjoyed a remarkable subsequent history. Churchill, Roosevelt and Chiang Kai Shek conferred there in 1943 to decide the future of war and peace in the Far-East. Today it has 500 rooms, 40 acres of gardens and has 850 employees for 1,050 guests.

Mrs. Locke-King at the Mena Hotel

    Hugh and his rich wife Ethel were keen early motorists and, captivated by the early race track 'petrol-heads' with whom he mingled, rashly promised to finance the construction of the expensive Brooklands circuit at Weybridge on his late father's land. At the end of the construction period he was hard put to it, even with his wife and family's financial support, to pay off the contractors who threatened to foreclose on the Billingshurst property. He escaped ruin with help from his friends but sold the Five Oaks lands in Edwardian times to Robert Shepley-Shepley of New Gallowey, NB [Scotland] in 1908. Locke-King died still worth over a million pounds in today's money.

    Shepley-Shepley, in turn, sold the estate to Sir Charles Fielding KBE in 1912. He was Chairman of Rio Tinto, a prosperous mining company originally founded in Spain in 1873. He designed and had built, Ingfield Manor as his home with a private road from the junction to serve it. It was first called Five Oaks Hall and was not properly named as a Manor. The eight roadside cottages of various ages and a new gatehouse provided tied dwellings for his staff. Descendants of the Fielding family still have Okehurst.

Other Properties

The 17 acres of Slinfoldland, which was separated off as Little Slinfoldland, has been farmed by the Morris family since 1825. They bought it from a Major St. John.

Another interesting property was built on the west side of Stane Street on waste land towards Billingshurst. About 1810, when the new road was opening, a Richard Voice who lived at Buckman's Corner successfully applied to the Steward of Wiggonholt Manor as follows:

'To Mr. Tyler, Petworth: Sir I have meashured the ground that I ask you for at 5 Oaks For to sett up a cottage for Euse of the Weeling business the lanth of the Ground is 7 rods wheath 1 1/2 Rod Witch makes 10 1/2 Rode of Ground that is as it Was stumpt out I should take it as a Favour if you will geat it For me please to Return a noat by post yours Resply Richd Voice Carpenter Buckmancorner. To pheasants withe the Baskeat if you please to Except of them'

The Billingshurst parish Officers bought the wheelwright's workshop in 1813 for £30, built a chimney and tiled the roof ready for use as two two-roomed tenements for poor relief. In 1840 these two cottages were the only buildings on the west of the street between the Inn and Okehurst Lane. [Fieldings Cottages 5, 6 and 6a now occupy the site.] One tenant, James Greenfield, a pin-cleaver, got behind with his shilling a week rent in 1844 and was ejected by law. Another tenant, Richard Allen, farm labourer, had five children but lost four of them at 15 weeks, 14 years, 7 and 9 respectively. Life was not easy for people 'on the parish' in Queen Victoria's time. By then the Petworth District Workhouse was functioning and the Parish Vestry deemed the cottages redundant and sold them off by auction. They were valued by Wiggonholt Manor in 1860, judged 'very old, low and damp', let for 1 shilling a week to Benjamin Knight by Peter Towse, who owned them, and deemed 'not fit for habitation'. The Towse family still owned them in 1887 when they housed Albert Knight and Sarah Pavey. Albert Towse the grocer eventually sold them to Locke-King as part of the estate bought by Sir Charles Fielding. They stood opposite Checkers and Pond Cottage.

Mr. Cliff Griffin renovated the Old Smithy. There were no openings in the south facing wall, probably in deference to the traditional belief that southerly winds brought the plague from the dreadful Continent of Europe.

20th Century developments

Numerous other changes have occurred in the 20th century. The little shop and Post Office, opened in 1926 by Mrs Scattergood and followed by Mesdames Conner, who had a private school, Williams and finally Henderson at 1 Elm Villas (now Willowbrook), has vanished. The Mission Hut, used for monthly communion services by the Vicar of St. Mary's and fortnightly whist drives and 'socials in the 30s, heated by an iron tortoise stove and lit by oil lamps, went in 1989. The old Five Oaks Inn was largely demolished and remodelled. Mr. Sam Van den Bergh ran it for many years but it was totally cleared away when Mr Harwood's new garage and salesroom needed a prominent forecourt. This business was an extension of the former Poplar Garage built up by the Griffin family on land north of the Inn. There was at first a shop, tea garden and garage alongside the Inn started by a Mr. Pole in 1926. Mr. Salt took it over. The garage caught fire in 1949. As the result of a fight he was sent to prison. His wife and family emigrated to Australia and Cliff Griffin started his enterprise in 1950. Cliff won third prize in the Bonfire Society juvenile section of the fancy dress competition in 1936 where the Skinner children also won a prize as 'The Bisto Kids'. Cliff has made his contribution to Billingshurst life ever since. During WW II he drove prisoners of war from Kingsfold to Cowdray Park golf course to pick up potatoes from the ploughed up fairways.

Ingfield Manor was sold to the Spastics Society in 1961 for residential conductive education for children with cerebral palsy, now renamed 'Scope' when the term 'spastic' was considered insensitive and hurtful. Dame Vera Lynn is the famous patron of the Charity which also has a School for Parents to help them care for their own children.

Along the road to Horsham is Furze View, an extraordinary ribbon development of houses built up over the years on a side lane in a fashion which runs counter to modern planning rules and would be deemed quite 'unsustainable' in current development lore. The residents of this little community would not agree!

Carnivals, Parades and Marches

In common with thousands of other English villages Billingshurst has long evinced an enthusiasm for taking to the streets in fancy dress and riding on bicycles, wagons and lorries to celebrate a wide variety of community activities. In this fashion the people loved to celebrate Royal Anniversaries or historical events, so demonstrating patriotism, loyalty and a warm sense of village neighbourliness and togetherness. Over the years this practice has taken various forms. The Bonfire Night torchlight procession was an annual festivity and the Jubilees and coronations of the monarchs often enough began with a parade and ended in a party such as that at Gratwicke House for George V in 1911. The Home Guard marched to celebrate the end of WW II and each year the High Street is closed for the Armistice Day memorial parade. In recent years the annual Billingshurst Show has begun with a themed parade processing from the new Village Hall to the Recreation Ground.

Bleriot flew the Channel in 1909 . George V's Coronation Parade

Before the coming of the National Health Service and other aspects of modern welfare village people relied for emergency help on their clubs and friendly societies which offered a form of community insurance for the common good. To further this cooperation there was an annual Hospital Parade and a Club Day Parade and in 1910 a morale boosting Floral Parade. After WW I the Billingshurst Band enlivened such civic occasions. Nowadays the tradition is maintained by an annual Carnival Parade as the opening feature of the Billingshurst Show, jointly organised by the Scouts and the Rotary Club together with other parish bodies.

Float in the show parade   Tractor-pulling contest

Bonfire Night is still celebrated on Jubilee Fields, but without the procession.

Mr. Joe Luxford lent the money to start the Billingshurst Band in 1919. George Skinner was the bass drummer for 60 years, George Messinger played the euphonium. Archie Stanton 'was a great bandmaster. He was the one who got us through so many competitions'. Fred, George, Ken and Wally Radbourne all played. When the band folded Mr. Wilding, Parish Clerk, stored the 17 instruments in his barn. They were handed over to Mr. Terry Wheeler, Head of Music at the Weald School. They were overhauled; the pitch lowered and formed the basis of the school wind concert band.

Clare Luckin wrote of the traditional celebrations, of how the children gathered on the cricket field at the Coronation of Queen Elizabeth II for games and competitions and a free tea, the field being decorated with red, white and blue bunting and Union Jacks. On Bonfire night the procession would visit the supposedly rich and elevated members of the village, the Manor House, and then Gratwicke. The last call was at Clevelands House, a Victorian house owned by Mrs. Puttock. She always had a Bonfire Night party at which the guests, fortified with mulled wine, waited on the terrace for the arrival of the procession. It was a scene reminiscent of the French Revolution when the huge procession armed with blazing torches swept across the lawn, rattling money boxes while the assembled guests fumbled for their money in the flickering light of the torches.

Another procession was on Rogation Day, albeit only concerning the church community. The Vicar, Choir and congregation would process from the Church, led by the Cross, to Cedars Farm, then a working farm. The farmer had been persuaded to collect as many animals as possible into the orchard. Rogation Day always coincided with apple blossom time and the orchard was a mass of pink and white, a perfect setting with the 16th century house in the background. At that time goats were part of the livestock, and they often caused consternation among the choir as they seemed specially keen to nibble the surplices, The geese pecked, the cockerels crowed, the horses kicked up their heels and galloped round the orchard while the cows continued their quiet ruminating, The Vicar then blessed the crops and livestock, exhorting them to increase and bring forth more. The Farmer's wife became pregnant with awesome regularity during the year following these services.

Clare 'The Reluctant Farmwife'

Clare Luckin was a notable feisty character with a liberal spirit. She wrote poems on natural themes. In her old age she joined a group of Billingshurst ladies in processing, via Piccadilly and ending at Hyde Park, to protest, unsuccessfully, about the war against Iraq. She wrote of the unsuccessful proposal to allow 'War Games', paintball etc in Rosier Wood. "There is no hope for civilization if people (presumably men) have the need to fantasize war in a way which must include pretending to kill each other". Clare was uncomfortable with what remained of Victorian class consciousness in the Billingshurst community. Some were evidently content with it. A friend of Mrs. Rogers of Parbrook wrote warmly of a holiday in Billingshurst in 1935:- "The people in Billingshurst are so very different from London people. Almost everyone you meet talks to you. They are very friendly and they all mix together, the workmen and their masters."

The account in Mr. Charles Tiller's newsletter in 1937 of the Coronation

Games for George VI shows how the great and the good of Billingshurst, up to the Second World War, put themselves out to supervise community activities. Victorian class distinctions had become blurred by WWI but persisted in practice. People were well aware of their social position until the democratising effects of wartime comradeship after 1939 shattered the old class order. We can still witness its disintegration in the follies of *'Dads' Army'* and in the Labour landslide of the 1945 election. The pre-war well-to-do paid the serving working classes as little as the law of supply and demand allowed, but they felt an obligation to show some care for their welfare. It is doubtful if such a lengthy list of wealthy civic minded people could be made today in our more classless yet, curiously, less integrated village society.

Those who do still offer leadership in village affairs, the Parish Councillors, the Scout leaders, the Lions and Rotary members, the clergy, the Club and Society officers, the teachers and so forth, do so as private individuals rather than as 'toffs' or anyone's social superior. We no longer recognise the concept of 'workmen and their masters' even though there are still employers and employees. Before WWII no farm or middle class household could manage without a body of permanent and casual manual labour. This offered employment to 14 year old school leavers and to adults with limited educational qualifications but valuable hand skills. Nowadays farms and factories equipped with modern machinery such as combine harvesters, and homes with comparable labour-saving technology require little hand labour. Domestic servants, gardeners and farm labourers have given place to business contractors in those services, sophisticated machinery and domestic appliances. Maid-servants are now waitresses, nannies are au pairs or professionals with diplomas and butlers are as rare as flat irons and copper kettles. Consequently, for better or for worse, village society comprises people independent in character rather than necessarily interdependent. There are no longer employment opportunities for those with only their physical strength to offer as a source of income.

BILLINGSHURST was *en fête* last month. Coronation Festivities were celebrated on June 28th in grand style, and were well worthy of special and particular notice. My personal account will be given in narrative form, but in order to make it complete I have inserted in their proper places the *official* figures copied from "*Sussex Daily News.*" I will merely say a Committee was elected, and nearly £65 collected in the place by voluntary subscription. Now to proceed—

Chairman, Mr. E. T. Norris; *Hon. Treasurer*, Mr. M. W. Ireland; *Hon. Secretary*, Mr. J. Luxford; *Collectors*, Messrs. W. Carter, Evans, Headland, J. Luxford, and W. Myram.

FINANCE.—Rev. J. Stanley, Messrs. Cosway, Hubert, Holland, S. C. Halahan, Hardwick, Milward, Schwier, Wadey, and Webster.

FLORAL PARADE.—Rev. J. Stanley, Messrs. Carter, Cosway, Milward, Shepherd, Ware, and C. Wadey.

SPORTS.—Messrs. J. Argent, F. Black, R. Crisp, A. E. Clark, Craft, Frewen, Headland, Halahan, Hardwick, H. Hoadley, Isted, W. Joyes, C. Joyes, E. Lucas, H. Laker, R. Morris, W. H. Puttock, A. Sprinks, Schwier, W. Tribe, R. Voice, Wright, J. Wadey, and F. Woodcock.

TEA.—Mrs. Alvis, Mrs. Brooks, Mrs. Blake, Miss Blake, Misses Beck, Misses Burtenshaw, Mrs. Carter, Mrs. Churchill, Mrs. Fielder, Mrs. Gosnall, Mrs. E. C. R. Goff, Misses Gosling, Mrs. Hubert, Mrs. A. Hubert, Mrs. Hardwick, Mrs. M. W. Ireland, Mrs. Morris, Miss Muskin, Mrs. W. H. Puttock, Mrs. A. Puttock, Mrs. Pearson, Mrs. Preston, Misses Puttock, Misses Schroeter, Miss Smyth, Miss Strong, Mrs. Thorburn, Misses Thorburn, Mrs. Wright, and Miss Woodhams.

Kings' weather prevailed, and though fleecy clouds now and then veiled the blue sky—causing ... they finally passed away and left

Newsheet 1937 Coronation of George VI

The King comes to Five Oaks

Canadian troops were widely dispersed in camps in the whole district for training and to await embarkation to Normandy on D-day, 6th June 1944. They were at Wiggonholt, Ebernoe and Wisborough Green in great numbers, most often in tented camps in the woods. At Shillinglee they managed to set fire to the mansion of the Winterton family, and relics of their stay, ammunition, grenades and discarded equipment are still occasionally unearthed. At Wisborough Green they are proudly commemorated in St. Peter's Church.

Mrs. Dorothy Pullen, Granddaughter of James Wadey, writes:
"April, 1944 was an important month for the village. All round the district, at the time, were stationed the Canadian 2nd Division. Some of it was in a camp at Buckman's Corner [Five Oaks] and another big camp between Gleniffer House and Rookery Wood and down nearer Billingshurst, another big camp at Wooddale with the Headquarters at Rowfold Grange on the road from Billingshurst to Coolham.

Peter Newman remembers being told one day by the troops that the King [George VI] was coming to review them. There was great activity. The road was swept, grass cut and hedges trimmed all the way from Five Oaks to Billingshurst. The royal car was to park near the Old Forge, and though a red carpet was put down the King didn't walk on it. Now all the camps had their quota of stray dogs. On the day two of them decided to accompany the troops to be reviewed. The red carpet was just too much of an invitation. These two decided it provided a good playground. It took a lot of persuading by two very agitated officers to move them.

Much to the amusement of the local people the troops decided that the King might need to use the pub toilets which were outside on the end of what is now the Grill Room. Not only were they cleaned but repairs done and painted inside and out.

Peter remembers climbing a tree outside his home, No.1 Fieldings Cottages, to get a better view but the Military Police made him come down and so he had to watch from his bedroom window. I remember my father and uncle shutting the gates at the entrance to the yard and making a platform for the family and some friends to stand on. Again, like Peter, we were moved so we went inside one of the buildings that had a long window overlooking the road so we still had a good view.

All the children took the day off from school; after all the road was closed to traffic from 8 o'clock in the morning. When the King finally arrived he walked from Five Oaks to Hilland between Canadian troops 3 deep each side of the road. The royal car picked him up at Hilland to take him back to London. So ended Five Oaks Royal Review."

More Royal Celebrations

"One of my earliest memories was the celebrations of either King George V's Silver Jubilee or it could have been the Coronation of King George VI. We entered a float from Five Oaks to go in the parade at Billingshurst. The children of the village (there were about a dozen at the most) all wore red, white and blue caps and sat around the inside edge of a wagon-type trailer drawn by a tractor. Mr. Cullen, who lived where Mr. Stafford did [Grainingfold] lent the trailer and tractor and Mr. Overington drove it. He used to work for him at the time.

The Five Oaks Coronation Carnival Wagon, 1911

Mr. Bowring, the publican and helpers made a big boot and then he dressed up as The Old Woman who lived in a shoe. After parading through Billingshurst we were given tea and a celebration mug. Riding on that trailer-type wagon to Billingshurst was the best part of the day's events for us.

Five Oaks football club started in the 30s and played on three different fields. In 1939 they held the Horsham District 3rd Division Cup for a year after a tie with Horsham Council United. The Union Jack was waved by Mr. Pole and a crowd of locals to welcome the team home. The team reformed in 1946.

(Dorothy Pullen corrected and helped by Yvonne Wolzak.)

The Hamlets – Adversane

Two miles south of Billingshurst is the hamlet of Adversane, known as Hadfoldshern until the 1850s. In the middle ages lands there were owned by Tortington Priory. It is likely that the change of name came as a result of a mishearing of the name by a map-maker or official when pronounced in Sussex dialect. It is on Stane Street (A29) where the Roman road is crossed by the B2133, affording access to Petworth to the west and Ashington and Worthing to the east. The main business was always the pub and forge next door, naturally entitled The Blacksmiths' Arms. Gaius (George) Carley who lived at Griggs Cottages was the last smith, who wrote a book about his life. Eleanor Farjeon, the children's author, used the village as a setting for her 1921 novel 'Martin Pippin in the Apple Orchard'. This is an elaborate fairy tale where the children of the village are said to sing a ballad 'The Spring-Green Lady'. There was a post office and shop in the end house of Malt-house Cottages kept by Frank Sharville in the 1950s. Adversane has three notable ancient timber-framed houses, Old House, Southlands and the later Blacksmith's Arms. A former hotel called Newstead Hall run by Mr. And Mrs Cartner at the old Juppsland farm site was recently demolished and apartments erected in its stead.

Grigg's Cottages 2013

The Adversane cross roads is the most accident-prone junction in the parish. Originally the B2133 was a simple crossroads, the road crossing the green, but in an attempt to limit the danger it was decided to stagger the junction, so making matters a good deal worse. Strict speed controls currently curtail the number of accidents but the attractive Green would be seriously disfigured by building a roundabout.

'FromHadfoldshern...to Adversane'

Deborah Evershed's carefully researched account of late Victorian and early 20th century Adversane Hamlet and the four or more closely related families, the Miles, Taylors, Humphreys, Puttocks and Eversheds, who lived thereabouts goes some way to proving once again that truth can be quite as sensational as fiction. The general tenor of this study of an extended family is warm, romantic and engagingly comfortable with the busy, aspirational, neighbourly, harmonious bucolic lives the author presents to us.

But never long concealed are the inevitable blows of fate, the violence and tragic happenings that had to be stoically endured along with the delights of nostalgic reminiscence of flowery meadows, woodland walks and rides home by pony and trap under the stars. The childhood excitement of the annual fair is troubled by brutal boxing encounters and a gang murder, Adversane maltsters (the Allens) cheat the revenue by not paying malt tax and escape justice by flight to America, an alcoholic and debt-laden Alfred Taylor shoots himself, good women die in childbirth and young men fall ill and expire in their 20s. Amid the excitements such as the coming of the railway and the crystal wireless set and the comforting sights sound and smells of the rich countryside, the sweetshop and the toffee and aniseed balls, the feeding of lambs and the rearing of piglets, are mingled moments of sadness and pain such as Buzzy Wright's cane at Billingshurst School or a glimpse of disfigured soldiers at Billingshurst Station at the end of WW I and the lice in the army uniform of poor Uncle Jack.

The closing chapters give a warm account of the residents of the hamlet and the social life and film shows they enjoyed in the 1950s and 60s, focused on the pub, the blacksmith's forge, the Mission Hall with Social Club and the village shop, Lola Baxter, who kept a restaurant at Old House and gave ballet lessons and the teenagers who had their own Youth Club.

Lola Baxter, a divorcee, and her friend 'Noni' Frame had joined the Women's Voluntary Service in 1939 and organised theatrical revues for Wandsworth Borough Council. After the war they bought Old House combining the restaurant with an antiques business. Some 40 dealers were accommodated there. Lola ran her ballet classes and the Youth Club and held antique connoisseurs' soirees. After her death her collection of Staffordshire animal figures and ceramics, glassware and furniture in the Continental taste was sold by auction at Toovey's.

Adversane Hall

The maltings

Alfred Allen, maltster of Horsham, and Dennett, his brother of Colliers' Farm, Gay Street, West Chiltington where he had maltings, also owned malt businesses at Worthing and in buildings at Adversane, which are still there. The brothers flourished financially, becoming the equivalent of multi-millionaires today, but their success was based on fraud. They maintained a respectable business for the duty officers to inspect, duty properly paid, but at the same time they conducted a black market in duty-free malt, secretly prepared and stored in hidden rooms. They could pay farmers good prices for barley and sell malt cheaply, so undercutting their competitors. Their many workmen must have valued their well-paid jobs because they kept quiet about the tax evasion, just as people turned a blind eye on smugglers.

"Them that asks no questions, isn't told a lie, Watch the wall my darling while the gentlemen go by." [Rudyard Kipling]

They were rumbled in 1857 however, probably 'shopped' by legitimate maltsters whose profits were undermined by such illegal competition. Customs Officers raided the Worthing premises. Alfred swiftly organised wagons to clear out the illicit malt at Adversane and dump it into the River Arun at Newbridge. Local people salvaged what they could to feed their pigs and make some home-brew. The customs men confiscated £12,000 worth of malt which was sent to London by special train from Horsham.

Maltings Cottages, Adversane

The cunning brothers had a plan. They did not show up in the Court of the Exchequer where they were peremptorily found guilty and initially fined £375,000 on pain of imprisonment if the fine was not paid. This unrealistic figure was reduced by the Solicitor General to a feasible sum of £110,000. However the Allens outsmarted the law. They took a packet steamer to France, where pursuing officers searched in vain, as they had turned round at once on disembarking and returned to England. Then they took the trains to London and Liverpool and enjoyed their wealth in America until they judged it safe to return. They paid off their much reduced £10,000 fine and lived happily ever after! There are times when crime pays. The Allens 'had form'. During the Crimean war an extra duty was charged on malt to pay the military bill. The Allens fraudulently claimed £700 refund on duty they had never paid, claiming that they had lost stocks in their warehouses.

Public Houses in Billingshurst

Today there are 6 public houses, their signs here pictured. The Five Oaks Inn is the only recent closure at a time when, elsewhere, numerous inns have ceased trading and the sites been redeveloped. At earlier times there were several other pubs and beer outlets in the village. On the west side of the High Street stood the Rising Sun. To complicate matters there was an earlier King's Arms on the site of what is now Lloyds Bank. There was also an earlier King's Head which stood where Freemans, the undertakers, is. The pub 'crossed the road' to the present King's Head in the 18th century. The White Horse Inn nearby where Lloyds the Chemist stands has long since closed down.

On land called Lockyers along East Street another house was built which predated the later Gratwicke House. This building housed The Star Inn. There was also other beer house on the site of Southdown House named The Lyon House, and formerly The Bell or The Dog and Partridge. The Maltings and Gingers in the High Street, which stood where the entry to Jengers Mead is now, became polite tea rooms in the 20s, renowned for its home-made cakes, until demolished in 1964. ['Gingers' was built in 1370 and named after Oliver Gynguire. He was a Horsham man elected to Parliament in 1368].

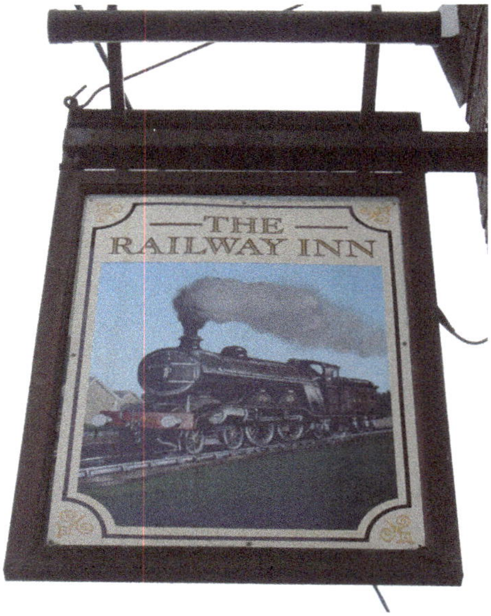
THE
RAILWAY INN

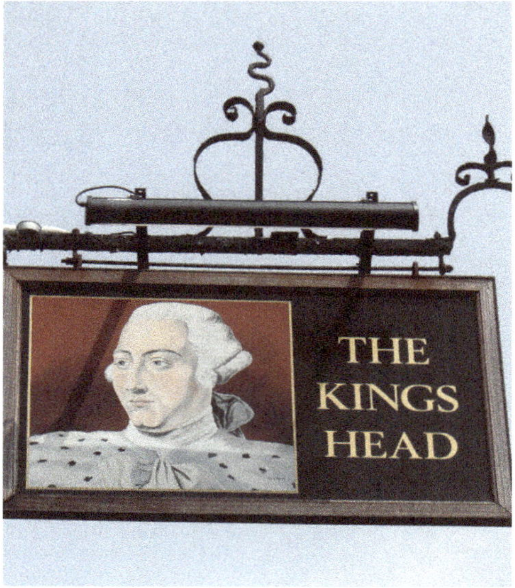
THE
KINGS
HEAD

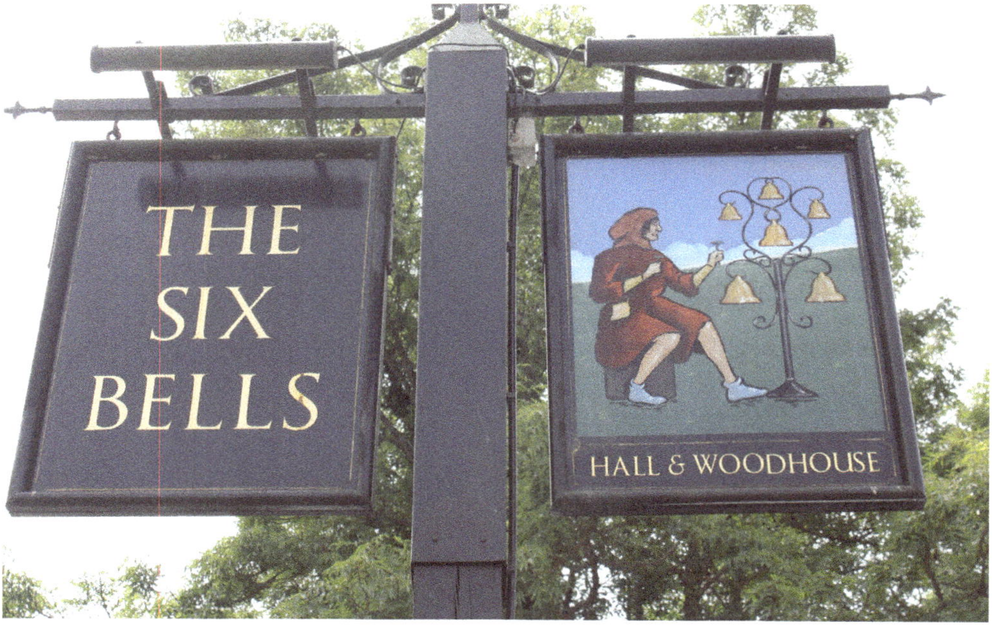
THE
SIX
BELLS
HALL & WOODHOUSE

THE RISING SUN was named as a beer house in 1862. In living memory it was converted to a private residence then demolished in the 1960s when the Malaya Garage was built. In the front wall of the Inn garden there were niches where drinkers could stand their pewter pots.

Though William Cobbett and J.B. Dashwood wrote handsomely about Billingshurst inns, one Arthur Becket, who was a journalist and founder of the Sussex County Magazine, wrote scathingly of one of them – "a certain evil spirit led us…to a certain roadside hostelry….but of the quality of that shelter and food I will say nothing, only praying that that self-same evil spirit that directed us to this inn, will direct thereto my greatest enemy when he comes upon that road".

Pauline Taylor wrote articles about the taverns. She tells of a travellers' guide by John Taylor, a Kings Waterman and the Egon Ronay of his day (1653). He wrote of John Agate the only listed licensee of the old KING'S ARMS. He praises the hospitality and refers to the destruction of the Inn sign some years previously by Parliamentarian troops, perhaps on the way to the siege of Arundel in 1643.

She presumes that when Cobbett visited Billingshurst James Fuller was the Licensee in 1820 of the present King's Arms. He was also the village butcher and in the 1831 Directory is listed as a basket maker. In the late 19th century the Arms provided the village Market room, was licensed to let horses and continued to be linked to the butchers' next door. The pub we know now as the King's Arms was

Billingshurst's Heritage

called The Carpenters Arms until about 1788. The Prince Regent was despised and when news came of the recovery of health of George III from his first illness William Greenfield renamed the Inn The King's Arms in celebration.

John Taylor wrote 'The travailles of an Uncertain Journey' in 1653 in the form of what can loosely be described as a poem with an undoubted debt to *The Prologue* to *The Canterbury Tales*:-

The year sixteen hundred fifty, with 3 added
Old Tib, my mare, and I a journey gadded.
August the tenth my bonny beast and I,
From Surrey travelled to South Saxony,
Now called Sussex, where at Billingshurst,
Six days I felt no longer cold or thirst.
'Twas the King's Arms, but shattering shot and flame
Did beat them down, as useless, of small stead,
For arms of no use without a head.
Mine host was mighty good, and great withal
And among hosts may be a general.
He's friendly, courteous, although big and burly,
Aright good fellow, no way proud or surly.
Six nights at Billingshurst I truly staid,
And all the charge for man and mare was paid
By a gentleman, to name whom I'll refrain,
Whose love my thankful mind still retain.
A Reverend preacher preached on Sunday twice
Directing souls to the Heavenly Paradise,
And, if we could but do as he did say,
His doctrine told us all the ready way.
Thus Billingshurst, thy bounty I extol,
Thou's feasted me in body and in soul.
There was rare music and sweet gentle airs.
For undeserved favours I am theirs.
My love to Mr. Fist and to mine host.
But love to T.H. deservest most.   John Taylor

Though hardly Chaucerian in quality, this doggerel is an entertaining narrative with a witty pun on the King's head which had been cut off from Charles I and it is a warm tribute to the people of Billingshurst. Fist suggests a Mr. Fiest, a local name. TH has been identified by John Hurd as Thomas Henshaw.

The King's Head had a poem under its 20th century advertisement:

Accommodation you will find
For travellers of every kind,
Most of whom who come from far
Appreciate a good cigar
Whilst wines *and* spirits *are to hand*
And served at anyone's command.
Bright sitting room and well-aired bed,
You'll always get at the 'King's Head'.

Pauline Taylor describes the present KING'S HEAD as an old timber framed building, some 400 years old, with a modernised frontage and the roof raised to give a third storey. The rear is 16th century, the front Georgian. It was used as a hostelry and dormitory together with the White Horse Inn. It was a staging post for the Comet coach which changed horses 'at a quarter before twelve every forenoon (except Sundays).' The archway and cobblestones of the stable yard survive. It was listed as a 'Commercial Inn'. On April Fool's Day 1839 the Tradesmen Club held their annual meeting there. "The dinner and attention of Mr. Aylward, the landlord met with acknowledged approbation'. In the 20th century (1903) it offered accommodation for cyclists. Earthenware footwarmers were found.

Of the SIX BELLS she writes of its varied history. Parts of the building have 14th century roots. It was once a yeoman farm, Taintland, a beer house, tannery, brewery and a '3d. Doss house'. Therein was the beginning of the modern pub, licensed since the beginning of the 19th century. Folk lore links it with smuggling. There is a 16th century fireback, a copy of one once used as a tombstone, in the saloon bar. The building is unusual among the old houses in the area having a continuous overhang storey or jetty along the whole first floor. The name was used before two more bells were added to St. Mary's to celebrate Queen Victoria's Silver Jubilee in 1897. It was called 'Ye Old Six Bells' until recently. 'Ye' was used by printers in place of the old disused letter 'thorn' (Þ), pronounced like 'th', as it most closely resembled a Y.

Mr. Bob Dames supplied additional information. In 1530 the building and land were known as Gillman, after its occupant William Gillman, whose kinsman, Thomas Gillman, was in residence at Great Gillmans. In 1563 the then owner and resident, William Tredcroft, a yeoman farmer, referred to it in his will as "Gylman otherwise named Tayntland". In 1673 it was known as Taintlands but by 1815 there was just a house and a yard, which in 1830 was referred to as a Tanyard. In 1851 the occupant, one Richard Mitchell was a carpenter and brewer – and the scene was set. In 1861 it was known as the Five Bells but by 1871 it was the Six Bells.

Aileen Walker commented that local tradition named the land between the Six Bells and the Post Office as Taintilands and there are 15th century documents using that name. The word, she suggests, may derive, as Tenterlands, from the word 'tenter', a machine for stretching out cloth on hooks round a frame, which relates to tainters or tenters who finished cloth, hence the expression 'on tenterhooks'. It is possible that the Six Bells once harboured a woollen cloth or linen finishing industry.

THE RAILWAY INN came with the railway and in 1862 was licensed as the Station Inn to William Harsant. The proprietors diversified their business. They were licensed to let horses, being convenient for arriving passengers and also ran a coal merchants business, being close to arriving coal trucks.

The other three village pubs, the BLACKSMITH'S ARMSs, the LIMEBURNERS and the demolished FIVE OAKS INN are described elsewhere in this book.

In Victorian times the most notable local brewer was Henry Michell. His immediate well-to-do ancestors owned Hermongers at Rudgwick. His father moved to Kithurst and Cootham Farms at Storrington where Henry was born, in 1809, the third of twelve children. He was schooled in Pulborough by a Mr. Billingshurst and then worked for his father brewing, malting and selling coal at Steyning. He had to earn his own living and became manager of a bank at Steyning and learnt the art of bookkeeping, so ensuring a shrewd and profitable business career. In 1834 he married, moved to Horsham and took on Mr. Allen's brewery on lease. He also had a malthouse in Gay Street but gave it up in favour of one in Billingshurst High Street. He expanded into the coal trade and made huge profits from brick-making. In 1838 he bought the Blacksmiths Arms at Adversane from Mr. R. Watkins for £750.

In 1841 he moved his brewery to West Street, Horsham on a dismantled site of a former brewery, let to him by Sir Timothy Shelley of Field Place, Warnham.

He could no longer do business with Mr. Allen 'on any fair terms' and gave up the lease, which included three pubs which he had to surrender, one of which was the Kings Head at Billingshurst. These Allens were the same infamous unscrupulous malt dealers.

We do not often think of the Victorians as growers of vines other than in greenhouses, especially the brewers. However there must have been a quantity in Billingshurst. In 1842, Michell records in his diary, 'we had 45 gallons of grapes brought home from the old malt house at Billingshurst and I trode them out in a tub and there were 27 gallons of juice which I put into a 36 Gn. cask and filled it up with sugar and a little water. This wine was like syrup at 20 years old.'

In 1845, in a masterly stroke of enterprise, he bought up the old Horsham County Gaol then sold off the materials, some land for building and some to the Waterworks Company. He built a new Malt house too, and 'made about ten million of bricks on the ground'. He cleared a £5000 profit on the deal, worth £5M today. Meantime he was brewing up to 1000 quarters of malt a year at some 60s a quarter. He became Chairman of the Gas Company and profited from the coming of the railway from Three Bridges to Horsham. He was able to buy cheap imported French barley from 1848 as 'the corn laws had been relaxed' making some £1000 a year profit. He could also send half a million bricks to the Crystal Palace at Sydenham. In 1850 he indulged his fancy to be a farmer and bought Stakers Farm, Southwater.

In 1852 the Gates Brewery at the Fountain Brewery collapsed and Michell bought it up together with five pubs, including the Kings Head, Billingshurst for £6000. He enlarged the Fountain Brewery rented from Sir Percy Shelley and 'at once gave up the old wretched Malthouse I had used for many years in Billingshurst'. He then gave up the coal trade.

Extra duty of 10s a quarter on malt at the outbreak of the Crimean War limited profit in 1854. By 1859 he had doubled his malt production to 2,500 quarters or so. Each year he bought more pubs, including The Rising Sun in Billingshurst for £260. In 1860 he bought Shiprods Farm, Itchingfield where he made bricks and drain pipes, built another malthouse and took over The Queens Head at Bucks Green. He was now getting his barley from Denmark and Scotland. His profits 1864 came to £5,000 when he built the Station Hotel, Arundel then he took on The King's Head, Slinfold. In 1868 'we did extensive repairs at Adversane, Billingshurst Station [hotel] and Billingshurst Street'.

Henry Michell died in 1874. His daughter Fanny was married to T.W. Cowan, an inventive engineer and famous as the Father of British Beekeeping. Fanny and Thomas inherited much of his fortune but his son Henry, 'a very weakly specimen' when born, carried on the business. It was taken over in 1911 by the Rock Brewery of Brighton.

Henry Michell was the very model of a Victorian middle-class capitalist provincial entrepreneur. He loved travelling. He was a stout Protestant, but of radical Whig political sympathies, opposed to the landed squirearchy, High Church activists and those who wanted to protect English farmers by reintroducing the Corn Laws. His revealing diary is available in Kenneth Neale's book, *Victorian Horsham*.

Michell, brewer, at the Railway Hotel

Billingshurst Characters and Celebrities

Most of the worthy public-spirited Billingshurst personages derived their deserved reputations in the annals of the village from their relative wealth, birth or office. Such leading citizens as the Greenfields, Puttocks, Sherlocks, Eversheds, Voices, Morris's, Lakers, Wadeys and Streeters leap to mind, not to mention the Gentry:- Goring, Ireland, Norris, Carnsew, Beck, Goff, and Renton; the entrepreneurs, Stiles, Wylde, Carter, Lugg and Merrikin; the shopkeepers, Crisp the hairdresser, Cripps the butcher, Lusted the grocer, Bernard Baker the outfitter, Gravett the confectioner, Jones the watchmaker, Rhodes the cobbler and Watts, the corn merchant at Hereford House by the Station. These are names that recur down the years, feature on the war memorial and are still to be found on the electoral roll. Many other well-remembered personalities are listed in the Appendices.

Numerous interesting characters have left their distinctive marks on the village history. One remarkable celebrity was Mr. Joseph Luxford, the Grand Panjandrum of the early 20th century. He was grocer and carrier, Secretary of the Working Men's Club, an original Parish Councillor, instigator of the building of the old Village Hall, sponsor of the Billingshurst Band, churchwarden, organiser of charabanc outings, actor in amateur dramatics, secretary of the Flower Show Committee, allotment owner and keen tennis player. He was surely the epitome of citizenship. Other remarkable figures included Henry and son, Buzzy Wright the schoolmasters, Dr. Moreton, master and actor, George Coombs, the oldest inhabitant, Frank Patterson the cycling artist and farmer, Billy Shepherd the fat grocer, Freddie Wells, angler, cricketer, gardener and Bonfire Society supporter, Dr. Hubert, G.P. and cricketer, Wally Wicks, champion gardener of Myrtle Cottages, Jack Leaman, Spike Milligan's commanding Officer and doyen of the British Legion, Jack Easton, Bank Manager and Chairman of the Parish Council, John and Renee Humphreys of the Dramatic Society, Lola Baxter ballet teacher at the Mission Hall, restaurateur and antiques dealer of Adversane and Hugh Wadey who saw Hammonds Mill collapse in a storm and kept his own museum of antiquities. Still flourishing are Cliff Griffin, ex-parish and district councillor and feisty business-man formerly of Poplar Garage, Five Oaks and Councillor Ken Longhurst who piloted the Western by-pass Committee. Nationally and rightly celebrated is the former West Sussex educational administrator, cycling tourist, author, wit and TV personality, Edward Enfield of Rowner and his gifted family which includes his son Harry, the comedian. William Richard, Mr. Ireland's shepherd, would stand on Billingshurst Hill at weekends in his working clothes and decorated hat, and salute passers-by with his walking stick.

Notable local people with Billingshurst Connections

Maggie Gee – novelist, daughter of the first Headmaster of the Weald School, V.V. Gee. Her autobiographical work '*My Animal Life*' includes fond and anxious recollections of her childhood and schooling in the village as well as brave, frank and profound meditations on her family and personal life.

Edward Enfield – Writer, educational administrator, wit, cycling tourist, professional stickler and paterfamilias, unswervingly loyal to traditional values.

Harry Enfield – Comedian and satirist of contemporary manners. Creator of TV characters Stavros, Loadsamoney, Kevin the belligerent teenager, etc.

Lizzie Enfield – novelist, journalist and contributor to 'The Oldie' magazine

Diana Dors, England's answer to Marilyn Monroe, actress and 'sex symbol', lived for a time in the 60s at Palmers Farm, Coneyhurst.

Mary Law, Actress, personal friend of Agatha Christie, once filmed with Diana Dors and played in *The Mousetrap* and with Laurence Olivier's company at Stratford-on-Avon.

Nancy Roberts – TV 'hostess' with Hughie Green of '*Double Your Money*' from 1955.

Paul Darrow – TV actor and author. Robin Hood, Blake's 7, Dixon, Z cars etc.

Dave Gilmour D.Mus, CBE- Singer of popular music and guitarist with Pink Floyd. The group are believed to have sold 250 million records.

Stroller – show jumping pony. A gelding once owned by Miss. Sally Cripps that won Silver in the 1968 Olympics, exercised by Mr. Des Wakeling.

Max Faulkner OBE (of Gay Street) – Open Golf Champion 1951 at Royal Portrush. Owned 300 putters. Flamboyant dresser who once walked on his hands to the next tee 'to get some blood to his brain'. Co-founded and designed West Chiltington Golf Club with son-in-law, pro golfer Brian Barnes.

David Sainsbury – National and International Level Rugby Union Referee

Arthur Paton OBE, M.C. – rugby footballer, soldier, and businessman.

Aileen Walker MBE of Stonepits – for services to Billingshurst. She was the principle founder of the Billingshurst Society. She designed the village signs.

Mike Read – radio disc jockey of Steepwood Farm. Twice bankrupt, the first time for debts to Horsham District Council.

John Wilding MBE – expert horologist, prolific writer on antique clocks, known as 'Meccanoman' because of his childhood enthusiasm and subsequent love of precision engineering. He played the French horn in amateur orchestras and formed his own chamber music group. Patrick Moore, the astronomer, composed a march dedicated to John's group. Mr. Wilding was Clerk to the Billingshurst Parish Council. They presented him with a watch on his retirement with the dates 1966-70 inscribed on it.

Post-war Billingshurst

The most striking changes to the village since 1945 have been the growth of housing and population. Decade by decade there have been fresh estates established. In the 1960s Jengers Mead was transformed into a shopping precinct, parking space and flats. Subsequently estates were developed east of Silver Lane and on the sites of former Glebe Land, Gratwick and Clevelands. The factory in Station Road was developed into Weald Court and Saville Gardens and another cluster of houses built off Forge Way in the west.

A remarkable, though strangely unremarked, contrast between village life in 1912 and in 2012 is the divergence of the people who conduct the trading business of the village and the people who make their homes there. A hundred years ago the pillars of the community were the shopkeepers and traders, often members of long-standing local families, such as those elected to the first Parish Council. Today only a single member runs a business in the village. Then most proprietors lived 'over the shop' or within walking distance of it.

Today a good many of them live elsewhere and several big shops are branches of chain stores run by managers. If they do not live in the village they naturally have a loyalty to their home place, its school, church and other social circles. Their 'roots' are therefore not in Billingshurst. In 1912 not only the shopkeepers but also the schoolteachers, the doctors and nurses who made home visits, the factory owners, the policemen, the station staff, the roadmen, the builder, the butcher and the baker, and most people offering services lived in the village and were likely to add 'and Sons' to their title, as a emblem of continuity. Such a quintessential civic figure as Joe Luxford epitomised an undivided spirit of committed citizenship typical of the old order. Today only Rhodes, the cobblers, have maintained the independent shop tradition. There are modern exceptions of course. The Vicar, the publicans, the ethnic restaurateurs and farmers still have a rational interest in dwelling in the place where they earn their living.

The obverse of the rule also applies. Many of the families now domiciled in the village earn their living elsewhere, Gatwick, Crawley, the coastal towns or London, and may well do their shopping and seek their entertainment somewhere other than Billingshurst. Fortunately many employees of local enterprises are still recruited locally to the benefit of the community spirit of the village. Nevertheless we must conclude, for better or worse, the railway, the bus service and most tellingly the motor car have created a 'commuting society' in Billingshurst just as significant as anywhere else in Britain. It is an inescapable fact that, in a mobile society, a great many people now living in Billingshurst were not born and brought up there. It is not surprising that the interests of the Chamber of Commerce sometimes conflict with those of the domiciliary residents. The latter tend to prefer to safeguard their exclusiveness and restrict expansion, the former look for growth and more potential customers.

In the mid 1990s, after forty years of delay and prevarication, a Western by-pass was built, and 550 new residences constructed within its boundary. This major expansion brought with it assets to boost the infrastructure at the developer's expense. Billingshurst gained the £8M by-pass, an all-weather pitch at the Weald School, educational funding, a new village hall or Community Centre and enhancements to the High Street, extensive sports facilities at Jubilee Fields and the Swimming Pool and Leisure Centre. More recently blocks of flats have risen near the Station and infilling with small estates has occurred wherever the District Council could be persuaded to grant planning permission. Five instances of this are off East Street alone. Apart from the older Rosehill development houses have been built at Caffyns Rise, off School Lane, at Luggs Close, in the grounds of Trees and at Hammonds Garden Field. Similarly six small estates have been permitted branching from the High Street and another off Forge Way. More details of post-war developments are shown in Appendix 1.

The pavilion at Jubilee Fields

Three industrial zones offer some employment to an ever increasing population. However where there were once four garages, filling stations and car showrooms in the High Street and a coach depot, all of these have now succumbed to alternative development so that the traditional function of Billingshurst as a coaching inn centre and transport hub is no longer so since the building of the western by-pass which relieved the High Street of the former intolerable traffic congestion in the summer months.

1966

In 1966 Mary Constance Trower died aged 82 and two years later, in 1968 Gertrude Amy Trower died aged 77. Both sisters had lived at Hammonds.

At an auction at Horsham Town Hall, offered for sale by the executors of Gertrude Trower of Hammonds, was 'a house of character, part-built in the 17th century, 4 bedrooms, bathroom, 2 dressing rooms, attic bedroom, entrance hall, 2 reception rooms, scullery, kitchen, store rooms, etc. Garage and barn.' The remainder of the estate continued in the ownership of the Trower Trustees who act in the interest of the heirs who live abroad. The fields have been let to tenant farmers for many years, and at the time of this writing is the subject of an application for a major development scheme by a consortium of building companies.

1969

The house and garden was bought by Dr. Evelyn Kilsby whose surgery was beside St. Mary's church.

1983

It was subsequently bought by John Griffin.

A steam engine entering Luggs Yard off East Street

James Lugg, a previous apprentice at Carter Bros. of Newpound, agricultural engineers, founded a threshing tackle and traction engine business on the northern side of East St. opposite to what was once called Lockyers Farm, and just west of the old Workhouse. This is now a small housing estate called Luggs Close.

The Bowling Alley in winter

Slope down the Bowling Alley

The Bowling Alley, north of Hammonds, now a wooded scrubland, was used for sledging and by the schoolchildren for ball games. Gratwicke House south of East St. was built about 1830 and substantially enlarged by Edward Norris. After WWII it was used for band practice and for a while provided premises for a fish and chip shop! It was demolished in the 1960s and an estate, Gratwicke Close, was built on the site. Gratwicke Lodge and the stable block still remain, as do Robin and Chime Cottages, built in the 18th century or earlier. Churchgate, a 17th century timber-framed house, had a shop wing added in Victorian times when Billy Shepherd was known, at 18 stone, as the fattest grocer in Sussex. It was later a guest house.

Building Developments in the 70s

In the 1960s and early 70s a large area of open land comprising farm fields of Broomfield and the parkland and gardens of Cleveland House and Gratwicke were transformed into the mature estates that we know today. Silver Lane is the 'spine road' linking Station Road and East Street. The south end was built first in the early 60s and as development spread north the road was completed on to East Street. Most of the roads in the area lead off it and only Broomfield Cottage and outbuildings of Gratwicke remain of the old mansions. The illustrative map here shows the present network of roads and how they relate to the rural scene before development began.

Trees in Silver Lane

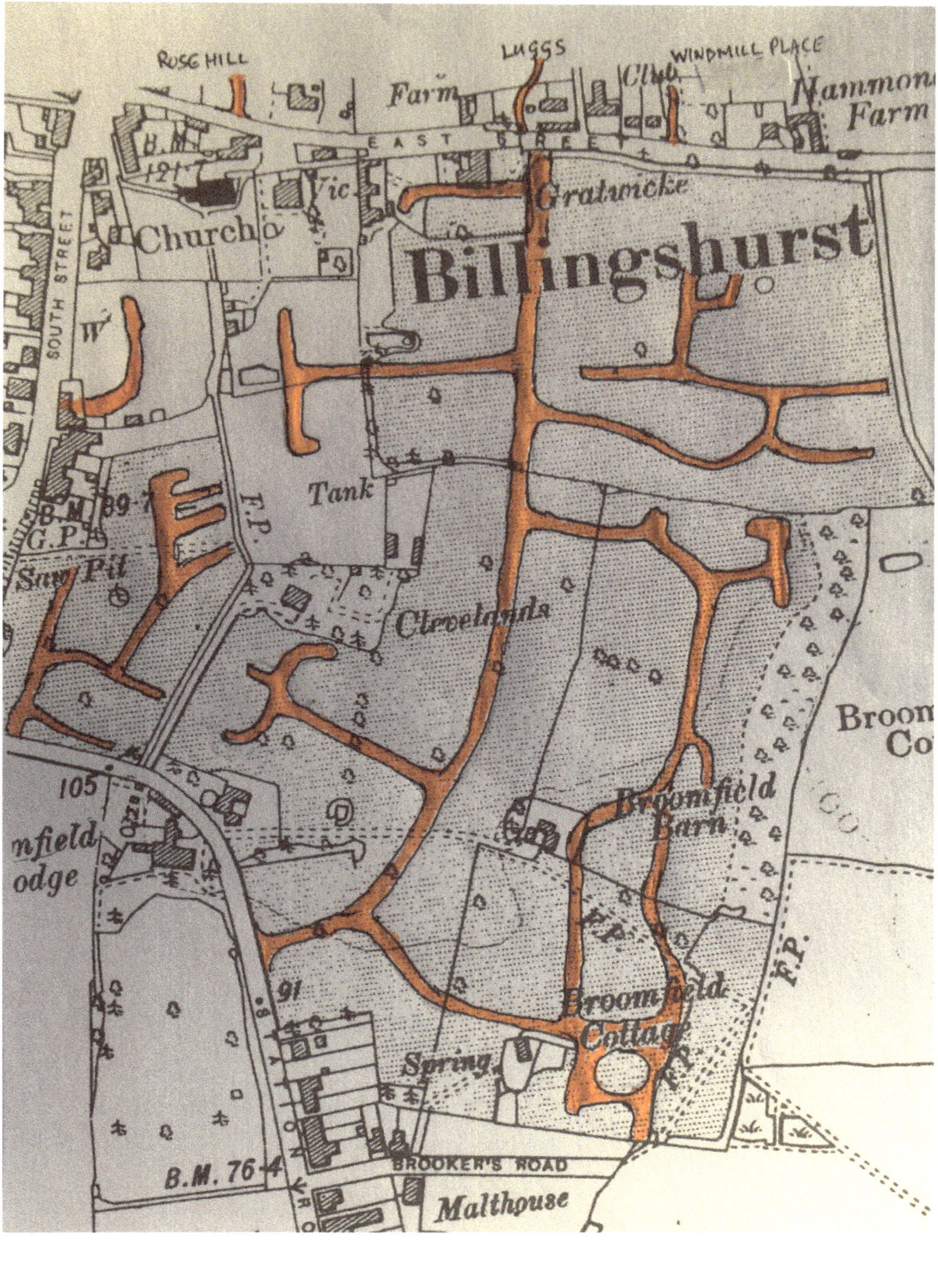
ROSE HILL
LUGGS
WINDMILL PLACE
Farm
Club
Hammond Farm
EAST STREET
Church
Vic.
Gratwicke
Billingshurst
SOUTH STREET
Tank
F.P.
B.M. 89.7
G.P.
Saw Pit
Clevelands
Broomfield Barn
Broomfield Cottage
Spring
91
105
B.M. 76.4
BROOKER'S ROAD
Malthouse

More recent developments

1977

After General Renton's death Rowfold Grange was sold and the mansion split into three apartments.

Aerial photograph to celebrate the Queen's Jubilee in 1977.

1. The Weald School from the air showing buildings and a tribute to the Queen at her Silver Jubilee

Rowfold Grange today

1978

Cleveland House, formerly the Puttock family home, was demolished to make way for affordable housing.

Shortly after this the Billingshurst Bonfire Society ceased, though the celebration of Guy Fawkes has recently been revived at Jubilee Fields. 'The Bonfire Boys' used to meet at the Six Bells. They staged the main event at Ireland Hill, the SCATS or Junior School sites, or a field at the end of Daux Avenue. The preliminary procession, headed by the Village Silver Band would start at the Old Village Hall where the Fancy Dress Competition was judged, circumnavigate the village via the High Street, Natt's Lane and the Station, finishing at the chosen venue, but stopping at every pub en route. Other Societies, The Haven, Adversane, New Pound, Loxwood, Shamley Green etc. would pay reciprocal visits so that participants were drunk for a week! The Bonfire Prayer would be said and the fire lit. Rabbits would emerge as they did when a field of corn was cut, as the pyre was prepared months in advance.

Bonfire Boy William Phillips as 'Old Bill', WW I cartoon character, by Bruce Bairnsfather

1987

In the early hours of Friday, October 16th 1987 a 120 m.p.h. gale swept through southern England. Access roads to Billingshurst were blocked, all trains cancelled and power supplies cut off for ten days or more. Food stored in freezers thawed out and shopkeepers sold off their deteriorating goods, candles lit the homes and chain saws chattered on all sides. Roofs were smashed in, cars crushed and the face of the church clock, which dates from 1884, was blown out. East Street and Station Road were impassable. Great areas of woodland and scores of magnificent old trees were uprooted. 40,000 trees were said to have fallen across traffic routes in West Sussex alone. Chanctonbury Ring was devastated and half the specimen trees at Wakehurst Place and Nymans Gardens were ruined. National insurers paid out £2 billion.

1. Fallen tree by Silver Lane blocking Station Road

2. Tower minus clock

3. fallen clock face at St.Mary's church

2011

Summers Place was restructured as apartments with a housing estate in the grounds.

1. Unrestored Mill barn

2. Today

Studies have proved that there are still twenty or more 16th and 17th century timber-framed houses and inns in good order in the village and eighty in the neighbourhood, whereas the more pretentious grand houses erected in Victorian times like Gratwick and Clevelands have succumbed to modern housing and Summers Place has been massively reordered. These premises were too expensive to maintain and stood in valuable grounds, ripe for development. Of recent years a number of studies have been conducted to assist housing estate designers in the future and to describe the vernacular architecture characteristic of the village. The Village Design Statement of 2009 is extant. It tells of the familiar tile-hung elevations, using hand-made and decorative tiles, occasional use of horizontal timber cladding and the red brick walls with interspersed bricks in other colours. Causeway and Tithe cottage beside the Village Green were together an example of a classic Wealden house of the late 14th century. Much new development has echoed these traditional styles in appropriate modern machine-made materials.

St. Gabriel's Catholic Church, also in East St. was built in 1962 on a site gifted by Mr. and Mrs. Maille of Marringdean Rd. some twenty years earlier. It was designed by Henry Bingham Turner of Uckfield and is described by local historian, Paul Smith, as 'in a watery Perpendicular style'. Pevsner judges it 'deplorable'. Tastes differ! The Mass had returned to Billingshurst, for the first time since the Reformation, in 1908 in a room over the late Cripps, the butcher's, in the High Street. The few catholic families who attended dwindled or moved away. Thirteen years later from 1925 about 40 Billingshurst and district Catholics worshipped in a building in Lower Station Road, originally The Gospel Hall, built in 1888 and used first by the Salvation Army and then the Plymouth Brethren. The

St. Gabriels Catholic Church

Hughes, Jukes and O'Reilly families gave generous help. Miss Shannon donated £100. From 1933 Fr. Walter Stone who became the resident priest boosted the growing congregation. He was followed by Father Candy. By 1949 Sunday Mass was attended by 150 people in Pulborough and Billingshurst combined. A single brick wall with shallow arches is all that now remains of the Lower Station Road building.

When Hammonds Garden Field was excavated, prior to the granting of planning permission for housing in 2011, a great deal of late Victorian and early 20th century detritus was revealed – jugs, marmalade jars, bottles etc. It had obviously been used as an 'amenity tip' probably by East St. residents and other village people. Excellent dumping facilities are now sited at the entrance to Jubilee Fields sports grounds.

Opposite Mill Barn is 'Trees', a house of ancient appearance, but of recent construction made up from materials salvaged from demolitions of other properties by the late Harold Wadey, a notable member of a local building family founded by Ephraim Wadey in 1884.

Possible future developments

In 2001 the population of the parish was 6531, in 2012 over 7000, more than three times its total in 1830. It is likely to continue to rise. Not least of recent expansions has been the building of care homes, sheltered accommodation and residential closes specifically for the senior citizenry. These late 20th and 21st century developments have dropped windfall financial fortunes into the laps of those lucky Billingshurst citizens who owned title to land, or development companies that were shrewd enough to buy it up, where the lottery of planning legislation allowed the right to build expensive houses, at times when such building land was in short supply. Although unwelcome to many people, planning permission has been granted for 475 houses and community facilities on Duckmore, Cocksbrook and Crouchers. Under active discussion are yet more development sites off Little East Street (the old allotments), Daux Road and areas off Marringdean Road. This is despite Pevsner's judgment that 'The Weald landscape near here is splendidly unspoilt, a continuously changing pattern of copses and small fields.' The village population was 7,820 in 2006, is currently estimated at 10,000 and is likely to reach 12,000 by 2020 AD.

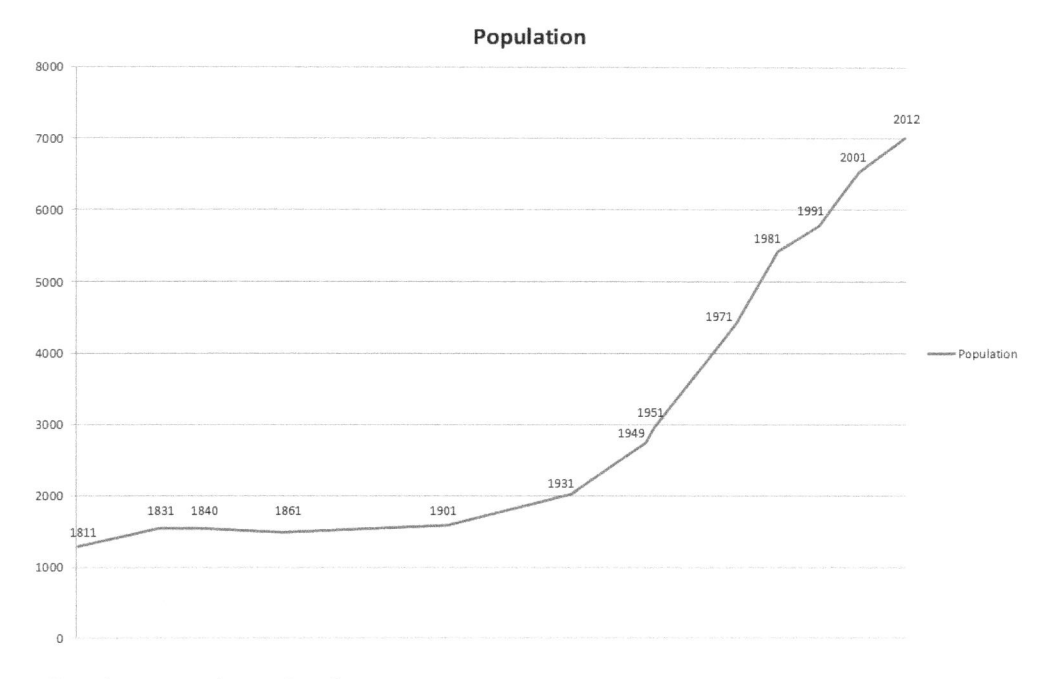

Billingshurst Population Graph

Of equal concern to many Billingshurst people are dangers arising from the potential exploitation of underlying oil and gas deposits in the neighbourhood. Hydrocarbon resources are preserved in the older strata beneath the Wealden clay upon which the village rests. This surface clay is the oldest layer in the Cretaceous group, laid down some 135 million years ago. Lying beneath it are some 20 layers of older sedimentary rocks, named Jurassic, Triassic and Permian, dating back up to 300m years ago. These, like the zest on an orange, are the outer skin of the planet. Earth has a 20 mile deep crust, itself comparable to the pith. Quite near the top of the Jurassic is one thick stratum named Kimmeridge Clay, which is rich in oil though allegedly not in gas. It was laid down some 160 million years ago. Hereabouts it begins some 610 metres beneath the surface. There are another two oil and gas-bearing strata lower down in the Triassic.

The Kimmeridge fossil fuel source at 3920 feet has long been tapped locally by the Island Gas Company at Cootham beside the A283. There three 'nodding donkey' pumps have extracted two tanker loads of crude oil each week since 1988. The shaft turns horizontally at its base and draws about 30 barrels a day.

Billingshurst parish extends over this same terrain and exploratory work is being done by Energie Centrique at Woodbarn Farm, Broadford Bridge. They are expected to drill 3km deep. Gas recovery is considered improbable by experts. However a crop of crude oil is a real possibility. Oil was originally formed from organic matter, mainly from shellfish and other invertebrates, together with crocodiles, turtles, certain dinosaurs and marine reptiles and subsequently subjected to pressure. However extraction could well prove uneconomic in competition with more accessible and plentiful world sources and in conflict with 'green' opponents of the burning of fossil fuel. Neither the landscape nor the financial well-being of the people of Billingshurst is ever likely to resemble that of Texas or Saudi Arabia.

Mary Mitford (in 'Our Village' 1824) has described our idealised concept of an English village as a place "with inhabitants whose faces are as familiar to us as the flowers in our garden...a little world of our own, insulated like ants in an anthill or bees in a hive...where we know everyone and are known to everyone... interested in everyone and authorised to hope that everyone feels an interest in us." This vision now has ended. Modern transport and technology have offered us instant global connection to almost anywhere on planet Earth but imperilled the hegemony of the village. It would be quite possible to live in Billingshurst without really knowing or having dealings with any fellow villager or interacting with any feature of the community. A century ago fellowship in neighbourhoods sprang automatically from a necessary interdependence. People frequently worked together in teams, they shopped locally and almost daily, they frequented a 'local' pub, they were schooled and made music together, they socialised at dances, 'socials' and whist drives. Pals enlisted and died together. The essential everyday provision of services, goods, shelter, food, medicine, worship and amusement created inescapable bonds of fraternity, common interest, and the conviviality of fellowship. Even the dubious distinctions of wealth and class still demanded face-to-face human intercourse. Even though people were categorised as 'master' and 'servant' those social groups could not lead separate lives. The milkman and the baker's roundsman, the village doctor, the vicar and even the policeman might call at your door. 21st century Billingshurst, like everywhere else, has largely lost these inexorable common ties. Villagers nowadays participate in the civic life by choice rather than necessity. It can be an easy option to duck out of any aspect of community life. There are no longer wealthy village 'worthies' obliged by custom to exercise their 'noblesse' for the common good. Lord Sainsbury does not sit on the Parish Council. Being public-spirited is optional, participating in villager life scarcely less so. But a fulfilled life demands some degree of flesh and blood sociability. It could well be argued that interactive social media have bounteously enhanced our capacity for making and maintaining an enriched circle of human relationships. However an image or text on a hand-held device or a voice on an earphone is an unsatisfactory substitute for physical camaraderie. It is bad for the human spirit to so restrict contact that we know none of our neighbours and no one knows us. People need to meet and find friends in order to find fulfilment in loyalty, pride and pleasure in one's local place. Whatever your birthplace, ethnicity, business or fortune, if you dwell in Billingshurst you have one thing in common with 8,000 other people, and would prefer to be an insider of 'no mean city'. "My name is Bloggs and I come from Billingshurst". A longing for a chance to express community applause is evident whenever a village football team has a triumph, or we take pride in someone living amongst us who achieves national celebrity.So the challenge for our village leaders is to find pathways that subvert any potential loneliness and isolation, like the solitude to be found when alone in a crowded city. It is owed to the people who choose to live in a village to provide for them the experience of the old village values that they hoped for and expected to find. Without positive and deliberate initiatives to bring villagers together we might well pass our lives in a standardised, featureless suburbia. 'Progress' would have concreted over our fields but also our souls. The message for long-term residents and incomers alike is: "If you value Billingshurst, then choose it, use it or risk losing it". Responsibility for village business will drift yet further from local control; yet more decisions on local issues will be taken by some remote 'authority'.

A disquieting trend in Billingshurst is for a steady decline in the stocking and marketing of basic goods with the limited exception of high quality products like butchery, floristry and bakery. Charities fill up the empty shops. This tendency is likely to be boosted by more internet shopping and home deliveries from stock depots and nearby hypermarkets. However the provision of services such as agencies, nurseries, catering outlets, finance and technological support is a growing compensation for the loss of retail shops. The village is evolving from a marketplace to a social hub.

Positive initiatives might be the promotion of music, film and drama, sports and games, carnivals and celebrations, clubs and societies, festivals, rallies, street parties, social centres for young and old, educational and recreational courses and other cultural enhancements as yet unheard of. Places need opportunities for employment too and an individual identity. At various times Billingshurst has been 'noted' for pretty girls, maltings, carpet sweepers and flea powder. Can it find a unique role in Information Technology, light industry, media services, restaurants or catering for tourists? If we do not aspire we shall never succeed. A 'Community Led Plan for Billingshurst' up to 2020 has been jointly produced by the Parish Council, the Billingshurst Community Partnership and the Chamber of Commerce. This comprehensive document analyses those aspects of community well-being which need safe-guarding or enhancement, under broad headings – The Economy, Transport and Parking, the Elderly, the Youth, Open Spaces and the Environment and Community Safety and Health. It identifies through what agencies, desirable goals may be achieved and a putative time-scale for implementation. It is an eminently worthy wish-list of unfulfilled needs and improvements, commendable targets and desirable extra facilities. If it has a fault it is that it poses imprecise challenges on some 28 different issues, the overwhelming scope of which invites scepticism in the light of limited resources of time, money and sufficient public interest. Although many desirable targets are identified, priorities and practical precise plans are avoided, as is the greatest and most vexed question of what, if any, expansion of housing and industry should be embraced. Fewer and more concrete detailed objectives await definition and common consent. Those objectives ought not to be narrowly 'parochial'. Economic and social settlement patterns in rural areas have, throughout Anglo-Saxon history, at intervals of ten or more miles, involved the establishment of one larger community which provides reciprocal services to its less-populated neighbouring parishes. Usually these have been trading hubs with specialised shops, manufactories and professional skills which their hinterland villages could not afford. In a word they were 'Market Towns'. Billingshurst village has always been such a hub surrounded as it is by extensive rural parishes. Kirdford, Wisborough Green, Ifold and Loxwood are remote from their District Centre of Chichester. Coolham, Shipley and West Chiltington have great acreages of woods and fields. They have their special attributes, farms, factories, auction houses, polo grounds, playing fields and pubs for example, but they need Billingshurst, just as Billingshurst needs them for mutual support. It is noticeable that along the A29 road to Adversane and beyond into Pulborough parish, by accident rather than design, four major businesses have recently been established – a builder's Yard, a vast fencing company, a modern brewery and a specialised plants nursery. When, in 1957 Billingshurst Secondary School was built to provide the education of nearly all the 11 to 18 year olds in the area, a new set of bonds of association were formed quite as embracing as that of any traditional Market Town. Billingshurst has the specialised churches, stores, banks, builders, the railway, leisure and travel facilities, estate agencies, legal services, medical expertise, and provision for the elderly and facilities for the young, together with the professional competences which are important for the economic health of the whole area. The Parish Council has recently launched another exercise in the shape of a Neighbourhood Development Plan. A Steering Committee to control proceedings has been established but has encountered initial difficulties over its composition and pessimism about public interest and involvement. Consultants have been appointed. It behoves Billingshurst residents to hearten and encourage the Committee by their interest in their research and support for its eventual proposals. Notwithstanding the doom laden message foreshadowed above, like a witch's warning from a blasted heath, there is every reason for the people of Billingshurst to trust that the sense of belonging to the place where they live and where their families can confidently put down their roots can be fully realised in the 21st century. The legacy of the 20th century is an adequate inheritance of public buildings and sporting facilities, good schools and nurseries, enterprising shopkeepers, roads and bypasses, four churches, banks and a plethora of eating places. The public houses have survived where elsewhere they have failed. The housing stock, ancient and modern, is attractive and fit for purpose, access to the surrounding meadows, public open spaces and the pleasures of the countryside readily available. Over and above all these assets is abundant evidence that our citizens continue to opt for fellowship and active participation in village community enterprises and cultural activities through scores of clubs, groups and voluntary activities. These are amply demonstrated elsewhere in this book. A few challenges remain such as inadequate parking and highway difficulties, the future of the High Street and Jengers Mead, employment needs and leisure facilities for young people. Nevertheless the basis of a home town to be proud of is there for the taking if leaders in the community guide developments with astuteness in attracting finance and wise planning.

The spirit of Billingshurst

The people of Billingshurst have long enjoyed their country sports as well as the familiar national games. Cricket had a long tradition at the ground in Station Road for some 180 years. Dr. Hubert was reputed to have struck a six on to the railway line and over the houses in Station Road. The ground is now superseded by excellent pitches at Jubilee Fields, created as a civic improvement when the Western by-pass was built, together with 550 new homes in the 1990s. Association football enjoys similar facilities after the club relinquished its Station Road pitch, originally created by the Parish Council from an old orchard. Plans have now been realised to create public gardens on these old sites where the new Children's Centre, Swimming Pool and Leisure Centre have left ample space. The old wall between the old pitches has been preserved but the derelict pavilion beside Station Road which originally stood on the south end next the Weald School boundary, has been demolished. The Weald School also furnishes playing fields for rugby football, a sports hall for basketball and a wide variety of other sports and games. The village boasts a thriving bowls club, founded in 1932 on land granted by Mrs. Alice Puttock, and it has a keen fraternity of anglers. The traditional Sussex ladies game of stoolball is no longer practised but lawn tennis is well provided for.

The oldest village club, the Horticultural Society is thriving. It has organised an annual show since 1882. There is a prospering Choral Society. The Billingshurst Dramatic Society, founded in 1941, stages remarkably proficient plays, thrice yearly, in the Women's Hall. Public spirited service clubs, the Lions and Rotary, give generous support to local good causes. The Lions staff a comprehensive bookshop and the Rotary, with the Scouts and Guides, stage an annual Village Show and Carnival Parade. The Women's Institute offers good companionship and in the 1950s created an excellent historical scrapbook to which this book is greatly indebted. The British Legion stages an annual Remembrance Day Parade, recalled by the War Memorial beside the ten Church Steps to the High Street, erected in 1921 commemorating 55 men who died in WWI and 9 in WWII.

The Parish Council meets in a handsome Community Centre in Roman Way which superseded the Old Village Hall in the High Street in 1991 before the opening of the western by-pass. It was built on a site that once had a hovel for cattle, converted into a house. The Council is active in the interest of the parish, together with its group of volunteers, known as the Community Partnership, which has a fine record of initiatives for the young, the elderly and the ordinary parishioners alike. There is a Fire Station manned by retained firemen and a conveniently sited branch of the County Library. The Village sign was erected in 1985 and The Heritage Plaque installed at the Millennium, 2000AD. Recent

The Village Community Centre, Roman Way

decades have seen, in the judgment of many, the building of more than enough accommodation for the care of the elderly but insufficient affordable housing for working families. Critics have also claimed to have lost count of the proliferating outlets for take-away meals and regret the struggle of independent shops to make a decent living. Six old inns continue to trade unlike the fate of many other public houses in the County and the Five Oaks Inn which has been demolished and replaced by automobile services. The pubs now depend on selling food as well as drink. However all the maltings which once nurtured the beer have long since disappeared. There are no longer any hotels since the Maltings Hotel and the last one at Adversane both closed but comfortable 'bed and breakfast' can be found and there is a motel and restaurant at Five Oaks at what was once Jane's Tea Garden.

During the middle 20th century the character of Billingshurst High Street, as a coaching inn stopping place on an important road, persisted in that it hosted four automobile garages and a coach company selling cars, fuel and services. By the millennium the effect of the western by-pass, congestion and more remunerative uses for the sites of these premises has resulted in a migration of the businesses to the outskirts at North Heath and Five Oaks, or in the case of repair shops, to the Station area or one of the three industrial estates.

What then can be said of the broad characteristics of the people of Cocksbrook and of Billingshurst and district? Though it is dangerous, indeed ludicrous, to generalise too readily about a diverse and constantly fluctuating community of human spirits, nevertheless certain attitudes to life, politics and religion are sufficiently evident to invite a commentary if not an explanation. The Billingshurst spirit is best explained by what it is not. It has never been an especially wealthy community. It is not well endowed with rich soils and valuable minerals, nor affluent industries and accessible markets. Local yeoman farmers and traders have always struggled to make a decent living. They have, in consequence become

The Village War Memorial. The Parish Council have advised that new roads should be named after the Fallen.

independent, self-sufficient and enterprisingly self-reliant. Neither has it had the benefit of the benign influence of the affluent landed gentry. This contrasts sharply with vast swathes of rural West Sussex. There, time out of mind, the great, semi-feudal estates of Cowdray, Leconfield, Goodwood and the domain of the Dukes of Norfolk have determined much of the way of life of the people who tenanted their lands and serviced their communities.

But the people of Billingshurst, farmers, traders and cottagers alike, were obliged to be their own men, owning or renting their land, poor but free to differ, Sussex-wise, reluctant 'to be druv'. Although consistently loyal to the established Anglican Church, nevertheless important sectors of the people have long shown a dissenting spirit, displaying a rich tradition of chapel-going and 'do different'. The arrival of the Huguenots, Calvinist protestants seeking refuge from Catholic persecution in the 1560s and settling at Wisborough Green where they made glass, may well help explain this local divergence from the pro-catholic sympathies of Arundel to the south and the siting of a Quaker meeting house at the Blue Idol a mile up the road from East Street towards Coolham. Here William Penn, namesake of Pennsylvania, preached on his return from America in 1691. George Fox who founded the Meeting House was imprisoned in Horsham gaol for three months. A new Family Church, the fifth village congregation, has but recently been established.

The Blue Idol Quaker Meeting House off the road to Coolham

The Parish Council, since its statutory establishment in 1894, has earned itself a reputation for cantankerous debate, albeit with constructive initiatives for the well-being of the parishioners. In politics, similar to their stance in religion, the voters have consistently elected establishment-friendly Conservative Members of Parliament, yet unlike the rest of the wards of rural Sussex, they have shown a divergent spirit in their choice of County and District Councillors, even electing Liberal Democrats in the 1990s. The feminist movement too has enjoyed local support. In 1924 the Beck sisters of Duncans, Ellen and Edith, friends of Mrs Pankhurst and keen supporters of Women's Suffrage, bestowed The Women's Hall and the mothers' garden next door on the ladies of Billingshurst as a potent symbol of their independence of mind. The Women's Institute had first call on it. They undertook much charitable work for hospitals and other good causes and were particularly busy during WWII in support of the war effort and were still helping issuing ration books until they were discontinued in 1954.

The Firemen's Family Christmas Party at the Women's Hall, in the 1950s

Billingshurst is a village, trembling on the brink of becoming a town. Under an Act of 1974 the parish has the power to declare itself a Town Council, but the elected representatives continue to prefer a village status. Had it hosted a regular cattle market in times gone by, it might well have grown into a country town, a trading hub for its adjacent villages, a service it now provides in a modest fashion, in uncomfortable competition with Pulborough to the South and Horsham and Crawley to the North. Shopkeepers have struggled to profit from a relatively small 'footfall', though the population continues to expand, and shows every sign of continuing to do so. The conjunction of roads, the railway, the sporting and social clubs, swimming pool and fitness centre, the churches, banks, restaurants, supermarkets, workshops and light industries, a surgery, dentistry and vetinary surgeons, nursery and primary schools and the Weald Comprehensive Secondary School and Sixth Form College, all set in a rolling wooded countryside, combine to offer a rich environment to families who are fortunate enough to inherit the living space of their half-forgotten predecessors.

Acknowledgements and Further Reading

John Hurd, Wendy Lines and Paul Smith- invaluable advice and generous willingness to allow use of their research, maps and photographs.
Geoff Rhodes, Patrick Perks, Duncan Reynolds, Tim Churchill, Julie Barnes, Peter Lines, Kim Hope, Des Wakeling, Alastair Morris, Roger Patterson, Gillian Yarham, Eric Clark, Durwin Banks, Ann Brooks, Jackie Charman, Di Burroughs, Mrs. Barraclough, Gordon New, David Lowe, David Thompson, Jackie Bench, Mr. Myers, Roger Lusted, Jim Burroughs, Sheila Van den Bergh, William Pickup, Peter Hooper, Ron Philbey for advice, research and photographs.
Helen Abbott – advice and research on Five Oaks, herself advised by Derek Sims, Roy Dumbril, John Morris and Yvonne Wolzak.
Jane Paton – advice, records of Kingsfold, maps photographs and Billingshurst Society Newsletters.
Phyllis Adam – Tedfold Estate, Billingshurst Newsletter No. 82
Wendy Holmes – records of Five Oaks.
Peter Etherington –loan of Ross booklet.
Peter Stockwood Remembers and advice on Angling Society.
West Sussex Record Office– Mrs.G.Maria Treland, 'A Memoire' and 'Tom Topper Remembers'.
Madeleine Woods – about Tom Topper.
The West Sussex Gazette.
The West Sussex Courty Times (and Standard).
Kelly's Post Office Directory, 1867,1969 and 1973.
Mr.Julian Morgan – Hon Sec Wey and Arun Canal Trust. www.weyandarun.uk. Contact - office@weyandarun.co.uk –advice and photographs.
Anna Doherty – Archaeology SE for Report No. 2013008
Pauline Taylor – Articles 'The Taverns of Billingshurst'.
English Heritage.
Sussex Archaeological Collections.
Billingshurst, Storrington and Horsham Libraries.
Malcolm Laker – Herbert Laker's Memories.
Billingshurst Parish Guide and leaflets published by the Billingshurst Community Partnership and The Historical Society..
WI – 1950s Scrap Book prepared with the Parish Council.
The Unitarian Chapel, Billingshurst. A Celebration'.
The Blue Idol –www.blueidol.org.uk
Billy Hoad – 'Diaries and Recollections'.

Wendy Lines – Two books, 'Billingshurst' and 'Billingshurst and Wisborough Green'.
Michael Jacob and Walter Parr – A Guide to Billingshurst Parish Church.
W. Sx. Federation of WIs –'West Sussex within Living Memory'.
Jane Robinson – 'A Force to be Reckoned With, A History of the WI'.
Peter Brandon – 'Sussex Landscape' and 'The Kent & Sussex Weald'.
J.R.Armstrong – 'A History of Sussex'.
W.E Tate – 'The Parish Chest'.
E.V.Lucas – 'Highways and Byways; in Sussex'.
Tony Wales – 'A Sussex Garland', 'The West Sussex Village Book'.
Rev Arthur Young –'A General View of the Agriculture of Sussex' 1813.
R.Thurston Hopkins – Old English Mills and Inns' 1927
Debora Evershed – 'From Hadfoldsherne...to Adversane'.
Valerie Porter – 'The Village Parliaments'.
David Arscott – 'Phillips County Guide to West Sussex'.
Martin Brunnarius – 'The Windmills of Sussex'.
Roger Birch – 'Sussex Stones'.
Diana Chatwin – 'The Development of Timber-framed Houses in the Sussex Weald'.
P.A.L.Vine –'London's Lost Route to the Sea', 'The Wey & Arun Junction Canal'.
Burgess & Saunders – 'Bombers over Sussex 1943-45'.
Jacqueline Simpson – 'Folklore of Sussex'.
Andreas Augustin – The Mena House Treasury'.
J.S.L.Pulford- 'The Locke-Kings of Brooklands, Weybridge'.
James Bishop – 'Social History of Edwardian Britain'.
H.L.Edlin – 'Trees, Woods & Man'.
Frank Holmes – 'Stories of Old Horsham'.
Kenneth Neale – 'Victorian Horsham, The Diary of Henry Michell'.
G. Lawes – 'The Weald School – 'A History' & 'Beemaster' with George Wakeford.
Maggie Gee – 'My Animal Life'
Gage, Harris &Sullivan- 'Going off the rails, The County Railway in West .Sussex.'
Mitchell and Smith- 'Crawley to Littlehampton'.
Hayley Nicholls –Archaeology Team Leader (UCL) for advice and guidance.
'Archaeology SE Report No. 2016168 Nicholls and Green'
John and Terry Griffin for meticulous proof-reading and the liberty of their 'Hammond's Messuage'.

My wife, Gillian and daughter Sarah Moloney with grateful thanks for their patience and boundless support.

Appendix 1
Billingshurst Roads and Estates 2016

This article was researched and written by Mr. Paul Smith.

Road and street names can reveal a lot about any place, commemorating national and local personages of note, the sites of long vanished buildings and natural features. Billingshurst has certainly been shaped by its road layout, being on the strategic Roman route of Stane Street linking London with the Romano-British tribal capital of Chichester. Most other roads run in the same parallel direction as the Roman road, with few routes from west to east. Many of these parallel roads originated in the Saxon period used as drove roads for livestock going to market or they were also used to reach pasturage on outlying land belonging to more distant manors on the coast or under the South Downs.

The route of the present A272 was developed as a Turnpike Road by stages during the beginning of the 19th Century, but it was the coming of the railway in 1859 that was to change Billingshurst forever. With a quick and convenient way of getting to the larger towns and London, Billingshurst was seen as a good place to live and the age of the commuter was born. Roads such as Station Road, and parts of Chestnut Road and Daux Avenue were laid out by the end of the 19th Century, while in Edwardian times rows of semi-detached houses were built at the north end of the High Street.

There was little building between the two World Wars but more dwellings were added piecemeal in Marringdean Road, Daux Avenue and Parbrook. In West Street, Downsview Cottages were built by Horsham Rural District Council (HRDC). These were the first Local Authority houses. More were built by the same Authority both in the early 1950s and early 60s. After Local Government reorganisation in 1974, the new Horsham District Council (HDC) constructed further homes in Forge Way between 1976 and 1983. In more recent years, social housing has been built for or by Housing Associations, such as Saxon Weald, who have contributed attractive houses and apartments for the young and elderly.

In addition to Local Authority and Social housing a post war boom in private homes attracted many fresh developers. Silver Lane was laid out in the early 1960s and subsequently many more. Each developer has added their own particular style of housing prevalent at the time of construction. The later 1960s are represented by the roads around Rowan Drive. The early 1970s are marked by the neo-Georgian of Rosehill, and the distinctive Sunley Homes styles of Broomfield Drive and Belinus Drive. In the early 2000s, Taywood Homes added styles reflecting the local vernacular on the Penfold Grange development, whilst Fabrica/A2 Dominion are currently building their homes in a more traditional Victorian style with integral roof solar panels as part of a general trend towards more energy-efficient living.

I would like to thank Alison Fearon at Saxon Weald and Mr Alan Setchell for their kind help in the compilation of these notes.

Adversane Lane – is the B2133 that leads eastwards out of Adversane hamlet. Adversane means "the hyrne or corner of the estate of Hadfold" and was first documented as Hadesfoldesberne in 1279.

Alicks Hill The origin of the name is obscure but probably is associated with a person who owned land or lived nearby.

Amberley Court, Brookers Road – is named after the village of Amberley. This block of flats was built by Bellway Homes in 2002-03 on the site of factories and includes **Arundel, Maplehust, Petworth**, and Sussex Courts of similar flats. The name Amberley may mean "the clearing by the river" and was first recorded as Amberle in 957.

Andrew's Hill – lies to the south of Billingshurst on the A29. This is associated with the family of Richard Andrew recorded in 1446.

Anvil Close – was built by HDC in 1976. It takes its name from the heavy metal block on which metal is beaten and shaped. The village forge and wheelwright's shop stood on the corner of the High Street and West Street and survived until the early 1980s when Forge House was built on the site.

Arun Court, Rosehill – is a retirement complex of flats and cottage style houses built at the end of Rosehill by Vinall in 1988-89. It is named after the River Arun which as a name is a back formation from Arundel – "Hoar-hound valley". The old name of the river is the Tarrant which was first recorded in 725 and is thought to mean "the trespasser".

Arun Crescent – The name of this road has the same derivation as **Arun Court** above. This interesting development is a crescent off Arun Road and was built by Saxon Weald in 2009-10. There are 6 Eco houses for rent that were built on the site of a garage compound. These were the first houses in the Country to gain level five of the Code for Sustainable homes (there were some flats to this level before but no houses). The underfloor heating uses ground source heat pumps off an 85 metre borehole and there are solar panels on the roofs. Rainwater is also harvested for the toilets. The development received grants of £80k from the Low Carbon Buildings Programme and £360k from central government.

Arun Road – The name of this road along with Arun Crescent has the same derivation as that of Arun Court above. This road is an extension of **Mill Way** and forms a complete loop. The houses and originally flats – Oak and Beech Court - were built by HRDC in the late 1950s to early 1960s. Whilst the houses remain, the original flats were demolished and replaced with new homes completed in May 2003 by Saxon Weald. These comprise 36 rented and 4 shared ownership properties. These smart new apartments feature different coloured bricks, tile hanging and dormer windows under a slate roof.

Arundel Court, Brookers Road – See Amberley Court, above. It is named after the town of Arundel. This block of flats was built by Bellway Homes in 2002-03. The name was first recorded in 1086 as Harundelle.

Ash Lane – was built off **Honeysuckle Drive** by a2dominion new homes/Fabrica in 2016 and marketed as Marringdean Acres. The setting, design and style are similar to other homes on this development. The name is taken from the Common Ash (Fraxinus excelsior) a tree threatened tree by Ash die-back disease.

Atlantic House – is an office over shops in **Jengers Mead** Shopping Precinct. It is named after the Atlantic Insurance Company who once occupied it.

Bakers Meadow – lies just off the High Street and comprises three 3 bedroom terraced houses and two 2 bedroom semi-detached homes that were built by Whiteoak Developments in 2005-06. The name will recall a celebrated local family of watchmakers, builders, drapers and outfitters.

Barrow Close – is on the Penfold Grange estate and was built by Taywood Homes in 2000-2001. Like all the houses on this estate, it was built in a style reminiscent of local, but especially East Sussex vernacular, with much use of cottage forms and painted weatherboarding. Many of the houses have attractively styled front doors under a lean-to porch. The brass house numbers set on a wooden block are an attractive little touch feature which were given to almost all the houses on the development. The name is likely to be the developer's suggestion..

Belinus Drive – is named after the Roman Surveyor, Belinus, who is supposed to have built the Roman Road of Stane Street. The road was part of the development built by Sunley Homes in 1974-76.

Berrall Way – The Berrall family were a local family commemorated by a stained glass window in the north aisle of St Mary's Church. Berrall Way was developed between 1999 and 2002 by Taywood Homes as part of the Penfold Grange development.

Birch Drive – was built in two stages. The earliest section off Silver Lane was built as part of that road in the early 1960s. This was given a concrete surface and a mix of attractive linear bungalows and detached houses. This would have ended in a drive to Pennybrooks, a timber framed house once known as Broomfield Cottage. The second section was built by Sunley Homes in 1970-71 with more of their distinctive style of homes and linked up with Broomfield Drive. The road takes its name from the Silver Birch trees (*Betula pendula*) that were planted along the road.

Bishopsfield – is an 8 home development by Legesgate Developments and built in 2002-03 on the site of two bungalows constructed at the end of Hayes Wood Road in Five Oaks. The name, probably a suggestion of the developer, appears to have no connection with the area.

Blackgate Lane – is mostly in Pulborough parish and was wholly so until 1933 when the extreme northern section of the road was transferred to Billingshurst. This section ends at Lee Place. The name is taken from Blackgate Farm which lies further down the lane well within the present Pulborough parish.

Blackthorn Avenue – is named after the Blackthorn or Sloe (*Prunus spinosa*), a common local hedgerow shrub. This road off Honeysuckle Drive was begun in 2013 and completed by the end of 2015 by a2dominion new homes/Fabrica under a marketing name of Cereston.

Bridgewater Close – is a cul-de-sac at the south end of the village at Parbrook. This road was developed in 1998-99 as part of the construction of the bypass and is mainly affordable housing. The name may be taken from Bridgewaters Farm which is to the north on Newbridge Road and close to the bypass.

Brookers Road – is named after William Broker, recorded in 1445 and later in land 1476. Land here was referred to as Brokers.

Brookfield Way – Takes its name from the Par Brook that runs close to the road. This cul-de-sac has detached houses in a Georgian style and was constructed between 1971 and 1974 on a site off Daux Avenue.

Broomfield Drive – Takes its name from the now vanished Broomfield Barn, Broomfield Cottage (now Pennybrooks), and a small wood that still exists behind houses in this road, Broomfield Copse. The name probably comes from the shrub Broom (*Cytisus scoparius*). Broomfield Drive is another of the prestigious roads to live in and was developed in 1970-71 by Sunley Homes in their distinctive period style.

Caffyns Rise – This short cul-de-sac lies off Rosehill and was built on a steep meadow that adjoins School Lane. The 15 homes here were built by Hillreed Homes (Sussex) Ltd in 1998-99. The name comes from a local family name. They included rich property owners, surveyors and preachers.

Carpenters – was named after a field called Carpenters Field. It was recorded as such on the 1841 Tithe Map and was part of the Glebe Land attached to St Mary's Church. Old maps also show a curious keyhole-shaped pond which would now be roughly behind the first houses on the left as you go into the road. Carpenters comprising 62 houses was developed about 1966-67 by Croudace whose distinctive and similar house designs can be found at Barns Green, Partridge Green and Horsham. The name John le Carpentir is recorded on the Subsidy Roll of 1332 AD

Cedars Farm Close – is a cul-de-sac built by HDC in 1976 off Forge Way. The name is taken from the nearby Cedars Farm. See The Cedars.

Centurion Close – was named with reference to the Roman road of Stane Street, the original alignment of which was exposed in 1981 during sewer works very close by. The 14 cottage style houses were built by Charles Church under a marketing name of Imperium Gate in 2013-14 on the site of Charles Wadey's Builder's Yard that had moved to a new site at **Andrews Hill**.

Cherry Tree Close – was built in 1963-64 and is a cul-de-sac off **Rowan Drive**. Consisting of a mix of semi-detached and terraced houses, it also contained a shop (Spar in my time) built in 1966 which has been a house for some years.

Chestnut Road – was laid out in the late 19th Century and has row of late Victorian houses, followed by a small development of individual houses built in 1987-88. There were a row of Horse Chestnut trees from which the road probably took its name behind the factory of Thomas Keating now occupied by **Station View**.

Church Path – is a pedestrian walkway leading from **Station Road** to the Parish Church of St Mary from which it takes its present name. The path was once a wider track-way known as **Holywell Lane**.

Clevelands – was built in 1979-80 by Chichester Diocesan Housing Association with terraced housing at the end of Cleve Way. The name is taken from the old mansion that formerly stood towards the north end of the road. **Clevelands** was a large mid-Victorian stuccoed house with cellars that became derelict until it was demolished in 1978. It gained a reputation for being haunted due to its neglected appearance in its latter years.

Cleve Way – is named after the mid-Victorian house that stood beyond the original end of the road. Many of the houses in the road are of a distinctive chalet style similar to others in Crawley, notably in and around Buckswood Drive, Gossops Green. These houses were built in the early 1960s.

Coombe Close – is a short cul-de-sac and actually pertains to one end only of this T shaped section of road and consists of 5 homes that were built in 1986-87. The name is derived from **Coombe Hill** of which it is a spur.

Coombe Hill – This road has a mix of home styles built mainly by HRDC in the early 1950s. The road also contains a number of Airey Houses built of concrete. These were designed by Sir Edwin Airey to the Ministry of Works Emergency Factory Made housing programme as a result of post war shortages of housing and materials. Due to their method of construction, these houses (to quote the terminology of BBC TV's *Homes under the hammer*) are of non-standard construction and can be difficult I understand to get a mortgage on. The components were pre-fabricated in the factory and assembled on site. They are becoming less common as many have been demolished and replaced as has happened in Horsham. Those that remain in Coombe Hill are therefore historically important. A coombe or combe is a dry valley usually found in chalk downland and as the road dips down may be the reason it was so named.

Airey House

Coneyhurst Road – the road to Coneyhurst – the present A272 beyond East Street. Coneyhurst, or originally Coneyhurst Common, is in the parish of West Chiltington. It was recorded as such in 1574 and may have been the home of William de Conyngherst or conyhurst of Sullington, recorded in 1327 and 1332. Coneyhurst means "rabbit wood".

Cranham Avenue – is just off Stane Street at Parbrook. It covers land that consisted of two cow meadows belonging to Groomland Farm between the road and the railway and once included a Gascoigne Milking Unit. The development was built in 1998-99 by Westbury and Westwood Estates Ltd. There are 60 homes built in a mix of a general cottage and Victorian style. The name seems to have no connection with the area. There is a residential area of NE London named Cranham which is also the name for the tune composed by Gustav Holst who lived in the Gloucestershire village of that name and set to Christina Rossetti's words, better known as the Christmas Carol - *In the Bleak Midwinter*.

Daux Avenue – was laid out by the end of the 19th Century off **Lower Station Road**. To the south is **Daux Wood**. The name has the same association as Daux Road. There is a mix of housing here, but most date from the early 20th Century, with some 1950s bungalows and some later infilling. By the spring of 2016, Bellway Homes, as part of their "Greenleaves" development, had added an eastward extension to the road that now turns to the south on the site of a field, known as Long Croft in 1841 when it was part of Great Daux Farm, owned by Peter Evershed.

Daux Road – This road takes its name from Great Daux Farm, a fine medieval timber framed house that lies at the end of the road. The name is probably associated with a William Daukes first recorded in 1369. There is also a Daux Wood and a Little Daux Farm close by.

Daux Way – links **Daux Road** and **Daux Avenue** and has the same name origin as these roads. As well as industrial premises, there are houses here dating from the early 1920s up to the 1970s and some 1950s bungalows.

Dauxwood Close – is a private cul-de-sac off **Daux Avenue**. Development began from about 1968 and continued through the 1970s. The road takes its name from Daux Wood behind the close.

Dell Lane – Dell means a small valley and this road lies at the bottom of a dip between the **Church Path** and **Silver Lane**. The initial section of the road was completed in the later 1960s and the rest was built by Fairclough Homes in 1979-1980. This attractive and quiet cul-de-sac came to fame in 1983-1984 when it was used for filming the BBC Sitcom *Ever Decreasing Circles*, using several houses in the road.

Downsview Cottages, West Street – were built by HRDC in the early 1930s.

There are a total of 12 homes that when they were built enjoyed an uninterrupted view of the distant South Downs, now largely obscured by later development. This house style was adopted elsewhere in the district. Large numbers were built along the Ifield Road in Crawley.

E**aston Crescent** – this cul-de-sac off **Nightingale Walk** comprises 10 houses and 2 bungalows and was built in 1994-95 by Gleeson Homes Southern on part of the garden and land attached to Trees, a house in East Street, owned by the Wadey family. It is named after local bank manager, Jack Easton, who was a long-serving chairman of the Parish Council.

East Street – takes the traveller east out of the village. Now part of the busy A272.

Farriers Close – a short cul-de-sac off **Forge Way** was built by Martin Grant Homes in 1982. A Farrier is a smith who shoes horses and the name is connected with the forge that stood on the corner of the **High Street** and **West Street**.

Field End – Literally the end of a field! In this case it was part of a field known as Long Croft in 1841, owned by Peter Evershed as part of Great Daux Farm. The cottage style homes here were completed by spring 2016 by Bellway Homes as part of their "Greenleaves" development. As a place name, End is very common in Central England and East Anglia and denotes a small settlement or farms at the extremities of a particular village or parish.

Five Oaks Road – leads from Five Oaks to Broadbridge Heath and is now the present A264 that begins at Five Oaks and ends on the eastern side of Tunbridge Wells in Kent. The section in question from Five Oaks to Broadbridge Heath was straightened and turnpiked by an Act of Parliament in 1811 and disturnpiked in 1876. The 1876 map still shows Hayes Turnpike or Toll Gate that was sited roughly where a pair of semi-detached houses stand, between Five Oaks and **Furze View**. Five Oaks is thought to have been originally a group of 5 prominent Oak trees but the name itself can only be traced back to 1622.

Forge House – is on the corner of the **High Street** and **West Street** and was built in about 1981 as an office block. In 2000-01 the block was converted into six flats and one house by S A Construction Co Ltd. It takes its name from the former forge and wheelwrights that stood on the site and demolished in about 1978 with the site derelict for four years.

Forge Way – is named after the blacksmith's forge that once stood on the corner of the **High Street** and **West Street**. The road links these latter two roads in an arc and was developed in stages. The section nearest **West Street** was built with detached houses in the mid 1960s, then the road was further extended by HDC and Sunley Homes between 1974 and 1976 when eventually it was joined to the **High Street**. In these developments flats and some terraced houses were built by HDC in 1976 and the reminder by Sunley Homes during 1974-76 and Hilbery Chaplin in 1982. In 1983, HDC had more flats and starter homes added to the north west of the road in a short spur.

Freemans Close – is a cul-de-sac off **Belinus Drive** and was built by Sunley Homes in 1974-76. It is possible that it was named after a local family or a name suggested by the developer.

Frenches Mead – was built by HRDC with good solid red brick houses in the late 1940s to early 1950s in a distinctive cottage style with originally metal Crittall windows. Part of the road is laid out around a green before it joins with **Coombe Hill** and **Mill Lane**. The name is taken from a nearby farm long since vanished under part of **Arun Road** and was connected with Robert le Franceys and Robert Frenssh in 1406.

Freshlands – is a crescent that joins at both ends to Morris Drive and was built by Bryant Homes/Taylor Woodrow in 2002-03 as part of the Penfold Grange development. The name is probably a developer name – fresh land.

Furze View – this cul-de-sac lies on the extreme north of the parish and established piecemeal after World War II. Furze is another name for Gorse and old maps show an area of rough ground on the south side of the stream where Gorse probably grew and houses were built on this land facing south over farm land.

Gorselands – was built in 1978-80 by Gleeson Homes on the site of two horse paddocks behind the Catholic Church and bordered by the track to Little Daux Farm. The detached houses here were built in a distinctive style which can also be seen at Turners Hill. The road is named likely after Gorse (*Ulex europaeus*) that grows in hedgerows and as scrub.

Gratwicke Close– Gratwicke was a large mansion house in its own grounds with a detached stable block that still exists as a house today. Sadly the mansion was demolished in the early 1960s. It had been built about 1830 and altered after 1898 by Edward Thomas Norris whose friend, Sir Edwin Lutyens, added a billiard room. The terraced houses here were built in the mid 1960s and the green in front has an old Mulberry tree which may have been in the grounds of the mansion.

Great Grooms – is a timber-framed house that displayed the date 1480 for many years. Originally Groomland Farm House, it has served as a restaurant before reverting to residential use in more recent years. It was recorded as the property of John Gretegrome in the Fitzalan Survey about 1400 AD.

Griffin Close – has frontage on the **High Street** and off **Coombe Hill** and was built on the site of **Townland**, most recently a care home, which was demolished at the end of 2007. The development by Saxon Weald comprises 19 properties for rent -7 houses and 12 flats. There was £515k grant from HDC and the rest was funded by Saxon Weald. Griffin Close was completed in May 2012. The contractors were Sunninghill Construction and the architects were Kenn Scaddan Associates of Portsmouth who designed an attractive terrace of properties which blend in well with the surrounding older houses using elements of local vernacular and Victorian styles with varying roof heights. Griffin Close was named after Cllr Griffin at the request of the Parish Council. Councillor Cliff Griffin had served as a councillor for the District and Parish Councils for 48 years at the time.

Grooms Court – is a converted barn and newer outbuilding attached, converted mainly into offices. The barn formed part of Groomland Farm and the premises served for many years as a successful antiques business which used the name given.

Groomsland Drive – takes its name from Groomsland Farm which is on the corner of **Natts Lane** and **Stane Street** at Parbrook, often shown on old maps as Groomland Farm. The road I understand was laid out in 1939 and interrupted by World War II after which building restarted by HRDC and not completed until the early 1950s. See also **Great Grooms** and **Grooms Court**. All names with Groom may derive from John Gretegrome, circa 1400.

Hawthorn Way – lies off Honeysuckle Drive and was built by a2dominion new homes/Fabrica in 2015-16. It is named after the Hawthorn, a common hedgerow shrub of which there are two main species – Common Hawthorn (Crataegus monogyna) and the less common locally Midland Hawthorn (*Crataegus laevigata*).

Hayes Wood Road – is a short cul-de-sac at Five Oaks. The houses here date from the early 1950s and were built by HDC. They use an interesting pale buff brick which is probably not of local origin. At the time of the 1841 Tithe survey, there was a Hayes Wood that was over 53 acres and owned and occupied by a Mary Hooper. The other nearest name with Hayes lies just over the parish boundary in Slinfold. What is known today as Slinfold Manor was in 1876 called Hayes House and along Five Oaks Road was the Hayes Turnpike Gate. Hayes is thought to have been associated with a William le Hay recorded in Slinfold in 1342. At the end of the road is **Bishopsfield.**

High Seat Copse – comprises 3 houses close to High Seat House at the northern end of the **High Street**. The site was once part of a nursery and the origin of the name is uncertain, though it was recorded as Highseat on the 1875 Ordnance Survey 6" map. The detached houses in a local style were built after planning permission was granted in 2000.

High Street – Many villages and towns have a High Street, just as German places may have a hauptstrasse or in an Italian village, via principale. It is the main street in a town or a village.

Hillview – is named after Hillview Garage that formerly occupied both sides of the High Street which was established at in the 1930s. There are 14 homes here all terraced with those on the west side arranged around a court. They were built by Taylor-Wimpey in 2010.

Holders Close – Another name with an uncertain origin, but probably suggested and chosen by the developer, Bryant Homes/Taylor Woodrow. This cul-de-sac has an interesting history. The site was originally intended for houses and bungalows for the over 50s, and construction of these began and a marketing suite set up. Then the developer changed the plans. The whole site was closed off and all the houses, whether completed or not, were demolished and replaced in 2005-2006 with houses and apartments with no age restrictions to completely different designs and layout, including some distinctive apartments blocks.

Holywell Lane – is the earlier name for the **Church Path** and was still known by this name up to the 1930s. Behind Dell Lane was once a pond, filled in about 1980 when this road was enlarged. The lane may have taken its original name from this pond.

Honeysuckle Drive – lies off **Marringdean Road** and is the principal road into a new development begun in 2013 by a2dominion new homes/Fabrica and marketed as Cereston. The show home was launched on 7th July 2013. By 2016 this road was largely complete and contains attractive Victorian cottage style homes and some flats. These also incorporate solar panels set into the roof. Much of this development has been built on derelict farmland, but the developers have retained almost all the hedgerows and trees. They have made a feature of the stream running through the site and created ponds to help with the ever present concern over drainage and flooding associated with the building of new homes.

Hurstlands – This short cul-de-sac was built about 1974 on the site of a house called Hurstland which was known as Hurst House in 1841 when it was owned by William Smart. However, the name goes much further back – to 1296 when the land here was occupied by Adam atte Hurst.

Ingfield Manor Drive – leads to Ingfield Manor School, Five Oaks. This is a school for pupils aged 3–19 with neurological motor impairment such as cerebral palsy. This road is a private road originally named **Marles Lane**. In 2007 a small group of houses were built at the junction of the drive and Stane Street and the Local Authority decided that the lane should have a proper name.

Ingfield Manor was built in 1908-10 by Lord, later Sir Charles, Fielding and the name is an anagram of his name. He owned all the land for some distance around the present site of the school. The story goes that he built the manor on his favourite spot so that he could survey his whole estate. During WWII the house and grounds were billeted by Canadian soldiers prior to D-Day. By 1961 when Scope bought the house from the Fielding family, the house was in some disrepair. The building was then restored and forms part of this important school. **Woodland Close** lies at the end of the drive near to the school.

Jengers Mead – takes its name from the medieval Gingers House and malt-house that once stood on the site. The name is a corruption of Gingers which in the 1930s was a tearoom. Jengers Mead was built in the mid 1960s as a shopping precinct.

Jengers Passage – is a pedestrian walkway linking **Jengers Mead** Shopping Precinct and the **High Street**. Part of it shares the rear entrance of Carlton House occupied by Austens Home Hardware.

Jubilee Court – is a complex of retirement apartments built by McCarthy & Stone who are famous for these developments often with the name element "Home" somewhere in their names. There are 29 apartments with a warden and the site lies off the **High Street** on the site of the yard and garage of the former Billingshurst Coaches. It was completed in 2002 and named in honour of Queen

Elizabeth II's Golden Jubilee.

Kenilworth Place – was named after a house named Kenilworth set in a large garden on the south side of **Natts Lane**. It was probably built in the 1930s and named after the town and castle of Kenilworth in Warwickshire. The house was eventually sold and demolished and 13 homes built on the site by David Wilson Homes in 2004.

Kingsfold Close – is a short cul-de-sac of large detached houses off **Marringdean Road** built in 1988. The site was originally part of the Italian POW Camp that eventually became the premises of a riding school before demolition. The name means "kings fold" or enclosure. It was first recorded in 1279 as Kingesfolde.

Kingsley Mews – is a small development along **Brookers Road** of 5 houses built by Bellway Homes (South East) Ltd in 2000. The origin of the name is unknown.

Knights Acre – was built in the grounds of what was once Broomfield Lodge, a large Victorian house with an extensive garden in **Station Road**. The house was occupied by a number of well-known Billingshurst families including the Puttocks. The building was remodelled probably around the 1920s when it was turned into a rambling mock Tudor house and later sub-divided with the major portion renamed Knights. In the 1990s an area of the garden was sold off and two detached houses built on the site.

Lakers Meadow – was built by Cala Homes in 1987-88 on the site of a field that was behind 82a **High Street**. 82a and **Laura's Garden** were once part of a butchery business owned by E W Cripps & Son and included the field and a slaughterhouse. The surname Laker is a well-known local one and this cul-de-sac was probably named for this reason. The field is nameless on the 1841 Tithe Map.

Larks View – Like nearby **Skylarks**, this cul-de-sac of 14 homes built by Taywood Homes in 2002-03 is named after the Skylark (*Alauda arvensis*) that was commonly seen and heard in this vicinity.

Laura's Garden – is a small development of four mews houses behind 82a **High Street**. They were built in 2011-12 on the site of the old slaughterhouse, the older part of which remains in use as a florist's shop. The florists shop is named Laura's Garden after the owner and as the name of this little group of properties.

Laura House – is a part of **Jengers Mead** built in 1989-90 and includes a number of shops and offices with some flats above. Laura House is named after the developer of the site, Laura Investment Co Ltd.

Lawrenson Mews – This small development by Martin Grant Homes was built between 2013 and 2014 just off **Myrtle Lane**. There are just 10 homes from 2 to 4 bedrooms. The developers wanted to call it Cobbett's Mews which was used as the marketing name, but William Cobbett did not come through this part of Billingshurst. It was suggested by Councillors that it should be called Lawrenson Mews as the Lawrenson family were proprietors of the concrete block making factory which was on the site until it relocated to Gilmans Industrial Estate in the 1970s.

Little East Street – is a short, dead-end lane off the **High Street** that runs parallel to **East Street**. The road ends at an area of wood and scrub known locally as the Bowling Alley, probably because it was used by the original village school for sports and balls would run down the hill. Rosehill crosses this road.

Longfield Manor, West Street – was originally an old people's home built by HRDC in the early 1960s and known just as Longfield. During the latter 1990s it was taken over by Sussex Healthcare who demolished the original building and built a much larger care home on the site, naming it Longfield Manor. On the 1841 Tithe Map the field here was indeed called Long Field and was owned and occupied by John Ireland. The field was then arable and measured 3 acres, 3 rods and 17 perches.

Lordings Road – was partly in Pulborough Parish until the boundary changes of 1933. The name also refers to a farm and a wood. It is associated with Francis Lording who first appears in 1602.

Lower Station Road – was laid out after the opening of the railway in 1859 as an extension to **Station Road**. Many of the houses are late Victorian with more added during the 1950s and 1960s. Now used as a take-away, the shop nearest the station on the east side was used for filming the sitcom "*Ever Decreasing Circles*" in 1983-84. See **Dell Lane**.

Luggs Close – is a cul-de-sac of 12 retirement homes and garages off **East Street**. The site was originally occupied by Gore Farm's buildings which were later used by the firm of J O Lugg & Son who were agricultural contractors and later boilermakers from which the road takes its name. The restoration of steam traction engines and rollers took place here until the business moved to The Haven, near Rudgwick. The houses were built by Lintott Property Development in 2002-03.

Luxford Way – was built in 1999-2000 by Taywood Homes as part of the Penfold Grange development. This is the main drive in from the old A29 and contains houses in the local vernacular style, a feature of the estate. The name comes from a local Sussex family name. Joseph Luxford must hold the all-time title of 'Mr. Billingshurst'.

Malthouse Cottages – are in **Adversane Lane**, Adversane. They take their name from a malt-house which was later converted to cottages that stood round the corner on what is now the A29. These particular houses date from the early

1950s and were likely built by HRDC.

Manor Close – is named after the Manor House close by – the ancient Manor of Bassett's Fee. This small development comprises four Eco Houses built in 2012 by Cross Construction, all sold before completion.

Maple Close – is a short cul-de-sac off Rowan Drive and was built in 1968. The name is taken from the local tree species Field Maple (*Acer campestre*).

Maplehurst Court, Brookers Road – is named after the West Sussex hamlet of Maplehurst in the parish of Nuthurst. The name means Maple-tree wood from the Old English 'maple hyrst', first recorded in 1485. This block of flats was built by Bellway Homes in 2002-03 on the site of factories and includes Amberley, **Arundel**, **Petworth**, and **Sussex Courts** of similar flats.

Maple Road – links **Birch Drive** with **Broomfield Drive** and was built in 1970-71 by Sunley Homes using many of their distinctive house designs. The road has the same source as Maple Close and shows that tree names are among the most popular for naming our roads.

Marles Lane – Most of this lane is in Rudgwick Parish that includes a short section that is metalled. Part of the southern section is now known as **Ingfield Manor Drive**. The name Marles was first recorded as Littlemarles, Midlemarle and Marlepitfeld in 1455, becoming Marles by 1616. Probably it was a place where marl was dug to help improve the clay soil.

Marringdean Road – Marringdean is also both a house and a wood. It was first recorded in 1288 as Merehonedene and is considered to mean "woodland pasture near the boundary stone" as the house and wood are close to the parish boundary with West Chiltington. At the north end of the road are 6 houses of 4 semi-detached that were built by HRDC in the early 1930s and are similar in style to **Downsview Cottages, West Street**.

Meadow Close – is a small cul-de-sac off the very end of Daux Avenue completed by Bellway Homes with cottage style houses in 2015-16 as part of their "Greenleaves" development. These houses were built on a meadow that had been unused for well over 30 years and was reverting to woodland. The field in 1841 was known as Long Croft and formed part of the land of Peter Evershed who owned Great Daux Farm nearby.

Mill Lane – See also **Mill Way**. Mill Lane appears on old maps up to the 1950s when it ran from the High Street and ended at Old Millhouse that was replaced by Local Authority housing in what became **Mill Way**. Early photographs show a rough track hedged on both sides.

Mill Way – is the later name for Mill Lane. It is named after a windmill that was burnt down on the 5th November 1852. Most of the housing here dates from the late 1950s to early 1960s.

Morris Drive – is named after the Morris family who farmed at Five Oaks Farm. Robert Morris was the first chairman of the Parish Council when it was formed in 1895. The road forms a major part of the Penfold Grange development and was built in 1999-2003 by Taywood Homes.

Myrtle Close – Completed by Thakeham Homes as their "Parbrook Walk" development in March 2016, this comprises a small development of cottage style mainly Shared Ownership homes. The land was previously occupied by industrial units. Myrtle Close is a natural extension of **Myrtle Lane** with the same origin.

Myrtle Lane – This short lane began life as a footpath and track that led westwards from between houses, now shops and the Railway Pub to the old A29 just to the north of **Hurstlands**. It remained a bumpy rough road well into recent times and is now surfaced throughout. It contains a mix of Victorian houses, an office building, some industrial and commercial premises and some new houses completed in 2015. Myrtle Lane is named after the Common Myrtle (*Myrtus communis*), a Mediterranean plant.

Natts Lane – is another road that is probably named after someone who had connections with land in the area. The road links **Stane Street** to **Lower Station Road**. It was formerly the only access road to Billingshurst and Newbridge from the south east.

New Road – is just that – a new road. It was however new in the early 19th Century when a road that went eastwards close to **Summers Place** was moved further south to give the enlarged house and grounds greater privacy.

Newbridge Road and **Newbridge Road East** and **West** – The original road is divided in two by the bypass with part re-routed to the north. The road leads to New Bridge which as well as being a bridge over the River Arun was also a farm and a small wood, now grubbed out. The wood was first recorded as La Nieubrugge in 1317. Until 1933 much of this part of the parish was in that of Pulborough.

Newstead Hall – is a development of 7 properties on the site of the former Newstead Hall Hotel at Adversane. These were built in 2001-02 by Fastnet Builders Ltd. Old maps show this to be on the site of Jupp's Farm which later became a large house known as Juppsland. This became Juppsland Farm Guest House and by 1968 as Adversane Guest House and Social Club. It seems to have been by the early 1970s that Juppsland became Newstead Hall Hotel and probably named by the then proprietors.

Nightingale Walk – was built by Gleeson Homes in 1978-80 comprising some bungalows and detached houses. The name after the Nightingale (*Luscinia megarhynchos*) was probably a suggestion by the developer. The site was once a playing field for the Junior School with two small horse paddocks between **Silver**

Lane and the track to Little Daux Farm and behind St Gabriel's Roman Catholic Church.

Norman Close – was a development of 59 properties built in the mid 1990s and has mostly Shared Ownership homes. The name takes its name from the Normans who ruled England from 1066 until the end of the 12th Century.

Oaklands – comprises a small private cul-de-sac off Station Road close to the Weald School. The road was built in the late 1950s and comprises 5 detached homes. The name probably refers to nearby Oak trees but the site formed part of the garden of Broomfield Lodge, now known as Knights. See Knights Acre.

Oak Road – was completed by a2dominion new homes/Fabrica in 2016 and marketed as Marringdean Acres. Accessed from **Honeysuckle Drive**, this road has similar houses to others on the development. The road takes its name from the Common or Pedunculate Oak (*Quercus robur*), the predominate species in this area and known as the "Sussex Weed". Oaks can be found all around the development.

Okehurst Lane – runs from the A29 to join Rowner Road and Okehurst Road. Okehurst is an ancient manor in the west of the parish and was first recorded in 1279 when Robert de Okehurst owned land here.

Okehurst Road – See Okehurst Lane above. Okehurst Road runs northward from the junction of **Rowner Road** and **Okehurst Lane**. It continues over the parish boundary into Rudgwick. The name has the same derivation as **Okehurst Lane**.

Old Forge Mews – is a development of 4 houses built about 2002-3 on the site of earlier properties in Five Oaks. The name suggests a Blacksmith's Forge here, but the OS 6" map of 1898 does not indicate the existence of a smithy, though it was marked on the 1909 edition. Luke Wadey, a prosperous Victorian builder was a wheelwright and his son Frank was a blacksmith. About 1810 Richard Voice built a wheelwright shop. Country life depended on well-shod horses and cartwheels.

Osmund Court, Rowan Drive – stands close to the junction of **Rowan Drive** and Coombe Hill. This is a large and attractively designed block built by Saxon Weald, providing 40 apartments – 10 of which are sold on an older persons shared ownership basis – they buy 75% and don't pay rent on the 25% which is retained by Saxon Weald. The need for apartments for the elderly was identified by HDC when the bypass was planned and built and this was the first extra care scheme to be built by Saxon Weald and received £1.7m of grant funding from the Department of Health. The name comes from Osmund, a Sussex Saxon King (c.760 – c.772). It was chosen by the then residents of **Townland** for this new scheme and approved by HDC and was completed in 2006.

Ostlers View – An ostler is employed to look after horses for people staying at an inn. The name is a continuing reference to the blacksmith's forge that stood on the corner of the **High Street** and **West Street**. Also, this cul-de-sac off **Forge Way** overlooked the farm buildings of **The Cedars**. This road was developed in 1982 by Hilbery Chaplin, a company based in Essex.

Owl Close - was completed by a2dominion new homes/Fabrica in 2016. Accessed from **Honeysuckle Drive**, this road has similar houses to others on the development. It takes its name from the bird of prey of which the most common locally are the Tawny Owl (*Strix aluco*) and the Barn Owl (*Tyto alba*).

Pegasus Court – is a block of Retirement Apartments at the junction of **High Street** and **Roman Way**. They were built by Pegasus Retirement Homes PLC in 2002, named after the developer and in turn named after the mythical winged horse. Pegasus Court was officially opened by the Rt Hon Francis Maude MP for Horsham on Friday 21st May 2004.

Petworth Court, Brookers Road – is named after the West Sussex town of Petworth the name of which means Peota's enclosure and first recorded in 1086 as Peteorde. This block of flats was built by Bellway Homes in 2002-03 on the site of factories and includes **Amberley, Arundel, Maplehurst**, and **Sussex Courts** of similar flats.

Pine Close – is a small cul-de-sac off **Rowan Drive** that was built in about 1965-66. It is named after the Pine tree (*Pinus spp*).

Platts Meadow – lies off **Newbridge Road East** and was a development of 30 affordable houses and flats by Quintonglen Ltd built in 1998-99. The name is of uncertain origin.

Pond Close – was also built as affordable housing in 1998-99 by Quintonglen Ltd with 20 houses at the end of **Platts Meadow**. As with the latter road, this was built as part of the package that went with the construction of the bypass and there were once ponds in the field that was developed for housing.

Possessionhouse Lane – is mostly in Itchingfield, including the farm of that name. The 17th Century farmhouse was badly damaged by fire in April 2016. It now forms part of **West Chiltington Lane** that runs from Coneyhurst to Toat and Bashurst Hill in Itchingfield Parish. It is likely that this was a drove road. Possessionhouse Farm was part of the Muntham Estate and was known once as Withers, Waves and Clouthers. After 1707 it was sold away from the estate and on recovery of "possession", it received its present unusual name.

Renton Close – is a cul-de-sac built in the period 1974-76 by Sunley Homes and lies as a spur off **Wicks Road**. The Renton Family lived at Rowfold Grange and played a prominent role in local affairs including a close association with the Horticultural Society. Major-General J M L Renton was chair of the Governors of the Weald School.

Roman Way – was built in the mid 1990s and contains many Shared Ownership properties. The name commemorates the Romans who built Stane Street. Recent excavations have revealed Romano-British farmsteads and settlements that predate the later Saxon village.

Rosehill – This cul-de-sac off East Street was named after a house with this name that stood here and once occupied by the village doctor. The road was developed in three stages with the first being houses built in 1970-72 by Sunley Homes in a neo-Georgian style. This was followed in 1987-88 by further homes at the bottom of the hill and the construction of **Arun Court** by Vinall in 1988-89.

Rosier Way – is a cul-de-sac off **Daux Avenue** and comprises bungalows that were built in the mid to late 1950s and back onto Rosier Wood behind. The name originally applied to the wood and a farm, now largely industrial on the other side of the railway. Rosier was first recorded as a name in 1379 as Roseresland, as Rosereslond in 1385 and Rosyers in 1535. It is thought that the first part of the name is probably the name of an early owner of the land.

Rowan Court, Rowan Drive – was built about 1973 as a 3 storey block of 14 1 bedroom flats with garages. It takes its name from that of **Rowan Drive** in which it stands at its junction with **Coombe Hill**.

Rowan Drive – was built about 1968 and runs parallel with **Coombe Hill** and is a mix of semi-detached and terraced houses. The name is taken from the Rowan or Mountain Ash (*Sorbus spp*).

Rowner Road – was in Pulborough Parish until the boundary changes of 1933. Rowner was first recorded in 1261 as Ruwenore and means "at the rough bank" and the River **Arun** is close by.

Saddlers Close – is off Forge Way and is named after the trade – the making and supply of usually leather riding saddles and associated equipment and tack. There are 59 houses privately built by Barratt Homes under a marketing name of Saddlers and some Social housing for Saxon Weald constructed in 2008-2009 in a mix of styles but mainly in a neo-Victorian. The construction of these homes was very controversial at the time as the site was a well-used playing field. However, as a compromise, part of the site was left as a children's play area and some open space.

St Gabriel's Road – is named after the Roman Catholic Church and its patron saint that stands nearby in East Street which was built in 1962 to the plans of Henry Bingham Towner of Uckfield. This road leads off Silver Lane and was built by Gleeson Homes in 1978-80 in their distinctive style.

St Mary's Close – off the **High Street** was built in 1988 and comprises a terrace of houses that adjoin the churchyard and front Ten Steps, built in a local vernacular style. The road is named after nearby St Mary's Parish Church. The site was occupied by two cottages which were demolished and generated opposition due to the effects on the health of beech trees in the churchyard which did indeed have to be felled over time.

Saville Court and Saville Gardens – take their name from a Victorian house known as Saville House and a malthouse owned by James King. This was burnt down in 1883 and replaced with a new one with a house attached. The conical roof of the malthouse was finished off with an octagonal louvered cupola. The house was demolished and replaced in 1972 with flats and houses. The flats are of three storeys and include a penthouse flat over an archway leading into Saville Gardens itself. The development includes a terrace of six houses in Station Road that are attached to the flats and have a distinctive mono-pitch roof. Originally 12 houses were built around a central open plan garden with the rest behind, but later a wooden bungalow was demolished in Brookers Road about 1978 to allow for the construction of three more houses that have access from both roads. I lived from July 1974 until July 1978 at Number 1 and the grounds at the front seem to have been owned by a Mr Burgess who may have been the developer and seems to have been regarded with some trepidation!

Saxon Close – lies off **Roman Way** and has a mix of homes of similar design to those in **Roman Way** built in 1989-90 and later homes at the northern end, completed by Lovell Partnerships (Southern) in 1995-96. The name refers to the Saxons who first established our village.

School Lane - is an unofficially named lane that once led to the original village schools built in 1865 and 1914. These have both been converted into dwellings and no 4 School Lane was built in 1984 and numbers 5 and 6 were built by Paris Construction in 1992-93 after the schools closed and consolidated on their present site in **Station Road**.

Silver Lane – When I came to live here in 1974 this was the premier road in which to live! Then it was the thing to have your double garage door up and show off your new chest freezer to the rest of the world – as an 8 year old I frequently heard comments like this!! Silver Lane was built in two stages – the first section in about 1958 - 1960 ends at the top of the hill, from the **Station Road** end, with a concrete surface. The remaining section to **East Street** was completed in about 1963 - 1964. All the houses are quite individual and many have been greatly extended over the years. The road is lined with Silver Birch (*Betula pendula*) trees.

Skylarks – is a road on the Penfold Grange Development, built under their Phase 5 in 2002-2003 by Bryant Homes/Taylor Woodrow. The houses are similar to others on the development. The name almost certainly comes from the fact that these birds could once be seen and heard in this vicinity. Skylarks (*Alauda* *arvensis*) like open country and the fields were very open with relatively few trees.

South House Farm Lane – is an unofficial name for the metalled road that ends at South House Farm. The lane is a turning off **Marringdean Road**. The farm lies in the south of the parish, so the name is appropriate. The lane ended at the farm itself and a nursery once owned by the Baines family who were breeders of Sweet Peas. During the late 1960s, South House Farm house was used as a Country Club and there are contemporary reports of much noise and slightly rowdy behaviour. It is a very quiet location today!

South Street – A name that has largely gone out of use. South Street ran from the junction with **East Street** to that of **West Street**, the street leading south from the centre of the village. Nowadays this stretch of road is part of the **High Street** and is so numbered.

Stane Street – This is the old Roman Road from London to Chichester and much of it is now the present A29. The earliest reference to this is in 1270 when a Ralph de la or ate Stanstret is recorded. In 1293 a charter relating to Horsham mentions a Richard ate Stanstrete who was connected to Slinfold and Billingshurst.

Station Road – runs from the top of **Alicks Hill** to the railway station. The road was built to link the station, opened in 1859, with the rest of the village. It was recorded at the time that the road ended in a ploughed field after the station was reached when first built!

Station View – was built by Thakeham Homes in **Daux Road** opposite the station and completed in 2012. There is a date stone set into the wall of one of the houses recording this. Named from the fact that it faces the railway station, it was built on the site of the original factory of Thomas Keating. The homes are remarkably convenient for commuting, are environmentally friendly and consist of 14 homes in a cottage style set in a mews type development.

Stemp Drive – is probably named after a local family as Stemp is a familiar local surname. This short cul-de-sac off **Belinus Drive** was built by Sunley Homes in 1974-76.

Summers Place – is so named from a Richard Somere first recorded in 1369. It was known as Somers in 1876. The present house was built in 1880 for Robert Goff by the architect John Norton. In 1945 it became a convent school – The Convent of the Immaculate Heart of Mary, founded originally in Newhaven. The convent school closed about 1985 and the house was bought by Sothebys, the auctioneers. In 2006 permission was granted for the house to be converted into 11 apartments with 21 courtyard dwellings. The work was carried out by Berkeley Homes. Sothebys continued to use the walled garden for Garden Statuary sales.

Sussex Court, Brookers Road – is named after the county of Sussex – the land of the South Saxons – *Sudseaxe* – Sussex. This block of flats was built by Bellway Homes in 2002-03 on the site of factories which include **Amberley, Arundel, Maplehust, and Petworth Courts** of similar flats.

Ten Steps – is part of a path leading to the Parish Church of St Mary from the High Street. There are according to my count 14 steps, but it has always been known locally as Ten Steps.

The Alders – is likely named after the Common Alder (*Alnus glutinosa*) tree which is common near water and on edges of woodland. The 27 houses here were built between 2011 and 2013 by Taylor Wimpey with some Social houses by Saxon Weald.

The Brambles – is named after the Blackberry or Bramble, common in hedgerows and waste places and of which there are many sub-species. This road was completed in 2015 by a2dominion new homes/Fabrica and is reached off Honeysuckle Drive.

The Causeway – This picturesque path lined with old cottages, one of which is a Medieval Wealden Hall House leads up to St Mary's Church. A causeway is usually a raised path or roadway and is likely to be so named as it is elevated above the **High Street** below.

The Cedars – is a development of 3 detached houses behind the old Grade II listed Cedars Farmhouse. These houses were built by Crownhall Estates in 1996. The name is a fairly modern one, as the original farm was known as Bondwick. It then became Clark's Land after Laurence Clark who married a Bondwick and was renamed The Cedars at the beginning of the 20th Century as the name first appears on the Ordnance Survey 6" map in 1909.

The Maltings – Part of the site was occupied by the malthouse attached to Gingers House that stood where the shops of **Jengers Mead** front the **High Street**. This development is on the corner of these two roads. Most of the site became a garage – Malaya Garage that sold Scimitar cars. The Maltings comprise 17 apartments and a shop and were built in a distinctive style by Barratt in 1999-2000 under a marketing name of Amberley Court. The name recalls the presence of the nearby malt-house.

The Wadeys – is a short cul-de-sac off **Belinus Drive**. It is likely named after the Wadey family who in 1884 founded a firm of builders based at Parbrook. The business founded by Ephraim Wadey still thrives today from a new yard at **Andrews Hill**. This road was built by Sunley Homes in 1974-76.

The Willows – is a short cul-de-sac off **Berrall Way** and named after the species of tree – Willow (*Salix spp*). This road was built as part of the Penfold Grange development in 2001-02 by Taywood Homes in their local vernacular style.

Townland – took its name from a house and outbuildings that stood roughly where **Coombe Hill** joins the **High Street**. The house was demolished in the early 1960s and replaced by a block of two storey flats for the elderly in semi open grounds. This was demolished towards the close of 2007 by Saxon Weald. The subsequent development was completed in May 2012 and is treated under **Griffin Close**. Many of the residents of Townland went to live at **Osmund Court**, also built by Saxon Weald.

Treetops – a cul-de-sac off **Easton Crescent** comprising 16 homes was built in 2011 by Hillreed Homes (Sussex) Ltd in 2011. The name likely comes from the fact that there are tall trees in the immediate vicinity and the road backs onto a house called Trees in East Street owned by the Wadey family.

Turner Avenue – is named after a prominent Unitarian family who lived in the parish for many years. It was William Turner who founded the Unitarian Chapel in the **High Street** in 1754 and many of the family are buried in the extensive chapel yard. This road is part of the Penfold Grange development and was built by Taywood Homes in 2001-02.

Valewood Close – lies just inside the parish and is a short spur off **Valewood Lane** to which the name shares its origin. The 4 houses here were built in 1968-69.

Valewood Lane – This lane is mostly in Itchingfield Parish, with a very small part inside Billingshurst. It leads from **West Chiltington Lane** to Barns Green. The route at the Barns Green end was straightened due to the building of the railway in 1859 where it runs parallel to the line. There is a mention in 1616 of Farlewoods Lane which is thought to have been the present Valewood Lane. Vale Wood is still a large area of woodland just inside Itchingfield Parish.

Weald Court – Weald Court is a three storey block of flats on the corner of **Brooker's Road** and **Station Road** that was built about 1973. The Weald is the geographical area between the North and South Downs and was first recorded in 893 as "se micla wudu" – the great wood. The name has sometimes been interpreted as "wild". Weald Court occupies the site of the former "Whirlwind" Carpet Sweeper Factory.

West Street – Quite simply the road leading west and is now part of the busy A272.

West Chiltington Lane – An old drove road, this lane lies in part in Billingshurst Parish. It runs from Bashurst Hill in Itchingfield and leads southwards to West Chiltington – literally the lane to that place via Coneyhurst and Broadford Bridge and over Woods Hill.

Wicks Road – forms part of the development off **Belinus Drive** built in 1974-76 by Sunley Homes. The road was likely named after the local family of Wicks who contributed to the local Horticultural Society for many years.

Willow Drive – is a very short section of road off Silver Lane leading into **Broomfield Drive**. Continuing the tree theme of many roads the majority of trees in the road are Silver Birches and Oaks! The distinctive houses here were built by Sunley Homes in 1970-71.

Windmill Place – was built in 2012-14 by Devine Homes PLC and consists of 14 2, 3, 4, and 5 bedroom homes built in a traditional style in a short cul-de-sac. The name comes from the presence of the nearby windmill – Hammonds Mill. Only the base of the mill, a smock mill that probably looked something like that of Shipley or West Chiltington survives and at the time of writing is being excavated and interpreted by Archaeologists.

Wood Croft – This cul-de-sac was begun by Rydon Homes in February 2016. It will have 46 2, 3, 4 and 5 bedroom homes and marketed as Woodland Place. It lies just off **Marringdean Road** behind Daux Wood. Although semi wooded, it has been farmland since 1841 when it was two fields called Daux's Wood Field and The Furze Field. During World War II the area was part of an Italian POW Camp which later was used as a riding stables. A croft in this sense is a small enclosed field often near a house and was probably suggested by the developer.

Wooddale Lane – Wooddale is a Victorian house a little over halfway along the lane that links the A272 with **New Road**. In 1841 the hill at the A272 or south end of the lane was known as Cats Hill and is sometimes still referred to as this. However, in 1841 the lane ended at a farm known as Dirty Dale Farm. I think that it is likely that when the later Victorian house was built on the east side of the now extended lane, the farm and house were re-named Wooddale as it sounded nicer to Victorian ears! By 1876 the farm had become Wooddale Farm – wooded valley.

Woodland Close – is one of the lesser known roads in the parish. It lies next to **Ingfield Manor School** at the end of Ingfield Manor Drive and was built to house staff at the school in 1961. As there is plenty of woodland around about it was an appropriate name to give this short cul-de-sac.

Woodlands Way – is a cul-de-sac of bungalows built in the 1950s off Daux Avenue. The name refers to Daux and Rosier Woods which are beyond the end of the road.

Appendix 2 The end of the Georgian years

The water mill wheel at Rowner Mill, William Carter, Miller

Pigot's Directory for 1832-4 states that 'Billingshurst's not remarkably productive. There are no manufactures unless that of tanning may be said under this head, of which there is one establishment'. The list of shopkeepers is shorter than 1839 but mentions Foice Champion, tea dealer, Richard Chennell, baker, Ann Miles, grocer, Phillip Puttock seedsman and grocer and James Turner, poulterer. The influence of the canal probably reflects the subsequent increase of trade. Most of the names quoted are still in office in 1839, but Cutfield & Co, Wharfingers are at Newbridge Wharf, Wm. Carter was a miller at Rowner water mill and Elijah Ford is also a miller. Maltsters are Maurice Farhall and William Towse. Stephen Evershed is called a farrier rather than a vetinary surgeon. Thomas Higgins is a currier [leather dresser] and Thomas Holman a tanner, Richard Mitchell is a carpenter, Luke Wadey a wheelwright and Henry Trower a gun and whitesmith [metal worker]. George Wells was then at the Kings Head, but he soon left for the Three Crowns at Wisborough Green. J.G.Read was the schoolmaster.

Clay, wood, leather, barley, wheat and iron are the basic raw materials of those making things in Billingshurst at the climax of the industrial revolution and who did not work on the land. These were the raw materials of self-sufficiency.

The railway had not yet arrived at the beginning of Queen Victoria's reign. When it came in 1859, it would open up great possibilities, as symbolised by all that was on show at the great Exhibition at Kensington in 1851. The introduction of parcel post in 1882 is often overlooked, but it facilitated national advertising of all the desirable new things being invented and marketed, all available by mail order from home and abroad. Victorian homes were notoriously cluttered with pictures and ornaments gathered from far afield.

Appendix 3
The early years of Queen Victoria

The Blacksmiths Arms, Adversane, today

Pigot's Directory of 1839 offered some interesting information. The fortnightly corn exchange meeting 'cannot properly be called a market'. Letters from London arrived by mail cart from Horsham every morning at five and were despatched every evening at ten. (The penny post began the following year). Rev Beath was the incumbent and there were 1,540 inhabitants.

John Napper of Maltham House was the Magistrate and George Wood of Summers was among the Gentry. William Boarer and Mary Voice ran day schools and Mary Medhurst also took in boarders, Peter Evershed was the surgeon and Henry Turner the Surveyor and Registrar of births and deaths. Matthew Caffin was land and timber surveyor and appraiser.

Fred Peskett ran The Blacksmiths' Arms, George Puttock the King's Arms and James Aylward the Kings Head.

[The close proximity of the two 'Kings 'pubs gave rise to the favourite jest of the 1660s. Charles Hindley in **Tavern Anecdotes** tells about a courtier of Charles II who asked a friend about a decent hostelry and was told, "You will find the King's Arms are always full while the King's Head is empty". The allusion is to Mistress Nell Gwyn.]

Shopkeepers and traders included John Allman, nursery and seedsman, David Baker, watchmaker, Wm. Brown, boot and shoemaker, two Carters at Adversane, blacksmith and grocer at Sayers and Edward Harwood, bootmaker, two Holdens, blacksmiths, Stephen Evershed, Vet., two Kensetts, butcher and grocer, draper and County Fire Office Agent, two Knights, grocer and maltster, three Lakers, tailors and hairdressers, currier and leather seller, Thomas Linfield, butcher, George Puttock, basket, sieve and hoop maker, Phillip Puttock, grocer, miller and nurseryman, James Puttock, fellmonger [dealer in skins] and glover, Thomas Puttock, grocer and draper, Wm Razell, saddler and shoemaker, Edward Robinson, butcher and grocer, Siward, Child and Henley, coal and lime merchants and barge owners, New Bridge Wharf, William Sprinks, miller, John Turner, lime burner and barge owner, New Bridge Wharf, two Voices, plumber and carpenter and boot and shoe maker and George Weller, boot maker.

The Comet coach from Bognor called at the King's Arms at a quarter to twelve every weekday to London via Dorking and Leatherhead. The return coach called at one, going via Pulborough and Arundel. The carrier, Levi Wade's **Waggon,** left for London every Monday. William King carried freight to Brighton and Guildford.

The picture here is of traders who made goods and provided services, rather than retailing items imported from further afield. The exceptions were groceries and clothing, doubtless brought in by the carriers. Georgian Billingshurst is largely self-sufficient.

An old photograph of the King's Head

Appendix 4
Mid-Victorian Billingshurst

Mill stone from the East mill used as a garden paving-stone at Hammonds

Melville's Directory of 1858 shows significant expansion, though little increase in population since 1839. Amongst the 'gentry' were Henry Carnsew at Gratwick House, Richard Denyer at Summers, John Ireland, Alfred Lloyd at Rowfold, Miss Ann Drinkwater, Thomas and Henry Baker, Charles Wonmer Ward and Joseph Kesterton at Great house. Rev Hugh Thomas was now Vicar, with a curate, Rev Cornwall. Rev. Leader was the 'Independent' clergyman.

Several names from twenty years earlier are still going strong. There are changes of landlord at the inns. Robert Bisshop was at the King's Arms Commercial Inn, licensed to let horses, Alfred Laker at the King's Head, and William Wood was a beer retailer at the Rising Sun, long since demolished. [This pub was opposite the Old Village Hall]. Edward Burchall was a retailer of beer as well as a grocer. Richard Mitchell combined building with brewing. Thomas Elliott was maltster and corn vendor. Strong drink mattered in Billingshurst! The brewing business required a resident Excise Officer to assess the tax; one was Peter Phillips and an earlier one, William Coulson.

David Baker, the watchmaker, had branched into building with his son, also David as plasterer and bricklayer. Henry King followed his father as carrier and Maurice Harwood too as bootmaker. Boots and leather goods also mattered. John Barnes, Albert Powell, William Streeter and William Voice were in the boot and shoe trade, and Caroline Puttock made gloves and gaiters. Jesse Laker was a currier. Another glover and dealer in wool was James Woods. Henry Laker made saddles, harness, rope and whips. The Puttocks were major players. John was a smith at the Blacksmiths Arms, Deborah a grocer and baker, Phillip a nursery and seedsman and Thomas a timber merchant. The Trower family too were significant traders. Mrs. Trower was a dressmaker, James a draper and grocer and William was a carrier to Horsham and Guildford. Other grocers were John Chart, also a draper and Insurance Agent, William Phillips, also a confectioner and baker and Peter Towse at the Five Oaks Inn. Peter Laker and James Turner were tailors. Others in the building trade were two William Wadeys, two Luke Wadeys, one a wheelwright and another James Turner. Other bakers and confectioners were Frederick Peskett and William Phillips. The butchers were Edward Robinson and William Grinsted. John Etherton and George Jupp were blacksmiths as well as John Puttock. [Deborah Evershed in her book about Adversane gives a warm account of a family Christmas party in 1856 at the home of George Puttock, wealthy timber merchant, in Billingshurst.]

William Boorer kept the academy and Miss Potter the seminary for young ladies. Evershed and son were surgeons, Stephen Evershed the Vetinary Surgeon.

Melville gives a useful list of mid Victorian farmers of the 5903 acres of productive land in Billingshurst as listed below:-

Thomas Barnes	Lordings
Thomas Botting	Oakhurst
William Bridger	Wood Dale
John Dean	Fewhurst
Thomas Evershed	Dunkins
James Evershed	Ridge
William Evershed	Tedfold
James Greenfield	Adversane, also mealman
William Gumbrill	
Thomas Ireland	
Walter Laker	Minses Wood
J. Meetens	Kingsfold
Hezekiah Miles	Soil Farm, Adversane
Charles Miles	Slinfold land
Henry Miram	Pratts
Charles Shepherd	Little Wood house
William Sprinks	also miller at Hammonds
Richard Towse	Hadfold, Adversane (married Sarah Miles 1807)
William Turner	Slatter
John Turner	Rosa

Billingshurst's Heritage

South Street before the building of the Women's Hall

Appendix 5
Kelly's Post Office Directory 1867

'Billingshurst is part of the Petworth Union and the County Court District of Horsham, 6 and a half miles SW of it, 41 from London by road and 45 by rail – Mid-Sussex Railway. The Church is now (1866) undergoing a thorough restoration and the old galleries and pews have been cleared away to make way for the more suitable open seats designed to suit the style of the church; a new chancel aisle has been added, the plaster ceilings have been cleared away and the old open timber roofs restored and exposed to view, and the stonework and walls throughout cleaned of their whitewash; new east windows of stained glass have been put in the chancel and chapel, one of which is to be a memorial one; both have been given by H. Carnsew Esq. of Somers, to whose liberality the restoration of the church is mainly due. The work has been carried out by local builders, viz., Messrs. Luke Wadey and Sons and the stonework, ornamental etc., by Mr. Owen Voice, from the drawings of Robert W. Edis, Esq., MRIBA, architect, of London. The church will seat about 520. The Register dates from 1630. The living is a Vicarage, tithes commuted to £200 yearly, with 13 acres of Glebe and a neat residence, in the gift of Sir Charles Goring, Bart. and held by the Rev William Howie Bull, MA of St. John's College, Cambridge. There is a National School for boys and girls, supported by voluntary contributions, and a handsome new school room has lately been created. It is a simple Gothic building capable of accommodating 150 children with playgrounds and master's residence attached. The building, which is of red brick with stone dressings, has been built at the sole cost of Mr. Carnsew who also gave the site from the designs and under the superintendence of R.W.Edis Esq.'

A considerable business is carried on in the manufacture of wood hoops.... the corn market is held at the King's Arms every other Tuesday evening. The Station Inn adjoins the Station. William Bigwood, Station Master. Somers, the delightful residence of Henry Carnsew Esq., is an extensive mansion in the Domestic Gothic style, with mullioned windows. Area of the parish, 675 acres; the population in 1861 was 1,495.

Parish Clerk: Thomas Baker and Sen. Relieving Officer, Postmaster: Peter Laker: Receiver of Post at Five Oaks: Peter Towse: National School: Henry Wright, master: Academy: William Boorer: Sarah Potter: Ladies' Boarding School: Rev. Joseph Harris: Independent Church.: Stephen Niblett MD physician at Brick House

Carriers: Charman from Pulborough every Saturday, Coombes from Wisborough

Green and Kirdford, Mondays and Thursdays

Gentry and notable persons.

William Axworthy, Thomas Baker, Rev. Henry Beath, Andrews Hill; William Berrall Esq. Duncans; Richard Bescoby, Gratwick House; Rev. Bull, Vicarage; Henry Carnsew Esq. Somers; Cornelius Carter, Adversane; Peter Evershed Esq., Capt. Finch, John Ireland at High Seat; Thomas Puttock, Carlton House; Edward Robinson, Mrs. Rogers, Mr. William Smart, Stallkart Esq.; Capt Anthony Triscott of Manor House.

Farmers
Benjamin Boniface – Hook Farm
Francis Botting – Oakhurst Farm
William Botting – miller and farmer, Rowner's Mill
Henry Burchell
Thomas Chesman – Graningfold
John Dean – Fewhurst
Richard Denyer – farmer and landowner, Goldings at Five Oaks
? Dubbins – Combe land
George Duke – Duncans Farm
James Evershed – Ridge's Farm
John Dendy Evershed – Cobbed's Hall
Robert and James Evershed – props of steam threshing machines at Jeffries Farm
Thomas Evershed – Slatter
William Evershed – farmer and landowner, Tedfold
John Naldrett Farhall, jun. – Clark's land
Richard Greenfield – Lower Wood House
William Grinsted – Hadfold Farm
William Gumbrill – Parbrook
George Ireland – farmer and landowner, Highfure Farm
Walter Laker – Mintrell's Wood
Alfred Lloyd – farmer and landowner, Rowfold
Charles Peacock – Adversane
John Petter – Woodsdale
? Shilcock – Kingsfold
William Sprinks – miller and farmer, Hammonds
James Strudwick – Andrew's Hill
Elizabeth Turner (Mrs.) farmer and landowner, Rosa Farm

Commercial and Services

David Baker, watchmaker and builder
James Batchelor, farm bailiff to J.Farhall
George Botting, draper and grocer –Insurance Agent, Liverpool&London&Globe
Joseph Brown, shoemaker and glover
Edwd. Burchall, shopkeeper and beer retailer
William Durrant, builder and shopkeeper
John Etherton, blacksmith
Maurice Evershed, corn and seed merchant
Mrs. Sarah Evershed, Vetinary Surgeon
William Grinsted, butcher
George Hammond, plumber and painter
Maurice Harwood, shoemaker
Huggett and Son, grocer and draper, Insurance agent, Atlas Fire and Life
George Johns, King's Arms, licensed to let horses and butcher
George Jupp, blacksmith, Five Oaks
James King, maltster, living in Betchworth, Surrey
Alfred Laker, King's Head
Henry Laker, saddler and harness maker
Jesse Laker, currier
Peter Laker, tailor and postmaster
Frederick Peskett, shopkeeper
Charles Petar, brick and tile manufacturer
Mrs. Elizabeth Powell, shoe maker
Charles Puttock, Blacksmiths Arms and smith
Philip Puttock, nursery and seedsman
Mrs. Deborah Puttock, grocer and draper, Adversane
Thomas Puttock, timber, bark and wood hoop merchant, hoop manufacturer
Mrs. W. Redman, shopkeeper
Spencer Reed, baker and shopkeeper
Albert Sprinks, Station Inn, licensed to let horses and coal merchant
John Sprinks, wharfinger and collector
Peter Towse, Five Oaks Inn, grocer and Post Office
James Turner, tailor
Edward Voice, plumber, painter and stonemason
William Voice, shoe maker
Luke Wadey and Sons, builders, Five Oaks
Joseph Wadey, bookseller, stationer and shopkeeper
Walter Wadey, blacksmith

Billingshurst's Heritage

William Wadey, wheelwright
William Wood, beer retailer

Appendix 6
Late Victorian Billingshurst

Outside Dr. Hubert's surgery at Brick House, now the NatWest Bank

Kelly's Directory of 1880 illustrates changes of people and developments stimulated by the coming of the trains to the village. It lists the gentry as James Wilson living at Gratwicke House, Charles W. Schroeter at Tedfold, Maurice Ireland of Broomfield Lodge, Lord of the Manor of Bassett's Fee, The Duke of Norfolk K.G. of Pinkhurst. Henry Hurst, G.C.Gibson, Henry Puttock of Clevelands, Robert Goff of Summers Place, H.F.Locke-King, W.Berrall of Stanmore, F.A. Schroeter and James Wilson are the principle landowners.

Harvey Jupp collected the rates and taxes; Job Saunders Clark was the Postmaster, vintner and keeper of general stores, William Wood the Registrar and Relieving Officer, W. Simmons Station Master and Dr. W.H.Hubert Medical Officer and Public Vaccinator at Brick House. Arthur Dale was the Vet. Luxford and Harman were the carriers. Rev. H.L.Norden was the Vicar and the Rev. Lee was at the Congregational Church. Emma Chart had a day school and Miss Harriet Grinsted a school for young ladies. James Thornton was auctioneer and surveyor.

Forty individual householders are listed. These include Mrs Caffin at Station Road, four Eversheds and Edward Underwood at Hammonds House.

The 'Commercial' entries reveal how much more diverse the trade of the village had become towards the end of the 19th century. Grocers were numerous. Frank Arnold was at Churchgate, also a draper, John Blake at Five Oaks, Edwin Cork, also an outfitter, at Adversane, Job Clark, Frank Price, also a baker, Edward Standing at Newbridge, W.T. Voice, together with horses and traps in Station Road and Mr. Luxford. Clem Etheridge kept a shop and Thomas Gray was a general dealer.

There were other bakers: Elizabeth Green at Adversane and Joshua Rowland. Alfred Songhurst and Harry Foice were the butchers. There were three tailors, Edward Seller, Charles Reader and James Turner and Miss Eliza Allman was a dressmaker and William Cranham an upholsterer. Boot and shoemakers and dealers included Joseph Brown, William Hurst at Adversane, John Joyes at Andrews Hill, William Voice and Wagstaff and Son.

Other trade outlets included Miss Fanny Herrington, the stationer, John Mills the chemist and Edwin Gravett, the mealman. Walter Joyes had the corn, seed and coal and plumbing business at the Station. Services were provided by Alfred Mitchell, the carpenter, Edward Voice, the plumber, Harry Read, the chimney sweep, William Wadey wheelwright and smith, David Wadey builder and decorator and Walter Wadey, smith.

The building trade was active. Job Robinson was a general builder and contractor, Mrs Jane Wadey and sons were builders at Five Oaks. Ephraim Wadey, brickmaker and builder was at Parbrook. He owned the brickyard at Gilmans, south of Natt's Lane [in the Manor of Storrington!] from 1890 to 1913 when it was known as the Station Brickyard.

Other businesses were malting by George Constable, saddlery by Henry Laker and Son, leather goods by Walter Laker, timber and hoops by Henry Puttock and coopering by Joseph Hughes. Walter Weller sold coal from Station Road. William King dealt in poultry at Adversane.

Two people sold beer in off licences: Clem Matthews and Amelia Wood. At the pubs there were Mary Sprinks at the Station Inn, George Wooldridge at the Blacksmiths Arms, David Yarrow at the King's Head, James Towse at the Five Oaks Inn who also ran a shop and J. Butterworth Sisman at The King's Arms.

Farmers listed in 1890 include the following:

George Alvis	Lordings
George Bradford	South Eden
C.W. Schroeter	Jeffries
Mrs Joseph Cheesemere	Andrews Hill
John Evershed	Fewhurst
Henry Garton	Frenches
Owen Garton	Great Daux and Grooms
Robert Goff	Priors
Hugh Ireland	Manor House
George Ireland	High Fure
William Kennett	Hook Farm
Mrs Louisa Maas	Goldings Farm, Five Oaks

Mrs Charles Mills	Southlands, Adversane
Maurice Myram	Denhams
Mrs Elizabeth Sands	
Samuel Richardson	Five Oaks
William Steele	Palmers Farm
William Wells.	

Thomas Holland was steward to R. Goff and Thomas Burchell, bailiff to C.W. Schroeter.

Appendix 7

Early 20th century Billingshurst

1. R.Rhodes & Son in 1935, still going strong
2. R.Rhodes & Son in 2012, with Geoff Rhodes

The shops and businesses of Billingshurst are superbly illustrated in Wendy Lines' compilation of archive photographs in her book *'Billingshurst'* published in 1995. The following list is derived from that source, detailing people and premises from about 1900 to 1939. It serves as a useful record showing the continuity and the changes from Appendices 4 to 6. The information here is augmented from a booklet, 'Billingshurst and District' issued by Douglas Ross & Son, estate agents, auctioneers and valuers in the 1920s. Then as now the village shops were subject to frequent changes of use and of proprietor.

In 1925 F.A Skinner was the farmer at Cedars.

R. Rhodes & Sons (Cecil) Bootmakers, South Street.

The Parbook Nursery, Tea Gardens. Cakes, ices, fruit and flowers, wreaths, tomatoes and cucumbers cut to order.

At Oak Tree cottage on the A29 Miss Tucker sold sweets, lemonade etc. Open on Sundays.

Charles Tiller, Fruiterer and Confectioner was at The Rosary Tea House and Garden, Alick's Hill. Board residence offered and 'Printing of all descriptions'. He issued the *Billingshurst News Free Newspaper*.

R. Crisp Hairdresser, tobacconist, films developed. Wireless engineer, Agent for HMV gramophones and records. Accumulators charged for the wireless.

Cooter's Wood Oven Bakery off South Street. Cakes and pastries made on the premises, teas, tobacco and minerals. Jabez James Peay had the shop from 1911

The Crescent School, South Street.

Leonard V. Jarvis, The Pharmacy, High St. Agent for Kodak. Developing and printing.

E.&W. Cripps Family Butcher, High Street.

W.Ward, plumber, gas and hot water fitter, tinsmith, mowers repaired and ground. High St. Works.

W.H. Etheridge, haulage contractor, sweep, well sinker, sheep shearer and water diviner, East St.

King's Arms. Landlord John Butterworth Sisman (about 1910).

At the Six Bells Stephen Garmon was Landlord (1907)

Laker's Refreshment Rooms, High St., next door to old bank buildings.

Luxford's Shop was at the corner of East St, now a restaurant. At one time, a grocer, variously Balls, Butler and W.J.Barnes

The Post Office 1902 formerly where stood a low wall, fronting the High St. Job Saunders Clark was the Postmaster.

Mill Lane meadow is now the Library car park. A large barn once stood there.

Brick House. Dr W.H.Hubert's surgery, subsequently that of J.Croft, Vetinary Surgeon. Westminster Bank was built on the site of Brick House.

Rice Bros. High St. garage, 1926, then it became Southern Counties garage, now Sainsbury's Local supermarket. 'Any make of car supplied'.

Field's Ironmongers, Crisp's Hairdresser, Tribe the butcher. All operated in what was the old Carlton House. Field gave way to Pilcher's, then R.S. Higgins and now Austin's. Serial ironmongers, 'Mowers, Valor oil stoves, Aladdin lamps etc.'

Tribe the butcher's first premises, then A.T. Jones the watchmaker, next the 15th century restaurant [now Blue India]. Tribe advertised, 'Our bacon is smoked on our own stoves. Families waited on daily within four miles'.

King's Head Landlords were variously J.Stewart and J.Howard Field.

Gingers House (Mediaeval) was still standing in 1930.

Gingers and the Maltings Hotel

The Maltings Hotel and tea gardens was converted in late 1920s from the original malt house.

The Malaya Garage was on the malting site, now demolished, stood at the entrance to Jengers Mead. It had earlier been Delaney's garage.[Now Truffles cafe].

The Rising Sun public house was opposite the old village hall, now demolished.

Whitehall was the Laker's home and leather shop, beside Rope Walk. (beside the present Roman Way).'Henry Laker, harness makers, bulk filtered petrol, footwear and shotgun cartridges'.

Whitehall garage (Alfred Laker).The house was demolished, the garage expanded. Now housing for the elderly.

The Manor House (of Bassett's Fee). A timber-framed building under a brick facade.

Old Village Hall 1906. Used by the community for meetings, whist drives, 'socials', dances, etc. until 1991, now converted to flats.

Gravett's Shop confectionary and bakery, now Oak Cottage.

John Argent's Shop, 1920s, grocer, baker, horse and trap for hire.

Bernard Baker, Draper and Outfitter, Argent's old place refurbished. 'If it's BB its good', footwear, shirts, corsets etc. Now Lloyd's Bank.

Queuing for a clothing sale at Baker's in 1949

Les Lusted's Shop, grocer and baker, High Street.

Voice's Monumental Works (19th century) demolished and rebuilt as Crisp's third shop. Part of the main house next door, became a florists.

Ben Moss, Fishmonger.' Fish sent direct from the coast, one day fresher than that sent to market'.

Churchgate, once a grocers, then a guest house, proprietor W.Cassie. Now an apartment.

Churchgate, East Street

Gordon Lugg's steam engine business, East Street.

W.T.Voice's shop, Station Road. Grocer, boots and shoes and Fly Proprietor. Just west of the railway. He was known as 'Bumper' Voice and carried passengers from the station to villages by horse and carriage.

Richard George had a General Store just east of the railway in the 20s and 30s, now Tescos He also had a butcher's shop opposite before Mr. Reynolds started his shop.

Malthouse, Station Road. James King owned that and the High St. plant.

Whirlwind Factory, on the malthouse site, now Weald Court flats.

The Railway Hotel (now Inn), Michell's Fine Ales. It has a new brick facade.

F.W.Watts, seed and corn merchants. End of Station Road. Formerly owned by Walter

Joyes. It had silos and a mill building at the rear with its own siding for rail wagons. It finally closed in 1992.

1. F.W.Watts & Sons, Station Road

2. Hereford House

Hoop Sheds, near the Station. Henry Puttock, proprietor. Immediately behind Great Daux farmhouse. It also had rail access with an inspection pit.

Keating's Factory. Originally flea powder. Came from London to Daux Road in 1927. Now demolished.

Gas works built in 1907 off Natts Lane, demolished with advent of North Sea gas. In the 1950s people could buy coke for 7s-6d a bag.

Great Grooms at the corner of Natts Lane and Parbrook. Originally a farmhouse and barn, retitled Groomland Farm. Subsequently a restaurant and antiques business, but now residential again.

Hurstlands corner, opposite, had a single bungalow owned by Mrs. Strong. The fine stone boundary wall still stands beside the A29.

Fossbrooks was the home and original building premises of Ephraim Wadey.

Griggs, Old House, Southlands. Ancient hall houses at Adversane, older than The Blacksmiths Arms (1630) where Gaius Carley was the smith.

Old House was a restaurant and antique business. Now residential once again.

The Limeburners Inn at Newbridge. HQ of Billingshurst anglers fishing the Arun.

Newbridge warehouse, built 1839, now restored.

Rowner Lock, last used 1871. Restored 1982 by the Wey and Arun Canal Trust.

Rowner water mill. Demolished 1968.

Okehurst west of the village dated 1606.

Five Oaks Inn, built 1850, now demolished and used as a display area for a large Automobile firm, Harwood's of Pulborough.

Ingfield Manor built in 1909 by the Fielding family, owners of Okehurst. Since 1961 a school for children with cerebral palsy.

Five Oaks Farm. Morris family dairy farm. Robert Morris was first Chairman of The Parish Council, 1895.

Summers Place Convent School 1945 to 1984. Subsequently Sotheby's.

The Haven School in Slinfold Parish. Closed 1948 and demolished.

Charles E Wadey Builder, plumber and sanitary engineer. Office and works at Parbrook. The brickyard off Natts Lane was called Gillman's Brickyard. Burchell & Sons ran it from 1930 to 34, then Gillman's Brick Company from 1936.

The playing fields north of Natt's Lane were used by Billingshurst Football Club. They changed in dilapidated cattle sheds in the north east corner. It later became the recreation ground, housing the tennis club, the scout hut, a play school and the Horticultural Society's Flower show held in a marquee.

The Weald School site was open fields with a block of tumbledown corrugated iron farm sheds and a well, said to have been used as a slaughter house. It was demolished and taken to Itchingfield Refuse pit by the author and colleagues in the 1980s. The Junior School site was an open field, sometimes used for Bonfire Night. A line of superb elms lined the A29 on the east side. All were felled in 1974, ruined by Dutch Elm disease.

At the corner of the A272 and the A29 Mr. Coe had a second-hand shop, with Redman's coal yard behind it. There was also the wheelwright's shop and forge.

Duncan Reynolds has plotted the sequence of High Street shops as remembered in the 1950s. On the west side going north (towards Five Oaks) were 1.Mrs Whitehead's wool shop 2.International Stores 3. Chemist, Mr. Gillibrand 4 Higgins, Ironmongers 5 Mr. Cheal's butchers/fish shop 6 an alley way 7. Mr. Ward's sweet shop 8. A pair of cottages (Mrs.Lines).

Opposite on the east side going south were 1. Ware's the drapers 2. Alley 3. Bernard Baker's drapers 4. Lusted the bakers 5. Alley 6. Crisp's Wireless/barbers 7. Mr. Barnes dairy 8. Alley 9. Mr. Freeman's greengrocers 10 Mr. Trevelyan's shoe shop 11. William Voice's tobacconists 12. Mr. Myram's cafe 13. Westminster Bank

Appendix 8 Post WW II Billingshurst

Wally Wicks, Maj. Gen. Renton, Allan Dugdale of the Weald and John Sutton at the Horticultural Show, 1969

Many changes have occurred in the village shops and on the farms within the memory of people still in the land of the living. The following data derived from **Kelly's Directory (1962)** may serve as a reminder of days some fifty years ago. Where figures are given they refer to numbering in the High Street.

The magistrates on the Horsham Bench included General Renton of Rowfold, William Pemberton of the Manor House and Rudolph Fielding of Okehurst.

Rev. R. Evan Hopkins was Vicar and Rev. Gerard Candy the Catholic Priest, living at the Priest's Cottage in Lower Station Rd.

J.B. Sherlock of Renvyle, Oakhurst Rd. and R. Ayre of Bridgewater Farm were Rural District Councillors.

There were Post Offices with groceries at both Five Oaks kept by Mrs. Rogers and at Adversane by F. Sharville.

Victor Gee was Headmaster at the Weald Secondary Modern School and General Renton Chairman of Governors. On the Board of Governors was Mrs. Pamela Foster of Greatham, sometime secretary to the poet T.S. Eliot and direct descendant of William Wilberforce. She was later Chairman for many years.

The West Sussex County Library was housed at the Trinity Congregational Hall.

The Doctors were Bousfield, Hope-Gill and Tillyard at Churchgate. Miss Phyllis Bradley was a District Nurse and another, Nurse Baines lived in Chestnut Road. On the corner at The Lindens the Registrar of Births and Deaths attended one morning a week. J.Symmons was the dentist and A. Pasfield the Vetinary Surgeon.

A private school stood at the corner of Daux Avenue run by Mrs Murat.

Whitehead &Whitehead were the Estate Agents, amalgamated with D Ross & Son.

Garages included Hillview at 107, Malaya, Poplar, Rice Bros., Billingshurst Coaches (Williamsons Removals), Lawrensons Haulage at the Station, and Laker's petrol pumps. Fred Stenning sold bicycles and mopeds. A.G. Williams & sons were agricultural engineers at Frenches Corner and Gibbons in Daux Rd., R. Crisp 33/43 dealt in radios as did Radio Traders in Station Rd., L. Brown, electrical engineer, W.G. Keyte & sons, precision engineers in Daux Rd. and Keatings were manufacturing chemists. Mr. Lusted and Albert Collin ran taxis. There were no supermarkets but many grocers; International Stores 50, Co-op 41, R.& J. Ball 59, Fishers (with a PO) in Station Rd., Sidney Reynolds, Lower Station. Rd., Walker Stores 70 and E. Ross, mobile grocer. A.E.Hearne 71 and Mrs. Freeman 47 were greengrocers and there were High Seat Nurseries and J.H. Way's nursery at Little Platt, Marringdean Rd. too. L.K. Fisher 48, appropriately, was the fishmonger. The Misses Dance had a shop at 2 East St next door to Brick House as did Mrs. S. Jaegar at 89. Mrs. Whitehead was a draper at 58.

S.C.Reynold's shop, formerly a butchers, then a grocers, subsequently became a sub-post office and is currently an Asian take-away and a fish and chip shop. Next door were two other shops. Mrs. Lawrence was the draper, later a bookmakers. Shirley's cafe stood on the corner but was demolished when the Daux Road corner was widened. The cafe moved to where the Travelodge stands at Five Oaks. Opposite Reynold's was a newsagents run by Mr. And Mrs Fortune who kept Saluki dogs, then by the Shaws and next the Humphreys and finally Dillon's. It is now a Tesco Express.

S.C.Reynold's grocery shop in Lower Station Road

E.W.Cripps 82 and W.Tribe 50 were butchers. Mr. Cripps had his own abattoirs behind the shop. P. Reeves 85 was also a butcher.

R. Brown was the barber and ladies had a hairdressing choice of Palm Court in Station Road, Louise (Morris) 49 or Helene 126.

A. Cannon 42, L.&D. Morley 72 and A.J.Voice 53 were confectioners.

Alex Lochie 54 was the chemist and Sheila and S. Caton Ltd had a drug store in Lower Station Rd.

R.G Oulds of Daux Ave. was the photographer and there was a studio at 124. Watts by the Station sold corn and seeds and garden sundries. R.S. Higgins was the Ironmonger 31 and 52 with Higgins (Toys) at 55. T.Pearson 29 and J.Shaw of Lower Station Rd. were newsagents. R. Rhodes & Son 112 and C.Trevelyan 51 dealt in boots and shoes. Dairy products came from Express Dairies at the Station Yard [now Duplex Engineering] or Mrs. A. Voice at 45. Brush-Vac Services swept chimneys from Little East St. E. Carley did plumbing from Adversane and G. Carley was the last farrier left. Chas. Wadey & sons was the main builder at Parbrook. Gillman's Bricks Ltd. made them at Parbrook. Fred Voice offered building and plumbing services. William Mees was landlord at the Blacksmith's Arms, Peter Bowring at the Five Oaks Inn. H. Temple-Jones at the Six Bells offered hotel accommodation at 7 and a half guineas a week (£7.35p) and bed and breakfast for 15 shillings (75p).

Apart from the Pubs, refreshments could be taken at the Shirley Cafe (Woods) in Lower Station Rd. or Jane's Tea Garden at Five Oaks. The cafe site was later used for car sales and is now residential. There were neither take-away stores offering 'fast food' nor ethnic restaurants of any kind.

The main outfitter was Bernard Baker 37 and there was Patswear for Ladies (A. Maynard) in Lower Station Road and a dry cleaners was to be found in the High St.

Antiques were sold by B. Hawes-Wilson at Great Groomes and by M.M. Frame and Lola Baxter at Old House Restaurant, Adversane. Mrs. Thurlow-Smith 95 dealt in antique copper and brass.

A.C. Walker farmed at Stonepits, Marringdean Road. His widow, Aileen, did the pictures for the village signs and was made MBE for hers services to the village in 1998. Mr. Gordon Simkin designed the shields which stand beside the roads entering the village.

At the station there was a Station Master, two porters and the signal man who opened the crossing gates manually.

Gillmans Brickyard closed during WWII and was used as a rifle range. It was revived after the war but finally closed late in 1960. Bricks were handmade and stacked in clamps in open sheds next to Natts Lane. The sulphur fumes killed off most of the nearby trees.

Appendix 9
Kelly's Directory – 1973

The 1973 publication contains valuable records of the village some forty years ago. The following selected information has High Street numbers shown in brackets. Items in square brackets are from the 1969 edition.

Officials
Lord Lieutenant – Duke of Norfolk, Chairman of WSCC – Sir Peter Mursell MBE. DL.- Wisborough Green

Justices of the Peace
T.C.N. Flynn MC. Beke Place, Billingshurst
R.W. Godden, Hilland Farm, Stane Street, Billingshurst and 15 others
Registrar – Miss R.E. Ogilvie (Thursday afternoons) Lindens, L Station Rd.
Clergy – Rev R.Evan Hopkins,MA (St.Mary's), Rev Geo. A Nunn (Trinity), Rev. Gerald J. Candy (St. Gabriels)
[Horsham Rural District Councillors 1969: J.B.Sherlock of Renvyle, Okehurst Rd.,
H.J.Stafford of Grainingfold, Five Oaks and C.J.Wood, 2 Birch Drive.]The Local Govt Act of 1972 had abolished the Rural District Councils by 1974.

Doctors: L.C. Bousfield, Evelyn Kilsby, T.A.Tillyard, 10 East Street.

Dentist:
J. Symmons (114)

Vetinary Surgeon:
[Pasfield] Rhan & Luckhurst (96)

Library:
Trinity Congregational Hall, High St.

Post Office [A.W.Briden post master] (88)

Grocers:
R & J Ball (59), G. Edwards, L. Station Rd, [Fishers &PO L. Stat. Rd.,] E.Fiddler (41) [formerly G. Voice], International Tea Co's Stores (56), Mrs. P. Rogers & PO Five Oaks, Mrs. D.M.Rugg & PO Adversane,

Greengrocers:
R.A. Allen [formerly Mrs. Freeman] (47), A.E. Hearne (71), Orange Grove 3 Jengers Mead

Nurseries:
High Seat (1), J.H.Way, Little Platt, Marringdean

Butchers:
E.W. Cripps (82), S.A Wilson 12 Jengers Mead

Newsagents:
Humphries Stat. Rd., The Paper Shop (D. & M. Wakeling) (36/38)

Hairdressers and Barbers:
R. Brown (43), Burnelle (49), Helene (126), Yvette Hereford Hse. Stat. Rd.

Clothing and Outfitting:
Fabrics Galore, haberdashery, (32), Ninety-four fashions (94), Patswear A.E. Maynard L. Stat. Rd., Raggity Jane, children, (51), Mrs. M. Whitehead draper (58), [recently Family Fabrics 2 East St.]

Cafes, Restaurants:
Bistro Cafe (92), Jane's Tea Gardens Five Oaks, Shirley Cafe L. Stat Rd., Old Hse. Restaurant Adversane

Radio, TV, electrical services:
Aerial Fitters L. Stat Rd., B.L. Barnes, 13 Carpenters, L. Brown appliances (31), R. Crisp radio (43), R.G. Oulds photographs Coneyhurst.

Turf Accountants:
Partington Norman L Stat Rd., J. Pegley (116)

Garages, coaches, service stations:
Billingshurst Coaches (Williamson) (85), Everest Garages & White Hall Services (3), Hillview Garage, High St., H. Johnson car breakers Coneyhurst, Malaya Garage High St., Poplar Garage Five Oaks, Rice Bros. High St., Southern Counties Garage (82).Estate Agents:

Bridger & Sons (70) [formerly Keymarket, grocers], Churchman Burt & Sons (44/46), Johnston Pycraft (34), Whiteheads (35).

Builders:
E.W. Carley plumber Adversane, Daux Ltd. Rosier Gate, Raymond Voice Little East St., Charles Wadey & Sons Parbrook. [C..W. Norton Five Oaks]

Other Goods and Services:
Arun Travel (85), Card & Candy Box greetings cards (53), Convent School Summers Place, The Flower Box florists (45), Higgins ironmongers (52), Horsham Dry Cleaners High St., Horsham Travel 2 Jengers Mead, Raymond Jackson Lily Pools, 17 Daux Rd., Juppsland Country Club Adversane, H. Johnson car breaker Coneyhurst, T & D Kelland stationers (29), Alex Lockie chemist (54), Lyons Fish Bar 12 Jengers Mead, Marsh DIY 11 Jengers Mead, Reta Launderette 13 Jengers Mead, R. Rhodes & Son, boot repairers (112), St. Christopher's PNEU School Beechwood Hse. Daux Ave., Stanmore Guest Hse. (118/120), [There was also an hotel at Adversane], F.W.Watt & Sons seed merchants Stat. Rd., R.J. Witt confectioners (72)

Other listed businesses:
Askeys biscuit mfrs. Daux Rd., Beverley Chemical Engineering, Station Yard, C. Braby antiques Groomsland Farm, Braemar Construction civil engrs. Daux Rd., J.A. Burroughs plant hire & haulage Daux Rd., Frame & Baxter antiques Old Hse. Adversane, Thos.Keating tool makers Daux Rd., W.G Keyte & Sons precision engrs., Daux Rd., E.J.Lawrenson Haulage Natts Lane, Lorlins electrical components Stat. Rd., J.O. Lugg & Son agricultural engrs., East St., Mermaid Swimming Pools Daux Rd., SCATS agricultural engrs., Frenches Corner, Southern Fuels coal & coke Stat. Rd., Stane St Press printers Daux Rd.,[Mrs. Thurlow-Smith antiques (95), Toyland (55)], [unlisted – Lannards Art Gallery, Okehurst Rd.}

Farmers and farm houses:
Harold Arnold & Son Copped Hall Okehurst La, Mrs. Ayre Bridgewater Newbridge Rd., R.D. Barnes Little Daux East St., C.E. Barron and Rupert Dunham Denhams Andrews Hill, Leslie Bayfield Southlands Marringdean, Eileen Blanch St. Andrews Andrews Hill, Norman Blunden Jeffries Coneyhurst, Nigel Bower Fewhurst East St., Mrs. K Braun Kingslea Marringdean, J. Breecher Jackman's Adversane, Alan Bryant Fold Farm Hse. Five Oaks, D.D. Carr Sayers, Adversane, Donald French Willow Coneyhurst, Geoffrey Garbett Westland Adversane, Miss Gauk-Rodger Great Daux, R. Godden JP Hilland, David Grist Valelands Coneyhurst, Harold Jackson Lower Hook. W. Chiltington La., S. Hiscock High barns Coneyhurst, G.A. Hook Little Gilmans Marringdean, A.J.R. Izat Eastlands and Lower Woodhouse, J.Maslin Kingsfold Marringdean, P.D. Morey & A Merison, Pratts Barns Green, Paul Merison Hook, Clarence Morris Longmead Marringdean, Jn Morris Little Slinfoldland Five Oaks, Roderick Norris Wildens East St., Victor Nutter Kynance W. Chilt. La., A.B. Patterson Pear Tree, F. Pinches Woodlands Adversane, Jn Rogerson Guildenhurst, A. Rowlet

Upper Woodhouse, Patricia Sherlock Renvyle Okehurst Rd., G. Sims Menzies Wood Okehurst Rd., W.H. Smith Borough Five Oaks, H.J.Stafford Grainingfold Five Oaks, Stanley Stocker Kingslea Marringdean, Jn Tomlin Tisserane Stane St., J. Treen Sunwood Adversane, E.C. Van den Bergh Southouse Marringdean, Percy Voak Gess Gates Adversane, Bryan. D. Voice Southlands Adversane, A.D. Walker Stone Pits, Marringdean, Lionel Williams Home Farm at Summers.

A number of implications of social and economic change can be deduced from a comparison of the use of premises as recorded above with what exists today. In those days most people were demanding their own cars as rail and bus services declined. Business was booming in supply, service and maintenance of vehicles. Garage premises in the village High Street were profitable and not, as now, more valuable as building sites, often enough specifically to house the retired and elderly.

Supermarkets had not yet captured the business of independent grocers and other traders and there were no empty stores or charity shops. Shopkeepers could offer groceries and clothing to a local clientele as well as a wide range of niche goods and services. Several valuable enterprises such as sellers of books, cards, antiques, sports goods, videos, DIY, white goods and the like have not survived the passage of years though others catering for up-to-date technical advances have started up. The advent of an undertaker may be a reflection of the increasing accommodation built for the elderly! The growing demand for home ownership and steady expansion of the village by incomers in the 60s and 70s is reflected in the number of estate agents.

The taste for ethnic food was quite undeveloped in 1973; neither did people 'eat out' much. There were few restaurants or cafes and the only 'take away' was the fish and chip shop, in marked contrast to forty years later. Light industry was then mainly in Daux Road and near the Station. Other industrial estates were still undeveloped. Private education was then available in the parish at Summers Place and in Daux Avenue but has now ceased. There were no children's nurseries but now there are three. Civic buildings were just The Old Village Hall, now apartments, and the Women's Hall. The doctors' surgery is now a vetinarian's. Builders were busy at the Weald School expanding it for comprehensive schooling and a growing Sixth Form.

Appendix 10
Occupants of Hammonds at Cocksbrook

Calms, diamond panes and old casement catches in window of Hammonds' attic

A synopsis of the people who occupied Cocksbrook, Hammonds and the mill as detailed in the main text:-

1327	John de Kockesbroke gave his name to Cocksbrook
1400	Wm Dakons (Daux) was paying for Cocksbrook
1530	Cocksbrook held by Greenfields
1557	Assigned to Richard West
1565	Francis Garton took a lease by copyhold on Cocksbrook
1581	Wm Lee holds a lease
1610	Wm Lee sold land to Edward Greenfield
1630	Anthony Haman I paid tax for Cocksbrook (m Susan Lee 1603)
1640	Anthony Haman I dies. Anthony II inherits Gilmans. Anthon II's brother Richard gets Cocksbrook when Anthony I's widow Susan I dies. Youngest sister is Susan II

1642	Richard Hammond holds Cocksbrook until 1680
1680	Anthony III inherits briefly
1682	Anthony III dies. Susan II, Richard's sister, inherits Hammonds
1685	Cow seized to pay Anthony III and Richard's debts.
1738	John Booker leases Cocksbrook. John Streeter pays Poor Tax
1767	Thomas Pacey had the lease and sold the freehold to John Streeter I
1779	Wm Streeter I pays Poor Tax for Hammonds and Cocksbrook
1795	Wm Streeter I dies, his widow inherits. His son Wm II gets Taintlands and Gingers. Wm III, James and John, grandsons, are to get the benefit of the sale when Wm II dies
1801	Wm II still paying tax on Taintlands, Gingers and Duckmore
1804	Wm II still at Hammonds but bankrupt
1806	Property alienated to farmer brother John Streeter II. Wm II fathers a natural son in the workhouse
1809	John Streeter II pays rent and Land Tax
1814	John II carting stone
1823	John II paying tax just for Hammonds House
1825	John Streeter II builds the mill. Richard Chennell is the miller
1827	Richard paying Poor Tax. Mrs. Evershed at Hammonds
1839	William Sprinks now the miller. John II still paying tithes
1850	John II dies having lived as a pauper. Daughter Mary Ann had married Thomas Trower. Wm Sprinks is a prospering farmer
1861	Wm Sprinks a widower at Hammonds
1867	Mary Ann Trower died. Her husband Thomas now owns Hammonds and Cocksbrook
1871	Sprinks still farming 140 acres, married to Ruth II
1874	H. Isted the miller
1878	W.F. Weller the miller
1881	Sprinks down to 26 acres
1881	Thomas Trower died. William Sprinks died and Edward Underwood now living at Hammonds
1891	Underwood still there – died 1923
1906	The mill cap blown off
	Early 20th century – the Trowers are at Hammonds
1920	All smock of mill gone, burnt. Base used as a store
1966	Mary Trower dies ages 82
1968	Gertrude dies aged 77, Hammonds auctioned off.
1969	Dr. Kilsby owns it
1983	John Griffin occupant.

Index

The Index lists surnames and places in the main text. Not included are names to be found in the Appendices, in maps and illustrations, other villages and many variant spellings.

Aella, 36
Agate, 303
   Albury, 54, 144
Alfold, 41, 174
Alfoldean, 29
Alick's Hill, 193, 198, 199, 201, 217, 258
Allen, 153, 157, 158, 288, 298, 299, 300, 306, 307
Allman, 131, 215, 282,
Alman, 194
Almond, 238
Alwyn, 84
Anderida Forest, 27
Andredesweald, 48
Andrew Hill, 252
Argent, 167, 214
Arnold, 114, 129
Atrebates, 26
Austin's, 215, 280
Ayling, 132
Aylward, 102, 112, 305
Ayre, 217
Baker, 89, 102, 104, 167, 309
Bank of England, 76, 210
Barclays, 77, 200
Barkhall, 155, 156
Barnes, 45, 46, 137, 169, 238, 310
Barralets, 122, 192
Bartellot, 51, 56, 284
Bartelott, 164
Bartholomew, 66, 83, 93

Bassett, 48, 51, 70, 86, 164, 208, 279
Baxter, 298, 309
Beath, 56, 102, 282
Beck, 10, 116, 129, 130, 149, 195, 217, 218, 309, 332
Beedings Castle, 23
Beke, 115, 152
Belcher, 282
Bell cottage, 210
Bench, 240
Bettesworth, 86, 283, 284
Betts, 234
Birch Drive, 163,
Bishopp, 103
Blackpatch, 25
Blacksmith's Arms, 10, 58, 244, 297
Blue Idol, 11, 331
Blundells, 255
Blunden, 202
Boarer, 102
Bohm, 158
Bolden, 268
Bondwick, 253
Booker, 81, 82, 83, 86
Botting, 54, 164, 181
Bousfield, 223
Bowling Alley, 26, 27, 31, 116, 119, 127, 134, 139, 200, 201, 215, 315
Bowring, 296
Bramber, 38, 51
Braose 38, 51
Brereton, 56, 219

Brick House, 55, 56, 130, 131, 132, 254
Bridgeman, 145
Bridger, 13, 99, 365
Bridgewater, 109
Brier, 147
Brinsbury, 9, 132, 134
Bristow, 133, 210
Brookers, 95, 198
Broomfield, 67, 81, 122, 129, 163, 192, 194
Brown, 58, 131, 183
Buckmans, 164, 282
Budgen's, 162, 181, 204
Budgens, 15, 112, 122, 127, 204
Bull, 56, 117
Bungar, 71, 208
Burchell, 228
Burge, 277
Burnt Row, 4, 7, 9, 186
Burntrough, 9
Burt, 3
Bush, 277
Byron Cottage, 167
Caffin, 102, 131
Caffyn, 84, 131
Campbell, 224
Candy, 322
Carew-Gibson, 145, 158
Carley, 297
Carlton, 127, 129
Carnsew, 56, 86, 114, 118, 119, 120, 285, 309
Carpenters, 55, 128, 140, 142, 162, 198, 233
Carpenters Arms, 304
Carter, 37, 90, 102, 121, 130, 181, 207, 309, 315
Cartmell, 241
Cartner, 297
Catshill, 80, 87

Causeway, 56, 168, 197, 210, 321
Cedars, 253, 291
Champion, 27, 43, 48, 83, 109, 148
Chantler, 90, 131
Charman, 72, 84, 224
Chart, 129
Cheeseman, 228
Chennell, 96, 98, 99
Chequer, 283
Cherryman, 159, 160
Chesemans, 70
Chesman, 282
Chime, 120, 200, 315
Chitty, 161
Church Path, 200, 212
Churchgate, 55, 129, 315
Clark, 83, 148, 160, 161, 253, 264, 270
Clarksland, 143, 253
Clayton, 282
Cleveland House, 198, 202, 316, 319
Clevelands, 24, 127, 130, 160, 225, 291, 312, 321
Clock Field, 58
Clock Gallery, 163
Cobb's Wood, 148
Cocksbrook, 26, 45, 46, 48, 65, 67, 71, 72, 83, 86, 87, 93, 113, 323
Cogidumnus, 29
Coleman, 131
Collins, 66, 208
Community Gardens, 10
Coneyhurst, 38, 92, 150, 163, 310
Congregational, 119, 134, 197, 200, 215, 284
Conner, 289
Constantine, 35
Convent, 87, 115, 207
Coolham, 11, 34, 92, 94, 135, 140, 148, 295, 327
Coombe, 10, 106, 200, 255

Coombes, 130
Coombland, 166
Coombs, 309
Cooper, 82, 131, 142, 144, 208, 282
Copped Hall, 166
Cornell, 149
Cosway, 152
Cowan, 103, 219, 307
Coxbrook, 37, 67, 79, 80, 83, 87, 88, 143, 162
Craft, 130
Crawford, 236
Cripps, 203, 217, 225, 255, 310, 321
Crisp, 107, 130, 223, 224, 225, 309
Croft, 128, 215
Croucher, 119, 284
Crouchers, 67, 68, 69, 207, 323
Crutchlow, 79
Cullen, 296
Dalbiac, 227
Dale, 104, 282
Darrow, 310
Dashwood, 179, 303
Daux, 20, 67, 68, 115, 137, 143, 190, 196, 200, 233, 319, 323
Daux Wood, 12, 24, 27, 148, 196, 200
Davis, 147, 223
Dawks, 81, 194, 207, 208
Deborah Evershed, 158, 188, 298
Dell Lane, 128, 212, 249
Denman, 246
Dors, 152, 202, 310
Downes, 54
Drew, 201
drove roads, 34
Drungewick, 41, 175, 179
Duckmore, 51, 80, 87, 93, 119, 137, 143, 201, 323
Dudley-White, 204

Duffield, 147
Dugdale, 218, 219, 236
Duke of Norfolk, 66, 102, 129, 172
Duncans, 149, 166, 332
Durham, 118
Dutton, 198
Easton, 223, 237, 238, 309
Easwrith, 65, 67, 106
Ede, 181
Edgar, 15, 210
Edis, 56
Elling, 277
Elliot, 234
Enfield, 203, 309, 310
Ephraim, 129, 252, 322
Evershed, 56, 68, 85, 93, 98, 102, 104, 118, 131, 132, 148, 158, 183, 184, 207, 227
Ewins, 112, 124
Falkner, 238
Family Church, 11, 331
Farguhar, 145
Farhall, 100, 103, 120, 157, 243
Farmer, 223, 224
Faulkner, 310
Fecamp, 51, 66, 183, 279, 280
Ferring with Fure, 41, 64
Fewhurst, 64, 150, 153, 163
Fielding, 164, 217, 287, 288
Fieldings Cottages, 282, 288, 295
Fiest, 305
Finlanger, 148
Fire Station, 135, 328
Firminger, 148
Flight, 89
Flynn, 115, 152
Foice, 127, 130
Fold Farm, 282
Forge Way, 233, 312, 313

Fossbrooks, 165, 166, 252
Foster, 261, 269
Fox, 331
Frogshole, 164
Frye, 52, 208
Fuller, 56, 84, 101, 104, 244, 303
Fure, 64, 92, 152, 153, 280
Furze View, 289
Fuste, 72
Garton, 66, 70, 144, 181, 208, 217, 253
Gatefield, 164
Gee, 202, 261, 262, 264, 310
Gierth, 224
Gillmans, 306
Gilmans, 79, 95, 133, 151, 152, 162, 210, 233, 252, 253
Gilmour, 310
Gingers, 87, 88, 93, 140, 279, 301,
Glaysher, 233
Glebe Land, 312,
Gleniffer, 237, 295
Goff, 86, 121, 129, 216, 227, 283, 285, 309
Goldings, 153, 214, 283, 284
Goodyer, 124
Gordon, 185
Gore, 87
Gore Farm, 89, 90, 166, 200, 210
Gorefield, 71
Goring, 51, 54, 56, 60, 102, 117, 119, 164, 181, 309
Grainingfold, 166, 282, 296
Gratwicke, 80, 130, 134, 137, 204, 236, 237, 285, 290, 291, 301, 315, 316
Gravett, 206, 209, 309
Gray, 160
Great Daux, 26, 68, 69, 85, 93, 164, 190, 207
Great Grooms, 165, 199, 252

Greenfield, 37, 52, 68, 80, 81, 83, 84, 90, 100, 142, 143, 144, 153, 155, 157, 208, 257, 288, 304
Griffin, 288, 289, 309, 314
Groomsland, 133, 198, 214, 252, 253
Guildenhurst, 181, 280
Gynguire, 140, 301
Hadfold, 50, 162
Halahan, 147, 148
Haler, 183, 282
Hammond, 72, 74, 80, 81, 82, 181, 219
Hard, 158
Harries, 158
Harrow Hill, 25
Harvey, 224
Harwood, 102, 206, 289
Hayes House, 284
Hayler, 282
Helsdon, 206
Henshaw, 54, 56, 66, 72, 208, 305
Herbert, 219
Hereford, 197, 215, 309
Hickford, 269
Hicks, 151, 275
Higgins, 225, 361
High Fure, 143, 152, 153, 157, 158, 207
High Road, 140
High Seat, 165, 202, 215
Hill House, 120
Hill View, 112
Hilland, 5, 72, 295
Hillview, 199, 201, 202, 258
Hilton, 54
Hoad, 256, 284
Hobson, 202
Hoile, 96, 123
Holden, 13, 88, 145, 212, 284
Hole, 152, 179, 185, 186

Holly, 267, 268, 269
Holmes, 134, 198, 334
Holy Well, 212
Hookers, 169
Hope-Gill, 138
Horelands, 208
Howles, 153
Hubert, 55, 130, 132, 205, 227, 309
Hughes, 84, 100, 103, 322
Humphreys, 298, 309
Humphries, 223, 224, 225
Hunt, 145, 255
Hurd, 67, 183, 207, 214, 305
Hurstlands, 252
Ingfield, 115, 135, 288, 289
International, 122, 245, 250, 255, 310
Ireland, 66, 102, 119, 127, 129, 131, 158, 189, 194, 227, 283, 284, 309, 319
Isted, 123
Jabeena, 151
Jane's Tea Garden 250. 329
Jeavons, 116
Jefferies, 131, 158, 163, 185
Jeffery, 85
Jengers, 26, 87, 119, 140, 200
Jengers Mead, 119, 204, 245, 301, 312, 327
Jenny Wren, 165, 199, 252
Jestico, 233
Johnson, 37, 93, 96, 101, 109, 158
Jones, 224, 240, 241, 255, 276, 309
Joyce, 237
Joyes, 215
Jubilee, 89, 224, 243, 296, 305
Jubilee Fields, 4, 8, 9, 10, 46, 221, 227, 228, 233, 238, 271, 291, 313, 319, 322
Jubilee Meadow, 196, 200, 233

Jupp, 283
Juppsland, 297
Keating, 122
Keatings, 196, 285
Kensett, 102, 131
Kerr, 237
Kilsby, 200, 314
King, 122, 137, 169, 192, 243
King's Arms, 10, 77, 98, 107, 131, 172, 194, 200, 202, 211, 244, 255, 258, 301, 303, 304
King's Head, 201, 236, 244, 301, 305, 307
Kings Arms, 54, 99, 102, 120, 179, 257
Kings Head, 102, 111, 132, 307
Kingsfold Close, 16, 134, 148
Kingslea, 149, 160
Kingston, 216, 218
Kitchener, 139
Knight, 85, 102, 288
Knob's Crook, 165
Lake, 218
Laker, 127, 128, 131, 167, 195, 200, 202
Lakers, 255, 285, 309
Lakers Meadow, 16, 203
Langley, 103
Lathy, 243
Law, 310
Lawes, 264, 267
Lawrenson, 236
Leaman, 152, 223, 309
Lee, 71, 72, 143, 175, 214, 221, 275
Leisure Centre, 4, 233, 242, 247, 272, 313, 328
Leyhold, 185, 186
Leyland, 86, 186
Library, 5, 6, 9, 85, 124, 195, 202, 265, 328

Limeburners, 137, 177, 221
Lines, 115, 122, 147, 207, 217, 242, 243
Lintott, 124
Lions, 9, 10, 245, 273, 293, 328
Little Daux, 96, 137, 138, 207
Little East, 127, 215, 323
Lloyds, 301
Lloyds Bank, 36, 77, 131, 167, 215, 301
Locke-King, 164, 285, 286, 287, 288,
Lockyers, 72, 80, 84, 100, 103, 109, 120, 143, 301, 315
Longhurst, 9, 131, 147, 309
Lordings, 121, 175, 177, 203, 236
Lorlins, 192
Loxwood, 174, 178, 179, 216, 319, 326
Luckin, 211, 215, 291, 292
Lugg, 200, 309, 315
Luggs, 313, 314, 315
Lusted, 202, 225, 228, 229, 309
Lutyens, 126, 204
Luxford, 56, 124, 128, 130, 158, 205, 216, 217, 235, 291, 309, 312
Maille, 134, 204, 321
Malaya, 112, 303
Malthouse, 76, 132, 192, 221, 307
Maltings, 192, 214, 236, 254, 300, 301, 329
Manor Fields, 10, 215
Manor House, 48, 58, 66, 129, 164, 233, 258, 279, 280, 283, 291
Marten, 196
Maslin, 151
Maude, 2
May, 269, 270, 272, 273
McMurrugh, 228
McVeigh Parker, 150
Mears, 243
Meetens, 145
Mena, 286, 287
Merrikin, 199, 309
Messinger, 291
Michell, 103, 219, 306, 307, 308
Miles, 104, 298
Mill Barn, 103, 137, 322
Mill Way, 6, 11, 89
Minstrells, 282
Mission Hut, 289
Mitchell, 97, 131, 132, 306
Molly Church, 223
Montgomery, 38, 65, 279
Moreton, 116, 223, 309
Morris, 45, 57, 89, 206, 216, 217, 288, 309
Mothers' Garden, 10
Murat, 115
Mursell, 211
Myrtle Lane, 9, 195, 225
Naldrett, 183
Natts Lane, 10, 26, 92, 140, 145, 252
Nevin, 223, 224, 225
New Road, 86, 92
Newbridge, 10, 36, 44, 85, 86, 92, 128, 140, 158, 174, 175, 176, 177, 179, 182, 194, 202, 203, 210, 221, 236, 252, 280, 299
Newcomb, 227, 233
Newman, 243, 295
Newpound, 121, 315
Newstead Hall, 297
Norris, 126, 128, 129, 130, 137, 204, 217, 228, 285, 309, 315
North Eaton, 185
North Heath, 29, 116, 252, 329
Nye, 79, 282
Oak Cottage, 167
Oak House, 214, 283
Oakdene, 160
Okehurst, 24, 51, 56, 163, 164, 166,

208, 236, 279, 284, 286, 288
Old Coach House, 167
Old Cottage, 165
Old Hayes, 185
Old House, 68, 297, 298
Old Pratts, 86
Old Reservoir, 133
Old Smithy, 288
Oram, 54, 131
Oulds, 223, 224
Overington, 296
Pacey, 86
Palmer, 142, 153, 160, 282
Parish Room, 77, 107, 225
Parminter, 160
Parr, 270
Paton 12, 151, 268, 310
Patterson, 129, 130, 169, 228, 229, 276, 309
Pavey, 233, 288
Peacock, 124
Pear Tree, 130, 169
Penfold, 54, 79, 142, 144, 153, 162, 208, 282, 283
Penn, 331
Pennybrooks, 163
Peskett, 102
Petras, 228
Philips, 228
Phillips, 319
Pickering, 247
Pilchers, 255
Pinkhurst, 48, 64, 65, 66, 80, 82, 86, 87, 93, 108, 113, 123, 129, 140, 162, 280, 283
Piper, 190
Pocokes, 152
Pole, 289, 296
Pollard, 224

Pond Cottage, 288
Poplar, 289, 309
Portbury 122
Post Office, 76, 125, 126, 127, 197, 200, 204, 255, 289, 306
Potbury, 150
Pound Cottage, 164
Pounds, 208, 280
Pratt, 86, 161, 162
Pruess, 224
Pryor, 54, 144, 145
Pullen 295
Puttock, 84, 100, 102, 112, 118, 121, 127, 128, 129, 162, 194, 215, 217, 225, 227, 228, 243, 244, 268, 270, 280, 291, 319, 328,
Quick's, 127
Quin, 2
Radbourne, 206, 258, 291
Railway Hotel, 103, 236, 237, 308
Railway Inn, 103, 104, 112
Read, 310, 361
Red Lane, 200
Reed, 277
Renolds Totham, 95
Renton, 56, 125, 128, 129, 202, 216, 217, 261, 309, 318
Rhodes, 77, 135, 200, 201, 202, 210, 255, 309, 312
Rice Bros, 127
Richard, 15, 275, 309
Ringwood, 186
Rising Sun, 194, 301, 307
Roberts, 202, 310
Robin, 120, 315
Robinson, 93
Roman Way, 3, 9, 10, 167, 205, 328, 329
Rose, 200

Rose Hill, 130, 202, 254
Rosehill, 55, 130, 132, 227, 313
Rosier, 20, 51, 135, 196, 279, 292
Rotary, 10, 290, 293, 328
Rowan Drive, 255
Rowe, 158
Rowfold, 41, 48, 96, 108, 118, 217
Rowfold Grange, 26, 56, 125, 129, 216, 261, 295, 318, 319
Rowner, 21, 36, 92, 142, 144, 164, 175, 178, 182, 200, 203, 286, 309
Sadler, 119
Sainsbury, 122, 204, 228, 229, 275, 310, 325
Salt, 289
Saunders, 234
Saville, 192, 198, 312
Saxon Weald, 4
Scats, 122
Scattergood, 289
School Lane, 114, 138, 200, 313
Schroeter, 129
Scolding, 149, 151
Scott, 282
Sendell, 85
Sharville, 297
Shelley, 72, 306, 307
Shepherd, 127, 212, 264, 309, 315
Shepley-Shepley, 129, 164, 287
Sheppard, 228
Sherlock, 217, 236, 240
Shilcock, 145
Shire Cottage, 283
Shirley Cafe, 250,
Short, 208
Sillett, 230
Silver Lane, 95, 312, 316, 320
Simkin, 14
Six Bells, 88, 89, 127, 194, 200, 202, 210, 255, 305, 306, 319
Skinner, 183, 233, 289, 291
Slaters, 153
Sleepy Hollow, 167
Slinfoldland, 282, 286, 288
Smart, 84, 257
Smith, 188, 210, 228, 321
Somer, 86, 210, 280
Sonny Harrison, 234
Sopp, 158
South Eaton, 186
South House, 92, 143, 144, 151, 152, 153, 157, 158, 164, 167
Southlands, 49, 153, 297
Sprinks, 73, 97, 102, 103, 104, 105, 109, 112, 119, 123, 124, 227
St. Gabriel's, 10, 11, 116, 321
St. Mary's Room, 10
Stafford, 296
Stammerham, 94
Stane Street, 13, 29, 30, 33, 34, 36, 41, 94, 140, 145, 147, 149, 150, 210, 252, 271, 280, 282, 288, 297
Stanley, 128, 129, 130, 205
Stanton, 291
Star, 131
Star Inn, 301
Stedman, 66
Steepwood, 147, 148, 158, 310
Steere, 257
Stiles, 122, 128, 192, 285, 309
Stocker, 149, 158, 161, 226
Stockwood, 202
Stone, 322
Stow Cottage, 167
Streater, 83, 86, 87, 88, 93, 94, 96, 99
Streele, 183, 184
Streeter, 73, 93, 94, 96, 103, 108, 113, 127,

Stringer, 79
Stroller, 203, 310
Stydolf, 142, 181
Summers, 26, 51, 80, 86, 92, 93, 102, 114, 115, 118, 119, 120, 129, 143, 162, 207, 210, 216, 217, 227, 280, 283, 284, 285, 321
Taintland, 87, 88, 93, 279, 305
Tarrant, 174
Taylor, 132, 159, 228, 229, 298, 303,, 305
Tedfold, 9, 104, 135, 183, 184, 185, 186, 200, 233
Ten Steps, 107
Tesco, 122
Teulon, 110
The Ship, 254
Thomas de Selhurst, 51
Thorne, 283
Three Houses, 92
Tidy, 109
Tiller 193, 211, 292
Tipping, 66, 208
Tithe Cottage, 168
Toat, 137, 162
Topper, 197, 201, 236
Tower's, 83
Towner, 196
Townland, 58, 194, 215, 279
Towse, 83, 104, 145, 148, 284, 288
Tredcroft, 306
Trees, 139, 200, 313, 316, 322
Tribe, 255, 375
Trinity, 11
Trower, 54, 96, 104, 108, 113, 123, 200, 244, 314
Truelove, 210
Tshabalala, 214
Tucker, 147

Twyford, 148
Underwood, 123, 124
Union, 101, 107, 108, 256
Unitarian, 11, 68, 84, 85, 200, 255
Upton, 228
Van den Bergh, 158, 289
Vestry, 56, 58, 59, 60, 61, 85, 95, 105, 106, 107, 194, 288
Vicarage, 54, 59, 83, 109, 110, 128, 130, 194, 195, 200
Village Green, 56, 168, 321
Vine Cottage, 89, 90
Voice, 45, 46, 89, 102, 109, 118, 133, 195, 196, 228, 254, 283, 288
W.G.Grace, 121
Wadey, 102, 112, 118, 128, 129, 158, 207, 212, 217, 225, 227, 228, 252, 258, 283, 295, 309, 322
Wakeford, 219, 220
Wakoos, 265, 272
Wales, 183
Walker, 14, 127, 306, 310
War Memorial, 210, 328, 330
Ware, 127,
Watts, 215, 217, 245, 309
Weald Court, 122, 312
Weavers, 210
Weavers Cottage, 9
Well, 186
Weller, 123
Wells, 54, 104, 109, 118, 243, 309
West, 69, 71, 181, 200
West Street, 9, 119, 128, 140, 203, 210, 306
Western by-pass, 12, 16, 309, 313, 328
Weston, 81, 144
Wheeler, 291
Whirlwind, 11, 122, 134, 192
Whitbourne, 134

White Horse Inn, 131, 301, 305
Whitehall, 167
Wicks, 217, 309
Wiggonholt, 48, 64, 66, 178, 280, 282, 288, 295
Wildens, 95, 128, 197
Wilding, 149, 291, 310, 311
Williams, 210, 289
Williamson, 278
Willowbrook, 289
Wilson, 54, 112, 119, 120, 124, 263, 284
Wolzak, 296
Women's Hall, 10, 11, 85, 195, 206, 223, 224, 259, 261, 328, 332,
Woodbarn Farm, 324
Wooddale, 26, 90, 92, 129, 135, 201, 285, 295
Woodhouse, 64, 100, 153
Woodman, 273
Woodworm, 230
Working Men's Club, 115, 124, 125, 128, 309
World Stores, 255
Worsfold, 103
Wray Brown, 58
Wright, 37, 56, 115, 124, 148, 228, 298, 309
Wylde, 309
Wyndham, 176
Wynstrode, 166, 236, 240
Young, 43, 44, 203, 233